LEABHARLANNA CHONTAE FHINE GALL
FINGAL COUNTY LIBRARIES

Items should be returned on or before the last date shown
below. Items may be renewed by personal application, writing,
telephone or by accessing the online Catalogue Service on
Fingal Libraries' website. To renew give date due, borrower
ticket number and PIN number if using online catalogue. Fines
are charged on overdue items and will include postage incurred
in recovery. Damage to, or loss of items will be charged to the
borrower

Date Due	Date Due	Date Due
26. 12.		
17. JUN 16		
13 SEP 16.		
13 SEP 16.		
28. FEB 17.		

Rugby in Munster
A Social and Cultural History

Rugby in Munster

A Social and Cultural History

By

LIAM O'CALLAGHAN

First published in 2011 by
Cork University Press
Youngline Industrial Estate
Pouladuff Road, Togher
Cork, Ireland

British Library Cataloguing in Publication Data
A CIP catalogue record for this book is available from the British Library.

ISBN-978-185918-480-6

Typeset by Tower Books, Ballincollig, Co. Cork
Printed in the UK by MPG books

www.corkuniversitypress.com

Contents

List of Tables
and Figures

Acknowledgements

Over the years of research and writing that culminated in this book, I have accumulated considerable debts of gratitude to many individuals and institutions. I would particularly like to thank the supervisory team who oversaw the PhD thesis on which this book is based. This work would never have been completed without the expertise, advice and encouragement of Professor Mike Cronin. His thoroughness, diligence and enthusiasm provided me with the self-belief required for a project of this nature. Professor Tony Collins has, through his support and expert reading of my research, contributed immeasurably to my research and analysis. Without his unparalleled knowledge of the social history of rugby, it would scarcely have been possible to put the Munster story into a broader context.

In the early stages of research, I wrote to every club and rugby-playing school in Munster founded before 1950 requesting any information and/or records that could be made available. I would like to acknowledge the following clubs for taking the time to reply and for making an effort to supply me with what information they had to hand: Bandon, Bruff, Dolphin, Presentation (Limerick), Shannon and Waterford City. Particular gratitude is owed to Dolphin RFC for providing me with a copy of the club's very useful centenary history.

I owe a considerable debt of gratitude to the rugby governing bodies for allowing me access to their records. At the Munster Branch, John Coleman very kindly lent me the branch's surviving minute books. At IRFU headquarters in Dublin, Gordon Black and particularly Éamon Sayers made much-appreciated efforts to accommodate my visits to the union's archive at Lansdowne Road. At University College Cork, the staff of the Special Collections Department of the Boole Library were always helpful. I am especially thankful to the university's archivist Catriona Mulcahy for her professional response to my repeated requests.

I have benefited over the years from the assistance of a number of individuals in various professional capacities. I would particularly like to thank: Donal Ó Drisceoil, Gabriel Doherty, Donal McAnallen, Vic Rigby, Dil Porter, Fiona Chambers, Julia Walsh, Val Walker (RIP), Marie Stinson and Dave Russell. I also wish to acknowledge the support of my colleagues at Liverpool Hope University, particularly Duncan Light for drawing the maps in this book.

My greatest debts are personal. I would particularly like to thank David Doyle for his friendship and immense proofreading skills. In Cork, my friends John Fitzgerald Kelly, Aaron Buckley, Ronan Goggin, Eoin McCormack and John Dennehy ensured that my social circle was always a welcome distraction from the rigours of research.

The successful completion of this project would not have been possible without the significant contribution of my family. My parents, Matt and Mary, my brother Ruairi, my sister Mairead, my sister-in-law Louise and my brother-in-law John all provided support above and beyond the call of duty. My grandmothers have always been an immense source of encouragement and wisdom and this book is dedicated to them. Finally, I wish to thank Sue Murphy for her empathy, affection and patience.

Introduction

When the Munster rugby team were crowned European champions for the second time in May 2008, the victory was arguably the highpoint in a period of unprecedented change in the nature of the game in the province. Neatly dovetailing the most impressive era of economic growth in the history of independent Ireland, rugby in Munster evolved from a minority sport with restricted geographical appeal to something of a 'mainstream' cultural product with the capability of attracting mass popular interest.[1]

Given the game's origins in Munster as an elite sporting extension of the British cultural influence in Ireland, the character of rugby in the province in the opening decade of the twenty-first century represented a striking metamorphosis. This was far from a gradual process. History rarely progresses in straight lines and rugby in Munster only ever changed spasmodically. Short periods of rapid modernisation were punctuated by long intervals where little changed at all. In addition, 'Munster' can never be treated as a monolith in sporting terms and one of the recurring observations of this book, reflected somewhat in its structure, is how the social and cultural function of rugby varied according to locale within the province. This book aims, therefore, not only to tell the complex story of rugby football in Munster but also to probe that complexity by extrapolating key themes from the story and analysing them within the broader context of the social and cultural history of both the province and the country as a whole.

The origins of modern sport

The arrival of rugby football in Munster in the early 1870s occurred in the midst of the British 'sporting revolution' of the mid to late Victorian era. Most historians agree that a certain number of social, economic and cultural patterns underpinned the nature and growth of modern organised sport in Britain in the second half of the nineteenth century.[2] Rapid industrialisation and a concomitant labour need fed urbanisation and population growth. The rapid expansion of industrial conurbations and resultant social change in the countryside marginalised traditional leisure patterns. The eventual regulation of the labourer's working week through the gradual phasing in of the Saturday half day and the passing of the Factory and Workshops Act of 1878 along with improvements in real income created a mass market for leisure and by extension modern, organised, commercialised sport. The codifying impulse (most notably in different variants of football) was initially given to sport in the public schools where games were imbued with organisational and ideological values.[3] Vast improvements in literacy, communication and transport gave sport vital media of popularisation, while enlightenment, legislative measures and an increased interest among elites in the leisure habits of the working classes contributed to the demise (but not the extinction) of animal sports and violent folk football.

In practical terms this translated into the spread of games with shared codes of rules, played in defined spaces and scheduled to the needs of various social groups' working weeks. These games were organised by administrative units of varying influence, from the local club up to regional, national and (later) international bodies. In Britain, sports such as cricket and the two main football codes, rugby and soccer, witnessed condensed periods of expansion where the upward curve of growing club numbers was steep. Interest was sustained by the creation of league and cup competitions, and by the turn of the twentieth century, the Football Association (FA) Cup, the Football League, the County Cricket Championship and the prestige events on the horseracing calendar were popularly entrenched features of British social and cultural life.[4] The promotion of competitions, in turn, fed the remarkable commercialisation of sport that also occurred in this era. The enclosure of stadia gave sporting contests a revenue-generating function where clubs traded on their ability to channel the partisanship of local identity and civic pride through sport.[5]

Many of the sporting patterns observed on the British mainland were replicated on a smaller scale in Ireland. Rugby, as it originated in the country at Dublin University for instance, had the same public school ethos that its sponsors so eagerly held onto in Britain.[6] Professional soccer, a sport of mass working-class appeal in the industrialised centres of the north of England in particular,[7] became popular in the north-east of Ireland, the only area of the island to successfully industrialise.[8] From the mid-nineteenth century the popularity of horseracing in Ireland was reflected in the enclosure of courses and their integration with the railway system.[9] The 1880s witnessed a 'cycling craze' in Ireland comparable to events across the channel,[10] while the numbers of tennis, golf and hockey clubs also expanded. Even the Gaelic Athletic Association (GAA), which as a mass sporting organisation, largely rural based and with a clear politico-cultural programme had no comparable equivalent in Britain, can be interpreted as being something of a product of the Victorian sporting revolution.[11] Processes that defined contemporary events in Britain such as the drafting of rulebooks for games organised around the unit of the club and governed by bureaucratic bodies at various levels, were wholeheartedly embraced by the GAA. A dedicated sporting press also emerged at this time. *Sport*, a wonderfully detailed newspaper published by the *Freeman's Journal*, covered most sports, while specialist publications in athletics, cycling and field sports also emerged. In Munster, the stylish *Cork Sportsman* was a marvellously written if short-lived publication that, again, gave attention to most sports.

The social and economic setting

As already indicated, two of the key interrelated social phenomena underpinning the popularisation of sport in Britain in the nineteenth century were industrialisation and population growth. Migration to cities and the mass market for leisure thus created saw the rapid and impressive commercialisation of sport. Indeed, scholarly works of the period always point out the sheer scale of change in the Victorian sporting world brought about to a great extent by mass working-class involvement. Codified rugby football arrived in Munster under social and economic conditions that contrasted sharply with the mainland British experience. In Munster, where by 1880, organised, bureaucratised rugby extended no further beyond the narrow band of elite clubs affiliated to the Irish Rugby Football Union (IRFU), economic and social patterns of a much different nature to the British mainland were reflected in sport.

Respective demographic trends were one of the most obvious platforms upon which Irish and British sporting patterns diverged. Unlike Britain, the Irish population had been in decline since the Great Famine. Though the proportion of city dwellers in Ireland increased between the Famine and the First World War, this was only relative to rural emigration rather than urban population increase.[12] Munster, the country's southernmost province, covered an area of 6,093,775 statute acres or 29.3 per cent of the country's area. The population of the province, having reached a high of just under 2,500,000 in 1841 and having witnessed average growth rates per decade of just over 12.5 per cent[13] since 1821, followed the national pattern of rapid decline in the decades following the Great Famine.

Table 1

Population of Munster 1821–1911[14]

Year	Males	Females	Total	% change
1821	960,119	975,493	1,935,612	—
1831	1,093,411	1,133,741	2,227,152	+15.06
1841	1,186,190	1,209,971	2,396,161	+7.59
1851	904,979	952,757	1,857,736	−22.47
1861	744,682	768,876	1,513,558	−18.53
1871	686,106	707,379	1,393,485	−7.93
1881	659,994	671,121	1,331,115	−4.48
1891	587,611	584,791	1,172,402	−11.92
1901	540,970	535,218	1,076,188	−8.21
1911	526,130	509,365	1,035,495	−3.78

Post-Famine emigration as well as falling birth rates and later marriages saw the population of the province almost halve between 1841 and 1871. By 1871, there were twenty-nine towns in Munster with populations in excess of 1,500, with an aggregate population of 314,085.[15] This represented just over 22.5 per cent of the entire population of the province and slightly below the contemporary national proportion of urban dwellers which stood at 22.9 per cent.[16] By 1911, this proportion had increased to 27.46 per cent but was relatively lower given that the overall national proportion had increased to 34.7 per cent. The province's largest urban centres were Limerick and Cork, both of whose populations fluctuated in the period 1831–1911. Tralee, Clonmel and Waterford were the only other urban centres with a population in excess of 10,000 by 1911 with towns such as Bandon showing spectacular population decrease in the nineteenth century due to industrial decline.[17] Whereas concomitant rates of urbanisation in England and Wales increased decade on decade from 50 per cent in 1851 to 78.1 per cent in 1911, Ireland's increased urbanisation was comparatively unimpressive, rising from 19.5 per cent in 1851 to 34.7 per cent in 1911.[18] Unlike continental Europe, which had experienced marked internal migration during the nineteenth century, excess population in the Irish countryside was more likely to emigrate than to migrate to towns. Of Munster's six counties in 1911, less than 10 per cent of the populations of Clare, Cork and Kerry were born outside the county with the respective figure for Limerick, Tipperary and Waterford being 10–20 per cent.[19] The failure of Munster's country towns and cities to attract inward migration in the second half of the nineteenth century is emphasised by the fact that in the same period, Dublin and Belfast accounted for 88–99 per cent of Ireland's net migration inflow.[20] What emerges is a relatively rural society with excess population leaving the country rather than being absorbed by native urban economies. Though rates of emigration from Ireland between the Famine and the First World War were subject to periodic lulls, the overall hemorrhaging of population remained remarkably

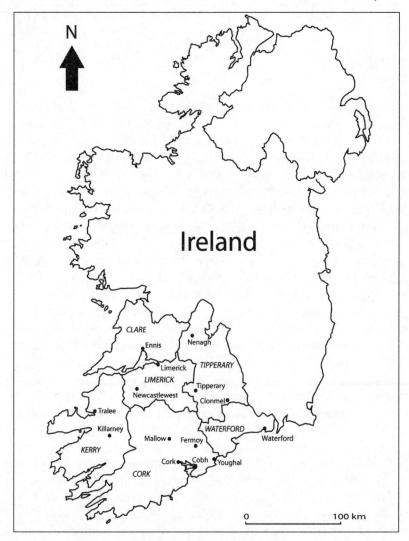

Fig.1. Munster: counties and principal towns

high throughout the period.

Determining precise regional proportions of overall emigration is not possible due to flawed data. Cohort depletion rates,[21] though imperfect (the overall depletion includes mortality), give some impression as to regional emigration trends. In Munster, the percentage depletion of the cohort aged 5–24 for the period 1861–1911 was consistently above the national average.

Table 2

Cohort depletion (%) in Munster 1861–1911[22]

Year	1861–71	1871–81	1881–91	1891–1901	1901–11
Munster	34.3	27.22	33.8	27.64	24.57
Ireland	30.99	25.84	29.98	23.33	21.47

High emigration was symptomatic of urban economic decline. The failure of industrialisation in Munster is evidenced by the demographic fortunes of the province's two largest urban centres, Limerick and Cork. Cork's population fluctuated throughout the latter half of the nineteenth century and it showed an overall decrease of just under 6 per cent in the period 1841–1901. In Limerick, almost consistent population decrease in the same period saw an overall fall of just over 11 per cent, with a slight increase recorded between 1891 and 1901. The significance of all the above figures (as will be made apparent in a sporting sense in subsequent chapters) becomes all the more evident in light of the fact that in the period 1851–1911, the combined population of England and Wales more than doubled.[23]

Table 3

Population of Limerick city and Cork city 1841–1901[24]

Year	1841	1851	1861	1871	1881	1891	1901
Cork	80,720	82,625	79,594	78,642	80,124	75,345	76,122
Limerick	48,391	48,785	43,924	39,353	38,562	37,155	38,151

Population decline in Munster's two largest urban centres becomes easily understandable in the context of their relative economic fortunes. Cork, with its impressive deep-water harbour (one of the finest in the world at the turn of the nineteenth century) was an established regional centre for financial services and the retail sector.[25] Industrial growth, however, was a tangible agent of demographic change in Britain and in this vital respect the nineteenth century was an era of decline for Cork. From the 1820s onwards, for instance, the textile industry (such a key industry in a British sporting context) in the Cork area went into rapid decline. Improved transport networks, technology and the removal of tariffs allowed the powerful British textile sector to muscle in on the Cork market. This development is illustrated by the fact that the numbers employed in certain types of combing in Cork fell from 6,600 to 478 in the period 1800–34.[26] Factors other than competition from Britain were instrumental in Cork's industrial demise. Failure to adapt to technological advances and a general resistance to change had an adverse effect on the butter and distilling industries, while over-dependence on the home market 'provided insufficient demand to sustain a substantial industrial base'.[27] The potential growth of heavy industry in Ireland was also fatally undermined by lack of proximity to natural resources, with coal and iron deposits being particularly sparse.[28] The fact that steam-dependent technology would require coal importation raised costs and compromised the competitiveness of Irish industry. All these factors, allied with a general lack of entrepreneurial spirit among Irish businessmen as well as a tendency towards the professions rather than industry among the middle classes, stymied Irish industrial growth.[29]

All of the above issues in the context of a rapidly evolving industrial world were clearly reflected in occupational fluctuations in Cork. For instance, the proportion of the city's male workforce engaged in manufacturing decreased from 40.88 per cent in 1841 to 19.15 per cent in 1901.[30] The same period saw increases in the numbers working in the transport, public service and professional sectors, none of which necessarily lent themselves to population growth. In a city where for much of the nineteenth century population far outran available employment and the working classes had to contend with such challenges as fluctuating wages and securing adequate nutrition and housing,[31] the growth of a large-scale proletarian sporting culture was always going to be adversely affected. Assessing levels of disposable income among the working class in nineteenth-century Cork is extremely difficult due to the seasonal nature of artisan work, fluctuating food prices, unemployment with resultant wage pressure and intra-class variations in all these issues. One could argue, however, that the relative failure to industrialise had a lasting effect on the city's sporting landscape.

In common with Cork, Limerick was an important regional port and service centre in the nineteenth century, where the produce from the agricultural heartlands of Kerry, Tipperary, Clare and County Limerick were exported to London, the north of England and Scotland.[32] Though efforts to promote cotton- and linen-related manufacturing failed, the lace and brewing industries grew in the decades prior to the Famine.[33] The city entered a severe economic depression in the latter part of the nineteenth century, with industry subject to the same pressures identified in Cork. Marked fall-offs in the brewing, distilling, linen and lace industries saw several factory closures and job losses. There was a slight recovery in the 1890s, however, with expansion in milling and tanning. The industry most synonymous with the city in the late Victorian and early Edwardian period, however, was bacon curing,[34] with factories such as Denny's, Shaw's and Matterson's being critical to the city's economy. Like Cork, where famine had brought with it migrants from the countryside, the 'vicissitudes of industrial production and provisions exports meant that manual and labouring jobs were not secure or permanent'.[35] Limerick and Cork, due to size, ultimately, were intimate societies where particular personalities and families could occupy positions of prominence and renown.[36]

What is clearly discernible from all of the above is that throughout the latter half of the nineteenth century and encompassing the key era of sporting modernisation in Ireland, the majority of the population of Munster lived and worked in the countryside. By comparison, agriculture occupations accounted for just 9 per cent of the British workforce in 1901.[37] The broad categorisation of occupations in Irish census reports hinders solid conclusions as to numbers working in the agricultural sector. David Fitzpatrick, however, using a selective reading of census reports to ensure greater accuracy, has calculated that in 1841, 76 per cent of occupied males in Munster were engaged in farming, with the proportion falling to the still relatively high 54 per cent by 1911 due to the rapid decline in numbers of men engaged as farm labourers in the post-Famine decades.[38] This was also symptomatic of the gradual decrease in the number of land holdings of between one and five acres in the same period.[39] Agriculture was primarily pastoral, with the raising of dry cattle seeing almost consistent increases year on year from the mid-1860s onwards.[40]

The preponderance of agriculture as the province's economic driving force was reflected in its impact upon provincial towns. Clonmel, for instance, the province's fourth largest town in 1841 (pop. 13,505) and fifth largest in 1911 (pop. 10,209) was hugely sensitive economically to changes in its agricultural hinterland. A decline in tillage following the repeal of the Corn Laws caused economic hardship in the town with the demise of the milling industry and the extensive local corn market.[41] The larger provincial towns had, however, become more economically complex in the early nineteenth century with the demand for professional services and more diverse forms of retail activity spreading from the principal urban locations.[42] The demand for professional services in particular would prove crucial to the later proliferation of rugby in the province, with the banking and legal sectors being staffed by those who would have had exposure to urban life.

In a sporting sense, industrialisation affected scale more than impulse. On the balance of evidence, Ireland, and in this case Munster, was far from unsuited to the establishment and diffusion of sport.[43] For instance, Ireland's cultural proximity to Britain was augmented in a sporting sense by the tendency among certain sections of the Irish elite to send their sons to English public schools – the sites which contributed as much as any to the codification of sport and the evolution of the amateur ethic.[44] The vast majority of late nineteenth-century indigenous Cork landlords had attended English schools and Oxford and Cambridge.[45] By 1885, it was estimated that at least 1,000 Irish boys (mostly Protestant) were attending such institutions.[46] This represented a significant number of potential sporting proselytisers with the former Cheltenham and Rugby boys introducing football rules of the latter to Trinity College Dublin being a conspicuous example.[47] Furthermore, English public schools actively competed with the elite native institutions by advertising in Irish newspapers towards the end of the nineteenth century.[48] Midleton College, a Protestant-run yet non-denominational school ten miles east of Cork city, attributed fluctuating enrolments in the mid-Victorian period partially to competition from across the Irish sea.[49]

The second factor contributing to Ireland's conductivity to modern sport was the country's remarkably extensive railway system: 'Ireland, one of the first European countries to rail-roadise, had 65 miles of track in 1845, 1,000 in 1857, 2,000 in 1872 and, with 3,500 by 1914 boasted one of the densest networks in the world.'[50] Cork city was linked by rail to Mallow as early as 1849, while rail links to Midleton and Queenstown (Cove) were opened in 1859 and 1862 respectively.[51] The Cork to Passage railway was opened in 1850, and later linked the city to popular leisure locations such as Monkstown and Glenbrook with a terminus at the harbour of Crosshaven.[52] The Cork Blackrock and Passage Railway Company also ran a subsidiary steamer fleet that linked the rail line to Queenstown, Haulbowline, Spike Island, Curraghbinny, Aghada and Ring.[53] By 1900, Cork city, principally under the auspices of the Great Southern and Western Railway, was linked by rail to almost every town in the county,[54] while the earlier building of the Mallow station had made rail travel to Dublin possible.[55] Railway lines from Limerick, meanwhile, were again developed from the mid-nineteenth century and services in the directions of Tralee, Ennis and Waterford were completed by 1880. Direct services to Cork were eventually worked into the complex morass of lines and companies within the Irish railway system, but in practical terms the most convenient services to the province's other major urban centre remained via Limerick Junction (County Tipperary).[56] Railway excursions, crucial to the popularisation of the GAA, also facilitated province-wide competition in rugby. The modernity of the country's transport system was matched by a comparatively far-reaching education system and high levels of literacy. Forty-seven percent of the population claimed reading ability in 1841 with this proportion rising to 88 per cent by 1911.[57] While the ability to understand advertisements nurtured consumer culture, the mass popularity of the land movement can partially be attributed to the spread of the newspaper.[58] As already indicated, a dedicated sporting press developed in Ireland in the late nineteenth century and gained in popularity as competitions and clubs garnered popular prestige.

Many of the acknowledged pre-determinants for the development of modern sport existed, therefore, in Munster. An expanding middle class embracing a wide range of professions with spare time and income as well as a comparatively well educated population in an area that possessed an extensive transport network were all key characteristics of any society where sport became popular. The lack of industrialisation, and by extension a proletarian mass, was the key point at which Munster diverges from the British model. The sporting implications of this divergent socio-economic model are the principal areas of exploration in the following analysis of rugby football.

Book structure

This book is both narrative and thematic in structure. The opening two chapters are organised chronologically while the remaining five chapters focus on specific themes deemed worthy of detailed analysis. The opening chapter describes the origins of rugby football in Ireland and Munster from the mid-nineteenth century to the end of the 1870s. Despite the gradual codification of games from the second third of the nineteenth century, football (in the generic sense of the word) was in a state of flux in Ireland. Rules were localised and the dominant social character of various codes had yet to take root. Rugby, therefore, is placed firmly within this context and is seen as a sophisticated strand of a broader football culture. Chapter 2 gives a broad narrative sketch of the development of the game from the 1880s to the beginning of the twenty-first century. This chapter will describe important events and processes not easily accommodated in a rigidly thematic structure. The numerical and geographical expansion of the club game, the proliferation of competitions and the internal politics of the game will be explained, with the chapter providing the narrative backbone for the themes subsequently explored.

Though the opening chapters cover a time period stretching from the origins of rugby football through to the present day, the chronological scope of the thematic chapters is generally limited to the seven decades from the 1870s to the 1940s. This was the era when social and cultural patterns of the game emerged that did not alter a great deal in subsequent decades. The rapid change brought about by professionalism is subject to more detailed analysis in Chapter 7 and the Conclusion.

Chapter 3 deals with the class implications of rugby in Munster. Focusing separately on Limerick and Cork cities, the game's adaptation to the social geographies of both of its urban centres of popularity is analysed. The game's varying communal function and ability to inculcate differing notions of locality in accordance with the socio-economic backgrounds of its protagonists will be illustrated. In addition, the social implications of rugby in provincial towns and its social networking function will be discussed. Chapter 4 takes violence and masculinity as its central themes. As a product of the British public school system and as a rigidly amateur sport, those who governed rugby in the British Isles had a very coherent perception of the game's masculine values. Data collated on violence in Munster rugby will not only expose the gap between discourse and practice in sporting ideologies but also build upon the theme of localisation developed in the Chapter 3.

In Chapter 5, rugby is analysed against the backdrop of modern Irish political and cultural history. The game's characterisation as an anglophile 'anti-national' cultural pursuit is challenged, with the fluidity of the game again underlined. As well as discussing rugby in terms of the political upheaval of the opening two decades of the twentieth century, the implications for rugby of the GAA's ban on 'foreign games' are explained. What emerges is a more complex portrait of sport and identity politics in Ireland than popular literature (particularly material by GAA enthusiasts) allows. Taking the management of the game as its area of investigation, Chapter 6 deals with the economics of rugby in Munster. The development of rugby as a commercial activity and the attendant infrastructural development of the game will be considered. The fact that the game had two centres of power in the province complicated the management of the game and officials' loyalty to their own cities frequently superseded the best interests of rugby in the province as a whole. The rivalry thus created was conspicuously played out in the context of the game's financial history.

The fate of rugby in the professional era will be revisited in Chapter 7. The transition to professionalism brought about dramatic structural and cultural change in world rugby. These developments were clearly visible in the case of Munster rugby, where a rapid shift in popular esteem from the club game to the professional provincial team occurred and where the commercial nature of the game evolved rapidly.

In the Conclusion, the twenty-first-century characterisation of Munster rugby is taken as a useful starting point for drawing the various themes of the main chapters together. Comparing the true complexity of the story with the contemporary impression of traditional provincial harmony will bring into sharper relief the conclusions of this book.

CHAPTER 1

Origins

The emergence of specific sets of rules governing different forms of football in the late nineteenth century and their social delineation was a gradual process. In Irish press reports, for instance, the generic term 'football' appeared above accounts of both rugby and soccer until well into the 1880s. R.M. Peter, in his 1880 *Irish Football Annual*, gave full accounts of the progress of both rugby and soccer – a lack of differentiation that would have been almost unimaginable a couple of decades later. Rugby originated in Ireland as a sophisticated strand of a pre-existing football culture. In order to acknowledge the complex cultural processes that led to the differentiation of broad sporting categories into specific codes, this chapter will examine the early history of football in Ireland and Munster in its totality. Highlighting the precise circumstances in which rugby emerged as a regulated, self-contained code in Ireland, something of the early social cleavages and cultural biases within Irish sport will be emphasised.

The origins of modern football

Before focusing on Ireland, it is important to briefly reflect on the codification of football as it occurred in late nineteenth-century Britain. The late Victorian and Edwardian period has rightly been identified as the crucial period in the modernisation of football. This was the era when the first formal clubs were founded, when administrative bodies were formed, rules agreed upon on a national and sometimes international basis, and competitions established. Furthermore, it was an era when football garnered mass, cross-class spectator appeal and became subject to commercial interest. From the outset, it is crucial to note that the modern codes of football share a common ancestry in folk variants of the game. Critical to a fuller understanding of the history of sport is an awareness of the tension between continuity and innovation central to the evolution of sport from its pre-industrial to its modern standardised form. One commentator has stressed that 'rugby and soccer were innovations. Both had deep and ancient popular roots.'[1]

It has been well established within sport historiography that the invention of modern sport in its codified and structured form in the British Isles was an evolutionary process that saw a vibrant culture of folk customs rooted in traditional society evolve through various agencies into a modern, regulated phenomenon more in keeping with an industrialised society. This striking metamorphosis saw the marginalisation in the first half of the nineteenth century of a rural and seasonal body of cultural practices, predominantly orally transmitted and open to sharp regional variation in a localised society.[2] Documentary evidence of football in Britain dates from the fourteenth century and surviving descriptions from that date to its eventual decline in the early nineteenth century depict a chaotic, amorphous practice, very frequently violent and varying from a relatively regulated practice with limited numbers of participants over a defined space to more unruly formats played over vast areas, with limitless numbers of protagonists and bound by little or no rules.[3] The precise nature of the game varied between locales with different levels of emphasis on handling and kicking the ball. It was also intimately linked to holidays, with matches frequently taking place on Shrove Tuesday or during Easter and Christmas. Given that both rugby and soccer were first put on a formal administrative footing in Britain, historians have been able to construct a coherent narrative that sees folk football, subject to various social and cultural stresses and changes, adapt to modern conditions and evolve into highly regulated codes with specific social and cultural connotations.

The works of Tony Collins, Tony Mason and Dave Russell all take folk football as their starting point and an understanding of pre-industrial football is clearly seen as being vital in interpreting the evolution of the modern codes.[4] The steady yet incomplete demise of folk football was a reflection of the decline of rural society due to the onset of industrialisation and was facilitated by various legislative instruments that curbed the perceived disorderliness and potential for social unrest seen to be engendered in practices involving large gatherings (particularly of those perceived to be on the lower rungs of the social ladder) taking place over vast spaces. Why and how folk football developed into different forms of modern rule-bound football with regional biases was attributable to various factors, none of which individually provide the rationale for such a striking process of change. Pre-existing regional emphases on handling or kicking assisted by the drafting of rulebooks within the public school system and subsequent diffusion aided the development of the two most popular codes, rugby and soccer. Problematically, however, the generational gap between the banning of folk football through the Public Highways Act of 1835 and the mass popularisation of its modern variants from the mid-1870s has raised questions as to the validity of historical links between the mass participation of pre-industrial and modern football. A crucial bridge in the chronological gap was provided by the elite public schools where football was consistently played throughout the nineteenth century. Indeed it was in the midst of the reforming spirit that engulfed these institutions in the first half of the nineteenth century that moves towards rationalising forms of folk football emerged.[5] While such institutions as Rugby, Marlborough and Cheltenham favoured a form of football in which running with the ball in hand was allowed, others such as Eton, Shrewsbury and Westminster promoted a kicking game.[6] The drafting of rule books within the public schools and the subsequent adoption of these rules by newly formed clubs was a vital precursor to the formation of the Football Association (FA) in 1863 and the Rugby Football Union (RFU) in 1871. It is important to note, however, that the demise of folk football was uneven and incomplete. In the economically diverse Stirling region of Scotland, for instance, there is evidence of an enduring culture of folk football lasting into the 1860s, clearly indicating some degree of chronological overlap between the formation of early formal football clubs and the fading out of folk variants in Britain.[7]

The clearly complex process of modernisation that sport underwent in the nineteenth century has frequently given way to crude myth-making, propagated by sporting organisations and individuals eager to represent the past as being in some way a logical and linear pretext for the modern development of particular codes. It seems anachronistic and unhistorical to distil the origins of a particular sport into a single event or to attribute its invention to the agency of one individual. In terms of rugby football, for instance, the idea that William Webb Ellis somehow conjured a unique style of playing football involving handling through one playground indiscretion has been adopted as the official version of the game's invention. The promotion of the Webb Ellis myth, therefore, completely dislocates modern rugby football from the older forms of folk football in which handling the ball was permitted. Tony Collins has argued that the middle-class homogeneity that has historically pervaded English rugby union has led to unwillingness to see the sport being in any way linked to a plebeian past. Hence, 'by implying that Ellis was playing a form of soccer when he picked up the ball, it unwittingly lent support to the claims of association football that it provided the continuation of the folk football for the masses.'[8] Collins' critique of the Webb Ellis myth clearly displays how the social mores, cultural and class implications that one particular sport later engenders can strikingly blinker interpretation of its origins.

Pre-modern football in Ireland and Munster

One peculiar adjunct to the Webb Ellis myth is the absurdly speculative contention that the inspiration for his playground indiscretion was young William's childhood trips to Tipperary (his father had been stationed in Clonmel as a British Army officer) where he witnessed the local game of *caid* – a form of football in which emphasis was placed on carrying the ball. This line of reasoning, first articulated by Fr Liam Ferris, a historian of *caid*,[9] was relayed with some circumspection by Edmund Van Esbeck, though the latter does accept that Webb Ellis 'in all probability' invented the game of rugby.[10] Fr Ferris' claims were seemingly accepted in some quarters, as evidenced by a correspondent to *The Irish Times* in 1962 who bemoaned 'the ludicrous position that rugby although it is as native as the McGillicuddy Reeks is denied the status of a national game . . .'[11] Notwithstanding the sheer tenuousness of the Webb Ellis myth in general, not one scintilla of evidence supports the claim that rugby football may have owed its invention to a form of folk football played in Munster!

The transmigration of rugby rules to Dublin University culminating in the formation of a club in 1854 via returning public schoolboys has rightly been interpreted as a critically important moment in the history of Irish rugby.[12] Clearly the establishment of the club at Trinity was an event of immense importance to the later development of rugby football on a formal basis in Ireland. Given the pre-existing tradition of folk football on the island, however, and the fact (as will be discussed below) that the form of football played in Trinity was proto-codified at best before the 1870s, the formation of the club should arguably be interpreted as an important staging post on an already existing football continuum rather than the unique starting point in the history of Irish rugby. In reality, games similar to rugby had been played in Ireland for centuries before the foundation of the club in Dublin. As will be discussed below, and in common with the British experience, the onset of the characteristics of modern sport in an Irish football context was a gradual process, not easily explicable through one single event.

Notwithstanding the relative chronological sparsity of references to football in Ireland in the pre-Victorian era, a culture of folk football not unlike the British version existed in Ireland, with games often played over vast spaces and with limitless numbers of participants and few rules and regulations. Literary and legislative references to sport from the sixteenth century onwards indicate that football was just one of many amusements that comprised folk sporting culture in Ireland. In addition, one can assert, anecdotally at least, that football appealed to both the rural population and townspeople, to the elite and to the peasantry, and was perceived by different quarters as being either benign or subversive.

The fact that sport drew attention from both the drafters and enforcers of law indicates its potential disorderliness. A famous early reference is contained in the Statutes of Galway in 1527, when locals were prohibited from playing the then primitive forms of hurling and handball that existed while no such ban was placed on playing with 'the great footballe'.[13] In 1695, the playing of football on the Sabbath was prohibited under the Sunday Observance Act. The extent to which this legislation was enforced is questionable given that the *Freeman's Journal* posed the following rhetorical question in 1763: 'Is there any day in the week that can cope like Sunday with all sorts of revelry throughout the nation. For guff matches, hurling matches, football matches, wenching matches?'[14] By 1793, the same publication had taken a rather less benign view of the folk pastime in a passage that saw football as part of a broader degenerate lower-class culture:

> Stephen's Green was never so badly taken care of as of late. It has become a general resort of all sorts of ruffians and vagabonds, every day. The Sabbath is there profaned by them with hurling and football matches – and in week days, herds of low ragamuffin vagrants . . . and servants disgrace the walks, playing pitch and toss and bellowing forth blasphemy and obscenity.[15]

In 1838, police in Dublin were ordered to clamp down on infractions of the laws relating to the Sabbath when a Constabulary proclamation declared that: 'No person or persons whatsoever shall play, use or exercise any hurling, commoning, football playing, cudgels, wrestling or any other games, pastimes, or sports on the Lord's Day.'[16] Given that the first half of the nineteenth century was an era of mass Catholic and national political mobilisation in Ireland, it seems scarcely surprising that the authorities looked upon football with some suspicion. That they may later have had some justification was evidenced by the claim, made during Fenian trials in the autumn of 1865, that football matches were being used as a cover for clandestine military drilling. According to one witness, 'vigilant sentinels are posted on the roads and paths, who give a peculiar signal when a stranger approaches. The moment the warning is given, the companies break up and begin to play hurling or football.'[17] Significantly, the fact that football could have been perceived by the Fenians as being a suitable cover for seditious activities potentially presupposes a general popularity of, or at least familiarity with, the game among the rural population in the mid-nineteenth century. A rather less subversive setting for a game of football was the country residence of J.D. Meldon at Coolarne, County Galway in October 1866, where the same gentleman 'gave his annual harvest home to all the tenantry and labourers on the estate' and where at 'twelve o'clock the sports commenced with an interesting game of football', this being followed by 'throwing the weights and sledge hammer'.[18]

As already indicated, the origins of football in Ireland have not been immune to myth-making. From an historiographical point of view, the sparse available references to football in Ireland prior to the nineteenth century have occasionally formed something of a contested lineage between historians of Gaelic football and Irish rugby. The already documented contention that *caid* inspired the 'invention' of rugby by William Webb Ellis is matched by claims that the same folk pastime was an important antecedent to Gaelic football. Jack Mahon, in his work on the history of Gaelic football, has unearthed a number of literary references to football in Ireland in the eighteenth century. In a fashion similar to the Welsh tendency to read the folk game of *cnappen* as a mythical precursor to that country's penchant for rugby football,[19] Mahon constructs a chronological narrative clearly implied as being somehow part of a pre-1884 historical lineage of Gaelic football, even though there was nothing uniquely Gaelic or Irish about folk football.[20] Interestingly, a poetic description by Matt Concanon the Elder, of a football game played in Fingal in 1720 between teams from the villages of Lusk and Swords is described by Mahon as 'perhaps the earliest description of an Irish football game', while the *Limerick Leader* in 1936 claimed that the football documented in precisely the same poem was 'obviously a form of rugby'.[21] The game described clearly allowed the handling and carrying of the ball as at one stage a protagonist 'intercepted the flying ball and joyful in his arms embraced the welcome prize. Running with eager haste and lustry strides.'[22]

In Munster, the form of football known as *caid* became popular in the south of the province and on the Dingle peninsula in the nineteenth century. Fr Liam Ferris from Kerry, who carried out extensive research on the game, described two distinct variants: field *caid*, played on a limited space with tree boughs used as goals; and cross country *caid*, where the play took place between parish boundaries and could last an entire day. A Kerry footballer from the 1940s, Dan Kavanagh, recalled his grandfather's description of *caid* in which his own parish, Dunquin, 'would play some other parish, Marhin or Ventry, and they'd go to the next parish and the ball'd be thrown in and it was a question of trying to bring it back to your own parish and it was played cross country'.[23] Wrestling, holding and carrying the ball were allowed and given its two distinct forms, *caid* is quite similar to the game of Cornish hurling referred to in the work of Elias and Dunning.[24] The level of popularity and geographical spread achieved by *caid* is difficult to assess but Ferris claimed that it survived to as late as 1888, when the parishes of Cordal and Scartaglen met in a match at Castleisland.[25] The legendary GAA writer P.D. Mehigan later documented descriptions of a game that was clearly orally transmitted and seasonal in nature. He prefaced his description with the rather spurious claim that *caid* was played 'with good humour' in contrast to England, where football was more violent. In any case, the game had some approximations to rugby football inasmuch as carrying was allowed and there also existed equivalents to scrimmages and specialist runners:

> Christmas time in particular and Winter generally, when the crops were cleared off the land, was the football season. Feats of individual players have been brought down from father to son and told at firesides today: tradition dies hard ... Carrying the ball and wrestling, in the form of tackling and holding were permitted. Fleet runners, specially placed on the outskirts of the crush, often gained considerable ground, or took the ball home for victory. The full manhood strength of each parish was marshalled for the fray, which often lasted the run of a Winter's day from Mass-time to dusk.[26]

An *Irish Times* sports writer, who had lived in Kerry in the early years of the twentieth century, claimed to have 'heard much of the old game ... a communal pastime played with great humour in holiday times'.[27] The seasonal nature of the sport combined with the lack of rules or regulated space demonstrates the clear parallels between folk football in Ireland and Britain.

If the effects of urbanisation coupled with legislation led to the marginalisation of folk football in Britain, it was subject to a different set of stresses in Ireland. Social and economic change in nineteenth-century Ireland came in the form of economic decline and rapid depopulation brought about by famine and emigration. One observer has noted, for example, that an '1871 proposal to allow hurling and football to be played in the proposed People's Park in Limerick city was ... countered with the observation that the hurling and football playing classes had all emigrated'.[28] Given this apparent decline, it seems hardly surprising that the impetus for the initial organisation of football in Ireland was provided by a narrow band of elites centred on the country's foremost bastion of upper-class education (see below, p. 23 ff.).

Despite the gradual spread of codified football in the form of rugby from the early 1870s, a culture of rural, localised football survived in Munster into the latter two decades of the nineteenth century. The rules varied, with some games possibly based on earlier local variants and others clearly played under something approximating to rugby rules. From a methodological point of view, press coverage of rural football was largely dependent on the initiative of individual spectators sending match reports to local newspapers. The precise extent and nature of football in rural areas and smaller towns is therefore difficult to determine. What is clear, however, is that merely following the historical trail of affiliated rugby clubs in the 1870s disguises the full social and geographical spread of organised or semi-organised football in Munster in that decade. In the form of a plethora of ephemeral and unaffiliated rural and small-town football clubs, the nascent rugby authorities in Ireland clearly had a larger potential constituency than they were capable or indeed willing to exploit.

It seems likely that the appeal of *caid*, like all folk sports, was heavily localised as multifarious forms of football seemingly existed in Kerry in the latter half of the nineteenth century. Like Britain, these rural games frequently involved gambling and were subject to elite patronage. In April 1874, a number of matches took place in the Killarney region between groups of young men from the town and surrounding rural parishes. In the first encounter, an eighteen-a-side match between young men from Killarney and the nearby village of Flesk, both teams agreed to play barefoot and when the apparent stalemate of the encounter led to some violent play from Flesk, the match was discontinued.[29] The sides replayed the following Sunday and the match was attended by a large crowd, among whom 'our Killarney young ladies were not backward in putting in an appearance and their presence on the field, no doubt, tended much to stimulate the highest efforts of several who took part in the game'.[30] Newspaper reports provide little detail of the nature of the action either in terms of the scoring system or the allowed method of propelling the ball, but it seems likely that a 'coole' was awarded for getting the ball past the opposition's defensive line.

In April 1879, the Clogher parish challenged any other parish to a game of football with a £100 wager being the winning prize.[31] It seems improbable that the peasantry of the parish alone would have been able to raise such an enormous sum without some patronage from the local elite. Elsewhere in the county, football seems to have been given a certain impetus by the Sunday Closing Act of 1878. Reporting on a football match between Castleisland and Cool in January 1878, a correspondent to the *Kerry Sentinel* commented that 'one of the many pleasing features that Sunday closing conferred on us is the revival of rural sports and manly exercises. Among the latter is that of football playing, which is one of the most popular as well as the most ancient of our national games.'[32] Later that year, what were termed 'the commercial and other young men of Killarney' formed a football club with a 'view to afford thereby amusement to the public, especially on Sunday when the public will be debarred from procuring refreshments in the public houses'. The Earl of Kenmare provided the new club with use of the local cricket pitch.[33] Again, the precise nature of these football matches in Kerry is difficult to discern from vague match reports but a certain level of sophistication was in evidence. In another match between the parishes of Cool and Castleisland in 1878, played with twenty players on each side, there were umpires, evidence of rules and set positions for players.[34] When the parishes of Tuogh and Listry clashed the following year in a match of twenty-five players a-side, there were two umpires, one representing each village, and two men on horseback to keep order among the 2,000 spectators present.[35] This footballing culture sometimes had a level of pomp and ceremony that would later be emulated by the GAA at major fixtures. When the Kilelton and Shannon clubs met in a twenty-one a-side match in October 1878, 'after mass at Ballylongford, both clubs marched to the appointed ground, headed by a fife and drum band and followed by a vast crowd . . . having first partaken of luncheon supplied by the Kilelton club'.[36] The game was possibly a variant of *caid* or 'rough and tumble' and bore similarities to rugby inasmuch as the method of scoring involved carrying the ball over the opposition's defensive area or 'cool'. What is clear, however, is that press reports do not carry adequate description to substantiate Eoghan Corry's assertion that the football played in 1870s Kerry was 'almost certainly of the rugby type'.[37]

One key example of both football's potential rural appeal and the methodological difficulty in fully documenting the latter is the existence of the Kilruane football club in north Tipperary in the mid-1870s. But for the preservation of its account and minute books at the National Library in Dublin, the club may have left no historical footprints whatsoever.[38] It has been observed, for instance, that no newspaper match reports appear on dates corresponding to fixtures recorded in the club's records.[39] Kilruane was one of several clubs that existed in the environs of Nenagh in the 1870s and again displayed the potential rural appeal of organised football. The parish had a population in 1886 of just 529.[40] Given that the club boasted a membership of fifty-five in 1876, all paying a subscription fee of four shillings,[41] it seems possible that some members of the club were drawn from other parishes in the area and from the town of Nenagh. Though the sheer generic nature of the Catholic names of the club's membership precludes empirical certainty, three of the seven individuals named as principal farmers in the parish of Kilruane in a trade directory in 1886 correspond with names (both Christian and surname) of club members in 1878.[42] Their opposition on two occasions was Carrigatoher, hailing from a parish of just 926 residents.[43] In 1880 Kilruane played two fixtures against Kilean FC. They fielded twenty-five players in their earlier fixtures, later reduced to fifteen, only to be increased again to twenty for fixtures in 1878. This does not represent relative lack of sophistication, however, as the IRFU only reduced team size from twenty to fifteen for matches under their jurisdiction in 1876.[44] Indeed, that the club strived to play some form of standardised football (probably rugby) is evidenced by the fact that among their expenses for the year 1876 was a book on football.[45]

A team had already existed in the town of Nenagh from as early as 1875, when the 50th (Queen's Own) Regiment provided opposition to the local team. A member of the military had explained the rules to the Nenagh team before the match. There is also evidence in the late 1870s of football in other villages in the environs of Nenagh. Though none of these clubs ever affiliated to the IRFU and seemed to have died out quickly, Nenagh Ormond RFC were members of the Munster Branch from at least 1886 onwards.

In the Blackwater Valley, there is evidence of similar inter-parish rural football in the 1870s. The *Cork Examiner*, for instance, carried the following report of a match between teams from Cork and Waterford in 1878:

> On Sunday picked teams representing both counties met at Waterpark near Ballyduff to play for a considerable wager. Those of the Waterford team came from Cappoquin, Lismore and Ballyduff, and the excellent physique of the men from the Knockmeldown hills was a theme of general admiration. The Conna Brass band played in a contingent in their interest in return for services rendered at the goaling between Lisgoold and Conna. The Cork team came principally from Clondulane and Ballinafana, but Fermoy sent some sturdy assistance. The assemblage was very large and reminded us of a third race meeting.

Several vehicles arrived from Lismore, Cappoquin and other minor towns in the Blackwater valley, heavily freighted, to swell the concourse in which the gentler sex was well represented. The ground was not all that could be desired, as was evidenced by the soiled garments of those who were worsted in wrestling. The superior physique of the Knockmeldown men was apparent to the most unobservant but the litheness and activity of the Corkonians told for them fairly in the goaling which was extremely spirited and dexterous. The accidents to mar the harmony of the sport were few, and may be summarised as merely isolated cases of bruised faces and battered heads. The ball was thrown up at ten minutes past 3 o'clock and at 3.30 the Waterford team scored a goal amidst cheers from the sympathisers. The ball was again thrown up and for fully two hours there was an incessant struggle to get the ball between the poles. Both sides being wearied, it was taken up and the Waterford team awarded the prize. The RIC on the ground had literally 'no occupation' a fair index to the peaceful disposition of our unrivalled peasantry.[46]

Though the report is sparse on detail in terms of the precise nature of the game, it clearly displayed characteristics of folk and modern variants of football. It had the potential for violence and there were no formal clubs involved. Furthermore, though a clear method of scoring existed, it seems plausible that both kicking and carrying the ball were allowed in furtherance of getting the ball between the poles. The presence of the RIC indicates official suspicion at large gatherings of rural, presumably Catholic, people. Most striking of all perhaps is the fact that these games took place after rugby football had been put on a formal footing in Ireland, displaying, perhaps, the resilience of folk pastimes in a society that remained predominantly rural in an era of urbanisation. The following week, another football match, this time between two parishes near Mallow was reported in the *Cork Examiner*.[47]

The early evolution of rugby football in Ireland

Meanwhile, and at a significant social, cultural and geographical refrain from this rural sporting culture, regulated football under rugby rules was developing slowly in Ireland. Football had been played at Trinity college Dublin since at least the 1780s as the poetry of Clareman Ned Lysaght speaks about frequent games at College Park between the commoners and pensioners of the College.[48] In 1854, former schoolboys of Cheltenham and Rugby established a football club at Trinity and hence initiated an incipient process of modernisation that would eventually see rugby football become a properly codified sport with a national governing body in Ireland by 1879. Indeed, recent research suggests that Trinity may be the world's oldest existing rugby club.[49] In its early days, the club at Trinity limited on-field activity to intra-college games with fixtures such as 'Freshmen v The Rest', 'Football Club v Boat Club', and 'English Educated boys v Irish Educated boys' filling the club's fixture calendar.[50] As if to underline the evolutionary nature of the codification of sport, the form of football played at Trinity, though probably an adaptation of the rules first formally decided upon at Rugby in 1845, retained some of the characteristics of folk football. Game duration, for instance, was clearly flexible. A match against 'Wanderers' in 1860, for example, and in common with contemporary matches at Rugby School, was played over two days, with the first day's activities only halted by the onset of darkness.[51] In 1867, a numerically lopsided fixture took place between a first-choice XV and thirty-three other members of the club. The numerical advantage of the thirty-three was seemingly negated by lack of skill, with some members of the team playing in a fashion that suggested they had mistaken the game for handball.[52] It also seems possible that many of the extra men were lost in the maelstrom of the mass scrummages for possession that characterised early rugby. As with the previous game, both sides played until 'night drew a curtain over College Park'.[53]

The game at Trinity did not become properly standardised until 1868, when Limerick aristocrat Charles Barrington was instrumental in the passing of an agreed set of rules at the club's AGM.[54] Of the unregulated form of football played at Trinity, theretofore, Barrington would later comment: 'the club had no rules, written or unwritten. They just played and ran with the ball, no touch line, no goal lines, our only paraphernalia being the Rugby goal posts.'[55] Furthermore, there had been no distinction between backs and forwards with players indiscriminately running with the ball. Incidentally, the practice of hacking was banned under the newly drafted Trinity rules. Crucial to the future growth of the game was its gradual adoption by elite schools in Dublin. From the mid-1860s onwards, the potential character-building benefits of sport had inspired the headmasters of the elite Rathmines School and St Columba's College to include reference to their football playing facilities in newspaper advertisements.[56]

Further north, former Rugby and Cheltenham boys were again to the fore in the foundation of the North of Ireland Football Club (NIFC) in 1868[57] and a club was formed at Queen's University Belfast in 1869.[58] The game was also expanding in Dublin with the formation of important clubs such as Wanderers (1869) and Lansdowne (1872). Debate surrounding the early administrative history of Irish rugby has centred on the fact that separate governing bodies were formed in

Belfast and Dublin. On the initiative of Trinity in 1874, a meeting was called of the principal clubs in order to form an executive with a view to arranging an international fixture with England. At a meeting on 10 December of that year the Irish Football Union was founded with membership comprising the Trinity, Wanderers, Bray, Engineers and Lansdowne clubs from the Dublin area and Monaghan, Dungannon and Portora from Ulster. In January 1875, the Northern Football Union was founded among the remaining Ulster clubs with football acolytes in Belfast apparently slighted at their perceived exclusion from the Dublin initiative. Edmund Van Esbeck, in his officially sanctioned history of Irish rugby, attempts to represent the existence of two bodies in the most benign manner possible. Van Esbeck's book was published in 1974, just two years after the 'troubles' in Northern Ireland had disrupted the international championship and at a time when the IRFU would have been especially eager to promote the apolitical character of Irish rugby. He therefore deliberately underplays the possibility that the formation of two bodies stemmed from a row lest it be interpreted as having been in any way politically motivated or would seem to contradict the IRFU's self-promoted status as an agency of sporting understanding between north and south. He criticises the apparent factual inaccuracies of the contemporary account of Irish rugby writer Jaques McCarthy, who claimed that after a match between Wanderers and NIFC in November 1874, 'the North men stood up and gave it very hot to the Dubliners for not inviting their co-operation'.[59] Van Esbeck countered by stating that: 'If that row arose, then the North were a little ahead of their time, for the actual foundation of the IFU was still a fortnight away.'[60] Given that the formation of an executive in Dublin had first been mooted in October, it is certainly not inconceivable that the Belfast clubs were indeed upset at being apparently omitted from a process that had already begun. That the IFU was Dublin-centric was underlined by the fact that clubs from Munster played a scant role in the formative years of the organisation, and clubs from Connacht none at all.

Press underreporting and the fact that Munster clubs seemed slow to affiliate to the IFU makes tracing the history of rugby in the province in the 1870s a methodologically challenging task. Though Munster clubs played no part in the formation of the IFU, the existence of the game in the province certainly predated that body's formation. Midleton College Football Club claim 1870 as their foundation date,[61] while IRFU records indicate that the Cork Football Club (also known as Cork Knickerbockers) was founded in the same year.[62] Midleton College had intimate links with Irish rugby's early cultural hearth at Dublin University and the headmaster of the school at the time of the football club's formation, Rev. T. Moore, was a graduate of Trinity (as were his predecessor and successor). Though ascribing causal links between Moore and the introduction of rugby to Midleton is not possible, he did bring an Arnoldian ethic to the college and is said to have encouraged games.[63] The precise nature of the football played at Midleton is unknown with the college's historian describing it as a 'rudimentary form'.[64] Queen's College Cork published a set of football rules in 1872. In February 1873, one of the few football matches advertised in that year's press was played between the college's rowing and football clubs.[65] There is evidence of a football club in Queenstown (Cobh) as early as 1874, when the latter secured a home victory over Cork, while sporadic press references to Montenotte FC (1874) and Summerhill FC (1876)[66] ensured that Cork's more privileged suburbs were not wanting for organised leisure in the game's formative years.[67] From 1874 a football club was added to the wide range of sporting interests of the large military garrison in Cork. Again, unfortunately, the task of gathering precise details of the personnel behind these clubs and the form of football played is undermined by scant press coverage.

As already noted, rugby in Munster initially remained aloof from the game's administrative centre in Dublin. In March 1875, Rathkeale became the first club from Munster to affiliate to the IFU, when a local RIC officer and the club's honorary secretary Captain Bowen wrote to the Union enclosing £1 as subscription.[68] The club was represented at the Union's general meeting later that month but seemingly did not persevere beyond one season as Munster was without representation at the October 1876 meeting.[69] The apparent isolation of rugby in Munster was further evidenced when *The Irish Times*, carrying details of the 1876 general meeting of Cork FC, was moved to comment that it was 'glad to hear of football in the south'.[70] That same year, Limerick FC was founded by the previously mentioned Barrington and another Trinity football pioneer J.G. Cronyn and was represented by C.B. Croker at the Union's general meeting in 1877.[71] The Limerick club, undoubtedly aided by their close links to Trinity, quickly established themselves as a leading club. Within months of their founding, they travelled to Dublin for a fixture with the well-established Wanderers club[72] and decisively defeated Cork in the maiden fixture between the two in April 1876.[73] In January 1877, the Limerick club issued a challenge to Leinster for a match against Munster and the first fixture between the two provinces took place the following March with Leinster claiming the spoils by one goal to nil. By 1878, Cork FC had also affiliated. Two of the latter's more prominent administrators, W.J. Goulding and A.R. McMullen, underlined the links between the modernisation of Irish rugby and exposure to the British education system. Goulding was heir to a large chemical concern in Cork and had earned a Cambridge blue for rugby while a student at St Catharine's College. McMullen, meanwhile, was the son of a large mill owner in Cork city, and had attended the prestigious Clifton College near Bristol where he had played on the first XV. Impetus was also given to the game by individuals educated at home. Tom Corker and Tom Harrison, two pioneers of the game at Queen's College Cork (QCC), had been educated at Perrot's School and Midleton College respectively. Both Protestants, Corker would later achieve the rank of surgeon general in the Royal Army Medical Corps while Harrison inherited a large farm near Fermoy, County Cork.[74] Harrison, among whose papers the 1872 Queen's College rulebook was later found, probably developed a taste for football while in school at Midleton.

With the merging of the Dublin and Belfast bodies in 1879 into the Irish Rugby Football Union and the creation of provincial branches, Munster rugby was put on a formal administrative footing and a representative team began competing annually with the other provinces. Furthermore, clubs were cropping up in towns beyond the game's two main urban centres. Formally constituted rugby football failed, however, to penetrate pockets of potential popularity in the countryside. As already described, variants of football with a mixture of folk and modern characteristics persisted despite the existence of a bureaucratised alternative in the form of rugby. In the context of this general appetite for organised football in the province, how does one explain the limited spread of rugby rules and relative slowness of affiliation to the game's bureaucratic body? Perhaps the apparent cultural gap that existed between these rural footballers and what one commentator has casually labelled the 'highly popular but unionist Rugby Football Union'[75] (it was neither highly popular nor self-consciously unionist) was enough to prevent the expansion of 'official' rugby into the countryside. This only partially explains a complex phenomenon. The reasons were at once demographic, cultural, social and economic.

Given the population trends outlined in the introduction, the comparative durability of a rural sporting phenomenon is scarcely surprising. Unlike Britain, where the labour demands of industrial conurbations had largely contributed to the decline of rural folk culture in the middle third of the nineteenth century, there was a tangible constituency for sport in the Irish countryside throughout the Victorian era. Besides football, a vibrant culture of rural athletics existed in Munster in the latter half of the nineteenth century, becoming particularly conspicuous from the late 1860s. Athletes such as the Davin brothers from Tipperary became figures of remarkable renown and became models of a peculiar type of pastoral manhood. Indeed, Michael Cusack saw Munster as the ideal location to launch the GAA, given the pre-existing vibrancy of athletics in the province.[76] The vitality of the Irish countryside's sporting culture was further evidenced (albeit outside Munster) by the phenomenal popularity of cricket as a rural pastime in Victorian Westmeath, with 68 per cent of the cricketing activity in the county in the period 1880–1905 taking place in townlands, parishes and villages.[77] Within the province, a study of Tipperary cricket has revealed a striking rural appeal throughout the 1870s.[78] Football, in its semi-regulated manifestation in the Munster countryside in the 1870s, clearly fits neatly into this rural sporting culture. Rugby football, with its early diffusion seemingly driven by those exposed to elite education both at home and abroad, was at a significant cultural distance from rural Ireland at that time.

The fertile football constituency that rugby failed to conquer was eagerly pursued by, and was overwhelmingly more culturally adaptable to, the nascent Gaelic Athletic Association. Tipperary, west Waterford, east and north Cork and west Kerry would all become GAA heartlands. This does not, however, endorse Mullan's 'bifurcation' paradigm as there is no evidence to suggest that the founding of the GAA was the inevitable product of Irish economic development. (See p. 142). Indeed, given ample time to diffuse, rugby may well have become a popular rural pastime in Munster. In France, for instance, rugby possessed a significant rural dynamic in its heartland in the southwest, far removed culturally from the game's centre of administrative power in Paris,[79] while in New Zealand, the game spread into agricultural areas from as early as the mid-1870s.[80] As later chapters will show, there was always ample overlapping between apparently incongruous sporting cultures in Ireland. Considering football in its totality, it seems clear that the early history of football in Munster, rather than being a process of uniform progression, was more of a maelstrom of tensions between formal affiliation and casual arrangement, codified centrality and local interpretation, pastoral culture and urban sophistication.[81]

CHAPTER 2

Overview since 1880

In the three and a half decades from the formation of the Munster Branch of the IRFU in 1879 to the outbreak of the First World War, rugby in the southern-most province of Ireland developed a durable club and competitive structure. By 1914, rugby had become enculturated in the province insofar as certain clubs had become 'traditionally' strong and competitions such as the Munster Senior Cup had garnered significant prestige. The position of Munster in the overall schema of Irish rugby had by then also taken root. From the post-war period through to the transition to professionalism in the mid-1990s, rugby was remarkable for its lack of ostensible change. The middle of the century, however, had seen the beginning of a slow and insidious process of change that would eventually render amateurism obsolescent. Before tackling the issues that comprise the thematic body of this book, a narrative sketch of how Munster rugby developed from the 1880s through to professionalism is necessary. We have already seen in Chapter 1 how the game evolved in Ireland from the mid-nineteenth century into the country's first properly codified and bureaucratised variant of football. At the beginning of the 1880s, when the current chapter takes up the story, rugby was the most sophisticated strand of football activity in Munster. This chapter will concentrate, then, on accounting for the development of the club game, the spread of competitions and the administrative politics of Munster rugby from the 1880s through to the dawn of the professional era.

The early evolution of the club game

By 1880, rugby in Munster had seen significant expansion both in terms of club numbers and geographical appeal. In his report of that year's rugby activity in the province, the previously mentioned W.J. Goulding claimed that though it had been a disappointing season, 'year by year the game has been making rapid strides in Munster.' Though impressive expansion was evident in Cork, the same could not be said for

Limerick where the game had seemingly regressed: 'lawn tennis has taken its [rugby's] place, owing to a lack of courage to sustain defeat, which has been their lot for the last few years . . . no energy has been displayed during the past season, and we fear that next year it will be a game of the past within the city of the "violated treaty".'[1]

The early promise shown by Limerick FC had evidently given way to apathy, with the club's efforts in 1879 amounting to a mere two matches, with both resulting in defeat to Cork FC and Queen's College respectively.[2] The adoption of the game in the local grammar school had seen the spawning of the Clanwilliam club in Tipperary, while in Clare, the presence of a football club at the elite Ennis College had possibly inspired the establishment of Ennis Town FC.[3] Incidentally, the respective headmasters of both institutions, R.H. Flynn and W.A. Lyndsay, were graduates of Trinity College Dublin and may have been exposed to the game in their *alma mater*.[4] In Cork, Goulding claimed that there were seven distinct clubs. Among them were the newly founded Cork Bankers (forty of whose sixty members were officials in local banks),[5] Queen's College, Blackrock, Knight's School (staffed by more Trinity graduates), Bulldogs, and Cork FC. Queenstown FC and Midleton College, both from towns infrastructurally well connected to the city, were the county's other official clubs. Other Munster clubs mentioned in R.M. Peter's *Irish Football Annual of 1880* included Waterford FC and The Abbey (Tipperary). Taking that publication as a guide (the comprehensiveness of which is not fully established), rugby was comparatively weaker in Munster than in Ulster and Leinster. The province's total of twelve clubs represented a mere 14 per cent of the overall total of eighty-eight listed in Peter's *Annual*.[6] Leinster, Ulster and Connacht had forty-three, thirty and three clubs respectively. The level of activity engaged in by Munster clubs could vary sharply. Cork FC, for instance, played sixteen matches in the 1879–80 season, a total greater than the combined tally of matches played by the neighbouring Queen's College, Queenstown and Knight's School clubs in the same season.[7] The absence of formal competitions left the arranging of fixtures to individual clubs – a process that was clearly dependent on levels of interest, communication and time that fluctuated from club to club. Moreover, the diffusion of the game to smaller provincial towns such as Ennis and Tipperary brought with it the problem of finding suitable opposition. Clanwilliam (Tipperary town), for instance, played just four matches in 1879–80, with three of those being against the same local military regiment;[8] while at Ennis College, J. Chartres Molony recalled of his school days that 'the old Doctor [headmaster

R.H. Flynn] endeavoured as best he could to teach us the rudiments of cricket and rugby football, but we had not the stimulus of competition to interest us. If the local Catholic schools played any systematic game of any sort, I never heard of it.'[9]

At the beginning of the 1880s, Limerick FC and Cork FC remained the leading rugby clubs in their respective cities. An annual contest between the clubs was still a *de facto* trial match for the Munster interprovincial XV and both teams, particularly Cork FC, usurped the best playing talent from any other local clubs. Indeed, Cork FC was probably the province's premier club in the period and co-ordinated much of the football activity within their native city. In 1881, the club had twenty-three paid up members and accepted eleven new members. They decided to make soldiers stationed in the Cork garrison honorary members and carried out their practices in conjunction with the Cork Bankers club – from whom they recruited players.[10] The Cork club followed the typical pattern of contemporary outfits by playing a lot of intra-club games. A match in February 1882, for instance, pitted the 'bicyclists' v 'the rest'.[11] Another match saw Cork City play against Cork County. Among the players on the county selection were Alf McMullen and Frank Levis, who lived in Rushbrooke and Bandon respectively.[12] More fixtures scheduled included 'Corkonians v Aliens' and 'Bank of Ireland v Other banks'. Clearly a limited pool of players, whose formal club was Cork FC, arranged these informal matches between scratch teams and used the local press as a method of advertising among themselves rather than to the general public. In October 1882, a county selection to take on the 'city' included players from Bantry, Mallow, Midleton and Queenstown. All of these towns were in convenient proximity to the city by rail and many of the players concerned appeared in contemporary Cork FC team lists.[13] A similar pattern of intra-club football was co-ordinated by Limerick FC.[14]

In 1882, just four clubs – Limerick, Cork, Queen's College Cork and Bandon – were represented at the Munster Branch annual meeting, as much reflecting sluggish affiliation rates perhaps, as lack of clubs. Though the IRFU recorded just five affiliated Cork clubs in 1885 (Bandon, Queen's College, Cork FC, Clonakilty and Bankers) a study of press coverage reveals at least twenty-three active football combinations (there were probably many more) playing a variant of rugby rules in Cork that season. Though this notionally represents a significant increase in playing numbers from the late 1870s, a study of various team lists suggests (but does not prove) that there was significant overlap between the playing staffs of the informal teams and affiliated clubs with the latter, particularly Cork FC, having

something of the character of representative teams. The pattern identified by Metcalfe in his study of football in the mining communities of
east Northumberland[15] and successfully applied by Hunt[16] to football
in Victorian Westmeath seems discernable to some extent in Cork with
on one level, a series of unaffiliated teams that existed on an informal
basis and a small number of well established, formally administered
clubs fully 'integrated into the practices of modern sport'.[17] In addition, the appearance of clubs in Kinsale, Clonakilty, Queenstown,
Bandon and Midleton in this era is further testament, perhaps, to the
impact of railways on the geographical spread of rugby in the Cork
region. Interestingly, O'Riordan's study of the diffusion of rugby in the
Cork region in the period 1886–1922 reveals that every town in which
a club was founded within that timeframe was linked by rail and that
the game experienced hierarchical diffusion from the core of Cork city
to the nearest towns along the area's rail network.[18]

The founding of Garryowen Football Club in 1884 was the most
important event in the history of the game in Limerick, foreshadowing
the future social diversity and cultural centrality of the sport in the
city. From the mid-1880s in Limerick also, a culture of parish-based
junior rugby began to emerge.[19] These developments saw a remarkable
broadening of the game's social base and contributed to rugby quickly
becoming a sporting means of expressing civic spirit in the city.
Garryowen, as the city's premier senior club, promoted junior football
by arranging and administering competitions. In turn the club gainfully recruited from their junior counterparts and a structure of mutual
dependence quickly developed.[20]

This expansion coincided with the gradual cultivation of competitive rugby through the arranging of knockout tournaments. The
inauguration of the Munster Senior Cup in 1886 was the product of
collaborative efforts between John F. Maguire of Cork FC and W.L.
Stokes of Limerick and Garryowen, 'two well known and enthusiastic
players determined that before retiring finally from the manly game
they would establish a cup, the want of which has been so long felt by
the rugby clubs of Munster'.[21] The Senior Cup, which would remain
the province's most coveted rugby trophy for over a hundred years,
brought unalterable cultural change to Munster rugby. Organised
competition gave clubs, the public and the media an exciting new
focal point through which rivalries and traditions were nurtured.
Clubs that put a premium on winning were rewarded and the concept
of 'playing for the sake of playing', so cherished by elements of the
game's contemporary bourgeois constituency, was challenged. The
inaugural tournament was won by an unfancied Bandon side but 'the

cup' was dominated for the rest of the century by Garryowen and Queen's College Cork.

It quickly became perceived wisdom that competitions were a vital means of promoting the game. The vitality of junior rugby in Limerick was bolstered by the organisation of a knock-out tournament in 1887 and the inauguration of the Transfield Cup in 1895, while from the same year, the Tyler Cup gave underage rugby vital impetus in the city. Cork schools rugby, a passionately followed strand of the game in Munster, was put on a competitive footing with the presentation of a Challenge Cup in 1888. When the founding of a junior competition for schools was mooted in 1897, *Sport* recalled how useful a breeding ground a similar competition had been in previous years and that 'much of the good that was accomplished [in promoting schools rugby] will . . . have gone for little if another cup be not secured.'[22]

The list of entrants for the maiden Munster Senior Cup tournament signified a notable spatial diffusion of rugby into provincial towns. Apart from the four clubs that represented the two urban centres (Garryowen, Limerick FC, Cork FC and Queen's College), county Cork was represented by Bandon, Tipperary by Clanwilliam and Nenagh Ormond, and Kerry by Tralee. By the mid-1880s, then, significant pockets of rugby activity were beginning to emerge in parts of counties Cork, Kerry and Tipperary. The initial impetus given to rugby in any provincial town came largely from those with prior exposure to the game in cities. In 1886, a club was formed in Mallow by one Mr McLeod, who moved to the town having been posted to the local bank.[23] In 1887 *Sport* gleefully reported that 'no less a personage than the popular ex-Clanwilliam player Bonnar Kennedy has started a club in Kilrush, where he is no less a favourite than at Tipperary or the Metropolis'.[24] In 1891, former Irish international Harry Spunner set up a club at Lismore, County Waterford while working there. His rugby connections allowed the club to earn a fixture with the well established Cork FC just six weeks after the Lismore club's founding. The team was comprised 'almost entirely' of boys from the local Lismore College.[25] In 1898, a club was founded in Kinsale with Dr W.G. Meade, a former UCC player, being elected its first president.[26] Jack Macaulay, the Garryowen and Munster Branch official attempted to start a club in Listowel in 1899.[27] In Waterford, the recently started local club did battle with Rockwell College in 1893 with a press reporter commenting that the city 'should easily support two good clubs, and these, if once started, would do a great deal for the game in the South.'[28] By 1910, the frequent overlap between the banking sector and rugby was evident in the same city with the institution of the Waterford Bankers club.[29]

The Royal Irish Constabulary and the army were more important agents of rugby popularisation in provincial towns than they were in either of the cities of Limerick or Cork. In Bandon in 1882, *Sport* 'noted that there was no less than four stalwart RICs on the Bandon team, who, true to their cloth, proved adept at collaring and when they got in possession, made gallant efforts to "run em in".'[30] In Killarney, in 1895, a match took place between the local constabulary and military teams with 'an easy victory for the blue jackets'.[31] In 1898, a Lieutenant Panter Downes, who had played with Garryowen, started a club in Clonmel with a Limerick correspondent hoping that 'next year he will affiliate the club to the Munster Branch, and enter the team for the cup'.[32] One club that certainly benefited from a strong local military presence was Queenstown (also known as Pirates), where a mixture of military personnel from the local naval base and civilians filled the club's ranks. In 1890, for instance, Lieutenant Harris of HMS *Triumph* was elected captain, with a local bank official, J.R. McNamara, taking the position of honorary secretary.[33] Later that season, the club was forced to postpone a match against Cork FC as 'in consequence of Lord Wolsey's visit . . . the service portion of Pirates could not play'.[34]

The backing of prominent citizenry was vital for the sustenance of rugby in provincial towns. When the Bandon club was reorganised in 1894, a solicitor and prominent local draper and wine merchant were at the forefront of the club's new administration.[35] In 1899, Skibbereen had a well-known local businessman and several solicitors on the club's committee. These smaller town clubs were also dependent on the benevolence of local land owners to provide playing facilities. When Mallow and Charleville played against each other in 1887, 'the latter were kindly presented with a ground by Mr Saunders of Saunders Park'. Bantry, a club that found plenty of opposition teams from the crews of locally docked navy vessels, secured the use of a field owned by a Mr Flynn of Caherdaniel for the 1897 season.[36] In some areas, the game was of sufficient strength at times to sustain several teams. In 1884, a match took place between Unicorns and Rangers in Killarney. Rangers represented the Protestant Hall School, while Unicorns were 'formed of the Catholic youth of the town'.[37] In 1896 in Skibbereen, two local teams, Skibbereen Rangers and Methodist FC, did battle.[38] This was a particularly active period in Skibbereen rugby. Later that year, the local club organised a match between the parishes of Creagh and Abbeystrowery.[39]

The men at the forefront of these clubs clearly had some exposure to urban life through professional training or education. Doctors, solicitors, RIC members and soldiers were all part and parcel of the

Irish town's occupational structure in this period and were all in professions that presupposed some level of mobility. When that mobility
was from city to provincial town, urban cultural pursuits could
easily follow.

In general, however, the strength of clubs in provincial towns was
uneven and many had little more than a fleeting existence. Having
enough interested individuals with adequate knowledge of the game
in addition to the administrative capacity to arrange fixtures from
relatively remote towns was a considerable challenge. Many well-
organised clubs frequently lapsed out of existence only to re-surface
when enough individuals of sufficient will and capability to organise
a football club emerged. Clubs such as Queenstown, Bandon, Nenagh
Ormond and Clanwilliam all had periods of inactivity in the 1890s. In
1906, Nenagh Ormond, a club that had competed in senior competition from the 1880s to as late as 1903, was re-organised. A group that
included a bank official, a solicitor, a doctor and a teacher were on the
initial organising committee and despite suggestions of ill-feeling
from the local GAA towards the project, one delegate recalled that 'in
the past Nenagh had a Rugby team that upheld the dignity of the
town'.[40] Clanwilliam FC from Tipperary town, who had also competed at senior level in the 1880s, were reformed in 1894 with the *Cork
Examiner* welcoming the development 'by recalling how "few people"
who are in the habit of patronising football matches some seven or
eight years ago in Cork, but can recollect the fine body of strapping,
stalwart, lithe Tipperary men who used to do battle for Clanwilliam
in those days.'[41]

Though levels of rail interconnectivity between urban centres and
smaller towns were very impressive in Munster in the late nineteenth
century, the logistics of sustaining a programme of fixtures between
clubs scattered over a broad area proved a considerable challenge.
This was evidenced by the indifferent operation of the Munster Senior
League. Initiated in 1900, the league was designed to increase the
number of first-class fixtures in the province and provide senior clubs
with a competitive programme prior to the Munster Senior Cup.
Clubs from outside the two cities had great difficulty, however, in fulfilling their league schedule. In the 1902-3 competition for instance,
Constitution and QCC had played five league fixtures each by
January, Limerick had played six, Garryowen three, while Cork had
played two. The remaining clubs, Nenagh, Clonmel and Tralee, had
played just three between them with the latter having played none at
all.[42] This problem persisted. In January 1910, for instance, Garryowen
topped the table having played seven fixtures, while Rockwell

College from Tipperary had played just two games of their league programme.[43]

Though neither club matched the achievement of Bandon in winning the Munster Senior Cup, Tralee and Rockwell were the most successful provincial town clubs in the pre-war period in Munster. Tralee had a more or less constant presence on the Munster Branch committee from the early 1880s and in 1888 had fifty paid up members.[44] In 1900, the club garnered sufficient support at the Munster Branch committee table to win the right to host that season's interprovincial between Munster and Leinster. Rockwell College became the hub of rugby in Tipperary from the early 1890s onwards. In 1891, having defeated the Tipperary garrison and, more notably, Garryowen, the club were said to have been 'crying to revive rugby around Clanwilliam'.[45] As a Catholic educational institution of some prestige, the club was guaranteed a steady supply of players and was credited with keeping the game alive in Tipperary: '*on dit* that new clubs are being formed in Clonmel and Carrick, and I think it is only fair to say that this in great part due to the energy with which Rockwell supported the game of rugby for the past few years, when it was the sole club of its kind in all broad Tipperary.'[46] The club was always competitive in the Munster Senior Cup and in 1897, the brothers Mick and Jack Ryan earned the first of their combined total of thirty-one caps for Ireland.

Rugby outside Cork and Limerick cities remained very much on the periphery and the game was dominated on and off the field by the players and officials of a small cohort of urban clubs. Indeed, by 1913, Rockwell were the only club from outside the two urban centres regularly entering the Munster Senior Cup. Garryowen and Queen's College Cork quickly surpassed Limerick FC and Cork FC as the leading clubs in their respective cities. Bandon's victory in the first Munster Senior Cup was very much an aberration. In the following twenty seasons, Garryowen won the trophy on thirteen occasions, including nine out of ten titles in the 1890s, Queen's College claimed five titles while the monopoly of the two major clubs was broken when Cork Constitution won the cup in 1905.[47] Though Garryowen's primacy within Limerick was not broken until the emergence of Young Munster as a force in senior rugby in the 1920s, Queen's College faced competition for dominance further south from Constitution. Formed in 1892 by the staff of the unionist newspaper of the same name, Constitution (benefiting, one would assume, from a considerable pool of administrative skill) was very efficiently run from early in the club's history and had become a senior club by 1900. By 1911, the Queen's College committee complained that their Cork rivals 'possess some strange fascination over us. We have now lost nine consecutive matches to Constitution.'[48] College, Constitution and Garryowen continued to monopolise the Munster Cup until Dolphin FC's victory in 1921.

The strongest Munster clubs also attempted to forge links outside the province. The prestige Irish club team of the era was Dublin University and the occasion of a visit from the Trinity team was cause of considerable excitement in the south. In 1895, the visit of the Dublin University XV to Cork yielded the following comment from a local journalist: 'such visits do good. They help to improve Southern football and they undoubtedly have a great effect in creating a feeling of friendship amongst footballers in Dublin and Cork . . .'[49] When they travelled to Limerick to play against Garryowen the following year, 'The event was the most notable that has yet taken place in Limerick football and the match was witnessed . . . by one of the largest concourses of spectators that ever gathered within the enclosure of the Markets Field.'[50] In the absence of formal fixtures between Munster and Leinster clubs within the competitive framework of Irish rugby, these friendly fixtures frequently excited considerably more interest than the interprovincial trial matches. Efforts to promote Munster rugby outside the province did not stop at national level. In 1900, Cork Constitution, then a very young club, was of sufficient organisational capability to fund a tour of Wales at a cost of £100 and still claim that the club was 'never [in] a better financial condition'. The object of the tour had been to forge links across the Irish Sea and promote 'South of Ireland' football.[51] Garryowen undertook a tour of Wales in 1909 and the same club hosted the Parisian club, Stade Francais, in 1911. Exemplifying the civic function of Limerick rugby, the French team were received by a welcoming committee chaired by the mayor.[52]

Around the turn of the twentieth century as well, the commercial function of the game was bolstered by the enclosure of grounds. In Cork, the vast open space at Cork Park was replaced by the purpose-built ground at the Mardyke as the rugby venue of choice while in Limerick, the Markets Field was properly enclosed from 1898. This signified the recognition in Munster of sport as a potential means of generating revenue. Competitions and the prestige that they brought to communities were now commoditised.[53] With better facilities, Cork and Limerick had the capability of attracting higher-profile fixtures. When Cork hosted the annual fixture between Ireland and France in 1913, it was the third occasion on which an international had been held in Munster. Considerable lobbying by prominent citizens and local rugby officials had seen Limerick host the Ireland v Wales fixture in

1898, while similar efforts saw Cork stage the Ireland v England encounter in 1905.[54]

The best efforts of rugby officials to promote the game in their respective cities did not, however, facilitate smooth administration at provincial level. Having two urban centres of power inhibited Munster rugby from acquiring anything other than marginal importance within the broader framework of Irish rugby.

The Munster Branch and the IRFU

The amalgamation scheme that brought the Dublin and Belfast bodies together to form the IRFU in 1879 led to the proper streamlining of rugby administration in Ireland. Three provincial branches were created, one each in Leinster, Munster and Ulster, and nominees from each province would comprise the IRFU's central committee. From the outset, administrative clout was tilted towards the Dublin/Belfast axis. Though the Dublin group had originally proposed a nine-member central committee with three nominees from each province, an amendment submitted by the Northern Union to the final scheme of amalgamation led to the creation of a sixteen-member body, comprising six representatives each from Leinster and Ulster with the remaining four from Munster.[55] This division of power recognised the perceived on-field weakness of football in Munster relative to the other two provinces. Munster would not be allocated two further places on the committee until the southern provincial team managed to secure either a draw or a victory against Leinster or Ulster, an achievement that had yet to be attained. Moreover, the composition of the committee reflected the relative numerical strength of the game in each province. The other provinces could display a subtle superiority to their Munster counterparts. In 1879 *The Irish Times* displayed something of the official Leinster attitude when assessing the progress of rugby in Munster: 'Football in the south, although much improved, still requires much organisation and careful watching . . . if the respective clubs are put on a firm footing, some of the Dublin Clubs would, no doubt, accept a challenge to play in the Southern province.'[56]

Though Munster's initial numerical underrepresentation on the IRFU committee was arguably based on a sound assessment of the province's relative contribution to Irish rugby as a whole, recriminations quickly surfaced. The IRFU's brief in the late nineteenth century did not extend much beyond co-ordinating the selection of the international team, a process that inculcated a sense of grievance among Munster rugby followers. Reflecting on this period in the mid-1920s, a

Limerick Leader correspondent had no doubt that complicity between Leinster and Ulster selectors kept Munster representation on the international team to a minimum: 'the Ulster six in those days usually included two Trinity men, who, with the Leinster representatives, selected a list of their own even before the interprovincial matches were played, and at the committee meeting the two northern provinces voted solid for the selected XV, though occasionally some Munster man played himself down the throats of the committee.'[57] From 1892, the international team was picked by a slimmed down selection committee of six, comprising two members from each province.[58] Despite being put on an equal footing in terms of selection power, Munster players struggled to gain international recognition. Of the 250 men who played on the Irish international rugby team before 1900, 220 were from either Leinster or Ulster clubs, with a mere twenty-nine hailing from Munster. In addition, Irish teams frequently had no Munster representatives. In January 1890, Garryowen FC wrote a bitter letter to *Sport* complaining that none of its players had been selected for the Irish team: 'We are disgusted. Garryowen kept football alive in Munster when clubs were dying like flies around . . . We beat Cork every way and every time, although we often had not half a team, and here is our reward.'[59]

The bitterness emanating from the south was deepened in 1895 when a serious row erupted between the Munster Branch of the IRFU and the Union itself. Munster had its representation on the Union committee reduced for not paying up full subscription fees and for not having comparable club strength to Leinster and Ulster. In addition, and of considerable future significance, the Leinster and Ulster delegates voted in favour of having Munster's voting power on the international selection committee reduced from two to one. The events drew stinging criticism from Branch official and professional journalist V.J. Murray, who accused the Union of 'prejudice and bigotry'. *Sport* reacted sympathetically to the Munster cause and while acknowledging that the Union had principle on its side, the paper commented on the unfavourable timing of the move, given that 'Munster has had a great impetus this season . . . yet it was such a moment was chosen to put a badge of inferiority on the southern province . . . it is also highly unfortunate that the moment Munster's representation on the selection committee was crippled that province was denied even the slightest representation on the Irish team of this year . . .'[60] The IRFU's decision quickly became a celebrated bone of contention down south. A *Cork Examiner* reporter related in 1895 that at an international match 'I heard a great many people say that a few of the Munster forwards would

have been just the men for such a day . . . the game was just another
buck-kicking, forward rushing game in which Munster did so well
against Leinster in Limerick . . . the result of the game is a slap in the
face to the selection committee . . .'[61] A perceived bias against Munster
players became a frequent theme in local press commentary. In 1898,
the *Limerick Leader* reacted to the announcement of an Irish team to play
against England by concluding that 'it would seem the committee of
selection did not act in an . . . unprejudicial manner. The very fact of
there being two representatives each from Ulster and Leinster on the
selection committee and there is but one from Munster is sufficient evidence that the Union does not treat this province in an impartial way.'[62]

Were it valid to weight voting power according to numbers of affiliated clubs, Munster did not have grounds for complaint. Figure 2
displays the relative vigour of each of the three main provinces
according to affiliated clubs in the period 1885–1910. The figures are a
limited barometer of real strength insofar as we do not possess reliable
figures for the 1890s and only affiliated clubs are accounted for. All
three provinces would have had numerous unaffiliated clubs
throughout the period. In 1885, for instance, a total of forty-seven clubs
in the three provinces included twenty-one unattached to the IRFU.
Incidentally, and perhaps reflecting the lack of urgency among junior
and provincial town clubs to affiliate, eight out of Munster's fifteen
clubs were unattached.[63] When it came to brokering at the IRFU committee table, however, affiliation was crucial and in this respect
Munster lagged behind the Dublin/Belfast axis. Moreover, Leinster
and Ulster clubs had far larger memberships, on average, than their
Munster counterparts. In 1885 the aggregate membership of the seven

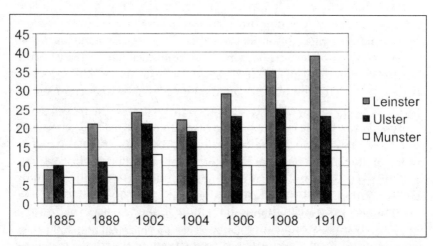

Fig. 2. Number of clubs affiliated to the IRFU per province 1885–1910

affiliated Munster clubs was 372, yielding an average number of members per club of fifty-three. The equivalent averages for Leinster and Ulster were eighty-eight and seventy-nine respectively.[64] Though it is not the prerogative of the historian to judge whether or not executive power should have been linked to these factors, the figures are clear evidence that the club game in Leinster and Ulster was on a healthier footing than Munster.

Beyond relative strength, the Munster Branch contributed generously to its own difficulties at national level. By the mid-1880s, the provincial committee was factionalised, with mutual suspicion between *de facto* Limerick and Cork camps inhibiting the smooth administration of the game in the province. Committee members had a clear tendency to use Branch membership to further the rugby interests of their own city over the province as a whole. In 1886, a farcical meeting took place to decide the venue of the Leinster v Munster interprovincial match for that season. When Cork Bankers failed to send a representative, another member of a Cork club left the meeting to find an individual who could act as a proxy voter for the Bankers. In response, Limerick representatives attempted a similar course of action for the absent Nenagh Ormond club. When the latter could only find two young boys, later described as 'street urchins', the proxy vote of Nenagh was not accepted and the Bankers' 'representatives' swung the vote in favour of staging the fixture in Cork.[65] Sectional interests influenced the selection of the Munster team, on which voting power for a particular city was weighted upon numbers of clubs affiliated. In 1886, Limerick representatives voiced concerns at Cork supremacy:

> We, the Limerick men . . . fear Cork will have the best of it as Midleton FC have joined the Union lately . . . Cork will be represented By Cork, Cork Bankers, Queen's College, Bandon, Clonakilty and Midleton; while we have Limerick, Garryowen, Tralee, Clanwilliam and Nenagh . . . we fellows fear this year that the picking of the Munster team will be the same as it has been for some time past, a mockery, delusion and snare . . . when it comes to voting, the idea of getting the best team is sacrificed for the purpose of each club striving to get greater numbers of their members on, and all idea of getting the best team totally ignored.[66]

The rivalry between Cork and Limerick in Munster was subject to derision from the Dublin press. In 1889, *Sport* spoke of the 'rotten wrangling of the southerners among themselves . . . how is it that Cork and Limerick people can find nothing more to their tastes than dissension and unfriendly opposition'.[67] This lack of harmony was reflected in the Munster team's performance on the field. In the fifteen matches played between the provinces in the period 1881–95, Leinster defeated Munster thirteen times, drew once, and lost a solitary encounter, in Cork in 1893. Some of the defeats were humiliating. In 1891, for instance, Leinster defeated Munster by one goal and five tries to nil despite having to call in five substitutes to replace men who could not travel, while playing against a Munster side that included nine of a very strong Garryowen outfit.[68]

The lopsided voting structure that militated against meritorious selection of the Munster team no doubt contributed to the province's poor record in the interprovincial series. When selections from the Limerick and Cork regions played against each other in a trial match for the Munster team in 1889, the superiority of Limerick players was not reflected in the eventual Munster XV, a fact not lost on media commentators: 'North Munster [Limerick clubs] beat South Munster [Cork clubs] by one goal and five tries to nil and on the united Munster team the proportion of representatives was altogether in favour of the Cork men . . .'[69] Quite apart from not fielding the strongest team in the province, Munster occasionally failed to gather together a full XV for interprovincial matches. In 1892 for instance, Munster travelled to Dublin without enough players to field a team and, having had to requisition local players to make up fifteen, were demolished by two goals and eight tries to nil by Leinster.[70] Two years later, *Sport* again bemoaned the Munster approach to the interprovincial matches: 'It was a great pity that Munster could not send up a stronger team this year . . . there is bound to be a lot of grumbling down south on account of none of the Munster representatives getting a place on the Irish fifteen; but really if the southern province don't send up its best men they can scarcely complain if their claim is not favourably received.'[71]

Suspicion among the Limerick rugby public at the selection of the Munster team persisted. In 1909, for example, the always colourful *Limerick Leader* rugby editorial bemoaned the fact that 'Joe O'Connor of Garryowen FC did not get a place on the Munster team', and was equally surprised that 'Paddy Walsh, Lansdowne FC was not picked. Both these men completely outclassed the Corkmen in Saturday's trial game and their brilliant football display according to the selection committee (on which Cork has the majority voting) has only merited their being appointed substitutes. The men who picked the team are indeed "generous" and their idea of fair play alarming.'[72] In 1911, though the pre-trial match to select the Munster XV had again resulted in a large victory for North over South Munster, the majority of the provincial team were still selected from Cork clubs. The *Limerick Leader* asserted that the selection reflected 'anything but credit on that rock of football "wisdom" the Munster five'.[73] In 1912, the *Leader* again expressed disquiet at what its rugby writer saw as the meagre Limerick representation on the Munster XV, complaining that 'Cork, of course, as usual got the lion's share of the pick'.[74]

From the early years of the twentieth century, the administrative brief of the Munster Branch became more complex due to its gradual extension into the club game. Amid concerns about the accountability of hitherto independently run cup competitions, the IRFU central committee resolved that 'all competitions in Munster be carried out under the auspices of the Munster Branch and that receipts and expenditure be included in the accounts of the Branch'. In a clear reference to the fractious nature of administration in Munster, the committee added: 'the system of alternating the officials from year to year between Limerick and Cork is very undesirable.'[75] Professor Connell Alexander of Queen's College, a prominent official in Munster, attempted to implement the IRFU's recommendations later that year but failed to garner sufficient support from the rest of the Branch committee. A second attempt the following season succeeded and was welcomed by the *Cork Sportsman*, whose rugby writer commented that 'the Munster Branch, instead of being a selection committee for the Munster team, are taking up their rightful position – the body managing, controlling and advancing Rugby Football in the South.'[76] The reforms saw the Munster Senior Cup (until then run by an independent committee) brought under Branch control, the re-establishment of the then defunct Munster Senior League and the creation of the Branch-administered Munster Junior and Munster Schools Cup competitions. These new steps were not without teething problems and prompted criticism in the press. This largely stemmed from the perception that the Branch's decision to take a more active role in the running of the club game was not matched by decisive action. One correspondent to the *Cork Sportsman* claimed in January 1909 that the Branch's negligence was resulting in a decline in the number of clubs in Cork: 'since 1905, Douglas, Wellington Rovers, Sunday's Well and Blackrock Road have succumbed to the mismanagement and neglect of the Munster Branch. The only junior club, seemingly, able to withstand the advances made by soccer and Gaelic, owing to an irresponsible and misgoverned Branch, is Dolphin.'[77] The Branch, having dissolved the individual committees that had hitherto run competitions, was seemingly sluggish in centralising this administrative function. The new competitions went ahead, however, and the three grades of rugby in Munster – senior, junior and schools – were now operating under the umbrella of the provincial body.

Rugby in Munster gradually became more effectively systemised. The previously chaotic nature of scheduling matches gave way to published fixture lists. At the beginning of the 1910–11 season, for instance, Cork County FC (the contemporary manifestation of the old Cork FC) were in a position to advertise a fixture list for the forthcoming campaign comprising twenty-eight matches with a mixture of friendlies, cup ties and contests with touring Welsh teams.[78] The new Branch-run cup competitions also gave clubs an incentive to affiliate to the central body. In 1910, Limerick City, Shannon and Young Munster, all of whom had previously limited their respective activities to local competitions in Limerick, affiliated to the Branch and entered the Munster Junior Cup.[79]

Neil Tranter has commented that 'the period between the middle of the nineteenth century and the outbreak of the First World War was characterised by a notable transformation in the scale and nature of British sporting culture.'[80] Though sharp movements in terms of scale were obviated in Irish sport by lack of economic development, the period identified by Tranter was also one of profound change in the sporting culture of Ireland. The nature of rugby in Munster on the eve of the First World War was vastly different from what it was in the 1870s. A sport that in the mid-1870s had been played on a semi-formal basis among a limited pool of players was, by 1914, firmly rooted in a network of formally constituted clubs with different grades depending on age and ability. The same timeframe saw the sport evolve from one played, for instance, on the vast and open expanse of Cork Park to a competitive activity played within the confines of enclosed grounds.[81] The *ad hoc* arrangement of fixtures among enthusiasts was replaced by a sophisticated administrative structure with provincial and national tiers. A gentlemanly pursuit gave way to a sport with an extensive competitive structure. A sport whose international structure involved cross-channel encounters between the then home nations from the mid-1870s evolved into one capable of hosting tours by southern hemisphere nations by the turn of the twentieth century.

Comparing the two most important rugby fixtures in Munster at either end of the chronological spectrum underlines the scale of change in this era. When the gentlemen of Queen's College and Montenotte played against each other in Cork in 1875, the game was most likely among men who were all acquainted with each other and neither side would have cared a great deal about the result. There certainly was no facility for charging gate money to view the encounter, and the events were of practically no interest to the media. Three decades later the Munster provincial team played host to Dave

Gallagher's famous All Blacks in Limerick. The game was played in the enclosed and stewarded Markets Field, tickets were printed and the press had a reserved area in the ground. In contrast to the private nature of the 1875 match, a campaign was initiated in Limerick in 1905 to move the weekly half-holiday to coincide with the New Zealand visit. Rugby had clearly evolved from a relatively neutral, almost private pastime to a cultural medium through which civic pride and identification with place could be channelled.[82]

As already illustrated, the primacy of place did not necessarily lead to efficient management at provincial level. Yet the one issue upon which the Cork and Limerick rugby blocs could consistently find common ground was a sense of bitterness and injustice at the perceived subjugation of Munster rugby at the hands of the IRFU. In a more restrained echo of a common theme, the *Cork Examiner* congratulated University College Cork's Vincent McNamara on his selection for the international match against England in 1914 by lauding the fact that 'No influences were worked; he had no press agents and he had no friends at court. In other words he has no-one to thank for his green cap but himself, and that is a very big achievement of which he may well be proud.'[83] Almost precisely a year later, Vincent McNamara was again the subject of praise. The context on this occasion, however, had altered dramatically. The relatively benign internal politics of Irish rugby had been replaced by international conflict. At a meeting of UCC RFC, Professor Alexander, having testified 'to the good qualities of the men who were about to depart to join their regiment', concluded his remarks by asserting that the 'German who would instil fear into the heart of McNamara . . . had yet to be born'.[84] The son of a Catholic solicitor, and a former schoolboy at Christian Brothers College, McNamara enlisted in the Royal Engineers and had attained the rank of lieutenant when he was posted to Gallipoli in June 1915. By the time McNamara was killed in a gas explosion in the Dardanelles in November,[85] Munster rugby had been officially dormant for almost a year.

Munster rugby and the First World War

The response of the IRFU to the outbreak of war had echoes of the imperial spirit displayed by the body's English counterpart and those who governed the game at national level responded enthusiastically to the call to arms. English rugby, collectively, felt that an acute sense of patriotic duty, expressed in this instance in ostentatious support for the war effort, was central to the sport's ethos. From October 1914 the international and domestic fixture list was suspended and official activity was limited to schools competitions. Senior clubs continued to operate on a limited basis with an unofficial league taking place in Dublin. In Munster official competitions were also discontinued from the beginning of the 1914–15 season, though local cups would continue to be contested throughout the war. In November 1916, for instance, a meeting in Limerick chaired by a Garryowen man, James Flynn, decided that a North Munster Junior Cup and the City Junior Cup would be staged in the forthcoming season.[86] Much of the rugby activity that subsequently took place was war-related. Just a couple of months into the war, Garryowen played a match against the Royal Army Medical Corps (RAMC) in aid of the Belgian Refugee Fund.[87] In 1914, the Royal Munster Fusiliers fielded their own rugby team comprised of officers. In Cork, UCC played Cork County in aid of the Royal Munster Fusiliers Fund.[88] In keeping with the comparable English situation, the war saw an upsurge in activity among military rugby teams, a development that kept some clubs busy. In 1915, the University College Cork first XV managed to play fourteen matches against primarily military opposition, 'including Munster Fusiliers, RGA (Fort Carlisle), and YOTC (Moore Park).[89]

Of the nine Irish internationals killed in the First World War, two were former Munster players.[90] Prior to McNamara's death in Gallipoli, Basil McLear had been killed in France.[91] An English-born career soldier, McLear had joined Cork County FC while stationed in Fermoy. A flamboyant three-quarter, McLear had been deemed not good enough to play for England by RFU official Rowland Hill when the latter witnessed him playing for Old Bedfordians in 1905. McLear subsequently earned eleven caps for Ireland and was one of the most revered backs of his generation.[92] As an ex-public schoolboy and a professional soldier, McLear conformed to the contemporary stereotype of the English rugby player whose involvement in the war was conditioned by selfless duty, manly vigour and courage. The RFU, in the words of Tony Collins, 'believed that rugby union had a higher moral purpose than mere recreation. Its goal was to train young men to be leaders of the Empire, to demonstrate the superiority of the Anglo-Saxon race in peace and war.'[93]

The sacrifice made by English rugby players in the First World War copper-fastened the RFU's desired self-perception of their sport being central to the imperial project. The game's war record was celebrated as an extension of the public school ethos. A similar sense of imperial duty ostensibly influenced the recruitment of rugby players in Ireland. Soon after the outbreak of the war, the IRFU president, F.H. Browning, set up the Irish Rugby Football Union Volunteer Corps. Recruiting over 300 mainly Protestant and professional men from rugby and other athletic clubs, the corps was formally constituted as 'D' Company of the 7th Royal Dublin Fusiliers.[94] The 'pals' left for Gallipoli in July 1915 and took heavy losses before leaving the peninsula in October with the company's strength reduced to seventy-nine. *The Irish Times* welcomed the formation of the company in language resembling that used by contemporary English commentators celebrating the contribution of rugby players to the war effort:

> The company includes within its ranks, barristers, solicitors, and other representatives of the professions, in addition to civil servants and bank officials, and it is naturally regarded as being typical of the spirit that animates the country as a whole. Its composition is symbolical [sic.] of the part that sport plays in war. Men who were prominent in the football field, and whose prowess was admired every Saturday at Lansdowne Road and other football centres, have thrown aside their interest in sport and devoted themselves purely to the affairs of war, in order that Ireland and other parts of the Empire may be kept free from the horrors of war.[95]

Middle-class men incorporating the lessons learned on the football field into a broader imperial mission was a popular discursive thread in conceptualising the involvement of rugby players in the war. Despite the seemingly faultless pedigree of the rugby pals in this regard, attempting to generalise on what motivated Irish rugby players to enlist in the British Army during the First World War is a hazardous exercise.[96] Notwithstanding the fact that their self-prescribed 'pals' status pre-supposed social cohesiveness,[97] the handful of Munster men who joined Browning's corps, for instance, comprised a sufficiently eclectic group to prevent any straightforward comparisons with the English experience. The three Cork-based rugby players in the battalion, for instance, were all Catholic and comprised a bank clerk, a shoe cutter and a grocer's assistant. Though all had attended elite Catholic schools, their social background was probably substantially different from the bulk of their comrades in Browning's corps.[98]

The number of Munster men who joined the rugby 'pals' was probably a statistically insignificant proportion of the overall number of rugby men from the province who served in the First World War. Though clubs did not keep records of members who served and newspaper casualty lists are not comprehensive, we know that men from institutions connected with rugby joined up in significant numbers. The University College Cork war record, for instance, contained the names of 352 men serving, or who had served in the war. Christian

Brothers College (CBC) in Cork published a list of 295 former pupils who had served. Considerable numbers of these men, in turn, had either played rugby or been members of clubs. At least seventy-three of the men listed in the UCC record had been associated with the college rugby club. The actual number is likely to have been far higher. Of the twenty-two players who won Munster Senior Cup medals with College in 1912 and 1913, nine served in the war. A list of club members for the 1906–7 season included thirty-seven war recruits, while at least seven former captains of the rugby team were serving by the end of the 1914–15 season.[99] In CBC, six members of the 1909 Schools Cup-winning team joined up.

To simply see these men as being an Irish extension of the British rugby war tradition would be spurious given the multifarious motivations that inspired Irishmen to join the war effort.[100] Intangible factors such as a desire to travel, a sense of adventure and camaraderie were probably as strong as any political motives.[101] The fact that those in favour of home rule or maintenance of the Union both had incentive to join precludes the notion that serving in the war presupposed any political disposition. That professional advancement was a clear encouragement for College men to join is supported by strong circumstantial evidence. Of the seventy-two members of the UCC rugby club identified in the college war record, forty-two were members of the Royal Army Medical Corps. A further fourteen were in the Royal Navy, practically all as surgeons; while of the remaining seventeen, nine were in the Royal Engineers and eight joined different infantry regiments or the RAF.[102] With work opportunities at home always limited, there was a long tradition of Cork-trained medics entering imperial service of some kind. The preponderance of UCC men among the military medical ranks, therefore, was merely a continuation of a long-standing tradition.

The devastating death tolls that decimated contemporary English rugby clubs was not repeated in UCC. Of the twenty-nine College men who died during the war, just six have been identified as members of the rugby club. The full horrors of war were only commented on from within the rugby community when a prominent figure lost his life. The death of Vincent McNamara, for instance, was a subject of considerable attention. Writing in the *Quarryman*, Professor Connel Alexander stated that 'When the call came for King and Country, Vincent McNamara felt it his duty to offer himself . . . a high sense of duty was the determining cause of his enlisting in the Royal Engineers.[103] Given his rather ostentatious unionist leanings, Alexander may have been merely expressing what he considered ought to have been

McNamara's intentions for volunteering rather than accounting accurately for the dead soldier's real motives.

The absence of records and the patchy coverage of local newspapers renders any assessment of the impact of the war on Limerick rugby difficult. It seems likely however, given the popularity of the game in the city, that the bias towards the commissioned ranks observed among Cork rugby players was not replicated in Limerick. A large proportion of the urban dwellers who enlisted in the Royal Munster Fusiliers came from the ranks of the semi-skilled and unskilled workforce and, given that rugby was capable of attracting individuals from these social categories,[104] it seems reasonable to speculate that rugby players from Limerick were dispersed across all ranks in the First World War. The small number of war obituaries in the *Limerick Leader*, for instance, included Timothy Carroll, a grocer's porter and the son of a labourer from Island Road who had played junior rugby for Shannon. He was killed in France in 1916 having joined the Royal Munster Fusiliers the previous year.[105] Another rugby player whose death was recorded was Augustine Neilan, a cleaner for the Great Southern and Western Railway and a member of Young Munster RFC. He was killed in the Dardanelles in 1915 and was also in the Royal Munster Fusiliers.[106] His brother Phonny would famously captain Young Munster to Bateman Cup victory in 1928.[107]

Recovery and the interwar period

The Munster Branch wasted no time in attempting to re-ignite rugby in the south after the armistice in November 1918 had brought the First World War to a close. In December a meeting was scheduled with a view to reviving the game and by May 1919 official competition in the form of the Cork Charity Cup was up and running.[108] In one fixture in the competition, the war veteran and poet Robert Graves played for the Royal Welsh Fusiliers against Young Munster in Limerick. Conceding that it was his last 'game of rugger', he ruefully recalled that 'our opponents seemed bent on showing what fine fighting material England had lost by withholding Home Rule. How jovially they jumped on me, and rubbed my face in the mud!'[109] That the war had not dimmed the local appetite for rugby in Limerick was evidenced by the concern in GAA circles at its successful revival in 1919.[110]

Despite the resumption of the Munster Senior Cup and the interprovincial series in 1920, however, the instability occasioned by the War of Independence and the Civil War somewhat hindered the progress of rugby in the early 1920s. In the aftermath of Munster's losses to Ulster in the first two interprovincial series since before the war, *The Irish Times* was moved to compliment the team for creditable performances considering conditions in the south. In 1921, for instance, Munster were considered to have played 'remarkably well' given that 'even practice games have been few and far between in the South this season'.[111] In March 1920, the Munster Branch delegate to the IRFU claimed that 'the game was in a dangerous state in the province' and he pleaded with the committee to schedule a high-profile fixture for the south.[112] In 1921, the University College Cork club claimed to have begun the season labouring 'under extraordinary difficulties. The tragedy that was then being enacted in Ireland had an affect [sic] on our club . . . Practices became impossible.'[113] Though matters had seemingly not improved one year later, the club were more optimistic about the future: 'The club like our country has a bright future, the clouds may be dark but they will pass away, and when the country has settled down to a happy and contented existence, I hope we will see the UCC RFC . . . take its place among the leading Irish clubs and keeping up our old traditions for sportsmanship and good fellowship.'[114] By 1923, however, the political situation was still capable of hindering the progress of the club. In January, University College Dublin cancelled a fixture with UCC 'owing to the troubled state of the south'.[115]

With two power centres, the successful renewal of rugby in Munster was more vulnerable to the vagaries of the troubles than Leinster or Ulster. The level of connectivity needed between Cork and Limerick to ensure optimum performance in terms of running and playing the game was most likely compromised by travelling difficulties. In Cork, for instance, the IRA carried out an extensive campaign of destruction on communications infrastructure from 1920.[116] Railway lines and bridges were blown up and travel was said to have become 'laborious and difficult'.[117] Proper trial matches and representative selection meetings allowing equal say for all interested parties were not possible – a fact evidenced by the composition of Munster interprovincial teams in 1920 and 1921. The XV that did battle with Leinster in Cork in 1921 featured thirteen players from Cork to just two from Limerick. When the same sides met again in Cork in 1923, all fifteen of the Munster team were from Cork. When calmer conditions were restored in 1924, the Munster XV took on a more balanced look, with ten players from Cork and five from Limerick.[118]

By mid-decade the game had largely recovered the ground ceded during the First World War and the revolutionary period. In addition, the reforms of 1909 were taking tangible effect. With the Munster Junior Cup now the prestige competition for clubs of that grade and with eligibility limited to affiliates only, the number of clubs joining the Branch expanded. From a position in 1910 of having a membership of just fourteen clubs including schools, the Branch received entries to official competitions from twenty-two different clubs in 1927. In one meeting in October of that year, five new junior clubs affiliated.[119] Clubs, particularly in provincial towns, frequently only affiliated spasmodically and the official number of Branch-aligned clubs was never a comprehensive measure of the game's true spread or strength in the province. An appendicised list compiled by the Branch committee from 1927 to approximately the mid-1930s included a total of eighty-six formally constituted clubs (including schools) that had existed at some point in that period. Most of these clubs had affiliated or had at least shown an interest in doing so and the list covered an extensive geographical area within the province.

As Figure 3 clearly displays, this was a period of energetic efforts to stimulate the game in provincial towns. From around 1925, a raft of competitions were introduced, mostly on a county by county basis, to accommodate smaller-town clubs. In Cork, the County Cork and Linehan Cups were inaugurated, while in Tipperary the Mansergh Cup was presented by the Clanwilliam Club in 1928.[120] The small

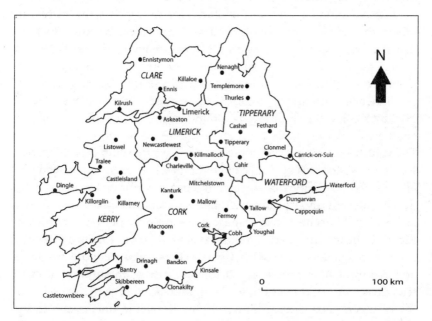

Fig. 3. The geographical spread of rugby in Munster c.1925–c.1935

number of clubs from rural Limerick were given their own competition when the Daresbury Cup was inaugurated by the Kilmallock club in 1928.[121] The vested interest that senior clubs had always displayed in promoting junior football persisted into the post-war era. In 1925, the Garryowen Cup was presented by the club of the same name 'in order to foster junior football in provincial towns of the northern portion of Munster'.[122] That the elite patronage more readily associated with sport of an earlier era still persisted was evidenced by the fact that the Mansergh and Daresbury families were substantial landowners in their respective localities. The Munster Branch was anxious to keep all rugby-related activity within the province under its control and all of these competitions, though originating in local initiative, were subject to Branch approval. In 1928, for instance, the Munster Branch refused an application from Kerry clubs to form an association titled the 'Co. Kerry Rugby Football Committee' 'whose objects would be the furtherance of the game in Kerry and take control of the McElligot Cup and any other cup that might be presented in the county'.[123] Ownership of the game in Munster was very much the Branch's prerogative.

Given that the number of clubs affiliated to the Branch at any one time in this period never approached half of the number recorded in the appendicised list, it seems clear that clubs in provincial towns continued to enjoy no more than a precarious existence. Though counties Cork and Tipperary always maintained a strong network of teams, other areas were inconsistent. Strangely, given the game's appeal in the city, rugby was weak in County Limerick where the GAA ban on foreign games may well have decisively stymied its potential development. Moreover, what clubs existed struggled for any level of permanence. Kilmallock Rugby Club, for instance, was founded in 1926 by a committee 'consisting among others of several professional gentlemen'.[124] The club lapsed in 1932, only to be revived in 1935.[125] The venture seemingly did not last long as when a club was revived in 1937 after an absence of five years in Rathkeale, it was commented that 'as they are the only playing rugby club in County Limerick, they deserve all the support the city clubs can offer . . .'[126]

As already argued with respect to the pre-war period, the administrative effort required to maintain what would have been a minority sport in any given town required a critical mass of potential members and players. Clubs that could not consistently maintain these human resources were always going to struggle. The average membership of the eighteen rural clubs affiliated to the Branch in one season in the early 1930s amounted to just thirty-seven.[127] Promoting rugby in towns where the game had little in the way of tradition or cultural resonance required the enthusiasm of individuals who had experienced the game either at school or while training for professions in cities. In that sense (again) those who worked in the banking sector were ideally poised to bring rugby from the centre to the periphery. In the Munster Branch list of clubs, compiled between approximately 1927–1932, the secretaries of the following clubs gave banks as their address of contact: Cork Bankers, Clanwilliam, Clonmel, Dingle, Fermoy, Kanturk, Killaloe, Listowel, Midleton, Newcastlewest, Skibbereen, Thurles, Tallow and Waterford.[128] Catholic rugby-playing schools trained students specifically for the banking profession and, once qualified, a bank clerk could easily be posted to a provincial town by his employer. Jack Liston, an ex-rugby player and pupil at Christian Brothers College, was stationed to nine different towns in six different counties in his career with Munster and Leinster Bank spanning the first half of the twentieth century and played his game of choice in most of them.[129]

With the impressive geographical spread of the game at junior level and the onset of an era when the Munster XV became more competitive on the field, the late 1920s and early 1930s were seen as something of a golden era for Munster rugby. In 1928, Young Munster had caused one of the greatest upsets in the history of Irish rugby when the club defeated Lansdowne in the final of the Bateman Cup in Lansdowne Road.[130] The tournament had been instituted as a war memorial trophy in 1921 and was put up for competition between the four provincial cup winners, becoming a *de facto* 'all-Ireland' rugby competition.[131] With a team comprising seven contemporary or future internationals and playing on home territory, Lansdowne were overwhelming favourites to defeat the Limerick club. Young Munster, however, sprung a surprise and took the trophy south for the first time with *The Irish Times* commenting that the win 'should do an immense amount of good for the game in Munster'.[132] Another landmark on the field was achieved in 1930 when the Munster representative team managed to defeat both Leinster and Ulster in the same series for the first time. The press saw the victory as being symptomatic of the contemporary health of the game in the province: 'Even before the war Rugby in the South was on the decline ... Recently, however ... throughout Munster new clubs have been appearing. Small towns in the southern counties have taken up the game with enthusiasm, while in Cork and Limerick rapid progress has been made.'[133]

Despite the apparent vitality of Munster rugby in the early 1930s, the game was still not as popular or as well organised as elsewhere. The

IRFU kept a close inventory of clubs' membership and gate receipts. The data on an undated tabular list (almost certainly from either 1932 or 1933) among the IRFU papers makes for interesting comparisons between the strength of club rugby in Leinster and Munster. The thirty-seven Munster clubs listed had an aggregate membership of 2,357. The four biggest Leinster clubs – Lansdowne, Wanderers, Old Wesley and Bective Rangers – had an aggregate of 1,902 members alone. Lansdowne and Wanderers, with a combined total of 1,346, had more than half of the entire Munster total between them, while Wanderers' total of 685 members was just thirty-nine fewer than the combined total of Munster's four biggest clubs: Garryowen, Cork Constitution, Bohemians and Young Munster. Some clubs operated from a very meagre membership base. Kinsale RFC, for instance, obviously did not compel players to join the club as their total membership of thirteen did not even amount to a full rugby team.[134]

The ostensible vitality of the game was also at variance with ongoing internal rancour. In a case of historical continuity, a feeling of affront persisted in Limerick centring on the selection of the Munster team. In December 1924, yet more scorn was poured over the Cork selectors by claims that 'the catch-cry of some of our Southern co-rug-byites about "selecting the team without fear of favour" seems to be a hollow mockery'.[135] Such was the feeling of injustice in Limerick rugby that at various points, the setting up of a separate administrative body to run rugby in Limerick was advocated. Along with the perceived injustice inherent in the selection of the Munster team, there was a general feeling that it was 'difficult to reconcile Limerick's proved superiority in the rugby world of Munster with their lack of superiority in administration'.[136] This feeling was expressed frequently in the *Limerick Leader*. In January 1933, the paper's rugby editorial claimed that 'if we ever hope to do anything constructive with Limerick rugby, we must have a working majority on the Munster Branch. This season's Munster XV was a clear example of Limerick's need for a majority.'[137] When Young Munster's international scrum-half Danaher Sheahan failed to gain selection for the Munster team that season, the *Leader*'s rugby writer decided that 'here now is an excellent opportunity for the Munster Branch to propose that the county method be adopted. It is proving satisfactory across the water, and in Ireland should prove to be even more adaptable.'[138]

At administrative level, the issue of grounds dominated the 1930s. At the beginning of the decade, the Branch became dissatisfied with the Markets Field venue in Limerick and decided to acquire and develop its own grounds in Limerick. A site at Hassett's Cross was purchased in 1930 and the painstakingly slow development of the ground that would become Thomond Park began. The logic of faction-alisation dictated, however, that if a Branch ground was developed in Limerick, one would also have to be bought in Cork. With the Thomond Park project unfinished and in financial trouble, the Branch decided to buy a site in Ballyphehane in Cork. In 1938 work began on the grounds that were later named Musgrave Park. Though a balanced consideration of the revenue-generating capacity of rugby in Munster would surely have precluded buying two grounds, the eagerness of rugby officials to push the agenda of their own cities overcame any financial considerations.[139]

Munster rugby and the Emergency

Though the outbreak of the Second World War in 1939 put paid to the international championship until 1946, Ulster was the only province in which the domestic schedule was suspended due to the hostilities. The Free State's neutral status allowed the provincial rugby authorities to continue planning competitions as normal. Rugby prospects were par-tially affected, however, by wartime supply issues. Fuel shortages interrupted both the playing and administration of rugby in Munster during the Emergency, particularly affecting fixtures between Limerick and Cork clubs. Fixture lists were seriously curtailed and the running of competitions on an 'open draw' basis became difficult. In January 1941, for instance, both Young Munster and Bohemians had fixtures in Cork cancelled due to petrol restrictions.[140] That season also saw the restructuring of the Munster Senior Cup on a regional basis for the duration of the war. In 1942, the Branch applied to the Ministry of Supplies for extra fuel rations and also pleaded with the IRFU for concessions on rationing orders applying to jerseys and togs.[141] Yet when the Munster Cup came around these difficulties were overcome and the customary five shilling excursion train to Cork was offered to Limerick rugby supporters for Bohemians' clash with UCC and Garryowen's tie with Dolphin in March.[142] In 1943, the *Limerick Leader* gave a positive assessment of the contemporary rugby situation. Though regretting the fact that travel difficulties had 'cut out the glamour of inter-city fixtures', it was noted that clubs had responded well to a Union circular regarding playing style and that there was 'a decided improvement in the play generally ... providing brighter football, which made the matches rather pleasant for spectators'.[143]

Tangible intersection between rugby and wartime events was manifested in other areas. The expansion of the National Army attracted a large number of recruits from rugby clubs in Munster – a fact that was seen as potentially detrimental to the prospects of Limerick clubs in particular. In the 1940–1 season, Young Munster were deprived of five of their starting XV who had joined up, while Richmond and Shannon were identified as other Limerick clubs affected by players enlisting.[144] The army's recruitment of substantial numbers of talented rugby players culminated in the immediate entry of the Army team to the Munster Senior Cup.[145] In April 1942, the Cork-based Army 3rd Division were allowed to enter the Munster Senior Cup and the Cork Charity Cup[146] and in 1943 the Army Southern Command were granted permission to enter two teams, one each from Cork and Limerick, in the Munster Senior Cup.[147] Links between the army and rugby were strengthened in 1942 when the Branch decided that all serving army personnel, in uniform, were entitled to free entry to all matches held under the Branch's auspices for the duration of the Emergency.[148] When hostilities ended in Europe, post-war demobilisation strengthened the ranks of Limerick's senior clubs. Several interprovincial players retuned to civilian life and joined Garryowen and Young Munster.[149] Young Munster, for instance, recruited future Lions test prop Tom Clifford from the army. With their playing resources depleted, the various army outfits dropped out of senior rugby.

Travel difficulties caused problems at administrative level, and from 1943 the day to day business of running rugby in Munster was left in the hands of two emergency committees – one each being set up in Cork and Limerick. These committees continued to sit until 1947 and the new structure facilitated the resurfacing of the old Cork–Limerick rivalry. In January 1944, for instance, a serious row erupted between the two temporary committees due to the exclusion of Limerick players from a Munster XV selected to play against the Defence Forces. When a Cork member of the selection committee, C.J. Hanrahan of Dolphin, was phoned by a Limerick member with a list of potential local players for the Munster team, Hanrahan apparently claimed that the team had already been selected and that none of the Limerick men could therefore be considered. A subsequent meeting of the Limerick committee concluded that 'the procedure by the balance of the Munster V in Cork was very high handed'.[150] A plethora of claims and counter-claims were made at ensuing meetings by Hanrahan and Garryowen's Morgan Costello. Eventually peace was restored at a full committee meeting and a proviso that all Munster teams had thereafter to be selected from a trial match was agreed.[151] Other disputes that arose relating to venues for fixtures and the selection of schools teams demonstrated the persistent lack of trust that prevailed within the politics of Munster rugby.

Mutual suspicion was one facet of a general continuity that prevailed within the governing of Munster rugby. By the middle of the twentieth century, and after seventy years of formal administration, little had changed in the fashion in which the Munster committee conducted its business. A small number of senior clubs had a monopoly on voting power. Despite the marked increase in junior club numbers in the inter-war period, senior clubs (now a small minority) still held sway. Though Abbey and Waterford both enjoyed brief stints at the top level in the late 1920s, administrative power was shared among a hardcore of seven senior clubs, three from Limerick and four from Cork. In Limerick, Garryowen's dominance was challenged by the promotion of Bohemians and Young Munster in the 1920s; while in Cork, Sunday's Well and Dolphin joined Constitution and UCC in the senior ranks. Each of these clubs sent one representative to committee meetings and, from 1928, were joined by two further delegates (one each from north and south Munster) to represent the interests of junior clubs. The senior clubs with a large voting majority, therefore, had sufficient clout to determine the fate of their junior counterparts.

A particular bone of contention between senior and junior clubs was a desire among some of latter for the introduction of a promotion mechanism. Agitation in this direction was initiated by Limerick's Richmond RFC from as early as 1943 and was later augmented by pressure from Presentation (Limerick), Shannon (Limerick) and Highfield (Cork). The Branch (i.e. the existing senior clubs) protested that increasing the number of clubs in the senior ranks would lead inevitably to a lowering in the standard of football in the province and therefore resisted the efforts of the junior teams concerned.[152] Junior clubs, for their part, suspected ulterior motives. Richmond RFC, always a happy recruiting ground for the Garryowen senior XV, reacted angrily to being denied promotion in 1943 and took the matter up with a letter to the IRFU stating that:

> The Munster Branch, as you are aware is comprised of seven representatives, from each of the seven senior clubs in Munster together with the usual officers of President, treasurer and secretary, who are also members of the senior clubs. On this occasion, Constitution had three votes, comprising president, secretary and their ordinary club representative. Garryowen – very much interested – had two votes comprising Mr McCauley, Hon Treasurer (who, in fact stated we had a thoroughly good record but voted against it) and the ordinary representative sent forward

by the Garryowen Club . . . Consequently [had circumstances been
different], Constitution and Garryowen, closely associated
through the old school tie, could in natural circumstances have
only recorded two votes, instead of five against us.[153]

The issue did not re-arise until 1952 when applications for promotion were received again from Highfield, Shannon and Old Crescent.
Despite the club's status as one of the province's leading junior clubs
over the previous six decades, Shannon were overlooked for promotion and the other two clubs, both founded in the previous decade,
were elevated to senior status. Under pressure, perhaps, from an
IRFU letter opining that Shannon's application had been the most
meritorious, the Branch granted senior status to the club in 1953.[154]
When Shannon justified their promotion by winning the Senior Cup
in 1960, they became the fourth Limerick team to achieve the honour.
Garryowen's hegemonic position in Limerick rugby was well and
truly a thing of the past.

Creeping modernisation

From around the mid-1950s onwards rugby in Munster, like Irish
society in general,[155] began an incipient process of modernisation on a
number of fronts. In terms of infrastructure, clubs began realising the
revenue-generating potential of developing their own facilities and the
Munster Branch was lobbied on a continuous basis to provide grants
or loans for the purchase of fields and the building of clubhouses. In
addition, dogmatic aspects of the game's amateur ethos came under
pressure from the onset of coaching and preparation as a culture
within the sport and the arrival of the broadcast media age.[156] This
process was augmented in the context of Munster rugby by domestic
economic policy. The opening up of the Irish economy to foreign
investment in the Lemass era brought multinational companies to
Ireland and saw a gradual proliferation of corporate culture.[157] Though
the economic factors that historically precluded professional sport in
Ireland still largely applied, the winds of change that signalled the
beginning of the end for amateurism in world rugby were also
apparent in Munster.[158]

The concept of coaching, much at variance with rugby union's
own peculiar brand of amateurism, first entered the lexicon of
Munster rugby in the mid-1960s. In 1967, the IRFU indicated to the
Branch that they would encourage and fund the setting up of
coaching courses in the province, though the provincial body
conceded difficulties in getting instructors for such courses. Coaching

committees were appointed in north and south Munster and courses were arranged in conjunction with the Leinster Branch for the start of the 1968/9 season.[159] At the Branch's general meeting in 1969, the secretary reflected of the previous season that 'coaching had become an important feature of the game in all grades and Coaching Committees in Cork and Limerick were organising courses during the summer months'.[160] Coaching took on a level of specialisation with the IRFU drawing up qualifications for coaching panels, and by 1970 an annual coaching congress was being held.[161] In Munster, the province's first residential coaching course took place in Rockwell College in 1973.[162] The Branch began taking proper preparation of the Munster team seriously and ex-international Noel Murphy was appointed coach in 1972. Though concerned at the potential cost of a co-ordinated programme of squad training, the committee felt that 'such coaching was necessary under present conditions'.[163] These developments were mirrored elsewhere. Long-established professional sports such as soccer in England only seriously began to engage with specialised coaching in the post-Second World War period.[164] Domestically, coaching and specialisation in the GAA intensified from the 1970s having previously reached a peak in the 1950s.[165] In England, the RFU had begun developing coaching structures from the early 1950s. Though the English governing body was traditionally suspicious of the concept of specialisation, broader social change had seen a gradual infiltration of new attitudes into the game. With increased importance being placed on international competition and the rise of France as a serious force in the Five Nations series, the home nations and Ireland ran the risk of falling down the international pecking order if they failed to embrace new methods of preparation.[166]

The encroachment of the commercial world upon rugby union, a cause of much concern for the International Rugby Board, was also perceptible in Munster from the 1960s. In 1965, for instance, having received a letter from the IRFU, the Munster Branch wrote to Waterpark to remind them of International Board amateurism regulations after one of their players accepted a 'Rugby Star of the Year Award' from the Town Hotel in Waterford.[167] Waterpark subsequently claimed that the award was made by the Committee of the Light Opera Festival.[168] In 1966, the Branch investigated a tournament in Cashel apparently being run by a commercial firm.[169] The IRFU subsequently wrote to the Branch outlining the International Board's policy regarding awards, gifts and sponsorship.[170] This gradual commercialisation of rugby in Ireland and Munster kept in step chronologically with developments across the Irish Sea. Barely a year after the RFU had softened its previously hostile stance on commercial sponsorship in 1971, the Northern Bank offered to sponsor a national knockout competition in Ireland. The increasing influence of corporate culture, coaching specialism and audiovisual technology on rugby was neatly encapsulated in one incident when the same firm presented a set of coaching videos to the Munster Branch at a reception hosted by the bank.[171] The following year a sponsored reception was held for a Munster v Wolfhounds match which would be titled 'the Munster Branch and Allied Irish Bank'.[172] In 1976, and roughly contemporaneous to the first official encroachment of the commercial world into Gaelic games,[173] the Munster Senior Cup was sponsored by Murphy's brewery in Cork.[174]

The intersection between rugby and the corporate world was also manifested in the emergence of inter-firm rugby from the late 1950s. Between then and the mid-1970s dozens of company teams affiliated to the Munster Branch, and in the mid-1960s the Shannon Development Cup was founded. The tournament attracted over thirty teams in any given season, with the final played in front of large crowds at Thomond Park.[175] In 1974, and with a third of the contemporary manufacturing workforce in the employment of overseas firms,[176] a company called de Beers presented a trophy for the industrial firms clubs of north Munster. That the league competition subsequently founded was again specifically geared to accommodate the firms of the Shannon Industrial Estate signified a direct link-up between rugby and a conspicuous strand of mid-century Irish economic policy.[177]

The competitive and administrative structure of Munster rugby had remained remarkably static throughout this era. The Branch-run schools and club competitions remained the popular focal points of the season. With the exception of matches against touring teams, the Munster XV rarely excited a great deal of public interest. For every season in which a rare highlight such as the 1978 victory over New Zealand focused attention on the representative team, there were several in which Munster merely plodded through the much-unloved interprovincial championship.[178]

An overhaul of the club game's competitive structure was not suggested until the early 1980s when the IRFU first considered the introduction of a national club competition. When first mooted in early 1984, the idea of an All-Ireland league was enthusiastically supported by the press. Influential *Irish Times* rugby writer Edmund Van Esbeck considered the old provincial cups and leagues outmoded and that an 'All Ireland league will improve standards and award achievement'.[179] The IRFU eventually proposed accommodating the country's forty-seven senior clubs in a five-division league. Reflecting a pecking order established over a century earlier, the top two divisions would comprise three clubs each from Leinster and Ulster, two from Munster and one from Connacht. The project was eventually shelved when the IRFU deemed the league unviable after twenty-three clubs voted against its introduction. Though the clubs involved advanced several logistical objections against the competition, such as the financial implications of extra travel and the demands placed on players by fixture congestion, a mixture of hypocritical conservatism and self-interest were at the core of the project's demise. Harry McKibbin, the secretary of Ulster club Instonians, for instance, opposed the league by advancing the archaic attitude that 'Rugby Union is an amateur game played for the enjoyment of players – all players. It is a participants' sport to be enjoyed. Higher and more competitive leagues can take away from this rather than enhance it. An All-Ireland League would lead to a scrappy, ill-tempered type of game.'[180] In response, Van Esbeck penned a brilliant article that dismantled all of McKibbin's arguments. With particular reference to the pretensions of inclusiveness implied by McKibbin's 'all players' comment, Van Esbeck pointed out that membership of Instonians was restricted to former pupils of the Royal Belfast Academical Institute. Countering the argument that a league would create an elite coterie of clubs that would poach players from weaker clubs with employment inducements, Van Esbeck pointed out that such had always been the case in senior rugby. McKibbin's fears of travel costs were deemed hypocritical given that his club had recently planned a tour of South Africa.[181] Rugby writers generally agreed that logistical arguments were a smokescreen for fear that mediocrity on the field would be more fully exposed in the context of a national competition:

> The againsts have trotted out some lame excuses for their opposition. But they are fooling nobody. The reason for opposition is simply the fear that they are not good enough at playing the game and they would lose status by finding themselves in the lower divisions of the league . . . the present set up in Irish rugby is a device developed over the past century to maintain the "private club" aura and to hold on, desperately, to the consequent perks that go with that status.[182]

The *Irish Independent* published the names of twenty clubs that opposed the league: nine from Ulster, eight from Leinster, two from Munster, and one from Connacht. In something of an endorsement of the press consensus, the two Munster clubs, Old Crescent and Sunday's Well, would certainly have been candidates for the lower divisions and would have been most at risk if a relegation mechanism to the junior ranks was introduced. As matters stood, both clubs were guaranteed senior status *ad infinitum*. One can only speculate, however, as to the motivation for either club's resistance to the new proposals.

The appetite for change was subsequently sharpened, however, by the Irish team's poor showing in the inaugural Rugby World Cup in 1987. With the national team clearly incapable of competing with the top nations, reform of the club game again became a live issue. When the idea of a national league competition resurfaced in 1988, the IRFU were altogether more forceful than they had been three years earlier and the project was eventually ratified that summer. The Insurance Corporation All-Ireland League eventually kicked off in the 1990–1 season and from the outset was a triumph for Munster, and in particular Limerick, rugby. Cork Constitution won the first title followed by two wins for Garryowen and one for Young Munster before an outstanding generation of Shannon players claimed four titles in a row. St Mary's College from Dublin became the first club from outside Munster to win the league in 2000 and by the end of the 2010–11 season, the title had been won by Munster clubs in all but four seasons of its history, with Shannon alone having claimed nine titles.

By 2011, the prestige of the All-Ireland League had, however, been long on the wane. The transition to professionalism from 1995 had brought about traumatic cultural change to Irish rugby.[183] Rupert Murdoch's proposals in 1995 to introduce colossal sums of money to rugby union for satellite television coverage of new competitions had effectively rendered amateurism moribund. With the southern hemisphere unions threatening to go professional with or without their counterparts in the British Isles and France, the International Rugby Board's (IRB) hand was forced.[184] In Ireland, given the structure of the game and the economy in general, the prospects for professional rugby were seen as bleak. Media commentators recorded a mixture of fears for the future. While the practicalities of professionalism being brought to bear on a game with a small domestic base was a legitimate concern, journalists also fretted sentimentally on the potential effect of commercialism and money on the game's apparent ethos of participation. One example of the trepidation with which change was anticipated was Seán Kilfeather's assessment that:

> Without its clubs, rugby union is nothing. If there is no place for the mediocre player who likes to go out on a Saturday or Sunday afternoon and get wet and muddy and bashed about, there is no rugby at all . . . It will become a television sport and more and more

people will sit at home or in the pub to see The Big Match and thousands will be deprived, partly through their own laziness, of that feeling of well being and camaraderie which rugby and other field sports like it engender in those who play.[185]

The IRFU did not initially possess any coherent plan to adapt to the game's new reality, and with large sums of money being invested in English clubs, elite players from the All-Ireland League began relocating across the Irish Sea. The Union eventually decided to effectively centralise the domestic professional structure. In 1997, rugby directors were appointed to the four provinces and set about consolidating the domestic professional game around the traditional provincial representative teams of Leinster, Munster, Ulster and Connacht. The viability of the scheme was bolstered by the introduction of the Heineken-sponsored European Rugby Cup in 1995. By attracting Irish players back from England and keeping developing native talent at home, the IRFU created a considerable pool of talent for the professional provincial teams to draw upon and thereby created a viable formula for domestic professional rugby. The subsequent development of provincial rugby in Ireland was startlingly successful. Ulster won the Heineken Cup in 1999 and Munster, having been defeated in the finals of 2000 and 2002, won the 2006 and 2008 titles. Leinster became the third Irish team to win the trophy in 2009, a feat repeated in 2011. Triumph on the field augmented success off it. In the case of Munster, reaching the Heineken Cup final in 2000 set in train a dramatic upward curve in the team's popularity that culminated in its Limerick base, Thomond Park, being redeveloped in 2007 to allow for an increase in its capacity from 13,000 to 25,000. In addition, 'Munster Rugby' became a highly valuable brand and in the 2007/8 season, the province signed a €2 million shirt sponsorship deal with Adidas.[186]

These developments had a rapid emasculating effect on the club game. The Munster Senior Cup's status switched from being the rugby season's much-anticipated finale to something of an autumn warm-up competition. The All-Ireland League, in losing its elite players to the professional game, surrendered much of its public appeal. The lively inter-club rivalries that once gave rugby in Munster much of its colour were overcome in the popular imagination by collective reverence of the professional provincial team. And the club delegates that uneasily shared power at the Munster Branch committee table took on a more ceremonial role with the employment of professional bureaucrats to run the game in the post-1995 era. Any popular twenty-first-century conception of the history of Munster rugby is simplified by the false impression that the contemporary success of the professional team is the inevitable outcome of a coherent tradition.[187] The themes examined in the following chapters will attempt to present something a good deal more complex.

CHAPTER 3

Class and Community

'Is not the artisan who plays football as good a sportsman as the gentleman? One stands to lose much, the other little.'[1] Such was the question posed by T. Desmond, the honorary secretary of Cork Constitution RFC, in the aftermath of controversial comments made by H.C. Sheppard, the then treasurer of the Irish Rugby Football Union, in 1903. In summing up the Union's financial position in February, Sheppard had embarked on something of a verbal solo run in which he claimed that the Welsh team were cheaper to host than their Scottish counterparts as artisans were happy to drink beer with their post-match dinner while gentlemen demanded champagne. The resultant stream of scorn from the Welsh press was matched at home by several repudiations from individuals and clubs. Dublin clubs Old Wesley and Bective Rangers publicly criticised Sheppard, while the meeting chaired by Desmond in Cork concluded that the 'inference suggested by the comparison made between champagne and beer should never have been made and the references to the quality of dinners offered to international teams was sorely out of place'.[2] A correspondent to the *Sporting Record* opined that 'few footballers know how to appreciate champagne and the money spent on it might be more judiciously used in fostering the game all over the country', while a contributor to *Athletic News* asserted that 'Mr Sheppard's views are not in sympathy with the best Irish Sportsmen'.[3] The casual snobbery inherent in Sheppard's indiscretion was possibly reflective of the fact that in his capacity as an official of the IRFU, he did not have much cause to deal with artisans. Indeed, the generalisation current in academic literature on the subject, which sees rugby in Ireland as an homogenously middle-class pursuit save for a degree of proletarian infiltration in Limerick, is broadly true.[4] In that sense it seems quite fitting that the sole Limerick representative on the Irish team that season was its only member likely to be directly offended by Sheppard's comment. Paddy Healy, a Garryowen front-row forward, was a prosperous butcher and who as a champion rower was denied entry to the Henley Regatta on the grounds of his occupation. A hugely popular character in Limerick, Healy most likely opted for beer or whiskey in Cowhey's, apparently his hostelry of choice in St Mary's parish.[5]

A corollary of middle-class domination was that Sheppard's comments were also notable for being a rare example of class being referred to in any kind of explicitly confrontational manner in Irish rugby discourse. Unlike England, where the bitter clash of working-class and elite sporting cultures leading to the split between the RFU and the Northern Union was heavily infused with class-based rhetoric and comment, Irish rugby has historically had a deceptively coherent social perception. As late as 2008, generalisations such as 'in the amateur era when rugby was a game for the gentlemen and the professional classes',[6] are buttressed by humorous caricatures such as those seen in the Ross O'Carroll Kelly series of books where rugby is part and parcel of an exaggerated middle-class decadence in suburban Dublin.

That artisans would not have entered Sheppard's domestic thinking was borne out of the fact that rugby at national level was dominated by middle-class players and administrators from Dublin and Ulster. As pointed out earlier, of 250 men who played on the Irish international rugby team before 1900, 220 played for either Leinster or Ulster clubs, with a mere twenty-nine hailing from Munster. Furthermore, sixty-nine of the 145 Leinster-based players were from the socially and culturally prescriptive Dublin University club.[7] Given this preponderance of Leinster and Ulster men, a sample of forty-four Dublin- and Belfast-based players, taken from the 1911 census, who were capped by Ireland before 1920 is indicative of the social tenor of the game at national level.[8] Of the twenty-seven Dublin men, twenty-one were Protestants (nineteen Church of Ireland, one Methodist, and one Weslyan), five were Roman Catholic, with the only non-Christian being the Jewish Bethel Solomons. Occupationally, the sample was clearly middle-class leaning. The health professions were represented by five doctors, two dentists and a medical student. Five subjects of the sample were at various stages of legal careers while a further three were in technical professions. Of the remaining eleven, there were three students, two civil servants, a landowner, a university professor, a wine merchant, a military officer, a clerk and an assistant cashier at a railway company. The seventeen Ulster internationals comprised eight Presbyterians, seven members of the Church of Ireland, one Quaker and one player who did not disclose his religious affiliation. The professions again dominated the social profile of the Ulster sample with two solicitors, two medical students, a doctor, a surgeon, an accountant, a stockbroker and a civil engineer. Industry was represented by two linen manufacturers, a linen merchant and a timber merchant. The remaining four subjects comprised a student, a buyer and two clerks.

Given the non-manual bias among the Dublin- and northern-based internationals, Paddy Healy's presence on the Irish team is a micro-example of a much broader trend that saw the social appeal of rugby in Limerick buck national and even provincial trends and in many ways illustrates the inherent difficulty in conceptualising class in Ireland. For though Healy would possibly have enjoyed greater material prosperity than some of his contemporary Dublin fellow internationals at the beginning of legal careers or working in clerical positions, education or perceived sophistication were also status defining agents in the social order. The complexity of the social appeal of Limerick rugby is much vaunted yet poorly understood and is one of the principal issues addressed in the following chapter. Munster rugby, elite in origin, evolved through a complex set of social, cultural and political circumstances. These circumstances, coupled with the key role of individual agency, bequeathed a dominant social function and appeal that varied depending on which part of the province one assesses. In this regard the diverging social appeal of Cork and Limerick rugby is the principal subject of what follows.

Elite origins

As already briefly outlined in Chapter 1, the social appeal of rugby football in Munster in the game's early years was limited to a narrow group of middle- and upper-class men. Before discussing the factors that led to the game's gradual democratisation in the province, it is necessary to expand the discussion concerning the early social milieu that dominated the game and outline how these adherents shared common backgrounds and social characteristics. As we saw in Chapter 1, rugby struggled to gain a foothold in Munster in the 1870s. A number of clubs had sprung up in provincial towns linked to endowed schools and local gentry, while rugby activity in Limerick had been limited to the mixed success of Charles Barrington's Limerick FC. Indeed, Cork and the towns immediately linked to the city by rail and other towns in the harbour area comprised the only meaningful enclave of rugby activity in 1870s Munster. Necessarily, therefore, the following section of this chapter deals primarily with rugby in Cork and its environs. Notably, a strong case can be built for asserting that key patterns that would come to dominate Cork rugby were established in the 1870s, with a mixture of elite education, suburban living and professional and business aspirations being common shared characteristics of the game's social coterie.

Elite educational institutions, both indigenous and British, were key agents of diffusion in Munster rugby.[9] In Cork, early rugby-playing schools such as Knight's, Fawcett's, Midleton College and St Faughnan's were staffed by graduates of Ireland's earliest football institution, Trinity College Dublin.[10] St Edmund's School, where 'the system is that of the larger public schools and the religious instruction is in strict accordance with the doctrines of the Church of Ireland', had two ex-Trinity men among its teaching staff.[11] Though the link between the establishment of rugby in these schools and the *alma mater* of their respective staffs is more circumstantial than empirical, the importance of Trinity to the early history of Irish rugby is such that it seems reasonable to assert that at least some of these teachers had exposure to the game while attending university. In Limerick and as already outlined, the diffusion of rugby from Rugby school via Trinity was direct, with Charles Barrington's founding of Limerick FC in 1876.

In terms of the influence of those who attended secondary and higher education in Britain, the case of Barrington was unlikely to have been an isolated one. It has already been noted that the substantial number of Irish boys attending British public schools represented a potentially powerful body of sporting proselytisers.[12] As already indicated, English public schools actively competed with the elite native institutions by advertising in Irish newspapers towards the end of the nineteenth century.[13] In Cork, influential Cork FC administrators and future Munster Branch presidents A.R. McMullen and W.J. Goulding, for instance, had been educated at Clifton College and Cambridge respectively. These individuals, along with Barrington, had countless equivalents across the British Empire, where it became customary from the late nineteenth century to channel civilised values through the 'games ethic'.[14]

Despite competition from abroad, it seems likely that Midleton College, as the first rugby club in the province, had a significant impact on the early diffusion of the game. In a series of articles on the early history of Munster rugby published by Queen's College Cork's student magazine the *Quarryman* in 1914, it was asserted that 'it is almost certain that its [rugby football's] nucleus in Munster was Midleton College, where it was played in the early "Seventies"; and all the early teams of which any record remains included old Midleton College boys.'[15] These recollections, possibly those of then Professor of Medicine Ashley Cummins, shed much light on the link between educational institutions and the early formation of rugby clubs in Cork. The spread of rugby football beyond the city limits to towns in the Cork region was most likely at least partially attributable to former city centre schoolboys. W.J. Knight's school, one of the first in Cork to embrace rugby football and the institution of choice for many of the city's early rugby players, usually placed separate advertisements in the Bandon, Charleville, Mallow, Midleton, Queenstown and Bantry sections of the annual county directory pointing out the achievements of former pupils from each town. Given that some of the school's graduates were likely to have returned to their native towns in a professional capacity, it is scarcely coincidental, then, that rugby clubs began to crop up in these towns from the late 1870s onwards.[16]

Of all the institutions that would dictate the early social tenor of rugby football in Munster, however, none was more significant than Queen's College Cork (QCC). Though the college's rugby club would later claim 1875 as its foundation date,[17] a college football rulebook dated 1872 was later found among the possessions of former international full back and Midleton College man Tom Harrison.[18] Assuming that the QCC experience replicated that of Trinity College and other British institutions where initial football activity necessarily predated the drafting of rulebooks, it seems reasonable to assume that some form of football was played at the college before 1872.

Significantly, the College club quickly established itself as central to football activity in the city, providing players for both formally constituted and ephemeral clubs. When a College XV did battle with nineteen players from Montenotte in March 1875, for instance, six of the latter were College men.[19] Similarly, in a fixture against a slightly later manifestation of the Montenotte club, Cork Knickerbockers, the following season, four Queen's College men were listed as the distinguished performers for the Knickerbockers.[20] Cork FC (a later name for the 'Knickerbockers'), for all intents and purposes a representative team and the city's other prominent rugby club, drew heavily on the College's playing resources. When College and Cork FC would play against each other, 'all other clubs, Queenstown, Bandon, Cork Bankers, and Midleton College with many "Queen's" men, and occasionally additions from Skibbereen, Tipperary, combined against College, but without success'.[21] The influence of Queen's College FC, therefore, extended beyond the city boundaries into nearby towns and created an insular sporting community with large overlaps between the playing members of early clubs.

The preponderance of university and privately educated rugby followers implies an obvious social exclusivity within the game. This exclusivity was also clearly manifested spatially. The early configuration of rugby teams in Cork, both formal and ephemeral, was decidedly suburban. The advance of industrialisation in nineteenth-century Europe led to substantial social and geographical changes in cities. Technological developments in transportation loosened the ties between home and work, and a growing perception that city life was somewhat unhealthy led those with sufficient disposable income and adequately flexible working hours to take up residence on the outskirts of cities.[22] The desirability among the middle classes of separating work and home life was matched by the attractions of the perceived privacy and security of the suburbs and further physical separation from those seen as social inferiors. Despite the city's adverse industrial performance in the nineteenth century, Angela Fahy's research has revealed a typical pattern of suburban development in Cork throughout the period:

> By the first decade of the twentieth century, Cork city had acquired many of the spatial and social characteristics of the modern European and North American city. The city centre was dominated by business activities, such as shops and offices: each having special zones of concentration. Residential areas near the city centre were generally poor, unsanitary and overcrowded. Members of the predominantly Catholic middle classes lived in the suburbs in substantial terraced and detached houses; set in neat gardens, behind walls, safe they hoped from poverty, crime and ill-health associated with much of the city's population.[23]

In a specific geographical example, Fahy has recorded that on 'the South Mall [a street in Cork noted as the centre of the city's legal and financial industry] offices and banks replaced homes. By 1852 fifty-four of the one hundred and four lawyers . . . in Cork had offices on the South Mall.' Ten years later this proportion had increased, with almost all having separate suburban residences.[24]

Initially, the new residential patterns were physically expressed in the mid-eighteenth century when impressive villas began to appear on the hillsides to the northeast of the city at Montenotte, Tivoli, Lota and Glanmire and the southern coastal area of Monkstown. In the early nineteenth century an expansion in bridge-building brought new areas within pedestrian proximity of the city with the result that 'aspiring professionals and business people moved to the terraced gentility of Sunday's Well in the northwest and Wellington Road and Summerhill in the northeast'.[25] Transport improvements brought yet further areas within the suburban orbit. The development of railway lines bolstered the prestige of Blackrock as a middle-class residential area to the southeast while the establishment of the electric tramway system in 1898 saw the Western Road and Douglas 'drawn into the terraced suburban network'.[26] Throughout this period, ultimately, patterns of wealth were matched by evolving residential ambitions and values among the aspirational middle classes. These developments, along with logistical improvements in terms of accessibility to the city-centre business districts, created the city's suburban landscape and recreational hinterland.

It was from within these middle-class areas that the early impetus of rugby football in Cork and indeed Munster emerged. This early genesis was the area of the northeast suburbs in the vicinity of St Luke's Cross extending from Montenotte down to Summerhill. Both of the latter-named areas had rugby teams of the same name at various stages in the mid-1870s.[27] It is likely that there were significant overlaps between the playing staffs of both teams. W.J. Goulding, for instance, was resident in Summerhill but appeared in team lists for Montenotte.[28] In St Luke's, a team known as Waterloo made up of schoolboys who later attended Queen's College was established in the mid-1870s. It was founded by future Irish international Oliver Stokes and Ned Byrne, who had attended the prestigious British Catholic school, Beaumont.[29] As neighbours on Waterloo Place, both men lived in close proximity to St Luke's Cross.[30] Initially confined to residents of the St Luke's area, the club was later revived under the 'Bulldogs' title to allow boys from other parts of the city to join, with the name Waterloo apparently a cherished possession of the St Luke's contingent.[31] The area would remain a popular football locality into the 1890s when further teams under the St Luke's and St Luke's Young Men's Society monikers would appear in press reports.[32] That these teams generally played against school teams indicates that they remained primarily breeding grounds for younger players aspiring to play in one of the city's senior clubs.

Significantly, these teams appear largely to have been casual arrangements with players opting for formal rugby with one of the city's properly constituted clubs: Cork FC, Queen's College or Cork Bankers. One could speculate that loyalty to place was superseded by the desire to mix with those of common socio-economic background. There is also evidence in this period of rugby in the southern suburb of Blackrock. A club of the same name was listed in R.M. Peter's *Irish Football Annual* in 1879 and a large contingent of Queen's College rugby players were said to have preferred playing for Cork FC over the college club including 'Blackrock men in general'.[33] Anecdotal evidence that rugby had early appeal further down the social ladder in

Blackrock came in 1896 when a team called Comrades played a fixture against Cork County. The apparent ill-tempered nature of the game was implicitly attributed in the press to the social background of the Comrades, with the *Cork Constitution* sneeringly observing that 'the comrades, who were mostly Blackrock fishermen seemed to have learned their football in a very rough and curious school.'[34] Further out the coast, rugby was played at Queenstown as early as 1874, when the local club played fixtures with both Cork and Montenotte in the winter of that year.[35] The Queenstown club was renamed Pirates in 1886, reflecting its embrace of the middle-class leisured townships of Monkstown and Glenbrook.[36]

That the northeast suburbs were the early cultural hearth of rugby football in Cork is quite indicative of the social makeup of the game from a demographic point of view.[37] In 1871 the North East Ward of the Municipal Borough, with a population of 10,149, was the second least populous of the non-city-centre wards. Moreover, it was just a little over a third of the population of its neighbouring, predominantly working-class and industrial, North West Ward. In addition, with a total of 3,346 (including Presbyterians and Methodists), equating to almost 33 per cent, the North East Ward had by far the highest proportion of Protestants of any ward in the Municipal Borough. Again, by contrast, the North West had a mere 1,532 Protestants in a population of a little fewer than 26,000. Though middle-class Catholics were well and truly in the ascendancy in terms of prospective wealth by 1871, Protestants were still disproportionately represented in business and the professions. Of the eighty-one practising doctors in the city that year, for instance, Protestants outnumbered Catholics by forty-four to thirty-five and enjoyed almost an equal share of barristers and solicitors.[38] Rugby's suburban impetus, therefore, provides strong circumstantial evidence of early social exclusivity.

Occupationally, given the educational and residential patterns observed, it seems likely that the majority of these early football devotees came from, or strove for, the professional and business sectors. Of twenty footballers who played for Queen's College in 1876, for instance, nineteen embarked on medical careers and one became a noted architect. Of the nineteen doctors, two became medicine professors in the college, one became a GP in Cork and another on Harley Street. The remainder entered imperial service of some form or another with eleven entering the army medical service (two of whom became surgeon generals), one entering the Navy and the remaining four establishing themselves in the Indian medical.[39] Though far from a thoroughly representative sample given the class implications that university attendance presupposed and the intellectual bent of Queen's College in the 1870s, the level to which the College team was interlinked with other city clubs strongly indicates a common early class profile in Cork rugby. As already indicated, a large number of rugby players attending Queen's College preferred to play for clubs other than the university team. Two noted Cork lawyers, Frank Levis and William Murphy, for instance, never donned the jersey of their *alma mater*, with the former opting to play for either Cork FC or his native Bandon.[40] Professor Cummins and the Townsend family of medical professionals preferred Cork FC, with whom they were both players and administrators,[41] while T.C. Butterfield, who combined a city centre dental practice with a suburban residence, devoted his early loyalty to Cork FC rather than Queen's College. Incidentally, this preponderance of medical students is not especially indicative of any religious bias in Cork rugby. Of the ninety-six medical students in Cork in 1871, for instance, forty-eight were Protestant and thirty-nine were Catholic – a statistic that supports John A. Murphy's contention that clerical disapproval of Queen's College Cork was no deterrent in the second half of the nineteenth century to ambitious secularly minded Catholics.[42] This was clearly a very insular sporting world. John Horgan, a Catholic lawyer from Montenotte, recalled that in his student days at the turn of the twentieth century, the college was 'little more than an excellent medical school' which had 'little or no connection with the life of the community in which it was situated . . . Outside the football field its students had hardly any opportunity for social intercourse.'[43]

Rugby football in Cork was also heavily linked to the financial sector. In 1879, Cork Bankers FC boasted a membership of sixty, two thirds of whom worked in the profession from which the club took its name.[44] As with the Queen's College rugby team, the Bankers were heavily bound up with Cork FC. The club captain in 1879 was the previously mentioned St Luke's native, Oliver Stokes, who would become a member of the Cork FC committee in the following season.[45] William Pierce, who lived nearby on Charlemont Terrace, was the son of a bank agent and divided his playing loyalties between Cork Bankers and Cork FC while holding the position of honorary secretary of the latter club in 1880.[46] In 1881, Cork FC fielded a team containing no fewer than six Bankers players for a fixture with Queen's College.[47] Beyond the professions, the commercial sector was also represented in early Cork rugby. The previously mentioned Goulding and McMullen combined playing and organising Cork FC with careers in their respective families' significant city businesses.

Two of the Montenotte team that did battle with Queen's College in 1875 were members of the Cade and Hungerford wine merchant families whose city-centre business lives were balanced with suburban home lives on Glanmire Road, in close geographical proximity to the Summerhill – St Luke's – Montenotte nexus.

By 1880, the lack of headway being made by rugby in Munster had become a source of concern for the IRFU. The problem was flagged that season by the Union's secretary R.M. Peter, who observed that 'In Munster football players suffer greatly from isolation, and the consequent difficulty in obtaining a sufficient number of matches to keep their interest in it awake. There are still, however, many fair sized towns near enough to Cork and Limerick possessing as yet no clubs . . .'[48] Rugby in Limerick had seriously regressed from its already limited popularity[49] and besides pockets of activity in Ennis and Tipperary, Cork city was overwhelmingly the sport's dominant centre of popularity in the province. It is clear that this sporting culture was remarkably insular and clearly reflected observable middle-class social and geographical patterns. Given the playing and administrative overlap between clubs and the compact geographical appeal of the game, it seems likely that the majority of those who comprised the rugby-playing community in Cork were acquainted with each other. Reflecting somewhat ruefully in 1915 on the changes brought to the game by expanding appeal and the proliferation of cup competitions in the 1880s, a correspondent to the *Quarryman* remarked that 'the old club friendly matches, which were really played between friends, as the old players will testify, have ceased to be of any importance.'[50]

Common educational, professional and suburban ambitions bound clubs together. The four doctors that comprised the committee of Cork FC in 1880, for instance, were either concurrently playing with, or had played for, Queen's College Cork. These trends were suitably encapsulated in the personage of W.A. Cummins. Having matriculated at the rugby-playing Knight's School in 1872 before studying medicine at Queen's College, he later set up a medical practice on the South Mall before taking up a professorship at his *alma mater*. By 1911, he still maintained a city-centre medical practice on St Patrick's Place while residing at Woodville, Glanmire in the city's northeast suburbs.[51] He was an enthusiastic rugby player with Cork FC, Queen's College and Munster and held administrative positions with both clubs and eventually held the presidency of the Munster Branch. Cummins shared a common social background with many of his Cork rugby contemporaries. Mike Huggins has saliently warned historians of sport against the risks of over-simplifying class identities and ignoring intra-class variations in social standing, wealth and professional ambition.[52] From the evidence gathered above, early Cork rugby seemingly appealed to a relatively narrow cross-section of society, largely limited to the local suburban middle classes. Though numerically limited and largely confined to a relatively small area of the city's northern and southern suburbs, the rugby fraternity included a heady mixture of those educated at home and abroad, heirs to large businesses and aspirant professionals, those with ambitions in imperial service and those who strove for local prominence. Indeed, this broad appeal based on the fundamentals of education, profession and suburban living largely ensured the later consolidation of Cork rugby.

Meanwhile in Limerick, elite domination characterised the game's social make-up for much of the decade following the establishment of the Limerick Football Club in 1876. As already noted, the game was an aristocratic import from Trinity College Dublin and the club founded by Charles Barrington seems to have played a large number of intra-club matches in its early years in the absence of local opposition. At the end of the 1870s, poor organisation and lack of local opposition for the city's only club saw the near demise of the game in Limerick and the club did not even bother to provide R.M. Peter with their playing record or list of officers for his 1880 football annual.[53] Unlike their counterparts in Cork, where rugby was very much given local impetus, Limerick FC was quite dependent on the city's military presence to fill its playing ranks. Indeed, the recovery of the club in the early 1880s was possibly attributable to the swelling of their playing numbers by military regiments. When the local garrison provided players in 1881, the press remarked that 'by their assistance this year, they have helped greatly to make the club a success.'[54] Something of the club's social tenor and dependence on the local military can be gleaned from the fact that an intra-club match in 1881 pitted 'The Banks and Garrison v The Rest of the Club' with the latter's forwards being recruited from the 57th Regiment.[55] The club, through evidence of membership overlaps, was linked to local institutions such as the Limerick Protestant Young Men's Association (LPYMA), Leamy's School, and the Limerick Lawn Tennis and Athletic clubs and thus created something of a narrow social world.[56] The individuals to the forefront of early Limerick rugby were, again, very much of the 'gentleman amateur' type. The football club and the local Limerick Boat Club were heavily linked and rowing contests took place between eights from each club.[57] Bruce Murray, a Protestant merchant, later recalled both playing in the first rugby match in Limerick in 1873 and being a member of the first crew to win an eight-oared rowing contest south of Dublin.[58] It was not until 1884, however, that rugby began to embrace a more diverse social demographic and take on its future civic function in Limerick.

Social expansion: the onset of Sunday rugby

An increase in the number of clubs and a broadening of the geographical appeal of rugby football in Munster from the latter half of the 1880s was matched by a broadening of the game's social appeal in the province. The following four decades would see significant social and political upheaval in Ireland. More specifically, the balance of wealth and power would continue to shift away from the Protestant elite towards the ever-expanding class of parvenu Catholics.[59] Aristocratic and middle-class Protestants had made a significant contribution to the establishment and early growth of rugby in Munster. The gradual marginalisation of these groups in Irish society, however, left the survival and further growth of rugby football in the hands of those with a meaningful stake in the country's future. In Munster, the dominant social character of the game in the twentieth century was linked to two distinct patterns initiated in the 1880s and related to broader processes of social and cultural change in Ireland. Firstly, an expansion of the Catholic education system from the mid-nineteenth century had seen the emergence of elite Catholic schools where prosperous merchants and professionals sent their sons in the hope that they would there develop contacts and networks that would aid their future careers.[60] Of particular importance in respect of this book were Catholic schools of varying prestige such as the affluent Cork schools Christian Brothers College (CBC) and Presentation Brothers College (PBC), Rockwell College in Tipperary and Crescent College, St Munchin's and Christian Brothers School (CBS) in Limerick. The significance of these schools in a rugby context varied, but the two mentioned Cork institutions along with UCC were crucial in defining the future social appeal of the game in the city. Meanwhile, social expansion took on a different character in Limerick where the onset of Sunday rugby and the concomitant development of a culture of local junior rugby ensured that a remarkably populist dynamic began to infuse the game from the mid-1880s onwards. This development, though ostensibly unusual in terms of Irish rugby in general, owed something to increased (though by no means uniform) solidarity among the working classes from the mid-nineteenth century where organised labour and nationalist politics often acted as cohesive forces and produced a breed of local notables whose involvement in public affairs was easily adapted to the sporting scene.[61]

By the mid-1880s, it seems clear that the social appeal of rugby football in Limerick and Cork respectively was evolving along two diverging tangents. In the southern city, a diverse group of middle-class suburbanites sharing a range of educational and professional ambitions had come to dominate the sport. The game was also socially exclusive in Limerick prior to 1884. The intermittent appearances of the Limerick Football Club had been the only activity of real prominence. Other clubs such as Crescent FC and Leamy's FC (both schools) and Phoenix had provided some local impetus[62] but the event of most significance in terms of the future broad appeal of rugby in Limerick was the founding of the Garryowen Football Club in 1884. Rugby was burgeoning in popularity from the early 1880s. In 1884, Limerick FC had claimed a playing membership of sixty players[63] and it was felt that the city needed another first-rate rugby team. After a series of meetings that year, the Rangers and Catholic Institute football clubs agreed to merge and Garryowen FC was formed.[64] That the social profile of the club would be diverse to an unprecedented extent in terms of Munster rugby was evidenced by the backgrounds of some of its pioneers. The first president was a local Protestant businessman W.L. Stokes, whose initial exposure to the game had been as a student at the exclusive Rathmines School in Dublin. Stokes, despite his new role with Garryowen, continued to play with Limerick FC and was elected captain of the latter club just one week after taking up his new appointment.[65] Among Stokes' fellow founding members were Mike Joyce and Tom Prendergast. Joyce, who worked initially as a square rigger on different sea vessels and eventually as a river pilot on the Shannon, was hugely respected among the city's working classes, eventually serving as a Home Rule MP.[66] Prendergast was an Edward Street baker, who, along with Joyce, was elected a city alderman in the 1899 municipal elections on the majority-winning Labour ticket. Both were elected with a mandate to improve wages and conditions for the city's working classes and were listed in contemporary RIC files as being members of the Irish Republican Brotherhood.[67] The club's first captain, Jack O'Sullivan, was a post office clerk and a future Irish international and would become a central figure in Limerick rugby.

Garryowen were unique in Irish rugby inasmuch as men with contrasting political beliefs and social backgrounds coalesced on the platform of civic pride to form a club. When assessed in terms of contemporary British sport, however, there was very little unique about the club's formation. Though Stokes' early exposure to the game in Dublin would most likely have been through masculine principles not dissimilar to those being promoted in contemporary British public schools, he contributed a great deal to the creation of a sporting culture that was both socially diverse and of great civic importance. He clearly jettisoned the more dogmatic aspects of Muscular Christian ideology by enthusiastically promoting competitions and placing value on winning above participation alone.[68] He was popular in Limerick and was described on his death in 1910 as having been a 'fine type of the tolerant, broad-minded Protestant'.[69] Garryowen FC was the sporting branch of a broad range of civic involvement that saw Stokes take membership of the Harbour Board, Chamber of Commerce and the City Council. Though pioneering perhaps in an Irish context, Stokes had many equivalents in the north of England, where prominent citizens of textile towns began channelling civic pride and rivalry into sport by establishing rugby clubs in the 1870s.[70]

Though contrasting greatly in terms of social and political background to Stokes, the personages of Joyce and Prendergast also provided a bridge between the hitherto social insularity of rugby football and a much wider portfolio of social, cultural and political interests. Leaving aside for now their involvement in organised labour and nationalist politics (dealt with in a different chapter), they were, as their political ambitions demanded perhaps, connected to a conspicuous triumvirate of urban working-class cultural pursuits: temperance, Gaelic games and civilian marching bands.[71] In St Michael's parish, they organised a Temperance Society which later established a band and a Gaelic football club.[72] Joyce, as captain, and Prendergast both played for St Michael's in the 1887 county Gaelic football final – a match they were forced to replay having been found to have included five rugby players in the starting team.[73] Though evidence of conscious design is thin, echoes of the British rational recreation movement are clearly present in the actions of Joyce and Prendergast, with activities such as football, temperance and bands all serving the function of diverting youthful and masculine attention into benign and purposeful pursuits.[74] In addition, as politically engaged skilled artisans, Joyce and Prendergast were in some ways akin to members of the British 'labour aristocracy' who, from the mid-nineteenth century, placed great import on working-class respectability.[75]

The club would continue to attract prominent citizens to its administrative positions, with the city mayoralty and the presidency of Garryowen being held by the same individual on many occasions. Joyce, for instance, held both positions in 1905 and 1906, while Timothy Ryan did likewise from 1910–12 inclusive. In addition, the curiously diverse church of local interests would continue to co-operate through Garryowen. Though Stokes' involvement decreased in the 1890s, one of the club's most prominent members and presidents in that decade was another Protestant and a fellow member of the Limerick Protestant Young Men's Association, Fred Hook,[76] while local bacon-curing magnate and future political rival of Joyce and Prendergast, Alexander Shaw, became a club patron in 1888.[77] Given its embrace of local notables of greatly varying social and political hues, it is not surprising that Garryowen quickly established itself as arguably the city's most prominent sporting club. Just ten years after its establishment, the club had already become embedded in folk discourse with the newspaper *Sport* moved to comment:

> There is no sport or pastime taken as much interest in by Limerick men as that of Rugby football, and at every match at the Market's [sic] Field, crowds of spectators, old and young, rich and poor, gather to witness the efforts of the Garryowen team to add further victories to their credit. Nor can local enthusiasts be wondered at for this, for the club has for years held a very high place among its contemporaries throughout Ireland . . .[78]

The club's early significance within rugby circles extended well beyond its own XV. It not only acted as a *de facto* representative team, but also functioned as a proxy administrative body for junior Sunday rugby. The significance of Garryowen will be dealt with in greater depth further on, but for now it is necessary to expand upon the significance of Sunday rugby – the organisation of which was one of the platforms upon which the divergent social imperatives of Limerick and Cork rugby initially took shape.

The staging of events and fixtures on Sundays in Ireland brought a potentially broad social constituency into the world of organised sport. Indeed, in an insightful assessment of the early popularity of the GAA, for instance, Neal Garnham has identified the fact that its athletic meetings and fixtures took place on Sundays as being a crucial dynamic underpinning the association's success. Sunday fixtures presented the GAA with a potential constituency, namely urban retail and rural agricultural workers, who were subject to *de facto* exclusion from other sporting bodies on the grounds of working hours.[79] Furthermore, the work of Fintan Lane and John McGrath on marching bands in Limerick and Cork respectively has added further weight to the contention that Sunday was the principal day of recreation for working-class communities in these cities in the years prior to the foundation of the GAA.[80] Though sport on the Sabbath was contrary to established practice in a broader British Victorian context,[81] the absence of sustained doctrinal objections from the Catholic Church and the dominant occupational patterns of a significant proportion of the Irish working population ensured that Sunday would continue to be a significant day of leisure in Ireland.[82]

Due to the fact that newspapers did not systematically report on Sunday rugby and were to a large extent dependent on sporadic correspondence from individuals involved, we cannot construct any patterns of spread or popularity of Sunday football or indeed identify its chronological origin. We have, however, adequate evidence to assert that a distinct and vibrant culture of Sunday rugby existed in Cork and Limerick from the mid-1880s onwards. The popularisation of Sunday rugby in Limerick occurred in the context of a broadening of the social and cultural appeal of the game in the city and owed a great deal to the interest shown in it by existing rugby bodies.

In 1887, a two-tier junior rugby tournament to be held over a succession of Sundays in the field behind Tait's factory in Limerick was organised. *Sport*, through the agency of its colourful rugby writer Jacques McCarthy, hailed the novel nature of the tournament by referring to it as 'one of the most distinct and hopeful features of the whole season'.[83] Crucially, the tournament was organised and endorsed by the local senior clubs Limerick FC and Garryowen. The already-mentioned Stokes was joined on the organising committee by Garryowen forward and Irish international Jack Macauley and it was presided over by Jack O'Sullivan, another Garryowen administrator.[84] The tournament was comprised of ten distinct clubs and was deemed a huge success, with fixtures attracting over 1,000 spectators.[85] Garryowen's second XV were joined by a plethora of local, community-based clubs including Parteen, Thomond, Kinkora, Shannon, Ramblers, Rovers, Star, Sarsfields and Faugh-a-Ballagh (later a Gaelic football club).[86] McCarthy again, who had referred to Sunday rugby in Limerick as a 'plucky and useful mission',[87] welcomed the formation of 'yet another club in Limerick' when Pirates were founded in September and announced that they had been 'practising away hard since the third of this month on the [predominantly working class] King's Island'.[88]

By the end of 1887, press reports were referring to these clubs specifically by the day on which they played as if to underline their divergence from established norms. One reporter, for instance, observed that 'to deal with Sunday clubs in Limerick would be to write a history. They are simply immeasurable. Every youth from five summers upwards has his club and colours.'[89] The junior tournament was held again in the following season and was again given a ringing endorsement by *Sport*, which not only celebrated the charitable function of the previous season's competition, but also encouraged support from the local senior clubs:

> I am delighted to perceive the Limerick Junior clubs tournament, which was so successfully inaugurated last year, will be held again this season. It is bound to prove most interesting and should be supported by every Knight of the jersey, past and present . . . They have no lack of clubs – The Rovers, Star, Shannon, North Liberty Rangers, Pirates, Kinkora 2nd, Ramblers, Parteen etc. Last year they took £9 in one day and of this generously gave £5 to Barrington's Hospital, medals and other expenses swallowing up the remainder. But they want a cup, and I think this is a thing they well deserve . . . I am sure that Mr W.L. Stokes would give the project his invaluable support. All the leading citizens could subscribe to the cup, and besides entrance fees of 5s (less than 6d a man) and gate money would be a source of income. If it were necessary, Limerick County, Garryowen and Kinkora 1st XV would, I am sure, play matches in the Markets Field for the benefit of their junior brethren.[90]

As will be shown below, the senior clubs (particularly Garryowen) involved themselves heavily in the advancement of junior rugby and played a crucial role in promoting what would become an enduring tradition of Sunday rugby in Limerick – a tradition that would characterise the unique social tenor of the game in the city.

Meanwhile in Cork, a roughly contemporaneous and equally vibrant Sunday rugby culture was emerging. From at least 1884 onwards, the local press began reporting on local rugby fixtures taking place on Sundays. Tellingly, the appeal of Sunday rugby stretched beyond the city limits into towns linked to Cork by rail such as Midleton, Kinsale, Bandon and Queenstown. Furthermore, the latter three towns also had non-Sunday-playing rugby clubs. In 1886, for instance, when Bandon FC became the inaugural Munster Senior Cup winners (a tournament played exclusively on Saturdays and weekdays), a completely different entity in the form of Bandon Shamrocks were playing rugby fixtures on Sundays. Queenstown Young Men's Society and Queesntown League of the Cross (rare examples of church-based rugby clubs in Munster) happily competed on Sundays as completely separate entities to the socially exclusive Queenstown Football Club.[91] In the city, clubs such as Ramblers, Shamrocks, Celtic, O'Connell, Lee Football Club and Nil Desperandum were frequently doing battle on Sundays. In November 1886, the Cork Junior Cup was inaugurated with seven teams entering and again with fixtures taking place on Sundays.[92]

This was not, however, before the Sunday football scene in Cork had already become somewhat fragmented with the establishment of the Munster National Football League with its component clubs playing under the newly created 'National rules'. This initiative was the brainchild of two GAA officials and members of Lee Football Club, John Forrest and primarily J.F. Murphy. The latter was a high-ranking GAA official and his framing of 'National' rules led to his suspension from the Association for forming a rival body with rules that were strikingly similar to rugby. At a meeting where Murphy attempted to defend himself, he admitted that the clubs affiliated to the Munster Football League had all previously played rugby. He asserted, however, that when the 'National' rules were drawn up, a resolution was passed that under no circumstances would clubs affiliated to the new organisation play under rugby rules.[93] A frustrating lack of press coverage precludes any generalisations as to the strength of the National Football League but a perusal of reports from the late winter and early spring of 1886 indicates that the majority of Sunday-playing football clubs in Cork and its environs continued to play rugby.[94] Three clubs that certainly took part were Lee Football Club, Nil Desperandum and Bandon Nationals. Surviving match reports indicate that an exasperated Michael Cusack may have been right in dubbing the new code 'the Murphy Rugby Association'. With the scoring method involving touching the ball over the opposition's defensive line and kicking for goal, and a preponderance of heavy forward drives, it seems clear that J.F. Murphy and his cohorts wanted to play rugby but did not want to be associated with it.[95] In the event, the experiment petered out after one season and by 1888, Nil Desperandum were playing under rugby rules again.[96]

Sunday rugby continued to prosper in Cork in the late 1880s even if prospects were grim for the higher-profile Munster Branch-affiliated clubs. In October 1887, amid concern for the prosperity of Cork rugby clubs in the coming season, one correspondent to *Sport* took solace from the fact that 'the Sunday-playing clubs are hard at work and nothing would surprise me less than that one of them should challenge and beat the Cork FC.'[97] Again, frustratingly, from then on press coverage of Sunday football in Cork becomes sparse, possibly indicating a decline in its fortunes. There was, however, still sufficient interest in Sunday rugby for the organisation of a tournament specifically for Sunday-playing clubs in 1894. The tournament was organised by the Ivy Football Club whose secretary, D. Murphy, gave Deasy's vintners on Buckingham Place as the tournament's correspondence address, indicating that Murphy was an employee there.[98] The tournament, apparently established for the 'lower orders',[99] had six entrants of whom only two, Shandon and Celtic, appeared in press reports from the 1880s, indicating the ephemeral nature of Sunday clubs in the city. In the event, the tournament seems to have been a one-off and

Sunday rugby appears to have petered out towards the turn of the twentieth century in Cork.

The distinctive nature of the Sunday rugby phenomenon was underlined by the fact that prior to 1910 (when the Munster Branch took control of most rugby competitions in the province), there is no evidence of any of the Sunday clubs affiliating to the IRFU. In addition, Sunday- and Saturday-playing clubs rarely played against each other, with the Sunday rugby culture remaining very much 'unofficial'. In addition, junior clubs in Limerick and Cork did not arrange fixtures against each other, as evidenced by the following question posed by a Cork correspondent to *Sport*: 'Why couldn't there be football matches arranged between the Sunday-playing clubs of Cork and Limerick? It would create the greatest interest here'.[100] Notwithstanding the apparent lack of connectivity between Sunday rugby in Limerick and Cork, collectively the junior clubs of both cities represented a distinctive sporting culture that diverged from the hitherto limited appeal of rugby in Munster and represented a potential broadening of the game's social base.

In Cork, for instance, the previously mentioned Munster Football League, which had comprised clubs that vacillated between rugby and 'national' rules, was specifically tailored to the needs of retail clerks.[101] John Forrest claimed that they had rejected Gaelic rules because 'in the city where they had to earn their bread behind counters, if they went into work in the morning with a black eye, they would be sent playing football for the other six days of the week.'[102] Nil Desperandum, who later as a Gaelic outfit numbered future Taoiseach Jack Lynch's father among their players, were linked to the drapery trade.[103] The *United Irishman*, in a polemical piece crediting the GAA for catering for 'commercial young men . . . who [prior to the Association's founding] were not eligible for membership of any athletic association if they played any game on Sundays under the canopy of heaven and within view of the hypocritical sabbatarian', castigated the rugby authorities by recalling (the uncorroborated instance of)[104] how the IRFU had apparently rejected an application for membership by the Cork Drapers football team.[105] In Limerick, what little we know about the spatial distribution of early Sunday rugby clubs is socially suggestive. Shannon FC, for instance, were inextricably linked to St Mary's parish, while Ramblers hailed from the Thomondgate area. Both areas, though inhabited by a broad social mix, had substantial working-class residential parts.

The divergent fates of Sunday rugby in Limerick and Cork were crucial to the future social trajectory of the game in the province. Junior

rugby in Limerick was consolidated by the establishment of cup competitions, whose fixtures invariably took place on Sundays. Crucially,
these initiatives garnered significant support from affiliated senior
clubs. Garryowen, for instance, saw Sunday rugby as a potentially rich
recruiting ground for their first XV and therefore enthusiastically took a
central role in its administration. The impetus given to junior rugby by
the establishment of the Limerick Junior Cup and later the Transfield
Cup in 1895 was aided immeasurably no doubt by the fact that
Garryowen officials supervised draws, mediated in disputes and provided referees. At the Transfield Cup AGM held in 1899, for instance,
three Garryowen officials, Tom Peel, Jim O'Connor and Jack O'Sullivan,
oversaw events.[106] When a fixture in the same competition between
Shannon and Rovers in 1900 had to be abandoned due to a pitch inva-
sion following a fight between the two teams, it was none other than
Tom Prendergast, in his capacity as president of Garryowen FC, who
was called to adjudicate.[107] Given his then recent election to the City
Council, it is not surprising, perhaps, that Prendergast found a formula
to keep both teams in the tournament. When a fixture bottleneck threatened the city's junior competitions in 1908, the *Limerick Leader* felt sure
that Garryowen's Jack O'Sullivan in his management capacity at the
Markets Field would do all in his power to stage the competitions 'as it
is to him the thanks of junior footballers is due for his efforts in fostering the game through all those years since the days of old
Garryowen to the present'.[108] By the turn of the twentieth century then,
junior rugby in Limerick was a firmly established and popular sporting
culture in the city with the *Limerick Leader* commenting in 1901:

> It speaks volumes for the future of football in Limerick to see the
> junior clubs playing so much football, and so early in the season.
> Sunday after Sunday for the past month or more matches have
> taken place at the Markets Field between the different teams and
> the form shown has – taking it all round – been very creditable to
> one and all. In fact, some of these matches have been better con-
> tested and have provided the public with better displays of the
> game than the senior teams have been able to produce. On Sunday
> next, Ramblers and Lansdowne will meet.[109]

Bolstered by its parochial appeal (as will be discussed below) and
benefiting no doubt from the rancour in Gaelic football circles brought
about by the Parnell split,[110] junior rugby was the key to the unique
popularity of rugby in Limerick. The facilitation of rugby on Sunday
allowed incursion into the social and cultural territory of the GAA – a
development further aided by the guiding presence of Garryowen FC
and its locally influential officers.

Despite competition from Gaelic games, the biggest threat to junior rugby prior to the First World War was petty inter-club disputes. The disputes were serious inasmuch as they threatened the viability of junior competitions. Shannon, for instance, having won the City Junior Cup in 1908, refused to hand it over for competition in either of the following three seasons,[111] while Young Munster delayed the handover of the Transfield Cup in 1910 to such an extent that the competition was not completed that season. The structural integrity of junior rugby in Limerick remained intact, however, and would inform greatly the social trajectory of Limerick rugby.

In Cork, by contrast, Sunday rugby appears to have faded out from the mid-1890s onwards and junior rugby would henceforth be largely limited to the second XV of senior clubs and a plethora of ephemeral suburban junior teams. The appeal of cultural nationalism, allied perhaps to the absence of a Garryowen-like administrative presence were the likely factors that led established football clubs such as Nil Desperandum, Lee Football Club and Bandon Shamrocks to throw their lot in with the GAA. There is no evidence of influential local rugby administrators or members of IRFU-affiliated clubs taking any interest in Sunday teams. The fruitful intersection between Saturday- and Sunday-playing clubs that occurred in Limerick was not replicated, therefore, to any great extent in Cork. Indeed, apart from very occasional fixtures between Nil Desperandum and Cork FC, the only solid evidence of interaction between the junior and senior clubs in Cork was when 500 footballers from all the local clubs gathered in 1886 for a celebratory procession to mark Ireland's first win over England in an international match.[112] Apart from these aberrations, the two rugby traditions in Cork remained firmly separated from each other and though the content of Cork rugby would continue to expand, the form would remain remarkably true to the patterns established in the 1870s.

Middle class consolidation: Cork rugby

The failure of Sunday rugby in Cork prevented significant social broadening of the game's constituency and rugby maintained its suburban tilt in the city. An interesting comment on Sunday rugby in general and specifically in Cork came from a correspondent to the *Cork Examiner* in 1913 who, in the context of concern for the organisation of junior rugby in the city, suggested that the formation of a Sunday League would help to popularise rugby by attracting a broader demographic to the game.[113] Such a move was not initiated and middle-class institutions and population centres were the principal arteries of rugby popularity in the city.

Continuing a pattern that had first emerged in the 1870s, clubs continued to sprout in the Cork suburbs in the decades prior to the First World War. Clubs such as Sunday's Well, Blackrock Road, Douglas, Rockboro Road, South Terrace, St Luke's and St Luke's Young Men's Society were all established with varying degrees of success in the decades either side of the turn of the twentieth century. In common again with the trends already observed for the 1870s, the second incarnation of Sunday's Well RFC, founded in 1910, had a Justice of the Peace, two solicitors and a doctor among its founding officers. In addition, three officers worked from premises in the South Mall business district while residing in the Sunday's Well area.[114] Rugby was brought to the developing western suburbs by Highfield RFC. Founded in 1922 by the sons of middle-class men living in the vicinity of University College Cork, the club's base was gradually pushed westerly by the development of suburban housing and by 1944 they took up permanent residence at a site near Model Farm Road.[115]

Whereas junior rugby in Limerick would become intimately associated with inner-city parishes, it was these suburban clubs along with a mixture of military-based XVs, other casually arranged ephemeral teams, schools and the second XVs of senior clubs that would characterise junior rugby and the large number of one-off friendly fixtures in Cork in the 1890s and early 1900s. Military teams, comprising a mixture of infantry regiments and the crews of naval vessels, flitted in and out of the Cork rugby scene and do not appear to have been important agents of diffusion or change in Cork rugby. Indeed, they rarely appeared in anything other than friendly matches and generally did not become formally constituted clubs. Exceptions to the pattern were the Cork Garrison FC, which intermittently appeared from the 1870s to the 1890s[116] and the Leicestershire Regiment, which briefly became an affiliated club and entered the Munster Senior Cup in 1912 having apparently made 'a very favourable impression on the public'.[117]

Of far greater importance to the future of Cork rugby was the evolution of the schools game from the mid-1880s to the end of the first decade of the twentieth century. Though private schools such as Skerry's College, Dixon's Academy, Latchford's Academy, Fawcett's and Knight's School had been active in Cork rugby circles since the 1880s, it was schools set up by religious orders in response to growing demand for quality secondary education among the Catholic middle classes that came to dominate schools rugby in Cork by the opening years of the twentieth century.[118] A Schools Challenge Cup had been inaugurated in the mid-1880s and was primarily contested by private venture schools. Indeed, an index of the strength of schools rugby can be gleaned from the fact that by 1890, a schools representative team was picked in the city comprising players from no fewer than eight different institutions.[119]

The Schools Challenge Cup was replaced by the Cork Schools Cup in 1895, while the needs of younger schoolboys were catered for by the initiation of the Cork Junior Schools Cup in 1900.[120] By this time competitive schools rugby became centred on a small number of Catholic institutions whose growing importance and popularity had no doubt stymied the prospects of their private counterparts. Indeed, the consolidation of rugby in these secondary schools in Cork was immensely important in providing a permanent constituency for the game in the city and became central to its cultural discourse. In 1900 for instance, private venture schools hitherto competing separately were grouped together in the cup competition as Skerry's Academy,[121] while Catholic schools such as PBC, CBC and North Monastery had sufficient players to enter individual teams. Though established Protestant schools such as Cork Grammar and Midleton College would continue to make occasional forays into competitive schools rugby, the fact that the three already-mentioned Catholic schools were the only entrants for the senior and junior schools competitions in 1910 illustrates their growing importance within Cork rugby.[122]

Presentation Brothers College (known colloquially as 'Pres') was established in the west of the city in 1878 and was followed ten years later by Christian Brothers College ('Christians') which was built on the site of what was a seminary on St Patrick's Place. Though the Christian Brothers provided education for a broad cross-section of society in Ireland, something of the target market for CBC can be gleaned from the following comment made by the mayor of Cork while speaking at the college's opening:

> There was no reason why educational establishments of the highest order should not grow up in our midst; and from this forward there would be no reason why any Cork merchant should send his children out of Cork to be educated . . . this was a want which had been frequently spoken of among the intellectual middle classes of our city.[123]

As a day school, the college's fees were considerably lower than comparable institutions in Ireland and Britain. The fee of eight guineas per annum for the University course in 1888, for instance, was much lower than the Clongowes fee of forty guineas in 1888 or the sixty guineas demanded by Stonyhurst in 1890.[124] Notwithstanding fees, however, the Cork schools were very much geared towards those seeking university qualifications and professional careers and were overwhelmingly middle-class orientated. Indeed, class above religion defined the school's clientele as Protestants in not insignificant numbers were educated at Christians and Pres. Notable examples included international rugby players Ivan Popham and Harry Jack.[125]

Given how competitive second-level academic standards became in Ireland following the passing of the Intermediate Education Act in 1878, one should be careful when comparing the sporting ethos of these institutions with the anti-intellectual athletic cult pervading the contemporary British public school system.[126] In saying this, however, schoolboy rugby became central to the sport's local culture in Cork with Pres and Christians quickly becoming the city's most important (and at times only) rugby-playing schools. Prior to the establishment of the Munster Senior Schools Cup in 1909, schools and underage clubs in Limerick competed together in the Tyler Cup. In Cork, by contrast, and as already indicated, competitions exclusively for schools had already garnered significant prestige by the time the province-wide competition had been inaugurated. Indeed, the establishment of the Munster Senior Schools Cup was greeted with scorn in Cork:

> The premier Cup, and the one for which the keenest rivalry will be shown is of course the Cork Senior Schools Cup. The Munster Schools Cup was only first put up last year and old prejudices die hard in Cork schools. If the final of the Munster Cup takes place before that of the Cork Cup, no inference whatever should be taken as to the ultimate winner of the latter . . . it is more of an obligation than anything else that makes the city schoolboys compete for the Munster Cup.[127]

When the same correspondent deduced that the Munster Branch was favouring the provincial schools competition on the fixture list, a somewhat more outspoken tone was taken:

> The Munster Schools Cup is an unmitigated nuisance. None of the Cork schools want it. It has not the faintest chance of usurping the pride of place held by the Cork Senior Schools Cup for the last twenty years. Then why in the name of common sense Cork schools do you participate in it?[128]

Nuisance or not, the competition would scarcely have taken place without the three Cork schools as they, along with Rockwell College from Tipperary, were the only entrants that season.

By the opening decade of the twentieth century, therefore, schools competitions had become firmly ensconced in Cork rugby culture.

Reflecting in 1931 on his days as one of the first generation of boys to attend CBC, an anonymous contributor to the college magazine recalled:

> And then we had Rugby. That still lives, and, from what the writer hears and sees, keeps still a lot of the spirit that we, the first gener-ation of 'Christians' put into it . . . The 'Pres' was the older college than ours, but in the words of Brutus – 'not a better'. The intellec-tual rivalry is something about which the writer remembers nothing; but on the rugby field, the rivalry in football seems to have sprung full blown and grown, from the brain of the newly born CBC. It almost looked as if our brand new College was the re-incarnation of the soul of some ancient College, long dead, that bore an enmity to the 'Pres' from eternity and was resolved to come to the Eastern end of our city in order to annihilate the insti-tution that dominated its Western extremity.[129]

Occupational background can be a slightly blunt instrument when determining social profile[130] and rugby in schools, as it was in later life, could be a binding agent or a mode of mediation between men from several sub-grades within the middle classes. Merely labelling Cork rugby as having been 'middle class' is far too bald an assessment to account for its social complexity. Exemplifying this are the interlinked careers of Harry Jack and Vincent McNamara. In the first decade of the twentieth century Jack and McNamara's names became synonymous with each other. As a star half-back pairing for CBC, they won the Munster Senior Schools Cup in 1911. Both went to UCC and having won a Munster Senior Cup with College, they were selected to play for Ireland – the first time Munster half-backs had managed such an achievement. After university, Jack entered imperial service and was posted to the Malay States, while McNamara, as we have already noted, was killed in the First World War. McNamara was the son of a prosperous Catholic solicitor from the southern suburb of Blackrock. Jack too was a suburbanite, coming from Audley Place in the northeast suburbs. Yet as the son of a Methodist saddler, his background was substantially different to McNamara's in an occupational sense. It was education and sporting preference, therefore, that drew these individ-uals into the same social world.

The club game in Cork was heavily bound up with the elite schools. In 1912 and 1913, no fewer than twelve former CBC boys featured on the UCC senior team. A UCC 'colours' team selected in 1927 featured seven players from Christians and Pres.[131] Highfield RFC was founded by Pres boys, while Cork Constitution's early twentieth-century Irish internationals Ivan Popham and W.F. Riordan had won schools honours with CBC. Other clubs similarly recruited from the schools.

The Dolphin cup-winning side of 1956 had six CBC men while the Highfield outfit of 1968 featured five.[132] Unlike Limerick, where the vibrancy of the junior game swelled the number of clubs of various grades in the city, the club game in Cork in the twentieth century was limited to a small number of senior outfits. Players whose ability limited their ambitions to the junior grade were swallowed up by the second-choice XVs of senior clubs. The neighbourhood ethic that gave independent junior clubs in Limerick a vital fillip was not apparent in Cork. Little or no evidence exists of rugby in working-class areas of the city, especially in the districts northwest and immediately south of the River Lee, where Gaelic games were particularly popular.[133] Clubs in Cork were more linked with social rather than community networks. Some evidence in this direction is discernable from clubs' origins. Cork Constitution was founded by the staff of the unionist newspaper of the same name and in 1910 still counted three journalists among their committee members.[134] Something of the club's social profile can be detected from the newspaper's hostile attitude to Sunday sport and Gaelic games. Dolphin RFC was initially the rugby-playing branch of a swimming and water polo club and among seven members in 1908 whose occupations were traceable, there were two accountants, two clerks, an engineer, a solicitor's clerk and one gasworks fitter.[135] As already noted, Queen's/University College Cork, as university attendance assumed, drew members exclusively from the middle classes while Cork Bankers had obvious links with the financial industry.

An impression of the spatial dispersion of Cork rugby is given by mapping the residences of eleven members of Cork Constitution RFC in 1910. Four subjects of the sample lived above business premises in the city centre. Irish international Mossy Landers was the only subject from what could be classified as a working-class area, living as he did above his parents in law's pub on Barrack St. By the time of his death, he had moved to South Terrace. The remaining members lived in various parts of the suburbs and no discernable link between the club and a particular area was evident. The sample comprised a relatively eclectic mix of middle-class occupations. As well as two journalists, there were three commercial travellers, a solicitor's clerk, an architect, a merchant, a land agent, an accountant and an engineer. The sample comprised seven Protestants (four Church of Ireland, two Methodists and a Presbyterian) and four Catholics.

As was evident from the case of Jack and McNamara, the rugby community in Cork channelled individuals from different religious backgrounds into the same social world. A sample of seventy Cork-based players and officials traced in the 1911 census comprised thirty-one Church of Ireland members, twenty-seven Catholics, ten Methodists and two Presbyterians. The sample is far from representative given that Protestant names are easier to cross-reference in census returns than generic Catholic ones. Yet clearly there was extensive social interaction between men of different faiths in Cork rugby. In addition, no religious bias in membership composition was evident within any of the clubs covered by the sample. One can speculate, therefore, that being part of the same broad social category, living in socially similar parts of town and sharing comparable educational experiences overcame any potential social cleavage that religion entailed. Moreover, this level of interaction was symptomatic of the level playing field on which Protestants and Catholics now operated when it came to professional advancement.[136]

Parochialism, populism and civic pride: Limerick rugby

Writing nostalgically in the late 1990s about the Limerick in which he grew up in the 1930s, Criostóir O'Flynn reflected that:

> Modern conditions of life, when people move house or county, or even country, with such frequency, have done much to weaken that feeling of local pride, but in my youth all the older areas of Limerick City – Garryowen, Irishtown, the village of the Thomondgate Soda Cakes on the Clare side of Thomond Bridge, Boherbuoy with its famous band, Park . . . the area around Wolfe Tone Street known as 'the back of the Monument' . . . Carey's Road and the neighbourhood of the railway station – each of these was like a little republic in itself, so far as sporting and other allegiances went and the inhabitants of each were just as proud of their quarter as were the inhabitants of the Island Parish.[137]

A degree of circumspection is required when consulting childhood memoirs as sources of historical evidence. There is a tendency among authors of such publications, as vividly argued by Roy Foster in his critique of Frank McCourt's phenomenally popular *Angela's Ashes*, to skew or selectively recall childhood with a view to pleasing the reading audience at the expense of factual accuracy.[138] O'Flynn, himself a native of St Mary's (or the 'Island') parish, was unquestionably writing with a specific agenda to romanticise the Limerick of his youth and freely admits that he saw his work as a response to the horrific portrayal of Limerick childhood in McCourt's work.[139] The evocation of parochial pride, as evident in O'Flynn's work, however, was central to the growth and popularity of rugby in Limerick.

The popularisation of junior rugby on Sundays in Limerick created the sporting structure upon which the social impulse of the game would take its divergent path in the city. Simply put, the promotion of local competitions brought rugby to the level of the parish and the street, with the most talented players having the prospect of playing senior rugby, initially with Garryowen and later with newly promoted senior clubs. Garryowen officials in turn lent their administrative skills to the consolidation of junior rugby and nurtured a sporting unity of purpose that predated similar efforts by other sporting organisations and thus allowed rugby to take root and establish emotional resonance in communities within the city. In terms of identity, this structure allowed rugby to fulfil both a parochial function and engender a marked sense of civic pride, both of which could easily transcend class and infuse the game with a remarkably populist (rather than essentially proletarian) function.

The local pride engendered in Transfield Cup success and the added carrot of the Munster Junior Cup (from 1909) had created a resilient sporting culture, while the establishment of the Tyler Cup[140] and the City Junior Cup had given underage rugby a competitive structure. The administrative maturity of junior rugby allowed this sporting culture to overcome significant potential obstacles. The severe interruption wrought upon rugby by the First World War and the subsequent revolutionary period clearly must have jeopardised the prospects of a sporting tradition that not only depended on a vulnerable mixture of formal and ephemeral clubs, but was also making inroads into what the GAA no doubt saw as its cultural constituency. In 1919, amid a post-war revival of the sport, Limerick Sinn Féin TD Michael Colivet bemoaned the popularity of rugby and the fact that Gaelic football, which he was now attempting to revive, had not been played in the city for many years. Colivet, who admitted to having played rugby as a schoolboy and whose party allegiance alone signified the break from the past and the new political atmosphere under which rugby now laboured, was clearly referring to Garryowen when he asserted that 'everyone will recognise the old club name that is familiar in all rugby circles, and knows what an influence its members' action will have on this matter.'[141]

As Colivet's complaint suggests, rugby in Limerick emerged relatively unscathed from the enforced hiatus. Indeed, junior rugby was remarkable for how little it changed. The City Junior Cup (which seems to have vacillated between being an underage and an adult competition) was back up and running in the early summer of 1920, when six teams entered.[142] This number had increased to eleven by

1925, eight of whom were independent junior clubs.[143] An example of the plethora of press comment on the popularity of junior rugby was the *Limerick Leader*'s observation in 1924 that it was 'both pleasing and surprising to note the numbers of people who are interested in junior matches in the city. The numbers of spectators who frequent the Markets Field on the occasion of an important City Cup contest on a Sunday afternoon proves that the rugby game, even if only indifferently played, is a very popular one indeed in Limerick.'[144] In a clear case of historical continuity, Garryowen maintained its vested interest in junior rugby and at the club's general meeting in 1924 'a discussion arose as to the advisability of appointing a committee, or governing body, to control junior football in the city.'[145] The Branch-controlled Munster Junior Cup was also revived in 1920 and Limerick entrants, unlike their Cork counterparts, continued to schedule cup ties for Sundays. A tradition of competitive Sunday rugby that had been initiated in the 1880s was now firmly re-established in the Limerick of the Free State era.

In social terms, the popularity of Sunday rugby, which had now spanned four decades, allowed the sport to become a key cultural signifier of parochial identity in Limerick. Indeed, arguably the most suggestive and significant by-product of the popularity of Sunday rugby in Limerick was its spatial manifestation. It has already been observed that the cultural hearth of Cork rugby lay in the modern extension of the city into middle-class suburbia. By contrast, rugby football in Limerick had a decidedly inner-city flavour, becoming rooted in the medieval Englishtown and Irishtown areas.[146] The eighteenth-century development of the Newtown district had seen a gradual southerly shift in commercial and industrial activity in the city. As a result, the medieval town and older suburbs such as Garryowen and Thomondgate declined in economic importance and became predominantly working-class residential areas in the nineteenth century.[147] Significantly, rugby was characterised by a parochial dynamic reflected in the city's medieval ecclesiastical geography.

Of the city's five medieval parishes, at least four had rugby clubs of the same name appearing in either junior or underage competitions at different periods, and all stemming from the Sunday rugby tradition. Teams named St Michael's and St John's appeared in the first decade of the twentieth century competing in juvenile and junior competitions,[148] and clubs of the same name became fully affiliated members (albeit temporarily) of the Munster Branch at different points in the 1920s.[149] A club called St Munchin's was among the members of the Munster Branch in the 1930s. Another club directly linked to St Michael's parish was Presentation. Founded in 1917, the club drew its playing strength from the laneways in the vicinity of Denmark Street. Richmond RFC, founded in 1909 and later to become an ambitious and well-run junior outfit, was based around the Clare Street and Lelia Street area.[150] Though St Mary's RFC was not founded until the 1940s, it was the parish of the same name that undoubtedly exemplified best the perceived cultural resonance between rugby and parochialism in Limerick.

St Mary's parish, located in Limerick's medieval Englishtown and colloquially known as the 'Island parish' because of its borders at either side with the Abbey and Shannon rivers, became synonymous with Limerick rugby from the last decade of the nineteenth century onwards. With Athlunkard Street and Sir Harry's Mall running around the perimeter of the island, the parish comprised a dense network of laneways and streets housing quite a diverse cross-section of the city's working and middle classes. Indeed, rugby was a clear platform upon which intra-class variations were expressed in Limerick city and quite conspicuously in St Mary's.[151] As already noted, the formation of Garryowen FC had signified a distinct move away from the game's elite origins in Limerick, and among the founders and early players of the club were residents of Athlunkard Street including members of the prominent O'Connor and Hartney pig-buying families.[152] By the late 1880s, the club had a significant surplus of players,[153] and clearly there was sufficient interest in the game for the development of different grades of adult and underage rugby. It was from this move towards junior and underage rugby that Shannon rugby club emerged – the first club to directly represent St Mary's parish.

Though the club claims 1884 as their foundation date, it was more likely 1887,[154] with the club's participation in that season's Sunday rugby competition likely to have been its first meaningful appearance on the Limerick rugby scene. From its very early history through to its promotion to the senior ranks in 1953,[155] Shannon was inextricably linked to Garryowen, proving to be a crucial breeding ground for the latter club's senior XV. In turn, Garryowen men from the parish took an active interest in the local club. When Shannon won the Junior Cup in 1908, for instance, they were trained by three local Garryowen men, Jim Keane, and the brothers Jim and Joe O'Connor.[156] The O'Connor brothers, two of whom would later represent Ireland, had begun their playing careers at Shannon. Another future Irish international who graduated to the Garryowen senior ranks via the Shannon junior team in the late nineteenth century was the aforementioned Paddy Healy, a butcher, who won ten international caps in the period 1901–4,[157] while

Tom Halpin, a plumber, followed a similar route to the Irish international team in 1909.[158]

Rugby adapted itself conspicuously to dominant occupational patterns in St Mary's parish. The pioneering research of John McGrath has revealed that, socially, the membership ranks of Shannon were principally composed of skilled tradesmen and the pig buyers from the Athlunkard Street locality.[159] Among early members were the already-mentioned O'Connor and Hartney pig buyers. Though this represented a striking divergence from the dominant class profile of Irish rugby in general, these individuals were something of a quasi-elite within the parish. The local pig buyers, generally congregated on Athlunkard Street, earned substantial livings through the buoyancy of the local bacon industry. They acted as a conduit between rural pig farmers and urban bacon-curing factories and augmented their income by breeding pigs in their own back gardens. As one parishioner recalled of the 1930s, 'those who had the least financial worries coming up to Christmas were the pig buyers. The fat cats from Athlunkard Street would have the most substantial kitty.'[160] The O'Connors, for instance, were one of several Athlunkard Street households of sufficient means through the pig trade in 1901 to employ a domestic servant.[161] These families, however, would have been parvenu Catholics, most likely of recently humble ancestry, and what they did not lack in material means they would most certainly have lacked in education and perceived status and sophistication compared to their rugby-following counterparts in Cork and Dublin.

The appeal of rugby was not confined to the more prosperous inhabitants of the parish's main thoroughfares. McGrath again, through a mixture of census cross-reference and oral testimony, has pieced together a distinct rugby culture among residents of the parish's laneways and tenement houses, particularly in the Abbey and Mary Street areas. Abbey RFC first appeared as a Junior Cup entrant in 1920[162] and catered for a different class of men than Shannon, with membership drawn from local fishermen and general labourers.[163] Proving that a broad portfolio of cultural interests was not the sole preserve of middle-class sportsmen was one of the club's founders and most prominent members Patrick O'Mahony, a general labourer, who at different periods held administrative office with Abbey RFC, St Mary's Band and Athlunkard Boat Club.[164] The club had a brief but colourful history and was frequently subject to heavy-handed treatment from the Munster Branch. In the club's solitary season as a senior outfit in 1928-9, for instance, it was disqualified from the Munster Senior Cup for refusing to change the scheduled

date of its first-round encounter with Sunday's Well. When the IRFU
intervened in Abbey's favour, the Munster Branch stood firm and
remarked that 'The players in this club are mostly fishermen and their
ever ready excuse is that they would be engaged in fishing on a particular date and could not play.'[165] The dispute had originated when
the Munster Cup draw had scheduled a tie between Garryowen and
Cork Constitution for the same date as an international match. The
latter clubs, with members eager to attend the international and
exerting their considerable collective influence on the Munster
Branch, forced a change to the cup schedule whereby the date of their
tie would be swapped with Abbey's. When the Limerick team applied
for a date change of their own, they were removed from the competition.[166] One of Abbey's grounds for appeal to the IRFU was an
apparent desire among its own members to attend the international.
The Munster Branch, in a letter to the national body, retorted that 'It
may interest your committee to know that I had not a solitary application from the Abbey club for International tickets for either Dublin
or Belfast internationals.'[167] Applications for tickets aside, it is
tempting to speculate that the men at the committee table, when re-
fixing the Munster Cup ties, felt that a group of fishermen from a
working-class area had less business attending an international match
than the members of well-established clubs.

Abbey were re-graded to junior status in 1929 and, having been
warned on several occasions for their disciplinary record, were suspended from the Munster Junior Cup competition in 1930.[168] Though
re-instated the following season, Abbey laboured under a warning
from the Munster Branch that the latter body steadfastly refused to
remove. Subsequent attempts to gain senior status were refused and
the club did not re-appear after the 1933–4 season.[169] During their brief
appearance on the Munster rugby scene, Abbey enjoyed a keen rivalry
with parish neighbours Shannon. Encounters between the clubs
always drew large crowds and were frequently marred by violence.
Despite the demise of their local club, rugby remained popular among
the men of the Abbey area, with many continuing to play the game
with Shannon. A new club, St Mary's RFC, was founded in the area in
1943 and was affiliated to the Munster Branch in April 1944.[170] They
famously used the fisherman's cottage of Paddy 'Haddah' Sweeney as
their clubhouse and the club's early membership was said to have
comprised 'descendants of the Abbey Fishermen's Guild, people who
worked in hard times at the timber yards, bacon factories, coal yards,
Rank's Flour Mills, Limerick Tannery and Limerick Harbour'.[171] Direct
evidence of historical continuity in the area's rugby tradition came in

1945 when St Mary's, obviously eager to bolster membership ranks, enquired of the Munster Branch if former members of the Abbey club were debarred from rugby activity.[172] This continuity was further expressed in the dubious form of St Mary's' frequent disciplinary wrangles with the Munster Branch.[173]

Within St Mary's parish, therefore, there was a clear class differential between the dominant membership trends of Shannon and those of Abbey and latterly St Mary's. This was far from a straightforward social divide, however, and embraced other aspects of local parochial culture. Moreover, social snobbery was almost certainly not an exacerbating factor in the contrasting membership rolls of Shannon and their sister clubs in the Abbey area. Members of Abbey and St Mary's, for instance, would have had a very clear sense of self-identity through either involvement or ancestry in the Abbey Fisherman's Guild or membership of cultural bodies such as the local St Mary's Band. They would also have lived in a specific geographical area of the parish. The social bifurcation apparent in the Shannon/Abbey divide was quite an organic development whereby men of similar background from the same locality chose to play rugby for their local team. Moreover, club loyalty was fluid and men from the Abbey area almost certainly played for Shannon in significant numbers in different periods.

This fluidity is clearly embodied in the example of the Hayes family from Flag Lane.[174] Over two generations, the family's rugby loyalties straddled uneasily between Shannon, St Mary's and Garryowen. Socially, the family was very much of the Abbey area, being occupationally tied to the Abbey Fishermen and the local sand-hauling industry. Stephen the 'Gullyman', the family head, was both a player and a vice-president at Shannon, while his six sons all played for St Mary's. One son, Matthew, played for Shannon in the late 1930s and was of sufficient ability to be selected for a Garryowen Senior Cup-winning team, while another brother, Mick, was also selected to play for Garryowen. The Hayes brothers had a fearsome reputation on the field, with one brother in particular, Augustine or 'Ducky', attracting a string of mythical anecdotes of his exploits in the St Mary's front row. In this case, the gap between myth and reality was seemingly bridged by Augustine's problematic disciplinary record.[175] The brothers' association with three different clubs displays the complexity of how rugby allowed men from St Mary's to express their identity as Limerickmen. While St Mary's RFC brought identity to the level of the street and the neighbourhood, association with Shannon implied a strong parochial ethic in general. By distinction, joining the ranks of the Garryowen Senior Cup team and the associated opportunity to do battle with the best teams in the province implied an obvious civic character, where one represented their city.

That rugby was undoubtedly a key agent of expressing both parochial identity and civic pride in the Island parish was neatly expressed in a reflective and sentimental article published in the *Limerick Leader* in 1932. Under the headline 'The glamour of the Parish', the writer claimed that 'there is a tradition in Limerick that there is a natural piety, an intensely religious fervour, and a simple unquestioning faith among the people of St Mary's parish that is to be found nowhere else.'[176] After referring to the incongruity of the 'chaste and beautiful' parish church in 'this far from prosperous area', the writer claims that, next to religion, rugby football is the other defining cultural characteristic of the area:

> To speak about the Parish and not refer to football would be an unforgivable, and, perhaps, dangerous offence, to a scribe whose identity would be known. To a Parishman, young or old, football is an obsession. What would Garryowen be without the Parish, and you might say, what would the Parish be without Garryowen? Without it the men at least would lose many of their distinctive qualities. For half a century back, the Parish was the feeding ground of the famous Garryowen combination. And what men it did, and does still supply! This much I must say, however, that the Parishman of the churches is quite a different proposition from the Parishman of the rugby field. The former cultivates the simplicity of the dove, but the latter assumes the quality of the caged lion let loose when charging on the field of play.[177]

The above statement, coming as it did several playing generations since rugby first became popular in Limerick, displays clearly how the sport had become culturally engrained in St Mary's parish. A *de facto* structure whereby men of all classes could compete for their local team and strive for a place on the prestigious Garryowen Senior Cup side undoubtedly helped to sustain the game's momentum. As already noted, some of Garryowen's early international players were former Shannon men. This tradition was resurrected in the inter-war period. When the *Limerick Leader* published a list of twenty players from which the Garryowen Munster Cup XV would be chosen in 1925, no fewer than twelve had played junior football with Shannon.[178] The captain, Rory Frawley from Ahearne's Row, made a precarious living as a sand hauler and perfectly exemplified how rugby afforded working-class men an opportunity to gain local prominence by his selection for Munster and his narrow failure to attain international honours. Another former Shannon man on the team, Tom Hanley, signed for professional rugby league club Oldham in 1931, with the *Leader* commenting that it was 'to be regretted that trade depression in our city should rob us of men of his type'.[179] Incidentally, there was not the slightest hint of moral denunciation of Hanley's decision to turn professional.

Contemporaneous to the division of rugby along parochial lines was a small, yet tangible, overlap between rugby and workplaces. Beginning in 1901, for instance, the city's bacon-curing factories initiated an annual series of rugby matches among employees. When Shaw's and Matterson's met in 1903 at the Markets Field, 'there was an immense attendance, the employees and the staffs of the firms turning out en masse to encourage and support their respective sides', with proceedings 'enhanced by the presence of the Workingmen's Band'.[180] The series again took place in 1905 when Shaw's, Matterson's and O'Mara's took part.[181] Though teams may have included members of management, it seems likely that the bulk of the participants were factory-floor employees benefiting from the contemporary predilection among Victorian businessmen to organise sporting events for their workforces. Moreover, it seems reasonable to speculate that middle-class men would have preferred the private club to the workplace as a site for personal leisure. The owners of these firms, for instance, were involved in rugby at club level in the city. A.W. Shaw was named among the patrons of Garryowen FC in 1888, while members of the (later republican) O'Mara family had a long-standing relationship with the same club as both players and administrators.[182]

In 1911, the Compositors and Allied Trade Football Club was formed and scheduled their first match for a Sunday, presumably to accommodate artisan working hours.[183] The sporadic nature of the sporting and occupational overlap in Limerick is illustrated by the fact that the next evidence of the phenomenon was the formation of the Neptune Football Club from among the employees of the Limerick Railway in 1923. Unsurprisingly again, the club had trained on Sundays on the Fair Green.[184] The affiliation of Railway United to the Munster Branch in the 1930s continued organised football among transport workers in the city.

The intermittent tradition of workplace-orientated rugby re-emerged in the 1950s with the establishment of an inter-firm tournament that catered for workers in the bacon, transport and financial sectors. The diversity of occupational interests is easily observable by examining the entrants for the 1953 tournament. Re-establishing a tradition of which they had been pioneers more than half a century earlier, the Matterson's and O'Mara's bacon-processing plants took part, with that sector's representation being rounded off by Clover Meats. More of the city's key industrial employers were represented in the form of the huge Ranks milling operation and Cement Ltd. Dock- and provisions-related workers saw action with Harbour United and Canal, while the financial sector had Bankers as its sole representative. The link between rugby and railways was resurrected in the form of CIÉ (Coras Iompar Éireann), with Shannon Airport being the transport industry's other representative.[185]

Though all the city clubs were represented, the large number of players from clubs such as Shannon, Thomond and St Mary's among the factory teams is in itself suggestive. In addition, there appears to have been a preponderance of Young Munster players in the CIÉ and meat factory teams, thus representing a clear correlation between the geographical location of these industries and that club's traditional heartland. Notable among the members of the Matterson's team, for instance, was Tom Clifford, the Young Munster prop, who in just the previous season had won the last of his eight caps for Ireland and who had made five test appearances for the British Lions in Australia and New Zealand in 1950.[186] The tournament was also aimed at veterans, with the Canal team fielding a forty-eight and fifty-year-old player. It therefore seems possible that the Danaher Sheahan who lined out for CIÉ was the former Ireland international scrum-half who had been a key member of Young Munster's Bateman Cup winning team of 1928. Sheahan, a railway worker, hailed from the nearby Hyde Road.

The periodic character of work-related rugby activity and the clear lack of permanence of these teams in Limerick arguably displays a divergence from the British experience. Workplace teams remained just that and club football always took precedence in Limerick. Unlike the north of England, for instance, where many industry-based teams shook off initial employer patronage to form independent and often high-profile clubs,[187] it was place in the geographical rather than the occupational sense that dominated rugby loyalty in Limerick.

Just as prominently as their fellow junior clubs in St Mary's parish, Young Munster RFC became a key sporting institution in the Boherbuoy, Prospect, Carey's Road and Parnell Street areas at the turn of the twentieth century. These environs, taken as a whole, comprised a large working-class residential area including some of the city's more impoverished slums. The club was founded in 1901 and, though the basis for the assertion is unknown, Michael O'Flaherty has recorded that Young Munster catered for boys who worked 'long hours in the Great Southern and Western Railways, the Sawmills or the Bacon fac- tories'.[188] Starting out as a junior club and therefore plying their trade in the Transfield, City Junior and Munster Junior Cups, 'Munsters' were promoted to senior in early 1920s.

Mythical anecdotes about Young Munster are legion and the club is recorded in the empirically unsound recesses of folk memory as being very much working-class orientated. The celebrated Irish sports journalist Con Houlihan, for instance, recalled a cup tie in the 1950s between UCC and Young Munster in which the respective appearance of the teams betrayed their contrasting social backgrounds:

> The College lads were immaculately attired; their shorts were snow white and their boots shone. Some of their opponents wore jerseys so faded that you could barely discern the colours. They didn't all wear matching socks. It was clear that some of their shorts had been made from flour bags. Some wore their ordinary shoes.[189]

One is tempted to suspect that Houlihan's anecdote possibly tells us more about a twenty-first-century concern with amplifying the supposed egalitarian nature of Munster rugby than it does about the social make-up of the Limerick rugby club, yet there is little doubt that Young Munster was historically a significant social outlet and cultural signifier for working-class people in a deprived area.

The foundation for much of the legendary discourse surrounding Young Munster was the club's victory in the Bateman Cup in 1928. This competition was initiated in 1921 and was played off among the winners of the provincial cup competitions, essentially functioning as an all-Ireland championship.[190] Young Munster had already beaten Cork Constitution to secure their first Munster Cup title that season before defeating a heavily fancied Lansdowne side in the final of the Bateman Cup. Feeding off the club's own popularity and the civic pride which successful rugby teams inspired in Limerick, 12,000 people greeted the team on its homecoming at Limerick train station.[191] The team were treated to a reception attended by the mayor and were led on a procession to the Glentworth Hotel by a selection of city bands. The civic nature of the event was underlined by the fact that the club's local band, the Boherbuoy, were joined on the procession by erstwhile political and parochial rivals the St Mary's Fife and Drum, whose contemporary rugby loyalties would very much have laid with Abbey RFC.[192] It was also an occasion for collective celebration in the club's heartland:

> Edward Street, Parnell Street and Prospect, the home of the Young Munster Club, were en-fete throughout the day. The colours of the team, black and amber, were displayed from every house and lamp post. Last night those centres were aglow with bonfires and

illuminations of various hues. Hundreds of people were on the
streets to the late hour sporting the 'favours' of the 'Young Un's'
singing appropriate dirges while the children enjoyed themselves
by sending sky high the sparks and embers of the various blazing
tar barrels and bonfires.[193]

The immense pride brought to the locality was no doubt augmented
by the fact that the players themselves were very much of the area. A
sample of ten players cross-referenced with 1911 census enumerator
forms revealed that all bar two were originally from streets and
laneways around the Parnell Street area. Four players, including the
captain, Phonny Neilan, were from labouring backgrounds, while the
remainder comprised the sons of a shopkeeper, a hotel porter, an
accountant, a carter and a clerk. Morley Nelson, a club official and a
Methodist shopkeeper, was probably the only non-Catholic associated
with the team.[194] One of the team's outstanding players, Charlie St
George, was later a popular publican while Irish international prop
forward Ter Casey was a general labourer who at different times was a
driver for a timber yard and a casual labourer at the docks.[195] The
Young Munster team, like countless successful Garryowen sides,
recruited from the junior ranks. Four of the Bateman Cup winning side
– J.J. Connery, Henry Raleigh, Mick O'Flaherty and future Irish international scrum half Danaher Sheahan – had won Limerick City Cup
medals with Pirates RFC in 1926 and 1927.[196] That Pirates hailed from
the same locality as Young Munster and were treated by the senior
club as something of a nursery was evidenced by the fact that Patrick
O'Callaghan, of Hunt's Lane off Parnell Street, was secretary of Pirates
in 1928 while simultaneously sitting at the Young Munster committee
table.[197] As was the case with so many Limerick rugby men, political
ambitions seemingly presupposed rugby involvement. O'Callaghan
was also a public representative, serving as a member of the city corporation for the Glentworth Ward and was seeking re-election just two
months after Young Munster's Bateman Cup success.[198]

Identity with place, whether it was neighbourhood, parish or city,
was also expressed through the reverence shown to star players.
Parochial teams produced parochial icons and famous rugby players
became heroes within their communities. W.F. Mandle has argued
vividly in terms of W.G. Grace that the emergence of the sporting hero
in Victorian Britain was a reflection of contemporary social and cultural needs.[199] More recent research has shown that the phenomenon of
the sporting hero was also expressed in Britain through individuals of
much less repute than Grace who were local rather than national
heroes, with Matt Taylor asserting that 'the earliest football heroes

were almost all local figures who managed to embody town, city or perhaps regional pride but whose celebrity rarely reached beyond the parochial to the national.[200]

A peculiar specimen of parochial sporting hero was cultivated in Limerick rugby that arguably had comparable emotional resonance with British Edwardian footballers such as Stephen Bloomer or Harold Fleming[201] or, in an Irish context, with GAA players in other parts of the country. Ultimately, these were local men who brought prominence and pride to their locality through exploits on the field. A dynastic example of this was the O'Connor family of pig buyers from Athlunkard Street, who first played rugby on Sundays with Shannon, and claimed a total of thirty-nine Munster Senior Cup medals for Garryowen spanning two generations of the family. The first genera-tion of seven brothers, roughly spanning the decade either side of the turn of the twentieth century, won thirty-seven medals between them, with Jack O'Connor claiming ten. His son Mick was the sole second-generation O'Connor to add his name to the trophy in the mid-1920s.[202] They were a family of diverse sporting interests. Beyond their conspicuous involvement in rugby, they were keen rowing and athletics enthusiasts. Regarding the latter, Jim O'Connor competed successfully in running events all over Munster and once surrendered a medal won in Cork under Irish Amateur Athletics Association (IAAA) rules in order to compete in the All-Ireland GAA champi-onships in Thurles in 1907, where he won two events.[203] The public profile of this family in Limerick was immense. When international scrum-half Joe O'Connor died prematurely in 1911, the funeral took the form of a civic event in the city and received a large volume of coverage in the local press. Among the attendees were notable local representatives and businessmen, including the lord mayor and the high sheriff, representatives of all the city's rugby and rowing clubs and members of the Bakers' Society and the Pork Butchers' Society. The procession to Mount St Lawrence cemetery was 'an immense train of people . . . eloquently expressive of the great hold the deceased had on the affections of the people and of the undoubted respect and popularity enjoyed by himself and other members of his family'.[204] Among the O'Connors' fellow Athlunkard Street residents was the already-mentioned Paddy Healy, of whom countless anec-dotes of physical prowess entered public memory and who was 'the pride of the Parish and reminiscent of the famous Matt the Thresher'.[205] The curious comparison between the Limerick rugby player and the farm labouring, pastoral and patriotic hero of Kickham's mid-nineteenth-century novel further serves to underline how class and cultural perceptions become skewed in the context of Limerick rugby.[206]

The O'Connors were far from the only Limerick sporting heroes to participate under both the GAA and IRFU banners. Charlie McGill, an immensely successful sprinter and hurler and a contemporary of the O'Connors, became a Garryowen stalwart in the first decade of the twentieth century, having previously played junior rugby for Lansdowne. Another man of the inner city, he was from Gerald Griffin Street and was employed nearby for almost half a century as a railway worker and at one time sat on the board of the Limerick Mechanics Institute.[207] Having resigned from rugby in 1910 to play Gaelic games,[208] he returned to the Garryowen ranks after the war to claim a third Munster Cup medal in 1920.[209] Successful Munster Cup campaigns that involved McGill were marked by one of the city's most prominent working-class institutions, the St Mary's Band, who would honour him by playing outside his house.[210]

If Limerick rugby heroes were exalted as exemplars of parochial manhood, they could also represent perceived subjugation of working-class men by those who were in positions of power in Irish rugby. Though explicit references to class were extremely rare in the media recording of Irish rugby, the controversy surrounding the selection of Young Munster front-row forward Ter Casey for the Irish fifteen became couched in such discourse. Casey, as already noted, was a labourer and a key member of the Young Munster Bateman Cup-winning team of 1928. On the back of impressive form in trials in 1930, the Limerick media began campaigning for his inclusion in the Irish team for the forthcoming internationals. The local press commented that the national media and influential commentators such as former international George Stevenson favoured Casey's inclusion.[211] When Casey was omitted for the opening game against France, Mick Hartney of Lansdowne (Limerick) RFC sent an angry letter to the *Limerick Leader*:

> Is it not now evident that it is a complete waste of time for Young Munster players to be obliging the Irish Five by providing an opposition in trial matches to find that Irish fifteen? . . . snobocrosy seems to be the ruling power in rugby circles and until it is dropped, men of the type of Ter Casey are merely wasting time in travelling to play trial games. A college education, Oxford twang, kid gloves and plus fours evidently are of more value than ability to play the game.[212]

When the selection committee finally yielded and included Casey in the XV to play against Scotland in February, the *Leader* quickly returned to civic celebratory mode:

It was with the greatest pleasure and pride that each and every one
of us, irrespective of club learned . . . that T.C. Casey, the Young
Munster forward . . . had been included in the victorious fifteen
who represented Ireland at Murrayfield . . . Ter, we hold is a real
product of Limerick City, and Limerick City rugby . . . and . . . his
fine sportsmanlike attitude throughout the season is no whit less
appreciated than our belief that he is a forward that we and the
province are proud to own as a Limerick City man and the product
of Limerick City rugby.[213]

That some form of snobbish conspiracy was held to have prevented
Casey from hitherto being selected for the Irish team was further in
evidence from a contemporary poem written in his honour: 'The time
at last has come along, They'll keep him out no longer, To pull his
weight no two men could, Like Ter Casey of Young Munster.'[214]

Casey's teammate at Young Munster, Danaher Sheahan, was
another of the city's most noted rugby players. When the scrum-half's
performance against England in his sole cap for Ireland was criticised
in the national press, a lengthy defence of the local hero in the *Limerick
Leader* again pointed towards perceived class subjugation as being at
the root of this unfavourable commentary. When one national press
report had commented that Sheahan was 'out of his class' in international rugby, the *Limerick Leader* mockingly took this statement as a
commentary on the player's social background rather than his playing
ability and asserted that:

It would appear that the situation of his own town on the map
would immediately come nearer to the equator of class if this
Limerick player had, for example, played for United Services or the
jolly old Army or jolly old Oxford, or if he had four initials and a
hyphenated name.[215]

Sheahan and Casey were men of significant profile in their neighbourhood and city and were part of the enduring folk legend that
Young Munster's Bateman Cup win created. Cristóir O'Flynn recalled
an incident in his childhood when his father pointed out a man on the
street to him and said: 'that man's name is Sheahan, and he played for
Young Munster in the Bateman Cup.' O'Flynn continued: 'As I grew
older, I would read and hear often of that glorious day for Limerick
rugby in 1928 when unfancied Young Munster went up to Dublin and
beat the cocky Lansdowne in the final of the Bateman Cup, and I would
relish the memory of having met Danaher Sheahan.'[216] There is no evidence to support the contention that class was a barrier to the selection
of Limerick players for the Irish team. What is significant, however, is
the perceived feeling of prejudice in Limerick at the non-selection of

local players of note and the willingness of the press to highlight this adversity. Men such as Paddy Healy, the O'Connors, Charlie McGill, Ter Casey and Danaher Sheahan were local heroes, very much *of* their communities, who helped to sustain the popularity of rugby and exemplified how ordinary individuals could achieve fame and create pride in their localities.

The cultural phenomenon that held Limerick rugby together was civic pride and populism and both became embedded in the game's folk discourse. The *Limerick Leader*, always aiming to steer a neutral course through inter-club rivalries, traditionally strove to underline how rugby was a collective source of city pride and a civic unifier. In a preview piece for the 1912 Munster Cup final between Garryowen and UCC, for instance, the paper pleaded for collective support for the Garryowen team: 'what a grand thing 'twould be to have past differences allowed to die out and the present is an opportune time, so let us all join in a ring of friendship and remember we all hail from Limerick.'[217] A year earlier, when Lansdowne needed to defeat UCC to win the Munster Senior League, the *Leader* declared: 'Let Lansdowne remember that they are Limerick's only remaining hope in this competition, and with the honour of the city at stake, all that is in them will be sure to come out till the referee, by the sound of his final whistle, declares Limerick the resting place of the shield.'[218] The insularity of this sporting rhetoric was further exemplified in 1929, when in the wake of a heavy defeat for Ireland at the hands of Scotland, the paper's rugby writer took solace in the uniqueness of Limerick rugby:

> We returned [from the international match] down cast and full of gloom, but happy in the thought that we still had our own little rugby world. We wended our way towards the Markets Field, and saw a rather young and hitherto unknown Garryowen second string easily defeat the fancied Young Munster string. Later, word came through that Presentation completely outplayed and registered an easy victory over the fancied Nenagh side, which had overwhelmed Abbey not so long before. After that we began to feel like summer weather forecasters.[219]

Two weeks later, the same writer asserted of rugby in Limerick that 'practically no other subject is under discussion . . . passing up and down "town" you hear belated snatches of "if he let it out"; "he's not as fast as he was" . . . this enthusiasm has spread to an enormous extent to the fairer and weaker sex and club scarves are all in vogue at the moment.'[220] These sentiments were again expressed a year later in a rugby editorial from a different writer stating that 'a correspondent . . . assures us on his word that on a recent walk from the town hall to the Redemptorists Church, he calculated that he heard Rugger talk of some description or other from a fair average of eighty people or groups, out of a possible one hundred and further he stresses the opinion that the gentler sex represented of that total at least thirty.'[221]

The sporadic appearance of these vague musings was probably dependent on who exactly was doing the writing and the nature of the paper's editorial policy at any given time and can be read as something of an historical precursor to the mass of hyperbolic comment that would later accompany the professional Munster rugby team. Within the *Leader*'s editorials, however, there was frequently more direct evidence of a genuine populism and cross-class appeal in Limerick rugby. Determining the class profile of a particular game's supporters has proven hugely problematic from a methodological point of view for sports historians.[222] We have, however, strong anecdotal evidence that a significant proportion of rugby supporters in Limerick were working-class people. As early as 1891, the national press was complaining about working-class rugby supporters attempting to gain entry to the Markets Field without paying: 'I do not so much mind the humbler or less moneyed classes of Limerick reversing the traditions of their ancestors by scaling walls instead of defending them, but I do protest that bursting in a pay gate at which the admission charge is only sixpence is going a little too far.'[223] When a decline in gates was observed in the context of a local economic depression at the beginning of the 1931–2 season, for instance, the proposed solution of the *Leader*'s rugby editorial was informative: 'Personally, we believe that the terrible unemployment is the chief factor in the small gates, and we should respectfully suggest that in the present conditions that local clubs should arrange for the admittance of any unemployed man at a purely nominal charge.'[224] A similar proposal was voiced at the outset of the following season: 'At a time when unemployment is so rife, particularly among our hitherto regular rugby supporters, we think the home clubs should consider the admittance of all men in possession of an unemployment card at half price to all parts of the field.'[225]

Less specific evidence of populist support is evident in folkloric rhetoric surrounding the Munster Senior Cup. Lighthearted anecdotes referring to the unsuitability of Saturday rugby fixtures for certain rugby followers in Limerick were frequent. In 1930, one rugby writer humorously observed that 'so great is the enthusiasm for the cup that a statistician calculated that death rate of relations of those who work on Saturday evenings is so high that it was considered necessary at one time to invite the attention of the Medical Union and further this statistician calculated that dinner hours became so long on Saturday afternoons during the cup season that if put end to end would reach the long can from the back of the monument.'[226] Another writer, three years later recalled 'one instance in which a young fellow overstepped the mark by telling his employer that he could not be at work on a particular Saturday as his Grandmother was being buried that day. The mistake he made was that this was the third time that such a relative was being interred, and they were all being laid to rest on the day a cup match was on.'[227] In the build-up to the 1934 tournament the inner-city partisanship and emphasis on place that surrounded cup football was evident in the following assertion: 'each year, it is only natural that the partisan can only see his own pet team triumphant and from the various entrenchments down the "Parish" way, up the "Yellow Road" and "behind the Monument" come confidential whisperings of the best thing in the cup this year.'[228]

Rugby football's place in folk consciousness was enduring in Limerick, as more recent events exemplify. By the mid-1950s Garryowen had lost their monopoly of rugby's civic function in Limerick. In 1955, Shannon and Old Crescent had become senior clubs in their own right and joined Garryowen, Bohemians and Young Munster as the city's representatives in the Senior Cup. Rivalries hitherto expressed in the junior game were now given a higher profile in the senior ranks. Though inter-club rivalries remained keen, the prestige brought to the city as a whole by successful rugby teams remained evident. In 1960, for instance, Shannon won their first ever Munster Senior Cup title and Young Munster's second XV won the Munster Junior Cup over the course of one weekend. When the victorious Young Munster team arrived back at Limerick railway station, a contingent of jubilant Shannon players and supporters greeted them and both captains were shouldered through the streets of Limerick in a procession of thousands of people led by the Limerick Pipe Band and Boherbuoy Brass and Reed Band. The customary bonfires blazed while Shannon supporters showed their exuberance by setting a fishing boat alight with the apparent justification that 'you can buy a boat anytime but not the Munster Cup!'[229] The following evening, the unmistakably Young Munster partisans in the Boherbuoy Band congratulated their Shannon rivals by parading through the 'Parish' in civic celebratory mode.

Rugby football's populism in Limerick compared to its social exclusivity in Cork is underlined by childhood memoirs from the two cities. This is perfectly exemplified by the respective works of the already-mentioned Criostóir O'Flynn and his Cork counterpart Christy Kenneally.[230] O'Flynn, born in Limerick in 1927, and Keneally, born in

Cork in 1948, both grew up in working-class areas of their cities where inter-generational familial ties, neighbourhood relations and notions of community were remarkably similar. Despite the slight generational gap between the two men, their cases are comparable due to other similarities in their backgrounds. Though both families were far from well off (O'Flynn's father was a coal beller and Kenneally's a factory worker) they were sufficiently above the poverty line to consider themselves more fortunate than many of their contemporary fellow working-class families living in cramped tenements. Both benefited from secondary education thanks to the benevolence of the Christian Brothers and are keen to underline the sense of neighbourhood solidarity nourished in their respective communities.

In these working-class areas of Limerick and Cork, this pronounced sense of community identity was expressed through a love of nation and religious devotion and it was also played out in a sporting context. The striking contrast between the two cities, as articulated by both of the above authors, was that in Cork, local working-class identity was expressed through hurling, whereas it was rugby that performed a strikingly similar function in Limerick. For Kenneally, the local hurling club, Glen Rovers, and their rivalry with other city clubs such as St Finbarr's, Blackrock and Sarsfields engendered parochial identity. A typically Irish mixture of cultural engagement is revealed when Kenneally describes how 'the men in our lives went to the confraternity in the North Chapel on Monday night and gathered uncles, cousins, friends and an assortment of Glen Rovers aficionados for an autopsy of Sunday's game. The sermon might get the odd dutiful mention but the main item on the agenda was hurling.'[231] He further recalled that 'the household gods were the players in the local club and names like Jack Lynch and Jim Young could conjure thousands swathed in red and white, the blood and bandages, to Kent Station for the All Ireland pilgrimage.'[232] In the Limerick of O'Flynn's youth, as already detailed, it was rugby that produced local heroes. One further set of comparable anecdotes is particularly informative. O'Flynn recalled that 'we only got to handle a real rugby ball as soon as we were recruited into the clubs by older brothers or relations; so in our street version, five, six, or seven a side, we used the rag ball or the Cleeve's milk tin.'[233] In Kenneally's Cork, by contrast, 'as soon as a boy could stand he was measured for hurley', while rugby in the city is caustically dismissed as having been 'the preserve of those with adenoidal accents and money'.[234]

These childhood anecdotes, romanticised and florid as they are, neatly underline the divergent social and cultural development of rugby in Limerick and Cork. Whereas in one city the game was adopted early by local notables from a broad range of social, religious and political backgrounds and moulded into a vehicle of civic expression, in the other it largely maintained the suburban character from which it originated and where the relative privacy of the game's 'clubability' was more prominent than any populist function. In that sense, therefore, generalising in terms of the province as a whole is futile. Rugby was fluid and adapted to the social and cultural characteristics of various locales in different ways. Furthermore and as the examples of Limerick and Cork display, class as a concept in the sporting sphere was multi-dimensional in the Munster rugby context. In addition to the bare socio-economic identity engendered in what one did for a living were additional identities linked to community, place, religion and educational institution attended.

That the ideological content and social appeal of rugby union should vary within one province was a microcosm of the game's experience globally. The dogmatic edifice of middle-class values that the RFU historically attempted to maintain among rugby unions throughout the world through rigid adherence to the principles of amateurism was frequently not suited to local conditions.[235] While the attachment to place so evident in Limerick rugby had clear parallels with the regional identities built around the game in France,[236] it seems likely that the professional networking and suburban bias of Cork rugby was a good deal closer to the desired English social model for the game's development. Though demographic and economic determinants prevented any cash function from infiltrating the playing of rugby in Munster, one could validly argue that Limerick rugby was much closer culturally to the north of England than the rest of Ireland.

CHAPTER 4

Violence and Masculinity

In the build-up to the European Rugby Cup final in 2002, the legendary actor and one-time Young Munster and Munster schools second-row forward Richard Harris recalled his rugby-playing days in typically theatrical terms:

> Limerick rugby was – is – a parish thing. The junior teams were based around the parishes and local pride was always at stake. It was intense and bloody hard but, because we were neighbours and had to talk and work with each other the next day, people were respectful and forgiving. We were quite a parochial bunch in one sense. The players and supporters in far flung Cork – the posh – hated us and the feeling was vice versa. Deep deep down – so buried as to not be ordinarily visible – we also respected each other as fellow Munstermen but such solidarity was rarely displayed or articulated . . . The rugby was hard. I once played in a Munster schools final for Crescent College against PBC Cork. They had a fantastic player, Mick Brosnahan – he normally played full back but I fancied he would play out-half. For three hours one afternoon we practised cynically 'nobbling' the out-half. Father Guinane, our Jesuit priest and coach, had been delayed but caught the tail end of practice and called me over. 'Harris, I'm utterly appalled. We'll win by fair means or not at all,' says he puffing angrily on his fag. He savaged me. Anyway, come match day and the mighty Brosnahan is wearing ten, as predicted. 'Harris, a quiet word,' whispers Father Guinane, emerging from behind a cloud of smoke 'You may continue with your plan.'[1]

Though one must bear in mind that Harris's statement may have been influenced by the fact that it was made in a period when an historical mystique involving notions of toughness and provincial solidarity (with the aid of much hyperbole) was being cultivated around the professional Munster rugby team,[2] it is noteworthy on a number of levels. The cultural connotations and function of rugby as a marker of parochial identity in Limerick, with junior clubs doing battle in city derbies with immense levels of pride at stake, are significant in terms of how notions of masculinity were created through the game.

The competitive nature of the game is further illustrated by the figure of the Jesuit priest advocating cynical foul play in order to boost his team's chances of victory in a cup competition.[3] Notwithstanding Harris's penchant for drama, discernible notions of manliness and attitudes towards violence in Munster rugby can be gleaned from the above statement with an implicit glorification of toughness and rough play. What follows seeks to interrogate and analyse these conceptions and the cultural contexts in which they were created and sustained.

This chapter seeks to examine the distinct yet interlinked issues of violence and masculinity in Munster rugby. While much of what is written on the history of sport rightly concentrates on events off the field such as socio-economic issues, politics and commercialism, etc., this chapter will attempt to combine such issues with a detailed discussion concerning the significance of how the game of rugby football as an abstract set of rules was actually played in the province. Through an analysis of patterns of violence, official and media responses to violence and discourses surrounding masculine types, an attempt will be made to draw significant conclusions as to the function of rugby within certain locales and social milieus. In this sense, the playing of rugby in Munster will be seen as a site upon which varying versions of masculinity and male identity existed.[4] Violence will not be treated, however, as merely a by-product of various 'manly' ideas of how the game should be played but also as being intimately linked to notions of community and locality. The British Muscular Christianity ideology for instance – most clearly associated with forms of codified football and arguably of particular importance to the evolution of rugby union as an amateur pursuit – was certainly influential but by no means definitive in regulating how rugby was played in Munster. The manly values that the game was imbued with varied quite significantly depending on social and cultural context and thus defy grand explanations of violence and masculinity. It is the purpose of this chapter to locate the latter phenomena within their proper contexts and assess the extent to which they intersect historically in Munster rugby.

Rugby football and masculine sporting ideologies

The modern ascription of moral values to athleticism in Britain owed its origins to the public schools games cult of the nineteenth century where, for a myriad of practical and ideological reasons, a harmony was sought between physical and mental exertion. At Marlborough for instance, the reforming headmaster, G.E.L. Cotton, 'was careful to emphasise the correct moral imperative in physical effort', by asserting that 'God was the creator of our bodies as well as our minds. His workmanship included physical as well as mental powers and faculties. In developing both we served Him who made us no less surely than when we knelt in prayer.'[5] From this socio-religious starting point developed an entire set of beliefs relating to sporting participation that gave vital impetus to the codification of sport. Muscular Christianity as an 'ideal valued the quality of "manliness". Participation in "manly" sports was seen to engender the desired traits of self discipline, courage and a sense of Christian duty. It also encompassed the movement of humanism which stressed and balanced moral, intellectual and physical development and often found expression on the phrase *mens sana in corpore sano.*'[6] This doctrine became embedded in popular culture through writers such as Charles Kingsley and most famously Thomas Hughes whose *Tom Brown's Schooldays* was a hugely influential fictional treatment of public school life. This abstract set of beliefs translated itself into a practical perception of how one should conduct oneself both on and off the sports field. Athleticism, or the public school games cult, theoretically served the function of conditioning the ideal imperial man and was the model for moral gentlemanliness. Codified field sports were seen as being particularly amenable to this 'manly' doctrine. T.J.L. Chandler, a noted scholar of Muscular Christianity, has neatly summed up the innate values imposed upon football at the public schools during the Victorian era as follows:

> Being ethical in life became a question of 'playing the game'; and football, as a national game requiring a balance between individual elements and passion, ruggedness, hardness, temerity and might on the one hand and the universal requirements of patience, control, chivalry, good-will and right on the other, was the perfect vehicle for promoting moral gentlemanliness.[7]

Rugby was seen as an ideal platform to express the manliness of the middle-class sportsman who 'saw himself as someone who could hold his passions in check and for whom the enjoyment of the game was more important than the result'.[8]

The Victorian concept of amateurism, which went far beyond the mere economic relationship between a particular sport and its players, owed much of its origins to Muscular Christianity and provided the practical blueprint for the manner in which gentlemen should play and consume codified sport. Participation was prioritised with winning of secondary importance and monetary reward morally tabooed. Gentleman amateurs were expected to play fairly as part of a team and not to compromise the purity of the pursuit by, for instance, engaging in excessive partisanship or elevating the importance of victory by training.[9] Moreover, games were not designed to suit the commercial exigencies of pleasing spectators. In 1880, the RFU secretary Arthur Guillemard stressed that players should 'never sacrifice safety for effect. A man who "plays for the gallery" at football is . . . to be dreaded by his own side.'[10] In a British context, however, the gap between theory and practice could be quite significant in terms of these dogmatic concepts of 'manliness'.

Recent scholarship, for instance, has stressed the contrived and contradictory nature of Victorian amateurism. Far from being intrinsic to middle-class sporting culture and the logical extension of the public schools games cult, amateurism in its moral manifestation was invented to reaffirm class divisions.[11] This was most eloquently expressed in rugby with the formation of the breakaway Northern Union in England in 1895. Though ostensibly a conflict over pay for play, the split was largely attributable to the middle-class-dominated RFU's desire to maintain control over the game in the face of its burgeoning popularity among working-class men in the industrial conurbations of the north.[12] Monetary reward for playing rugby was very much the occasion rather than the cause of the split and the doctrine of amateurism was subject to refinement in order to balance a desire to keep the game pure with the need to boost its popularity in the face of soccer's burgeoning appeal and to stave off the threat of the Northern Union. The attitude of the RFU towards blatant infractions of the amateur code in the Midlands and Wales showed how strategy could easily supersede ideology.[13]

Apart from the central importance of the amateur/professional dichotomy and issues concerning commercialisation, differing class-related conceptions of masculinity were an important aspect of the split.[14] James Martens has neatly summed up this conflict by concluding that 'while southern gentlemen were educated to public school sporting values of play for its intrinsic benefits and character-building, the northern game came quickly to reflect a different type of masculine values that placed a premium on victory. Immediate success created community pride, bragging rights, personal reputations and reinforced community solidarity.'[15] The 'character building' championed through public school sporting values did not, however, eschew violence. Acts of foul play on the rugby union field were common, often celebrated, and were only subject to moral admonition if engaged in by working-class players.[16] For the middle-class rugby hierarchy, robust styles of play among those perceived to be their social inferiors was evidence of excessive and undesirable competitiveness. Conversely, there was an element of 'manly pluck' to physical confrontation among those of similar educational and social background. In 1880, then IRFU secretary and ex-public schoolboy R.M. Peter reacted to press denunciation of violence in Irish rugby by concluding that football was 'a healthy, manly, outdoor amusement in which they [players] have a perfect right, if they are so minded, as free men, to receive more kicks than a halfpence, and to run what dangers to life and limb it pleases them in their favourite pursuit'.[17]

At its most fundamental level, rugby football, like all modern codified sports comprised an abstract set of rules that could, through styles of play, attitudes towards violence, commercialism and class exigencies for example, be culturally manipulated and therefore exhibit varying social and masculine values. There are clear limitations, therefore, to ascribing definitive masculine ideals to flexible cultural formations. As Nauright and Chandler have noted: 'manhood ideologies are not immutable constructs but are adaptations to social environments which are part of the material conditions of life in the various societies during particular time periods.'[18]

Value-centred sport and Munster Rugby

How did the doctrine of Muscular Christianity and the 'gentleman amateur' ideal influence the emergence of rugby football in Munster? The transmission of ideals as culturally specific and complex as Muscular Christianity and amateurism from one country to another is difficult to assess. The imperial, industrial, class and religious conditions under which Muscular Christianity developed in Britain were vastly different from Ireland both in terms of impulse and scale. There were, however, numerous potential agents of transmission in the form of the returning public schoolboys who originally brought rugby to Ireland. Furthermore, the press and official language surrounding rugby football in Ireland was heavily leavened with the sound bites of the 'gentlemanly' approach to the game. Given, however, the extent to which middle-class ideologies of masculinity in Britain were largely illusory in practice, circumspection is required when assessing their influence in Ireland.

If the playing rules of rugby football were successfully imported from Britain, it is far from inconceivable that the same could have happened with the associated idealised values and certainly many of the pioneers of Munster rugby were Muscular Christians. As already noted, the aristocratic founder of the Limerick Football Club, Charles Barrington, had attended Rugby school and had been an influential member of Dublin University Football Club and also one of the key early promoters of rugby football in Ireland. His Limerick FC colleague, the butter merchant W.L. Stokes, was also the product of elite education having attended the exclusive Rathmines School in Dublin (not to be mistaken as being an early manifestation of the rugby-playing St Mary's College of the same locale). In Cork, the Cambridge-educated W.J. Goulding, who played on the early Munster representative teams of the late 1870s and became Munster Branch president in 1879, was theoretically the gentleman amateur *par excellence*. As outlined earlier,[19] in Victorian Britain, Goulding's story of elite education matched with a notable public life and far-reaching sporting interests was typical of the contemporary stereotype of the gentleman amateur. Goulding's Cork FC and Munster Branch colleague A.R. McMullen, heir to a large Cork milling concern, had played on the first XV at Clifton College in Bristol. These were examples of a much larger phenomenon as the tendency among wealthy Protestants (and to a lesser extent Catholics) to send their sons to school in England gave Muscular Christianity ample potential agents of diffusion in Ireland.

That rugby football's elite origins in Ireland informed its desired ideological content is evidenced by the IRFU's attempt to promote something akin to Victorian manliness in Irish rugby. Aiming, perhaps, to ape the British model, they saw a potential platform for promoting their vision of the game through the education system. This policy evidently struggled in the early years. As late as 1880, the IRFU's president, W.C. Neville of Trinity College Dublin, pleaded with the country's schoolmasters to

> recognise that a lifelong brainwork cannot be built up on flimsy bones and flabby muscles; let them look for a sound mind only in a sound body, and let no disastrous attempts be made to treat either on the forcing principles of the hothouse. The animal wants of the growing boy demand attention, and they are to be wisely directed towards the enjoyment of invigorating sports, rather than let run riot in the pursuit of treacherous pleasures.[20]

That this statement, in response to the Union's feeling that rugby had not been adequately fostered in Irish schools, should come six years after rugby was first bureaucratised in Ireland signifies, perhaps, the lack of a native organic growth of Victorian sporting principles among the country's elite schools. Significant in terms of the envisaged masculine function of the game was the IRFU's advocating of cup competitions as a means of promoting football in schools. As early as 1876, a meeting of the Union recommended the presentation of 'a challenge cup to be competed for by schools – members of the union – in such a time and in such a manner as the committee may think fit'.[21] This represented a noteworthy compromise with the purer aspects of British Muscular Christianity as it clearly was at odds with the idea of playing for the sake of playing. Though inter-school cup competitions had existed across the channel since the early 1870s, the RFU harboured significant moral misgivings and suspicions surrounding the concept of competition.[22]

The Irish education system was arguably not very well predisposed to the tangible spread of the games ethic. In the nineteenth century, the Irish system of elite education was in something of a state of flux. The disproportionately wealthier Protestant elite preferred to send their sons to British public schools at the expense of the native-endowed and private classical schools. In Munster in 1856, for instance, Bandon Grammar School had just twenty-five boys enrolled; Midleton College had twenty-two, while Lismore College had gone three years without any enrolments.[23] These establishments would have been the closest to an Irish equivalent of the British public school. Within these institutions, the curriculum remained stubbornly classical, yet there was some evidence of at least a marginal athletic culture. In Fermoy College in County Cork, for instance, football and cricket were popular and a gymnasium was built in 1832 where boys practised drill. It was, by all accounts, an insular sporting culture with a contemporary staff member commenting that 'it was natural, of course, that there should be no dealings whatsoever with the Catholic school [St Colman's] whose ground adjoined ours – the idea of playing cricket and football with them would have been outrageous.'[24] Rev. Berry, appointed headmaster in 1888, promoted a broad athletic programme: 'sport and drill formed an important part of his educational philosophy. Older pupils were encouraged to play "manly" and gentlemanly games and were instructed by the Garrison instructor, Staff Sergeant Derby in gymnastics and drill, imbuing the boys with self-control and discipline.'[25] Elsewhere, many of the schools inspected for the Royal Commission on Endowed Education in Ireland in 1858 had ball-alleys and other sporting facilities.[26] At Midleton College, the headmaster in the 1870s, Rev. Thomas Moore, brought an Arnold-ian ethic to the school and is said to have encouraged games.[27] Both Moore and his mid and late-century counterparts in Fermoy were graduates of Dublin University, rugby football's cultural hearth in Ireland, and may have been familiar with the game's rules. Indeed, Midleton College Rugby Club's alleged formation date of 1870 makes it the oldest existing rugby club in Munster.

This elite athletic culture, which somewhat reflected British developments, was marginal in influence in terms of the broader context of rugby within Munster schools. In reality, rugby within southern Irish educational culture has historically had a decidedly Catholic and competitive flavour. Indeed, the focal point of schools rugby in Munster has always been competition, as evidenced by Harris's statement reproduced at the beginning of the chapter. Though developing the moral character of boys no doubt underpinned the promotion of the game within schools to a certain extent, the prestige of winning competitions was a far more palpable motivation. In Limerick, the Tyler Cup competition, open to both schools and underage clubs, was contested from 1895 onwards and quickly generated levels of partisanship between players and spectators and inter-school rivalry that defied moral ideologies of 'manliness'. In 1900, for example, Brother Baptist Walsh of Limerick CBS reported on the competition as follows:

> The contests for the Tyler Cup between the city schools and colleges took place in March and April. Our boys were defeated by the Leamy's School team and by the [St Munchin's] College team but they beat the team of the Crescent College. In the report of the match between St Munchins [sic] College that appeared in the 'Munster News', April 9th, it was stated 'as the College team left the field, they were pelted with stones and mud by some of the opponent's [sic] backers.' In the report of the final match between the College and Leamy's School it was stated 'the boys carried the Cup to the College in Henry's [sic] St cheering and followed by the opposing crowd shouting in opposition. Stones were thrown in some cases and one of the College boys got his head badly cut.'[28]

Boys from Limerick CBS (albeit eliminated earlier in the competition) were blamed by the bishop for the disorder and the permission for the school to hold its annual collection was withheld pending an apology for the conduct of the pupils. The previous season, when Limerick CBS had won the trophy, the Bishop again accused the victors of having taunted St Munchin's.[29]

The Munster Schools Senior Cup was established in 1909 and has historically been dominated by Catholic schools. Indeed, Abbey Tipperary's victory in 1921 was the only occasion in the competition's history that a school run by a Catholic religious order did not win the trophy.[30] Levels of violence in schools rugby were, on occasion, a source of concern for the Munster Branch. At a meeting of schools representatives in 1946, a row erupted between the north Munster and south Munster schools as to the selection of the provincial XV. In the course of the meeting, Fr Dennehy of Crescent College Limerick accused Presentation Brothers College Cork of engaging in foul play with the meeting ultimately deciding to recommend to 'the Referees Association that they employ the greatest severity with schoolboys indulging in rough play and that all such incidents should be reported to the Branch Committee'.[31] According to the then headmaster of PBC, Brother Evangelist, a further meeting of the schools committee in 1953 'developed into what he had termed "a pre-arranged and concerted attack on Presentation College,"' in which all of the other schools, bar one, 'had charged the College teams with rough play and doubtful tactics in games and illegal methods of training'.[32]

By contrast with the organic growth of the games ethic in Britain, the emergence of a schools football culture in Ireland post-dated the popularisation of modern codified sport in the country. The relationship between modern sport and elite education in Ireland was, therefore, something of an inversion of the British case as in chronological terms, the playing of football in schools was a later development than the establishment of the club system. With the Munster Senior Schools Cup being the Branch's third largest source of income, schools rugby easily lent itself to the promotion of competition and spectatorism – two phenomena at odds with Victorian notions of amateurism. It also seems likely that boys attending elite Catholic schools in Ireland did not have ascribed privileges in life to the same extent as British public schoolboys. Academic achievement was incentivised and was therefore of paramount importance to schoolboy and institution alike. The Intermediate Education Act placed a premium on examination success. As Senia Pašeta has related: 'Immense pressure was placed on schools to win results fees and prove their high academic standing. Catholic students felt this competitive and even combative atmosphere in their everyday school lives.'[33] Though the rugby playing field was no doubt seen as a medium of moral conditioning to some extent, the prestige of winning the Schools Cup fittingly dovetailed the competitive academic atmosphere. Advertisements for schools highlighted examination results and rarely made reference to athletic facilities. Indulging in anti-intellectual moral glorification of games was a luxury that elite Catholic schools in Ireland could scarcely afford.[34]

In the club game, something of the Muscular Christian ethos clearly informed discussion and debate on the state of the game. The rivalry and intensity associated with cup football, for instance, led to palpable concern in certain quarters as to potential adverse effects on the game. The tension between those who advocated the 'participation above winning' maxim and those who saw the benefits of infusing the game with competitive spirit soon surfaced after the establishment of the

Munster Senior Cup in 1886. The introduction of the cup was clearly an opportunity for the two rugby centres in Munster to garner prestige for their respective cities. In the weeks preceding the opening fixtures of the inaugural competition it was rumoured that the two Limerick entrants, Garryowen and Limerick FC, were intending to pool their playing resources and enter the strongest XV that the two clubs could muster. It was also rumoured that, in response, Cork clubs were going to engage in similar activity. The press, reflecting on the foundation rationale of the competition, reacted with hostility:

> The object in view was not, as they [the clubs] seem to think, to discover which two clubs could beat another two, or even what one club could beat the next, but rather to give a healthy stimulus to football generally throughout Munster, to ensure the constant practice and regular training of as many players as possible and as a consequence to raise the tone of the game, if we may be allowed that expression, and all with the object of enabling Munster to take her proper position by the side of her sister provinces.[35]

Competition, however, was always likely to bring cultural change with it. In Limerick, comparable in some respects with contemporary developments in the north of England, the concept of competition was a vehicle through which the game of rugby bolstered its ability to promote civic pride.

Those reflecting sentimentally on the game's quaint origins, however, held stubbornly to the belief that cup competitions encouraged some form of moral decay in sport. Reflecting in 1915 on the then thirty-year history of the Munster Senior Cup, a writer in the *Quarryman* questioned the benefit of the competition:

> The old sporting spirit in which games were played for the sake of the game itself has disappeared and in its place there is excited and ill tempered 'cup fighting' with constant and deliberate 'foul' play. The increase in the number of clubs, which would have undoubtedly taken place, has been prevented by the concentration of players with the sole object of winning 'cup ties'. The number of clubs now competing for the cup is no larger than it was in its very first year, while old teams and real lovers of the game like Limerick FC, Cork Bankers, Bandon and Clanwilliam have been robbed by Cup competition . . . Cup competitions appear to be a sort of half, or even three quarter way house between the old game played by sportsmen for the sake of the game irrespective of the result, and the game played by Welshmen or paid performers, in which the pleasure of the game itself is quite subordinate or absent, and everything hinges on a win obtained very often by foul means. The 'competition' formula is so universal nowadays that any objection to it is hopeless.[36]

The above statement crudely exposed how the elite values of the game's initiators could scarcely exist outside the realms of ideology. In this case, those who qualified as 'real lovers of the game' were quite limited in terms of social and cultural background and the author arguably displayed, by implication, disapproval at the game's populist function in Limerick.

With the consolidation of league and cup competitions as the dominant features of the annual fixture list, however, concern as to how the game was being played became widespread by the opening decade of the twentieth century, particularly in Cork. In March 1906, the referee of the recent Dudley Cup fixtures, V.J. Murray, wrote to the QCC club complimenting

> the three colleges for the great assistance they gave me by playing the game in a clean sporting spirit right through. The matches were the most keenly contested it has ever been my lot to referee, yet with all the keenness and determination displayed, there were no deliberate fouls. What pleased me more than anything was the fact that the games were devoid of any of that trickery or sharp practice which has been I am sorry to say imported to Ireland by some clubs during the past few years.[37]

As well as being a long-standing Munster Branch official, Murray was a journalist – a position that allowed him to influence and shape public opinion. And it seems evident that the type of quasi-moralistic concern about violence in rugby that he displayed in the letter was a dominant motif among his contemporary press colleagues and rugby officials alike.

In 1909, Professor Connel Alexander (most certainly a Muscular Christian of some description himself), president of the Munster Branch of the IRFU, wrote a letter to the *Cork Examiner* launching a general broadside against the manner in which the game of rugby was being played in the province at the time and expressing hope that matters would improve for the coming season of his presidency. Two of his main sources of grievance were, firstly, the attitude of players towards the referee and secondly, what he saw as unnecessarily rough play:

> Players are inclined at times to question the referee's decisions and to pass remarks thereon. The referee's authority on the field is absolute, no player is permitted to criticize or question his decision . . . In many of our matches, there is a great deal of rough and dangerous play – I refer to wild buck rooting in rucks, to savage charging and vicious tackling. These tactics may win matches, but they prevent the games being played with any skill, they rob it of any real enjoyment, they alienate support and they stir up the

worst passions, instead of training men to self-restraint and control
. . . I am sure that we all desire earnestly to see this [Rugby] puri-
fied of the defects which damage it so much at present and to see it
characterized by skill, stamina, resource and a spirit of good
sportsmanship.[38]

Invoking a frame of reference cherished by Muscular Christians,
Alexander described what were in his terms, the ideal functions of
rugby football. As well as his desire to see respect for officialdom and
his criticism of competitiveness in identifying rough tactics as a means
of winning matches, the idea of playing for playing's sake and the fostering of self-restraint through sport – ideas central to the doctrine of
Muscular Christianity – are quite apparent in Alexander's letter.
Alexander expressed these ideas even more explicitly in an article in
the college magazine that year:

> Rugby, when played in the right way and spirit, is not only one of
> the best possible games for developing a man's physique in an all
> round way, but also for inculcating within him moral qualities
> which are invaluable, nay, indispensable, in after life. In these days,
> when life is arduous, and a professional man's hours long and
> exhausting, physical endurance and a robust constitution are just
> as necessary as any qualification the University can confer . . . To
> those who have never played the game or who have only seen a
> Munster Cup tie, the moral training will be hard to estimate. But
> isn't there something in learning to bear defeat, to accept victory
> quietly . . .[39]

Yet, and as was evident in English rugby union, moral judgements on
methods of play arguably reflected the immediate subjective conceptions of those doing the judging, rather than accurately assessing any
objective values of the games themselves. This can be clearly seen if
one closely assesses the context in which Alexander made his comments. The letter to the *Cork Examiner* was published just one week
after a serious row had erupted in the pages of the *Cork Sportsman* in
the aftermath of a Cork Minor League match between Presentation
College and Wanderers. Indicting the tactics of the Wanderers team,
the paper's reporter surmised that:

> They buck-rooted, hacked, and mauled in such a dangerous
> fashion that any attempt on the part of their opponents to handle
> the ball became a most risky undertaking. And to make matters
> worse the language of at least two of their players was such as to
> merit their immediate removal to the touchline.[40]

The secretary of the Wanderers club, J.H. Murphy, mounted a spirited
refutation of the charges levelled against his club and protested

sarcastically in a letter to the *Sportsman* the following week that 'what is invisible to the eye of the average sportsman is perfectly clear to the impartial and keen-sighted optics of your correspondent'. Murphy continued to strongly imply that class bias had precluded the writer from fairly reporting on the match: 'it is quite fashionable in certain quarters to treat us with contempt, as we do not aspire to that region where the "upper ten" rule supreme.'[41] When those members of the Wanderers team with sufficiently esoteric surnames to allow accurate census cross-reference are examined, the presence of a boot maker, an accountant's assistant and a draper's assistant on the team represents something of a divergence from the dominant class profile of contemporary Cork rugby.[42] That this was a factor in the *Sportsman*'s criticism of the club, however, was fervently denied by the reporter concerned: 'in judging a gentleman I never make any distinctions whatever as regards class, but I certainly do as regards morals . . . I would consider tactics of the Wanderers' type as anything but gentlemanly.'[43]

The episode ultimately displayed how two witnesses could watch the same rugby match and, owing to contrasting conceptions of the manly values of sport and divergent motivations for expressing these values, could write strikingly conflicting accounts of the same events. For the reporter, the use of bad language by a Wanderers player was 'one of the most scandalous pieces of blackguardism' that he had ever witnessed. Murphy, however, saw matters differently and claimed that the player concerned had just been struck and had merely 'abruptly addressed' the linesman in the 'excitement thus occasioned'.[44] The controversy rumbled on over a number of weeks with the reporter 'L' ultimately claiming that 'I am glad to be able to say that this is the only team of which I have ever had the experience that would countenance such conduct.'[45] In a postscript that must have felt like vindication for 'L', Wanderers were suspended for a month, and one of their players for life, when a referee was assaulted two months later in the aftermath of a match at the Mardyke.

That there was an element of bias in the reporting of the *Cork Sportsman*, however, seems beyond doubt. In March 1910, letters of protest were sent to the paper at what was seen as sensationalist reports of schools rugby matches. The reporter concerned, 'Liner', was accused of writing 'malevolent' accounts that indicted Christians and North Monastery in particular, and making false accusations of rough play.[46] When a particularly vitriolic attack was launched against Garryowen in the paper in 1909 (see below), a Cork player wrote a letter in defence of the Limerick club, claiming that 'They [Garryowen] played a fine, strong, vigorous game – what you would naturally expect from men; and after all, when a man goes to play rugby football he must remember he is playing a game where the *man* [emphasis in original] is brought out. If some men are afraid of masculine football, well they can fall back on Ping-Pong, Diabolo or similar harmless recreations.'[47] When a similar attack was launched on Lansdowne in the same season (see below), the *Limerick Leader* referred to the reporting of the *Cork Sportsman* as being 'selfish and unfair' and that it was 'Cork criticism . . . quite untrue and unworthy of notice'.[48]

The reporting of the *Cork Sportsman* and the criticism that it received had both immediate and broader significance. It can be argued that the opinions of the publication represented a reaction to the consolidation of the game around competitive structures and the growing significance of rugby as a mode of identity expression with the resultant marginalisation of its status as a 'mere pastime'. On a more general level, the subjective nature of judging what constituted 'manliness' on the football field is clearly displayed. What was considered 'ungentlemanly conduct' by one observer was merely 'robust play' and an inevitable part of the game for another.

The comparative situation in Limerick was influenced by the broad popularity of the game in the city. In a rather ambivalent sense, the celebration of partisanship and competition in Limerick rugby was tempered by moral judgments on the level of roughness or acts of violence in matches. The *Limerick Leader* championed the cultural specificity of Limerick rugby while simultaneously condemning acts of violence on the field. The city's main newspaper evidently did not recognise a possible connection between the two. When Abbey and Young Munster met in the City Junior Cup in Limerick in 1924, the match preview nodded to the typical toughness of junior football by predicting 'a rattling good game provided the players take the tip "play the game" as it is only through players doing so that there is any pleasure derived by players and spectators alike from any form of sport'.[49] One year previously, in a fixture in the same competition between Shamrock and Star, the *Leader* 'hoped that the game will be conducted in a proper spirit of sportsmanship so that it will not be necessary to appeal to players to "play the game"'.[50] By the same token, the *Leader* hailed the apparent exceptionalism of rugby in Limerick. In a celebratory preview to the Munster Senior Cup competition in 1934, for instance, the *Leader*'s rugby writer stated that: 'down here [in Limerick] rugby cup competitions have a flavour all of their own – and a pretty strong one at that. Cup time is the time when pretty football, with its frills and furbelows, is put aside and Cup fighting, in the real sense of the word is the dominating feature.'[51]

Violence in Limerick rugby

If there was an inevitable gap between theory and practice when it came to elite sporting values, this disparity became a chasm when applied to rugby in Limerick. Limerick rugby has historically been tough. It has already been observed in some detail elsewhere in this book that the social and cultural development of Limerick rugby took a divergent path relevant to the rest of the country. In a city where rugby enjoyed incomparable levels of popular cultural identification in the broader Irish context, it was a medium through which internalised notions of parish rivalry and class identity were given their masculine expression by both players and spectators alike. The partisanship and popular appeal of Limerick rugby went hand in hand with styles of play, expressions of masculinity and modes of spectatorism that were not unlike those witnessed in other areas where rugby acquired a populist function (for more of this, see concluding paragraph). By extension, it was a rugby culture much at odds with the professed ideals of contemporary Muscular Christians and gentleman amateurs. From the last decade and a half of the nineteenth century, when the social appeal of rugby broadened in the city, it was already evident that the Markets Field had a reputation for being a hostile venue for visiting clubs. This is quite evident in the *Cork Constitution*'s reporting of a crowd disturbance at a Munster Senior Cup match between Garryowen and Queen's College Cork in 1889:

> It certainly seems that whenever Corkmen travel to Limerick for sport, they do so with their head in their hands. During the second half it certainly looked as if the students, especially the jovial big secretary, would not leave Limerick with a whole skin – as arising out of an unsportsmanlike action on the part of one of the Garryowen forwards, Meade, the captain of Queens [sic] called on his men to leave the field. The students were immediately surrounded by a howling, threatening mob, several of them brandishing sticks and making things anything but pleasant for the wearers of the black and red. However, by the united action of the stewards and the rest of the Garryowen team, the mob were induced to disperse, the offending forward to apologise and the captain of the college to finish the game. During the remainder of the match, play was carried on in a gentlemanly manner.[52]

In 1898, Rockwell College's international forward Jack Ryan was assaulted in Limerick after a cup match against Garryowen. The referee 'was followed almost into the city and hooted'. These incidents were explicitly attributed to working-class spectators as 'a great many of the rougher element came over the walls and created a disgraceful scene at the end of the match'.[53] The IRFU held an inquiry into the incident and subsequently decided that no further representative fixtures would take place in the Markets Field until the grounds were properly fenced. In addition, Garryowen were reminded that the club was responsible for the behaviour of its supporters.[54] By 1908, the unwelcoming reputation of ground and club alike extended across the Irish sea where, in his review of the preceding rugby season, the English writer E.H.D. Sewell remarked upon 'the fashion of the Garryowen club in the famous "Garryowen corner" in the football ground at Limerick, where, base rumour hath it, teeth have ere this met in the flesh of the enemy!'[55]

The *Cork Sportsman* unsurprisingly took a malign view of Limerick rugby. With its usual penchant for pontificating along the lines of the 'fair play' maxim, the publication subjected Garryowen to particularly vitriolic condemnation in the aftermath of a Munster Senior League fixture in 1909:

> Did Garryowen 'play the game' in this match? Do they ever 'play the game'? Are they a dead weight on the progress of Munster football? Every time the ball was punted by a Constitution man he was recklessly charged (with knees up usually) by a Garryowen player, if it was at all possible . . . Every sort of obstruction was indulged in. Hipping was common. Hacking was the custom . . . the whole ideal of the Garryowen team seemed to be – first 'lay out' (it means broken leg, dislocated shoulder, or concussion of the brain) your opponents and then score . . . We have seen Garryowen play fouler football (!) than on Monday, and we have seen them when they are in more lamb-like mood. But the fierce, foul, fighting, kick-out-their-brains spirit is always there . . . We assert that Garryowen always have been and are at present the cause of the wretched state of Munster football and we suggest that serious steps (suspension on the slightest provocation) should be taken by the branch, and that referees, when Garryowen are playing should leave the fine points of the game alone and confine their attentions to watching the dirty tricks of the club in question.[56]

The highly acerbic nature of the description is an illustrative commentary on how the masculine function of the game could be interpreted in contrasting social contexts. The same writer had previously made clear his differing perceptions of how he expected the game to be played in Cork and Limerick. When Cork Constitution and Lansdowne (Limerick) met in a League tie in 1908, he acknowledged that while both sides were at fault for rough play, it was quickly pointed out that 'this "football" is more or less expected from a Limerick club . . . [but] it should not be seen from a team of a club like Constitution. This club can play very good football; unnecessary roughness and open or concealed fouls are totally unnecessary for them to win their matches.' The report concluded that rough play was 'tolerated in the Northern Union [what became professional Rugby League], where players are paid; but rugby is a game that is supposed to be played by sportsmen.[57]

All this is not to say, however, that violence in rugby was confined to Limerick. In a league match between Cork Constitution and UCC in 1923, several players were removed from the field suffering injuries resulting from acts of violence, with one player sustaining a broken collarbone. Contrary to the likely outcome of comparable events in Limerick, however, the incidents provoked an almost hysterical response from press correspondents. One letter writer to the *Cork Examiner* asserted that the encounter had 'thrown back Munster Rugby by a quarter of a century'.[58] Another correspondent drew criticism from local soccer officials by making the suggestion (with blatant class bias) that the players and supporters concerned should take up association football instead of rugby. In a more measured response, the UCC club felt that the incidents called for a reconsideration of 'our ideas as to what rugby should be . . .'[59] Rugby matches degenerating into cycles of violent acts in this fashion were more common in Limerick and rarely triggered the level of mutual recrimination in the press in evidence here.

This does not imply, however, that the Limerick press condoned violence on the field. Within the city, and as discussed below, junior rugby in particular was notable for roughness and the depth of parochial rivalry that it promoted – a perception augmented by the press. The following description, of a match between Shamrocks and St Michael's in 1900, was typical of much comment on junior football: '. . . the players made no attempt to play the game as it should be played but seem to think that their lack of many niceties with which the code abounds can be made up for with over-energetic tackling and rough and tumble play.'[60] When Shannon and Young Munster met in the City Junior Cup final in 1908, one press reporter commented that 'the game was in every respect up to the usual standard of junior finals, roughness and bullying being at all times in evidence.'[61] The following season, the Junior Cup semi-final between Young Garryowen and Shannon was abandoned after twenty minutes due to a series of free fights.[62] In 1910 a match between Young Munster and Great Southern and Western Railway made national news when fans threw stones at each other and the police had to intervene 'to quell what promised to develop into a serious conflict'.[63]

When rugby returned after a hiatus of almost a decade brought on by the First World War and the revolutionary period, one press correspondent singled out junior players for particular attention in an indictment of how the game was being played:

> In view of the welcome revival of Rugby Football in Limerick, it may not be out of place to give a little advice to the players, especially the juniors . . . to endeavour to play the game according to the rules and without any undue roughness. All rugby followers – and the majority of the citizens are keen enthusiasts – are aware that in the past, the charm of the game was invariably spoiled by the bitterness displayed between local rivals; and after seeing some of the games recently played, one is forced to admit that there is little or no improvement in that respect.[64]

This apparent continuity between pre- and post-war rugby in Limerick can easily be gleaned from an examination of disciplinary records, which are only available in any systematic form from 1927 onwards.

The patterns of violence quoted below have been derived from a quantitative study of players suspended for offences committed in matches under the jurisdiction of the Munster Branch of the Irish Rugby Football Union in the period 1927–42.[65] It is worth noting that at the beginning of the period which these figures cover, violence in Munster rugby was seen to be on the decrease. A 1928 newspaper report, for instance, claimed that 'within recent years much of the roughness which formerly characterised Munster Rugby football has been eliminated . . . due to the efficiency and alertness of referees.'[66] Disciplinary issues were dealt with at Branch Committee meetings and are documented in that body's minute books. Almost all of the players suspended in the period covered had committed some form of physical attack on a member of an opposing team, with striking, kicking an opponent on the ground and fighting being by far the most common. These incidents were punctuated by the less common phenomenon of crowd disorder with both on and off field violence frequently occurring in the same matches.

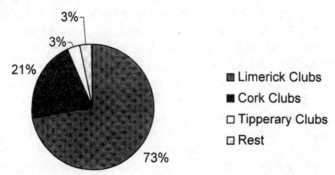

Fig. 4. Suspended players per region in Munster 1927–42

Of the 331 recorded suspensions imposed by the Branch in the period 1927–42, 234 (73 per cent) of them were against players representing Limerick city clubs. A further seventy-one (21 per cent) were against players representing Cork clubs. The remaining twenty-two suspensions were attributable to representatives of the various junior outfits from Tipperary, Waterford, Clare and Kerry (See Figure 4)

Table 4

Suspensions imposed on players from Limerick city junior clubs 1927–42

In matches against	Total	Percentage
Limerick city junior clubs	78	60.3
Limerick city senior clubs' junior teams	43	32.8
Tipperary teams	3	2.3
Limerick county teams	1	0.8
Unknown	5	3.8

Table 5

Suspensions imposed on players from the junior XVs of senior clubs from Limerick city 1927–42

In matches against	Total	Percentage
Limerick city junior clubs	52	65.9
Limerick city senior clubs' junior teams	17	21.5
Cork city teams	4	5.0
Limerick county teams	1	1.3
Waterford teams	1	1.3

Table 6

Suspensions imposed on Limerick city senior teams 1927–42

In matches against	Total	Percentage
Limerick city senior teams	14	56
Cork city teams	11	44

Furthermore, and as already alluded to, 209 of the 234 players from Limerick city that were suspended committed their transgressions while playing junior rugby, while 190 of the 234 suspensions stemmed from incidents that occurred in Limerick derby matches. As illustrated by Tables 4, 5 and 6, violence was comparably rarer in senior rugby. To further underline the disproportionality of the violence in Limerick rugby in the overall Munster context, a specific study of suspensions handed out in the Munster Junior Cup, the prestige competition for junior clubs in Munster, reveals that though clubs from Limerick city rarely comprised more than a third of the total number of clubs competing in the competition in any given year in the period under examination, 85 per cent of all recorded suspensions in the Munster Junior Cup were attributable to Limerick teams.

The disparity between levels of recorded violence between Limerick and Cork rugby is solidly underlined when the total number of suspensions are examined on a per club basis. As Tables 7 and 8 illustrate, Young Munster managed alone to equal the total number of suspensions imposed on all Cork clubs in the period 1927–42.

Table 7
Suspensions per Limerick club 1927–42
(*clubs from outside the city)

Club	No. of suspensions
Young Munster	71
Shannon	26
Presentation	24
Richmond	24
Garryowen	19
Old Queen's	17
Abbey	16
Bohemians	12
St Munchin's	8
Limerick County	5
Old Crescent	3
Askeaton*	3
Ramblers	2
St John's	2
St Michael's	2
Lansdowne	1
Newcastlewest*	1
Wanderers	1
Crescent	1
TOTAL	238

Table 8

Suspensions per Cork club 1927–42

(*clubs from outside the city)

Club	No. of suspensions
Cork Constitution	20
Sunday's Well	18
Highfield	9
University College Cork	7
Dolphin	7
Kanturk*	3
Bandon*	3
Skibbereen*	1
Mallow*	1
Cobh*	1
Christians	1
TOTAL	71

The Munster Branch responded with stern measures, frequently imposing long suspensions on offending players. At a meeting on 19 March 1927, for example, one P. McInerney of Presentation was suspended for life for biting more than one Waterford player.[67] On 28 January 1932, a certain J. Lyons of the St Munchin's club received a five-year suspension for kicking a Garryowen opponent.[68] One would have to assume that Lyons had previously offended as kicking opponents was an offence that usually merited a more lenient punishment. In a particularly ill-tempered Junior Cup affair between Limerick County and Garryowen in 1935, Sheehy of County was suspended for life and a further three players from the same club received suspensions totalling seven years. The previous year, another Limerick County player, W. Cunneen, was sentenced by the Branch Committee 'not to play for life for one of the foulest offences they ever investigated', with the nature of the offence never specified in either the minutes or press reports.

In March 1942, arguably the most serious disciplinary crisis in the history of rugby in Munster occurred when almost an entire meeting was given over to a Munster Junior Cup replay between Young Munster and Old Crescent, in which the referee, Paddy Sullivan, saw fit to send nine players off the field. It was reported that the referee 'stated that he was subject to continuous abuse from spectators, and on leaving the field after the game, he was assaulted by a playing member of the Young Munster club who was a spectator and by one of the Young Munster players already sent off during the game'. The *Limerick Leader* reported that:

> From the kick off to the final whistle the referee, Mr Paddy Sullivan had a most unenviable time not alone from the players but from a section of the spectators whose chief hobbies were to hurl insulting epithets at his every decision given against the Young Munster team and to invite the members of that side to commit acts not in accordance with the rules of the game. This in itself was bad enough but when the game was over the referee was surrounded and attacked by the playing and non playing members of the defeated club.[69]

Though a motion advocating the permanent suspension of the Young Munster junior team failed to receive a seconder, the Branch eventually decided to suspend three Young Munster members for life, four players for a period of two years and the remaining eight Young Munster players, not sent off during the match for a year. The latter were re-instated in October, meaning that the majority of their suspension was served during the summer, when no rugby fixtures took place.[70] In reaction to the entire series of events, the president of the Branch, D.J. O'Malley, himself a former referee and a member of the Bohemians club, resigned his position as he saw the punishments as being too lenient.[71]

The potentially hazardous nature of refereeing rugby in Limerick was previously underscored when a similar incident had occurred twelve years earlier in another Junior Cup match involving Young Munster, this time against Abbey, when two Young Munster players and a spectator assaulted the referee.[72] Concern at the behaviour of Young Munster supporters had been expressed in 1927, when the Branch wrote to the club requesting their secretary to take 'the necessary steps to control the attendance of certain supporters of the club'.[73] When Garryowen and Bohemians met in a brutal Senior Cup encounter in 1927, the referee wrote to the Branch complaining that officials from the Garryowen club had done nothing to stop their supporters from threatening him and that as he was leaving the field he was informed that 'if Garryowen had not won, I would not have got off the grounds so safely'.[74] In November 1929, District Justice Flood criticised 'unruly elements' within junior rugby before giving a dock labourer, Thomas Lynch, a two-month suspended sentence for being part of a mob that assaulted a referee and vandalised the car he was travelling in following a junior rugby match at the Markets Field. Apparently, the crowd had resented the referee's decisions in the match.[75] This was not the only brush with the law that followers of junior rugby had. In September 1927, twenty-six men comprising the players and travelling support of the short-lived Rangers junior rugby team were arrested after a public house on the outskirts of Limerick to which they were refused entry was vandalised.[76] The party were returning from a fixture in nearby Killaloe.

As already evident from the above incidents, on-field violence in Limerick rugby was matched by a similar, though not as frequent, pattern of spectator disorder. Almost all the incidents that could fall into the category of crowd violence in the time period under study occurred in derby games in Limerick. In response to the general on- and off-field disorder associated with junior football in the city, the committee decided in 1930 that 'all matches between Limerick City Clubs [sic] in the Munster Junior Cup [are] to be played in week days'. This decision was in response to excessive violence in a Limerick derby match between Young Munster and Presentation, with the *Limerick Leader* bemoaning the fact that 'there seems to be a blight on this [Munster Junior Cup] competition'.[77] Due to fixture congestion, however, they quickly had to change their decision but warned Limerick clubs that they should steward their grounds 'and ensure that no unseemly conduct occurred as in the event of disorderly conduct occurring, the sub committee of the Branch would report same and permission for future Sunday games would be withheld'.[78] Indeed, it was often deemed worthy of comment if there was no disorder at a junior match. When Limerick City and Shannon met in the Munster Junior Cup in 1911, it was noted that the game 'was contested in a good spirit . . . despite the fact that a rather "hot" feeling has existed between the teams'.[79] While when Richmond played against Presentation in a junior match in November 1931, the *Leader* was moved to comment that 'the game was played in that fine sporting spirit which asks for no quarter and gives none either . . . well played juniors, and mark you on a Sunday too.'[80]

In addition to the above measures, Old Queen's, St Munchin's and Limerick County football clubs found themselves temporarily suspended from Branch competitions for failing either to control their players or supporters.[81] What one can clearly see from both the statistics and the anecdotes just mentioned is that in terms of Munster rugby overall, violent incidents either on or off the field were most likely to occur when Limerick city teams played against each other. Moreover, violence appears to have been more likely to occur in the context of a competitive atmosphere such as the Munster Junior Cup.

Violence, as these patterns prove, was part of the flavour of Munster, and particularly Limerick, rugby. How can one rationalise the peculiar configuration of violent incidents in Munster rugby? The British sociologists Eric Dunning and Ken Sheard, applying the ideas of Norbert Elias, have argued that the evolution of rugby in the late nineteenth century was defined by decreasing levels of violence toleration which found expression in the drafting of rules by administrative bodies specifically designed to curtail violence within the sport.[82] Specifically, they point to the banning of 'hacking' in rugby football as an example of this 'civilising process' at work.[83] 'Hacking' was a practice whereby opposing players would kick each other on the shins while attempting to gain possession of the ball. Dunning and Sheard also saw the fact that referees could award penalties and players could have sanctions imposed on them as further testament to rugby's 'civilisation'.[84]

In the case of Munster rugby, this paradigm is clearly questionable. Though violence was circumscribed in rugby both by the game's rulebook and its gentlemanly ethos, the game could be tailored to the cultural norms of specific localities. In Munster acceptable levels of violence can be more accurately gauged by the enforcement of rules rather than their abstract creation. Though previously mentioned incidents indicate that the Munster Branch did not tolerate rough play or crowd disorder, in reality the Branch's approach to violence, and more specifically disciplinary matters, was of a chaotic, uneven nature. For instance, in the period covered by available records, no co-ordinated policy was forthcoming from the Munster Branch to eliminate, or at least reduce, levels of violence among Limerick junior teams. Throughout this period, the Branch never once flagged levels of violence in Limerick rugby as a fundamental problem that needed specific attention. In October 1927, it was noted by the committee that many players sent off in Limerick in the previous season had not even been reported by referees.[85] As already pointed out, some *ad hoc* measures were taken. The temporary suspension of relatively weak clubs had its deterrent effect undermined by the fact that players from such clubs could simply re-register with other teams and continue playing. Furthermore, Young Munster, whose disciplinary record was far worse than any of the clubs that found themselves suspended, were seemingly spared this sanction because of the club's status as one of the most popular in the province. When it came to imposing sanctions on the club after the conduct of their players and supporters in the previously mentioned Junior Cup match against Old Crescent, it was decided that suspending the club would not be in the best interests of the game as a whole.[86] In addition, the prohibition of Limerick teams from playing Munster Junior Cup ties at weekends was quickly rescinded when the possibility of resultant fixture congestion became apparent.

Had the Munster Junior Cup (a competition with tangible disciplinary issues) been run on the basis of an 'open draw' rather than having the earlier rounds regionalised, matches between Limerick teams would in all likelihood have been fewer and hence the potential for violence both on and off the field would have been reduced. This format, however, was tried and failed and was marked in 1927 by 'very poor gates and repeated alteration of fixtures'.[87] Furthermore, each time a Limerick or Cork team travelled outside their native city to fulfil a fixture in a cup competition, the Branch was bound by its own rules to compensate the team for any travelling expenses incurred.[88] In other words, it was in the best financial interests of the Branch for Limerick teams to play against each other as frequently as possible. The Munster Junior Cup was, for the period under examination, the Branch's second largest source of gate income and this, one could confidently assume, was largely due to Limerick derbies. Bearing these factors in mind, it seems plausible that the financial viability of the Munster Junior Cup, the smooth running of the competition and the overall strength of the game (as exemplified by the Branch's relatively lenient stance with Young Munster) were greater priorities for the Munster Branch than any attempt to 'civilise' the game as it functioned under their jurisdiction. The Munster Branch, through their lack of action on this matter, arguably believed that violence was an undesirable yet acceptable by-product of the Junior Cup.

One disciplinary controversy that clearly displays the ambivalent attitude of the Munster Branch towards violence occurred in 1928 when, in the course of their Munster Senior Cup final victory over Cork Constitution, Young Munster had one of their forwards, H. Raleigh, sent off for kicking an opponent in the face.[89] The Munster Branch suspended Raleigh for a mere two days. The match referee, Noel Purcell of Leinster, indignantly wrote to the Leinster Branch claiming that the decision of the Munster executive to impose such a lenient sentence was tantamount to 'condoning the offence with the natural implication that I, as referee, had without sufficient cause, ordered the players off'.[90] The IRFU quickly got wind of the controversy and secretary Rupert Jeffares wrote to his Munster counterpart, Bill O'Brien, stating that '. . . my Committee feel that a suspension of two days was quite an inadequate punishment and trust that if such an incident occurs again, your Branch will deal in a more drastic fashion with the offenders. My Committee are exceedingly anxious to keep the game free from foul play and feel that the referees must be supported in their decisions.'[91] The Munster Branch's apparent lack of support for the referee's decision is mysterious given that kicking an opponent would ordinarily have merited a stiffer punishment. One could confidently speculate, however, that given Young Munster's status as champions of Munster and the province's representative in the Bateman (all-Ireland) Cup series the following weekend, the Branch did not want to impose a suspension that would deprive them of a starting player and in any way diminish their chances of victory. Young Munster famously defeated a much-fancied Lansdowne side and won the Bateman Cup with strict disciplinary measures possibly sacrificed on the altar of cup success for the province.

A similar series of events occurred in 1932 when Young Munster's Ter Casey was suspended for four months from May to September for kicking an opponent. The punishment was not really a punishment at all given that no rugby was being played in those months. When the IRFU wrote to the Branch asking them to reconsider the suspension's leniency, the Branch refused, claiming that 'the punishment fitted the crime.'[92] Subsequently the Branch proposed a minimum suspension of three *playing* months for players sent off in competitive matches.[93] The mandatory nature of the measure proved something of a blunt instrument and was reduced to one month in 1936.[94]

It is not possible to determine if players derived any pleasure from engaging in foul play but it did, at times, meet with the approval of the crowd. In 1924, a press article condemned 'the common fault of tackling a player long after he has parted with the ball, and which some of the spectators seem to acclaim as wonderful'.[95] In 1929, the same publication condemned the fact that 'we have seen players sent off the field being accorded a vociferous ovation by spectators'.[96] In addition, the deeds of players seen as having been robust and tough are recorded in folk memory with a degree of warm nostalgia. The Hayeses of St Mary's attained legendary status for their front-row exploits in the 1940s and 1950s. As Table 9 demonstrates, the brothers had a colourful disciplinary record that spanned three decades in the middle third of the twentieth century. Augustine and Michael were members of particularly notorious St Mary's teams while Matthew had played for Garryowen and Shannon. In the period spanning the offences documented in Table 9, the clubs were subject to repeated warnings from the Munster Branch committee as to the behaviour of both their players and supporters.[97]

Table 9

Disciplinary record of the Hayes brothers
of St Mary's Parish[98]

Family member	Club represented	Offence	Date of suspension	Duration of suspension
Matthew	Shannon	Rough play	27 February 1936	Three months
Augustine	St Mary's	Kicking an opponent	26 February 1948	One week
Augustine	St Mary's	Kicking an opponent	13 October 1949	Ten weeks
Augustine	St Mary's	Striking an opponent	2 April 1952	One year
Michael	St Mary's	Assaulting an opponent	22 April 1955	Five and a half years

Yet for all their disciplinary foibles, the Hayes brothers are remembered with affection in Limerick. Denis O'Shaughnessy's sentimental collection of anecdotes about St Mary's parish, for instance, dedicates a chapter to the brothers' rugby exploits. Rather than being the subject of admonition for rough play, it was claimed that Augustine Hayes 'was one of the great characters of Limerick rugby and there was little doubt that the coffers of the North Munster Branch was swelled any time he played in the cup at Thomond Park . . . Skin and hair flying was guaranteed'.[99] As the sons of a factory worker and a labourer and hailing from the laneways of St Mary's parish,[100] the social and cultural distance between the Hayes brothers and the Irish rugby establishment could scarcely have been greater. That they were tough and played rugby accordingly was a product of where they came from.

The decrease in violence so central to the 'civilising' thesis promoted by Dunning and Sheard presupposes increased repugnance at violent acts. The above evidence gathered with regard to Limerick rugby indicates that violence was in some ways accepted by player and supporter alike with the crowd frequently partaking in disorderly behaviour.

Violence in Munster rugby can be more easily explained through varying ideals of sporting masculinity. Taken as a whole, one could argue that within the context of the Limerick urban sporting landscape and underpinning the disproportionate levels of violence in rugby in the city was a masculine ideal that championed vigour, aggression and competitiveness. Parallels can be drawn with Richard Holt's description of the gender implications of football in England where he asserted that 'sport was a kind of subtle and ubiquitous male language . . . interfused with ideas of territory and grace was an ideal masculinity. Football enshrined older forms of toughness and rudeness, which stoutly resisted the "civilising process" of fair play and sportsmanship in which the crowd "happily transgressed the limits of decent partisanship" in terms of middle-class language, gesture and style.'[101]

When assessing the territory component of this masculine ideal, the context of junior rugby is again vital. It seems reasonable to assert that inter-parish rivalry amplified by the intensity of a prestige competition and partisan crowds augmented potential for conflict in Limerick rugby. In Limerick city, at any given time in the post-First World War era, anything up to between fifteen and twenty clubs were affiliated to the Munster Branch. Of this number, only Young Munster, Garryowen and Bohemians were senior for any considerable length of time before the mid-1950s. Furthermore, and as previously discussed in this book, many of the clubs were intimately linked to specific geographical areas within the city. The contrast with Cork rugby was stark. Cork city teams entering the Munster Junior Cup, for instance, were generally the second XVs of senior clubs. The same affiliation to locality did not prevail in Cork rugby and it is this key disparity between the two cities that mirrored contrasting levels of violence in the two areas with the apparent 'clubbability' of Cork rugby contrasting with the community dynamic so palpable in Limerick.

This contention is supported by another aspect of the pattern of suspensions in Munster rugby. The high levels of violence in junior rugby diverged widely from senior rugby. In Limerick, just 25 of the 238 suspensions recorded stemmed from senior matches. Furthermore, the Munster Senior League and Cup competitions accounted for a mere 17 suspensions from a total of 331. Why was there such a discrepancy between senior and junior? A potential answer lies in the respective grades' competitive structures. Young Munster, whose staggering total of seventy-one suspensions for the period under review (see Table 7) was higher than any other club by a distance, could attribute almost all of their disciplinary problems among players and supporters to games involving their junior team. Young Munster's seniors, incidentally one of the finest teams of their generation in the late 1920s, were not exposed to the same inter-parish rivalry as their junior team. The competitive structure of senior rugby included a league and cup competition comprising the three Limerick teams and four from Cork. Given these factors, it is arguable that Limerick rugby was not fundamentally violent and trouble only occurred under specific circumstances.

Thinking again in terms of masculinity, the particular brand of rugby played in Limerick was of the forward-orientated, robust vintage in which no quarter was given. In a letter to the Munster Branch in February 1928, Garryowen FC wrote in 'protest against the ordering off the field of some of our players in recent matches . . . apparently it is quite in order for our opponents to play as vigorously as they please while our players are compelled to play "tig" (or some other parlour game) and one need not be surprised that we resent such an arrangement.'[102] They further objected that 'referees insisted on encouraging too much namby pamby play and discouraging robust play'.[103] These claims were repeated by Garryowen official Jack Macaulay at the club's dinner the following May when, in a statement directed at referees, he stated that 'Rugby Football . . . is a man's game in the truest sense of the term, but when we play a strenuous game, there is no necessity that it should be a foul or rough game . . . It is not a kid-glove game or a drawing-room game.'[104]

In addition, evidence suggests that a culture of disrespect for the authority of the referee prevailed. Beyond the documented incidents of physical violence against referees, newspaper reports frequently judged the level of sportsmanship in a match by the respect or lack thereof shown to the referee. In describing a junior cup match between Abbey and Young Munster in 1930, the *Limerick Leader* commented with more than a note of surprise that 'the attention to his [the referee's] whistle was extraordinary and he had only to whistle and both teams turned round to listen to what he had to say.'[105] Quite clearly masculinity in Limerick rugby flouted the Victorian public school ideal of fair play and self-restraint.

Violence in Limerick rugby was centred on an observable parochial ethic and ultimately defies grand explanation. Philip Dine's study of French rugby has shown that levels of violence can be a reflection of specific local context. In that regard, the junior game in Limerick was truly the Irish equivalent of the French *Culture du Rugby* of the 1920s where violence in the game became culturally embedded in south-western France.[106] Though it was not quite *le rugby de muerte* as no player, to public knowledge, ever died from injuries received on the field in Limerick, it was certainly brutal and, in common with France, occurred within a very specific cultural, geographical and social context. Rugby as a game that championed the values of the British public school had limited success. Though authorities and press alike idealised this vision of gentlemanly conduct, the success of the game was always contingent upon its adaptation to local conditions.

CHAPTER 5

Politics and Culture

In March 1966, the Munster Branch of the IRFU granted permission to Westport RFC to field Munster players in a rugby match commemorating the fiftieth anniversary of the 1916 Easter Rising.[1] An innocuous decision, one could argue, given the nationwide festivities held for the same reason that year. In the context of the all-island administrative structure of Irish rugby, however, it is possible to ascribe deeper symbolic significance to the idea of a rugby match commemorating such an iconic watershed in the history of Irish nationalism. This is clearly apparent in the context of the internal structure of Irish rugby given that the Easter Rising was prosecuted primarily by the Irish Volunteers, a paramilitary body set up in response to the founding of the original Ulster Volunteer Force (UVF), who in turn were strongly supported by rugby players in Ulster.[2] In addition, a certain paradox exists in the idea of a sport that had been historically ascribed anglophile connotations commemorating physical-force republicanism.

Paul Rouse has commented that the paucity of academic research on the history of Irish sport 'has allowed a series of stereotypes and caricatures to prosper, while distortions of history have blossomed as inherited truths'.[3] Though intended as a general statement, Rouse's observation is arguably most applicable to the historical intersection of sport and Irish political culture and in the case of this book, rugby football. If cultural nationalism was the dominant foundation rationale for the Gaelic Athletic Association, then negative campaigning in the form of unpatriotic or 'anti-national' characterisation of sports that originated in Britain was to become an important weapon in the organisation's ideological armoury. The resultant discursive division of Irish sport into 'native' and 'foreign' categories disguises the fluidity of the relationship between sport and political symbolism and identity in Ireland, a fluidity that this chapter will attempt to display within the context of Munster rugby. As already hinted, the relationship between Irish rugby and political identity was not merely a matter of external imposition, however, and factors peculiar to the game are also significant in this respect. As a sport with a non-partitionist administrative structure and international selection policy, and with a broad cross-section of adherents from different social and cultural backgrounds, the game's potential to become embroiled in controversy of a political nature was quite extensive and will be the focus of the second half of this chapter.

Gaelic games, 'foreign' sports and cultural perception

In a Dáil Éireann committee session on estimates in science and arts in 1922, Professor W.M. Magennis stated that 'the spirit of the shoneen . . . is propagated largely through certain sports that are regarded as peculiarly the privilege of the wealthy classes and belong to a British tradition.'[4] In another Dáil Éireann debate on entertainment tax in 1930, Fianna Fáil's Seán MacEntee declared pejoratively that 'there have been political associations and political implications attaching to the rugby game that we [sic], as a legislative assembly, cannot shut our eyes [to].'[5] Almost three decades later, the GAA enthusiast Pádraig Puirséal wrote: 'In Ireland, from the time of the Catholic Emancipation and right through to the Victorian era, there was a tendency to think of all things good as coming from England. Irish people, taken as a whole, suffered from an inferiority complex and were apt to follow where England led.'[6] Without any hint of ironic reflection on the GAA's wholesale adoption of British methods of sporting codification and administration,[7] this was the rationale put forward by the author for the growth of rugby in Ireland in the second half of the nineteenth century. Negative characterisation of British sports existed to varying extents since the first GAA ban on foreign games was introduced in 1886,[8] yet the stridency and historical pretension inherent in these statements was facilitated, no doubt, by the contemporary atmosphere in which the GAA's institutionalised antagonism towards 'foreign' sports had gained an unprecedented ideological potency. Indeed, as the leading historian of the 'ban' has asserted, 'it was only in the decades after independence that it [the ban] attained extreme ideological importance.'[9]

The idea of a 'bifurcation of sport into Anglo and Gaelic camps' has been promoted academically in the work of Michael Mullan.[10] The apparent marked duality of cultures in late nineteenth-century Irish sport is seen as being due to the failure of certain class configurations to take root in Ireland stemming from industrial decline and the penal laws. What emerged, in Mullan's view, was 'a dual system of sport', relying on 'traditional patterns of conflict and opposition'.[11] Apart from the fact that the current state of knowledge on nineteenth-century Irish sport and its adherents precludes any such clear demarcation as propagated by Mullan, his treatment fails to ascribe any agency to the nascent Irish Catholic elite and neglects to acknowledge the fact that most of the so-called 'foreign games' quickly drew significant support from sections of the native Catholic community. That there was a strain of unionist sentiment within British sport in Ireland is likely. Though ascribing any political significance to Irish involvement in the First World War is a fraught exercise, it seems probable that a certain proportion of Irish rugby players that joined the war effort were in some way inspired by a sense of imperial duty comparable to the ostentatious patriotism of English rugby players. Moreover, sections of the unionist media were critical of the GAA. The *Cork Constitution*, the unionist publication that would later spawn a rugby club, frequently criticised the GAA 'for having little to do with athletics and much to do with politics'.[12] The same paper campaigned against the GAA's scheduling of fixtures on Sundays, commenting that 'some people do not like to be reminded of their sins'.[13] Commenting on an ill-tempered rugby match between the Post Office and HMS *Black Prince* in 1900, the *Constitution*'s rugby reporter stated that 'hand ball, passes forward, knocks on, every illegality was allowed until in the end, the football became a species of the Gaelic game.'[14]

In reality, however, the attachment of politico-cultural significance to different sports in Ireland was an evolutionary, contested process – the success of which was both regionally and chronologically varied. The pretence of broad historical legitimacy that can be taken from the utterances of Magennis, MacEntee and Puirséal, therefore, amount to little more than crass simplification and generalisation. Given that the labelling of certain sports as being 'foreign' was the ideological corollary of the 'ban' mentality, it is necessary to briefly revisit the history of the 'ban' itself. It has already been observed in this book that Garryowen FC's role as a proxy parent body for Sunday rugby in Limerick decisively facilitated the game's relatively egalitarian evolution in the city. This is a typical example in the history of sport where mundane administrative issues supersede more engaging social or cultural explanations for a particular trend. It is within these terms that one should consider the early history of the 'ban'. For instance, the adoption of a rule in September 1886 precluding from membership of the GAA persons playing rugby or other non-Gaelic sports was a specific response to unimpressive rates of club affiliation and fee payment and 'carried no political or ideological connotations'.[15] When, in 1896, it was believed that the 'ban' was having an injurious effect on the Association's popularity, it was duly dispensed with. Indeed, it was only after 1900 that the 'ban' began to slowly evolve into the instrument of dogma that it would become in the post-independence decades. In 1901, it was re-introduced with an appeal to 'young men of Ireland not to identify themselves with Rugby or Association football or any form of imported sport'. In the event, implementation was to be left to the discretion of individual county boards.[16] In 1905, the measure assumed its permanent form when a narrowly passed motion imposed a compulsory two-year suspension for 'persons who play rugby, soccer, hockey, cricket or any imported games'.[17] Even then the 'ban' was far from unanimously popular among GAA members and it was only in the context of the political tumult of the 1912–21 period that it became a fundamental guiding principle of the GAA.[18] It was within this background that the 'ban' shed its purely utilitarian purpose and became an instrument that symbolised the final separation of the Gael and the garrison.

The ideological evolution of the 'ban' was, as one historian has termed it, a 'process of invention',[19] which facilitated the GAA's position as 'a sporting organisation that has become central to historical myth of the late nineteenth and early twentieth century reawakening of the Irish nation'.[20] The consequence of all this was that an entire system of rhetoric had to be 'invented' to negatively characterise rival 'foreign' sports. Given the above outlined chronology of the ban's evolving function, however, it is hardly surprising that the discursive and practical bifurcation of sport into 'Anglo' and 'Gaelic' camps was a far from straightforward process and significant shades of grey would always exist between the apparent polarities. This becomes clear when one assesses the experience of rugby football in Munster.

Gaelic games, rugby football and cultural conflict in Munster

The extent to which political beliefs dictated one's sporting preferences in Ireland at any given time is impossible to accurately measure and certainly varied from place to place. Moreover, untangling social background from political persuasion as a deciding factor in one's sporting destiny further complicated the process – an issue underlined in Neal Garnham's astute speculation that 'the GAA may have drawn a great deal of its early popularity from the simple fact that its members could not participate in sports elsewhere.'[21] The safest generalisation that can be made on available evidence is that the GAA's negative campaign against sports that originated in Britain was uneven, gradual and far from unanimously accepted prior to the turn of the twentieth century. A clear cultural delineation between 'native' and 'foreign' in the case of Munster rugby was obscured by the early fluidity of codes and affiliation, frequent overlaps between rival codes in terms of personnel, and the contested nature of the 'ban' mentality.

It has already been observed in this book that the popularity of Sunday rugby in Munster – temporary in Cork, enduring in Limerick – was a striking example of rugby making incursions into the GAA's potential social and cultural constituency. Prior to the adoption of Gaelic football by certain erstwhile rugby clubs in Cork, it seems exceedingly likely that they played the 'foreign' game free of any political or cultural frame of reference. In April 1885, for example, the *Cork Examiner* carried a report of a busy day's sporting activity at Cork Park the previous Sunday in which 'some hundreds of the young men of the city' took part in some 'very lively events in the way of football, cricketing and hurling'. The hurling was played under GAA rules, while the football, which included a match between Nil Desperandum and Queesntown Young Men's Society, was rugby. The events, attended by thousands of people, were clearly festive and communal with potential political connotations of sporting rules not figuring as an issue of any import.[22] The 'denationalising' effect of rugby football was clearly not yet apparent.

The following spring, the newly instituted Munster Football League at least ostensibly had a distaste for the cultural implications of rugby as one of its founding principles. Yet it seemingly failed to attract the majority of Cork's Sunday rugby teams and when it folded due to antagonism from the GAA, at least one of its component clubs, Nil Desperandum (colloquially called 'Nils'), quickly returned to rugby rules. Nils, in many ways, demonstrated the level of fluidity between codes and affiliation that existed in the early history of Irish football. Having already been a rugby and national rules outfit, the club returned to the former in 1887 and in February of that year, members of Nils joined with rugby players from a mixture of Saturday- and Sunday-playing clubs including Queen's College and Cork Bankers in a celebratory procession to mark Ireland's first international rugby victory over England.[23] Nils continued under rugby rules for at least another season before eventually converting to Gaelic football and winning the Cork county title in 1889 and again in 1890.[24] The club had not, apparently, dispensed with the idea of playing rugby at this point, as evidenced by a notice in *Sport* in November 1890 which claimed that Nil Desperandum had merged with Trinity Football Club and were 'going for the Munster Cup'.[25] Nils quickly, however, seem to have developed into an exclusively Gaelic football club and went on to become one of the most successful exponents of that code in pre-independence Cork. Other examples of former rugby clubs that made significant impacts in Gaelic football were Laune Rangers from Kerry and Arravale Rovers from Tipperary.[26] In the absence of definitive evidence, one can speculate that the clubs' eventual choice of code was as much attributable to a greater availability of Sunday fixtures in the Gaelic code and a social distance from the local rugby authorities than any politico-cultural considerations.

The early cultural neutrality of football codes was humorously demonstrated in west Cork in February 1887 by the farcical outcome of a fixture between clubs from Baltimore and Skibbereen. The Skibbereen team had been under the impression that the match was to be played under rugby rules and when the umpire signalled for a scrimmage after the ball had been thrown forward by their full back, the Baltimore team indicated that they did not understand what a scrimmage was and claimed ignorance of rugby rules. Furthermore, the latter club insisted that the match should be played under the local 'Baltimore rules' known as 'kick and tear away'. The Skibbereen contingent subsequently challenged their opponents to another fixture 'any day either *Rugby or Gaelic rules* [emphasis added] but not the Baltimore rules that nobody knows only themselves'.[27] A comparable situation had occurred in Ulster six years earlier, when schools from Derry and Coleraine met in a friendly football tournament with one team prepared to play under association rules and the other under the rugby variant.[28]

Within the maelstrom of different available codes in the late 1880s, therefore, it appears that there was little room, as yet, for political sentiment to encroach upon the sporting sphere. Moreover, the transition of 'football' from its generic to specific meanings was gradual, as was the acquisition of the social and cultural connotations that various sports would become associated with. Within this context, therefore, the apparent incongruity of Gaelic football clubs fielding cricket teams in 1890s Westmeath was clearly an anomaly only in retrospect, while the defection, for organisational reasons, of T.P. O'Connor's Gaelic Football Club to soccer in Athlone in 1893[29] clearly displays that the necessary association of sports with cultural identities was also an evolutionary development. This fluidity of codes was replicated elsewhere. In England, Northern Union clubs were forming soccer sections and affiliating to the West Yorkshire FA at the end of the nineteenth century. In 1903, a leading Northern Union club, Manningham, dramatically took up soccer and joined the Football League as Bradford City AFC.[30] Up to a certain chronological point, which varied depending on country or region, sporting codes remained flexible enough for clubs to seamlessly switch allegiance without much in the way of social or cultural constraint – the GAA, at least prior to the turn of the twentieth century and perhaps slightly later, was no exception to this trend.

Even where no such ambivalence as to a club's code affiliation existed, significant overlaps in personnel between codes were possible. In Limerick it has already been noted that two of the most important founding members of Garryowen FC in 1884, Tom Prendergast and Mike Joyce, also founded and played for the St Michael's Temperance Society Gaelic Football Club. The club fielded five rugby players in their 1887 county final team and were subsequently forced to replay the fixture rather than incurring expulsion. Both Joyce and Prendergast continued their involvement in rugby long after their entry into Gaelic games.

The broad sporting experience of Joyce and Prendergast was frequently replicated in Limerick. Con Fitzgerald, one of the city's most highly regarded Gaelic footballers and captain of the Limerick Commercials team that won the All-Ireland title in 1896, played rugby in the Transfield Cup for Lansdowne in 1899 and was congratulated in the press after a fixture against Richmond 'on his more than successful debut at the "handling code"'.[31] In 1905, Lansdowne RFC publicly congratulated 'one of their most prominent members', Michael Hartigan, on his appointment as captain of Shannon Rowing Club while also noting that he was currently captain of Young Ireland Hurling Club.[32] In 1907, the *Limerick Leader* published an obituary for one James Howard, who had died in the USA having emigrated from Limerick twelve months previously. Particular mention was made of his sporting career and it was noted that 'at the initiation of the Gaelic League Football Club, he was a staunch member and took part in many a hard fought match', while also being 'an old and valued member of the Young Munster Football Club'.[33] Significantly, the press reports from which the above examples are taken seemed oblivious to any inappropriateness in these individuals' involvement in both Gaelic games and rugby. It seems clear that the mental division of sport into 'native' and 'foreign' categories was a mode of thought that was not universally shared in Limerick.

Within the context of rugby's broad social appeal in Limerick, obvious challenges faced those GAA supporters subscribing to the 'ban' mentality. The strong local and civic function of rugby allied to its popularity as a mode of masculine expression gave it a distinct advantage over the GAA and appeals to the patriotic imperative of playing Gaelic games failed to make any significant inroads into the popularity of the handling code. Allied to this was the vicissitudes of GAA organisation in the city at the turn of the twentieth century. One correspondent clearly attributed this problem to the popularity of foreign sports in language as romantic as it was acerbic:

> A few short years ago Limerick boasted of thirty odd teams, today six fairly good hurling and football clubs cannot answer a referee's whistle . . . The cause is not far to seek. Unsystematic working, an unseemly leaning towards a few favoured teams . . . and fluctuating, fitful decisions . . . Games that have come down to us through bloody centuries over the graves of our kindred dead, over age, over the Druid cromlech . . . and past the Carnaha of the Fianna over the accursed dust of the mongrel sassanach and Vikings must be preserved, otherwise the anglo-maniacs and anglicised dandies . . . will form such feminine clubs as lawn tennis and cricket and a choice set of 'Chawlies' may have the moral stamina to inaugurate Association football teams here and there. Already I have noticed a small but sure excursive from our games by a few of the milk and water class whose fealty to the land of tears is of a misty character.[34]

Though something of a revival in Gaelic games did occur at this time, the cultural resonance of rugby was already strong enough to maintain its popularity, notwithstanding the game's hiatus during the First World War. During and after the independence struggle – a period when the 'ban' had already evolved from an administrative tool to being central to the GAA's nationalistic programme – it was clear that advocates of Gaelic football in Limerick were fighting something of a rearguard action. In 1919, Limerick's Sinn Fein TD, Michael Collivet, wrote to the *Limerick Leader* appealing to the young men of the city to take up hurling and Gaelic football and not to aid the post-war revival of rugby. With the broad appeal of rugby in mind perhaps, Collivet avoided scathing admonitions of the city's rugby devotees and conceded that the 'game was very much suited to the Irish temperament' and that there was nothing de-nationalising about the game itself.[35] Moreover, he was moved to comment that 'Limerick rugby players have taken a part in the history of the last five years which is a source to them of pride, not shame.'[36] Clearly, temperate language was designed to avoid insulting his rugby-supporting voters, of whom there must have been a significant number. Admitting that the then poor state of Gaelic football was partly attributable to the popularity of rugby and that the latter was the only game he had ever played himself, Collivet argued that rugby should not be revived in the city on the grounds that it stymied the growth of Gaelic games and that it facilitated fraternisation with the forces of occupation. Repudiating the argument that 'sport is sport', Collivet was clearly attempting to attach political connotations to sporting preference by concluding that the choice between rugby and Gaelic games was comparable to the choice between the enemy's flag and 'our own flag'.

Collivet's pleas seemingly did little to increase the popularity of Gaelic football and by 1925, the annual convention of the Limerick County Board of the GAA had the promotion of the 'native' code as a key item on the agenda. W.P. Clifford, in his chairman's address, urged that 'all true Gaels should do their utmost to rejuvenate the game of Gaelic football', as it was 'better than those football games which had apparently insidiously crept into the country . . .'[37] Clifford made a similar appeal at the following year's AGM, in the aftermath of which a correspondent to the press complained of how strange it was that in the city of Limerick there was 'so much apathy among our young men in the matter of playing the old national game [of] Gaelic football'.[38]

Despite these various pleas, Gaelic football was unable to supplant rugby as the city's football code of choice. Indeed opposition to the 'ban' was evident from within the city's GAA circles. In December 1923, a correspondent under the pseudonym 'Hurler' wrote a letter to the *Limerick Leader* advocating the adoption of rugby by the GAA, arguing that 'since the game is played in Ireland at all, let the country take it up all round in whole earnest and then we will be in a position to cut a figure in international rugby competitions that will bring us additional credit as a nation . . .'[39] At the 1924 AGM of the Commercials Gaelic Football Club, a resolution was passed calling on the GAA to remove the ban on foreign games as the club believed that 'it would be to the advantage of Gaelic football in the city if same were withdrawn'.[40] Five years later, Claughaun Hurling Club made a similar move at the county board's annual convention. Claiming that retention of the 'ban' was injurious to the promotion of Gaelic games, the club's representative called on the county board to 'prove their love for freedom and their tolerance by giving freedom where games were concerned'. In a clear reference to rugby, he spoke of how in Limerick city 'it was not hurling or football that their young men were playing at present' and that this apparent defiance of the 'ban' was attributable to the fact that these young men 'were Irish and a characteristic of the Irish was that . . . they would not be compelled'.[41] Rouse's argument that in the post-revolutionary period ideology had firmly superseded pragmatic considerations as the GAA's motive for retention of the 'ban' is firmly supported by the Limerick County Board's reaction to the motions submitted by Commercials and Claughaun. Commercials' proposal was defeated by seventeen votes to seven at a special ordinary meeting of the county board, with Clifford commenting that 'it was time Limerick . . . took a stand against the forces that were out to Anglicise Ireland'.[42] The Claughaun motion was defeated by fifty-one votes to twenty-two with one retentionist delegate claiming that 'there were two outlooks in Irish life . . . the Gaelic outlook and the outlook of the invader', concluding the playing of foreign games by Irishmen 'was mainly due to environment and wrong outlook'.[43]

Meanwhile in Cork, conflict between rugby and Gaelic circles took place on both the pragmatic platform of competition for players and, augmented by political context, the ideological platform of antipathy towards 'foreign' games. The extent to which the dominant bourgeois character of Cork rugby and a resultant social divide with the Gaelic constituency defused potential conflict is difficult to determine. What can be assessed, however, is the degree to which politico-cultural discord in the sporting scene affected secondary and tertiary educational institutions that did not fall within the jurisdiction of the ban on foreign games.

In late nineteenth-century west Cork, where smaller populations in towns meant keener rivalry between codes for players, negative campaigning against the 'foreign' sport was intense. This was no doubt exacerbated by the traditional strength of rugby in the region. In 1892, for instance, there was evidence of rugby teams in Clonakilty, Bantry, Timoleague, Skibbereen and Kinsale. Additional teams were provided by military garrisons and the crews of naval vessels.[44] It was the re-establishment of a rugby club in Clonakilty in the winter of 1892, however, that inspired public reactions of various levels of opprobrium from GAA devotees.[45] Commenting on rumours that efforts were being made to revive rugby in the town, one Gaelic games writer asserted dubiously that rugby had previously been 'sent into oblivion by the introduction of the Gaelic game, in which, strange to say, there seems to be something too "National" for certain Irishmen'.[46] Less strident views were taken by another commentator who posed the question 'Why has this Rugby club suddenly sprung into existence in Clonakilty? Echo answers why? We don't desire to get into a "tangle" on the matter but we would say to all local Gaels "stick to your colours, don't be deluded by the new game now introduced; let it pass . . ."'[47] Noteworthy in all this commentary is the extent to which rugby was seen as a genuine threat to the vitality of Gaelic games in the west

Cork region. It seems arguable, therefore, that there was at least some blurring of the lines between the perceived cultural and social constituencies of 'native' and 'foreign' pastimes, a hypothesis further evidenced by the following comment:

> But though rugby is not an innovation now, yet it has its attractions, and many a Gael will have allurements held out to him to make him 'change his colours.' We think the Clonakilty Gaels may be relied on, and also of the other Gaels of the West to be 'up and doing' whenever called on.[48]

In Bandon, where the existence of Bandon FC and (the Sunday-playing) Bandon Shamrocks rugby clubs in the 1880s had indicated the one-time broad popularity of the code in the town, the adoption of Gaelic football by the local Shannon Street National School was seen as 'a most praiseworthy effort' on the part of the teachers to 'infuse a healthy Gaelic spirit amongst their pupils. No rugby for these boys . . .'[49] Competition between codes persisted in Bandon, however, and in the aftermath of a Gaelic fixture between clubs from Dunmanway and Bandon in 1896, the captain of the Dunmanway side, despite being victorious, objected to the constitution of the beaten team on the grounds that some of their players had played rugby three weeks earlier.[50]

Significantly, this episode occurred just weeks before the Cork County Board expressed concern regarding 'the action of certain members of the board stated to be playing rugby'.[51] One of the members most certainly being referred to was Tom Irwin, a member of the Redmonds club, who was expelled from the GAA shortly afterwards for playing rugby. This move in Cork seems likely to have contributed to the somewhat clandestine decision by Central Council in April to suddenly remove the ban on foreign games. Dick Blake, the Association's secretary, had written to the Cork board expressing the central authority's disapproval at the action taken against Irwin, while at a Central Council meeting in August, the president, F.B. Dineen, defended the ban's removal, suggesting that Cork officials 'should draw a line across expulsion and start afresh'.[52] Cork had not been represented at the April meeting and later objected, through their Central Council delegate Michael Deering, to the removal of the rule that stated that 'persons playing Rugby football could not be permitted to be members of the Gaelic Athletic Association'.[53] Interestingly, the desire in Cork to maintain exclusionary policies was framed in terms of potential competition from rugby: 'the Rugby game was a game that had not in the county of Cork served the Gaelic Association. They had had a big struggle to stem its progress a few years ago and the result was eminently satisfactory.'[54] Explicitly attributing the popularity of Gaelic games in Cork to the 'prohibition of men playing rugby and Gaelic alternately', Deering read letters of support at a Central Council meeting from J.K. Bracken and Michael Davitt. And though a certain level of cultural disdain was evident in this correspondence, the Cork County Board were predominantly motivated at this point by fear that the removal of the 'ban' would potentially dilute the popularity of Gaelic games in the county.

In Tipperary, where rugby always enjoyed a level of popularity in the county's larger towns, the 'ban' could also be a frequent cause of controversy. Overlaps in playing staffs between rugby and GAA clubs were inevitable. In 1913, Templemore GAA club objected to the awarding of a match to Nenagh on the grounds that the latter had fielded both a player from, and the secretary of, the local Ormonds Rugby Club.[55] In 1925, Portroe were awarded victory over Nenagh in a junior hurling match when the latter were found to have fielded one Charles Fitzgerald who not only played rugby but was also an 'encourager' of the game.[56]

Cork colleges and the 'ban'

A more flagrantly politically infused desire to keep rugby and Gaelic games in separate cultural camps emerged in the city's education system from the first decade of the twentieth century. The non-extension of the 'ban' to schools and colleges potentially allowed a situation whereby institutions could field teams in both Gaelic games and sports that were British in origin. Rugby had a chronological head start on Gaelic games in the city's schools. By the time the first formal Gaelic competitions were established for schools and colleges in Cork in 1902,[57] rugby had already become the game of choice in three of the city's most important Catholic educational establishments: PBC, CBC and North Monastery (both of the latter being run by the Christian Brothers). Debates surrounding the sporting affiliations of these three schools and those of UCC provide a fascinating micro-history of the relationship between the 'ban' and political context and the gap between the politico-cultural discourses that justified the instrument's implementation and the actual fluidity of sport and political preferences in Ireland.

As already indicated, Gaelic games were established on a formal basis in Cork schools in 1902 and at a conference held in Mallow in 1907, a committee was set up to organise hurling and football in schools at provincial level.[58] Given the prospect of competition from 'foreign sports', these events inevitably led to the spurious infusion of identity politics into school sports in debates that were notable for the levels of untruth and crass characterisation that accompanied them. In a letter to the *Southern Star* in June 1906, for instance, one correspondent commented on the sporting preferences of the North Monastery in language that typically placed the GAA at the centre of the national project: 'None but Irish games are played by the students attending the Christian Brothers Schools. The Brothers will have nothing to do with rugby and cricket, although very great influence was brought to bear on them to make up a rugby team. There will be time enough for that when we are a nation, was the answer of the Brothers.'[59] The statement was startling for its factual inaccuracy. When the letter was published, North Mon (something of a nursery for republican revolutionaries) were Cork Schools rugby champions and would continue to field a rugby team for more than a decade. Later that summer another correspondent wrote along similar lines, scarcely countenancing the idea that the Christian Brothers would support foreign games. Commenting on the fact that the GAA was organising a tournament for the North Mon, he inferred that 'it is clear that rugby or any other English game is not tolerated by the Brothers.' The point was embellished by the denigration of the rugby-playing Presentation Brothers College, which apparently was 'entirely for pupils of anti-Irish feeling'. It was further claimed that 'a large number of soldiers' children are pupils of this school and if these play rugby, practise cricket and attend in processional order all the garrison fetes held in Cork, the Brothers cannot help this.'[60] All these claims were made despite the fact that both North Mon and Christian Brothers College were rugby-playing schools – a point that the correspondent can scarcely have been unaware of.

A similar line of controversy arose in the pages of the *Cork Sportsman* in 1908, when the paper's GAA reporter, under the impression that North Mon had switched allegiance from rugby to Gaelic games, commented that 'we on our part are satisfied to forget the past and think only of the present and the future', adding that the school's hitherto preference for rugby was 'strange' given that 'nine-tenths of the Monastery boys have been brought up in Gaelic atmospheres.'[61] Three weeks later, the same reporter happily recorded that 'what I wrote a little time ago about the Gaelic inclinations of North Monastery has now . . . been verified . . . To Rev. Brother Walker our very best thanks are due, and we assure him, as well as Brother Leahy and many others who have sacrificed old associations for ours, that nothing shall be left undone to furnish an attractive programme for the new and welcome adherents.'[62] The foundation for these claims becomes mysterious in light of a stinging rebuke co-penned by C.J. Shaw, the School Captain and J.J. Kelly, the honorary secretary of North Mon RFC, which was published in the *Cork Sportsman* the following week. The letter was a response to references made 'to the North Monastery Football Club that were both inaccurate and misleading'. Clearly, not willing to yield to cultural duress, the correspondents announced that:

> On behalf of the boys [of North Mon] we wish to state that there is not foundation whatever for the assumptions of your correspondent. Rev. Bro. Walker also desires it to be known that he has given no authority to anyone to use his name in the matter. He never interfered, and will not interfere with the boys in their choice of games.[63]

The controversy surrounding North Mon's continued participation in rugby reached something of a bizarre apogee in 1911 when J.J. Walsh, a prominent Cork GAA official and IRB member, made personal representations to the school's authorities. Having failed to secure a seconder at a county board meeting for a motion pressurising North Mon to switch allegiance to Gaelic games in June, Walsh was said to have been rebuked by Brother Walker when he visited the school. Walsh's own account differed dramatically and had him at the head of a hurley-carrying procession that protested at the gates of the school and successfully convinced the North Mon superiors to abandon rugby.[64]

The positing of North Mon as an institution of Gaelic inclinations as opposed to the 'anti-national' bias of Presentation Brothers College and Christians was part of a broader contemporary phenomenon that saw elements of nationalist opinion in Ireland create a discursive division between different classes of institution within the Catholic education system. At the forefront of this development were intellectuals such as D.P. Moran, who famously described elite Catholic schools as being 'bereft of nationality' owing to, among other factors, choice of sport.[65] In reality, this division was social rather than political. Though Pres and Christians were not as prohibitively expensive as other Irish Catholic schools such as Clongowes, they were certainly perceived as being higher-class institutions than North Mon, an institution whose apparent profile would have been more akin to the typical Christian Brothers school.

Aspersions cast about the cultural inclinations of these schools were spurious. There was nothing fundamentally 'anti-national' about Pres and Christians. In addition to the fact that there was no evidence of a coherent pro-British outlook in these schools, they readily and enthusiastically embraced Gaelic games when given the opportunity. When the idea of promoting hurling and football in Cork schools was first mooted in 1902, Pres was mentioned among a group of institutions that already embraced hurling. They first entered Gaelic games competitions in 1910. In 1918, and having played the game for almost three decades, Pres discontinued fielding a rugby team in favour of Gaelic games. This was possibly on the initiative of a former pupil, then teacher and IRA man Pádraig Ó Caoimh (O'Keefe), who counted fellow IRA volunteer and future literary figure Seán O'Faoláin as a member of the college's first hurling team.[66] Pres re-entered the rugby arena in 1927 and won the Munster Senior Schools Cup at the first attempt with a team of which seven members had won Senior College hurling honours in the previous year. Another Pres alumnus was noted Kerry Gaelic footballer Dick Fitzgerald, who would later write a famous manual about his chosen code.[67] Though O'Faoláin and O'Keefe clearly expressed cultural nationalism through setting up a hurling team (and jettisoning rugby), sporting preference was not politically prescriptive within the school. Frank Gallagher, later an Anti-Treaty republican and the first editor of the *Irish Press*, fondly recalled rugby matches at Pres and how his lack of playing ability reduced his role to that of boisterous supporter: 'those Cup matches were indescribably fearsome affairs for those who watched. A rush by Christians or North Mon towards our lines was white with agony.'[68]

Christians first fielded a hurling team in 1917 after a deputation of students had campaigned for the inclusion of the game in the school's games programme. The college president acceded on the grounds that the hurling devotees did not have the supplanting of rugby as their aim. A contemporary pupil enthusiastically commented that:

> The two games are now played, and several students figure prominently in both. It remains to be seen how far they can be carried on successfully together, but the beginning augurs well. It is not within the range of possibility that hurling and the football [rugby] that so eminently suits the Irish character, rechristened if you will, may become the national games, and that bye-and-bye [sic] we shall all be playing hurly and burly.[69]

Christians were instantly successful on the hurling field. In their maiden season, they had the notable achievement of reaching the inaugural Harty Cup (Munster secondary schools) final only to be beaten by (the rugby-playing) Rockwell College. On their way to the final they had taken the considerable scalps of experienced Cork hurling schools Rochestown and Farrenferris. John Murphy O'Connor, who would later get a final trial for the Irish rugby team, was among five boys who played for both the hurling and rugby teams that year. Political context is likely to have contributed to the college's embrace of hurling as there was clearly some element of nationalistic sentiment at Christians. College magazine editorials and debates, probably somewhat reflective of overall sentiment within the school, were dominated by contemporary political events and ideas with subjects such as 'Irish Ireland', 'Conscription' and 'Republicanism versus Monarchy' being aired in 1916. By 1919, the tone of these debates reflected political change and hardening sentiment with 'Exploitation by England' and 'Abstention from Parliament' now dominating discussion.[70] Though the link between Christians and the revolutionary period was apparently not extensive, Billy Collins recalled two of his classmates at Christians being in trouble with the RIC for Sinn Féin membership.[71]

The level of vitriol that contemporary school sport could rouse was illustrated in 1918 when ties in the hurling and rugby schools cups were fixed for the same April afternoon in the Mardyke. In a subsequent article in the *Southern Star*, the Cork journalist, GAA official and revolutionary Tadhg Barry noted that:

> The referee of the rugby game was one of the stay-at-home imperialists whilst the teams were drawn from the 'imperialist' schools of the Christian Brothers and the Presentation Colleges who with the help of the anti-Irish sporting section would have our youth forget their nationhood. These youths are more inclined to hurling and are drawn from a class whose knowledge of English games is nil . . . boys are enticed to play alien games by teachers who do not know the harm they are engendering in the minds of Irish youth.[72]

Barry went on to claim that most of the spectators present abandoned the rugby game when the hurling teams of Farrenferris and North Mon entered the parallel field, while complimenting a Brother from the latter institution for 'shepherding his boys on Saturday to shield them from any contamination'.[73] That both of the schools involved in the rugby fixture fielded strong teams in the hurling competition was clearly not enough to abrogate the stench of imperialism. Incidentally, the fact that Barry was moved to pose the question of the rugby fixture: 'was it this that men were dying in gaol for?' lends further evidence to Rouse's hypothesis regarding the effect of political context on mentalities surrounding the 'ban'.

It seems more than merely coincidental then that it was not until 1919, the year after hitherto rugby-dominated schools embraced hurling, that the sporting inclinations of the city's educational institutions became an outright source of debate in official GAA circles. In the winter of that year the Cork Colleges Board decided to extend the Association's ban on foreign games to boys who played rugby in the city's schools. The GAA had theretofore not applied the ban to secondary schools and when the Cork Colleges Committee communicated its decision to the Central Council, the Association's secretary, Luke O'Toole, replied informing the committee that a motion calling for the extension of the 'ban' to schools and colleges had been withdrawn at the last All-Ireland Congress. As it stood, therefore, the Cork Colleges Committee was willing to close a pragmatic loophole that the national body had decided to maintain. O'Toole's communiqué led to some debate among committee members. Rev. Fr. Tobin, for instance, no longer saw any pragmatic basis for allowing schools to play foreign games:

> . . . when the Gaelic games were in a weak position in the schools the GAA, in order to foster them, departed from the general rules. But he didn't think that the reason for that departure existed any longer, and the Committee would be acting quite reasonably, in face of the strength of Gaelic games in the schools, in saying that they no longer wanted any departure from the rules of the GAA.[74]

Yet there were clearly grounds for accommodating schools with diverse sporting interests in Cork. Establishments which played both Gaelic games and rugby, for instance, would now be potentially excluded from the former. The Youghal representative, Liam Owen, in arguing that the Cork committee should fall into line with the GAA's position, pointed out that the new rule 'would kill one hurling club – the Christian College [Christians] – members of which also played rugby', adding that the regulation 'was not going to get Rugby out of the schools, and it would kill one Gaelic club'.[75] Notwithstanding the potential alienation of certain institutions, the Cork committee decided by ten votes to four in favour of implementing the new rule. Christians were not represented as Rev. Bro. Egan had withdrawn from the committee in protest against the measure at a previous meeting. North Monastery effectively abstained by splitting their two votes – one in favour of the rule and one against – while Pres signalled their intention of abandoning rugby when O'Keefe voted in favour. The seven votes shared by St Coleman's, Rochestown and UCC tilted the balance decisively in favour of the 'ban'. The weighting of voting powers in favour of schools campaigning for the 'ban' made the result something of a foregone conclusion.

A certain elasticity of logic was clearly in evidence when two committee members who had supported the 'ban' admitted to playing golf and tennis – a fact that led to lively debate in the letters page of the

Cork Examiner. The enthusiastic golfer Rev. Dr Edwin of UCC had the ambiguity of his position cleared up by a correspondent who pointed out the Celtic origins of the game while also (naturally) ascribing it to peasant origins: 'a sport which originated with the shepherds in the Highlands of Scotland cannot be English by tradition.'[76] This claim was countered by an opponent of the Colleges Committee decision who pointed out that 'Golf, it is well known, is a far more denationalising and Anglicising game in this country than perhaps any other – certainly far more so than Rugby. The mainstays of every golf club in this country with one or two exceptions are Unionists.'[77] In the eyes of those who opposed rugby in schools, the Anglicising influence of tennis was somewhat mitigated, apparently, by its inability to directly compete with Gaelic games.

Within three days, the schools that had voted against the 'ban' (Youghal and Fermoy), the *de facto* abstainers (North Mon), along with Christians, Midleton and Sullivan's Quay CBS formed a breakaway group, the Cork Secondary Schools Committee. The inaugural meeting decided upon matters such as competitions and affiliation and did not make reference to the 'foreign' games ruling. Significantly, however, schools affiliated to the new body would only have one vote each when it came to deciding upon motions.[78] Reflecting on these events that year, the Christians annual magazine, *The Collegian*, outlined the rationale behind breaking from the Cork Colleges Committee:

> The main cause of our opposition was due to the reservation we made when invited to enter for the hurling competitions two years ago. We had been playing rugby football for twenty-five years then, and it become the traditionary [sic] College game. It was definitely understood that there would be no interference with our traditions on the games question. The Central Council of the GAA, to which the Cork Colleges Committee owes allegiance respects those traditions and rejected the motion excluding rugby players at its meeting last Easter . . . the conditions are made such that we cannot continue without abandoning our traditions, a course that does not commend itself to wisdom.[79]

As pointed out in Chapter 3, the function of rugby in more exclusive fee-paying schools extended well beyond any physical or mental utilitarian function. For middle-class-orientated institutions like Christians, rugby was a potentially important networking avenue for former pupils as they embarked on professional and business careers after school. In addition, it was central to the school's prestige and identity. Apart from class concerns,[80] rugby enjoyed a considerable chronological advantage over Gaelic sports when schools came to embrace games in the latter decades of the nineteenth century and therefore became culturally ingrained as the traditional sport of certain institutions, as was clearly the case with Christians.

Despite the school's apparent preference for rugby, there was considerable regret in CBC that the schism with the Colleges Committee occurred. During the debates, an uncorroborated suggestion that a majority of CBC boys preferred hurling and were playing rugby under duress was strenuously denied by college staff. Denis Lyons, a representative of the fervently anti-rugby University College GAA club (see below), claimed, on the authority of Denis Cashman, a former hurling captain at Christians, that a vote was taken on choice of games at Christians in 1917 in which hurling polled a majority. Cashman, according to Lyons, further claimed that the Brothers did not accept the result and threatened to withdraw the college from GAA competitions if boys did not play rugby.[81] This version was emphatically denied by staff members including Liam Owen, a GAA official at county level and certainly no advocate of rugby.

Something of the fraught atmosphere that defined sporting debates in Cork schools in 1919 was encapsulated in a poem written that year by a former pupil at Christians. Entitled 'The Munster has his Talk-out', the poem both celebrated the sporting success of the college and ruefully commented upon the contemporary strife among Cork schools:

> But what's this cry of the Gall or Gael
> Dividing the children of Granuaile?
>
> Oh, I love the click of the quick caman
> For it's that gives swiftness where I give brawn.
> I strengthen the bones of my pack;
> I stretch the limbs and I square the back;
> And while hurley makes them fleet of foot
> Pluck is my chiefest attribute.
>
> And the proof that we can work hand-in-hand
> Is that glorious year when the Christian band
> And their rivals old, in their 'maiden year'
> Swept the hurling field of opponents clear,
> And for Munster honours won each half,
> Save that Rockwell's proved the latter half.
>
> But now it seems some would stir up strife
> And put Christian scholars at knife to knife,
> And annul that grand old sporting rule;
> Play all the games that are played at school.
> But I know that the Christian staff are wise
> And will think of their boys before the prize.[82]

Poetically repeating the frequently made argument that rugby was quite suitable to the Irish temperament, the verse continued: 'How the Fenian hosts would have loved a scrum! . . . Its a game just after the Irish heart/For it weds great strength with the subtlest art.'[83]

Again, contemporary political context certainly played its part in this controversy. The fact that the new rule prohibited rugby-playing schoolboys rather than rugby-playing schools *per se* from competing in Gaelic games possibly indicates that the Cork Colleges Committee were opportunistically attempting to kill rugby in Pres and Christians. A divide and conquer strategy whereby choice of sport would be left to the boys themselves was potentially based on the gamble that the majority, bearing in mind the contemporary political atmosphere, would opt for hurling and render themselves ineligible for rugby.

A more explicit reflection of political context permeated cultural division along sporting lines in UCC. Such tension was hinted at in 1913 when the first editorial of the new college magazine, the *Quarryman*, stated that:

> We have noticed with regrets that the first impression of the maga-
> zine idea was not a favourable one with what is wrongly termed
> the 'Gaelic element.' Now, at the outset, it is well that the
> Quarryman gives an opinion on this point. We all look upon our-
> selves as Irishmen. Every student in the College realises that he is
> justly claimed by the country as a member of the Irish race.
> Whether he proclaims himself an Irishman or not, does not cost the
> Quarryman a thought. Consequently, the question of representa-
> tion of this element must always be a settled matter. The games
> wherein alone the question may arise shall always be catered for
> as items of the utmost importance, not to one section only but to
> the whole body of students. Hurling, Rugby, Gaelic Football,
> Hockey and Camogie, are departments in College Athletics, and as
> such shall each receive in the *Quarryman* a proper amount of atten-
> tion by students who practice them.[84]

Friction emanating from the 'Gaelic element' was not surprising given that UCC was something of a hotbed of competing political and cultural outlooks. The college had its own branch of the Irish Volunteers and there had been a strong element of support for the 1916 rebels within the college student body. This was exemplified by the replacement of the Union Jack with the Tricolour by a medical student, Flor O'Leary, as a response to the execution of the Rising's leaders. The ire of GAA devotees was probably raised more directly, however, by the fact that two high-profile professors and office holders in the rugby club, Charles Yelverton Pearson[85] and Connell Alexander, were openly pro-British.[86] Pearson, who had famously acceded to requests from the rugby club to change his anatomy lecture schedule to accommodate students taking part in rugby practices,[87] was subject to threats from the IRA in 1921.[88] Sir Bertram Windle, the college president from 1904 to 1919 and a supporter of the rugby club, was subject to criticism from nationalists within the college for his membership of the Irish Convention.[89] The flames of conflict between the rugby and Gaelic clubs in UCC were, in all likelihood, mostly fanned by the behaviour of Alexander. Professor of civil engineering from 1906 to 1920, Alexander devoted more energy than any other staff member to rugby affairs, serving as both a player and committee member with the UCC club and holding the presidency of the Munster Branch of the IRFU in 1908–9.[90] He was an outspoken admirer of college men who had served in the First World War,[91] and displayed his anti-republican tendencies by posting Bishop Kelly of Ross's condemnation of the Rising on a departmental notice board. When this was torn down, he threatened to refuse testimonials to the students responsible.[92] Directly linking the political outlook of these academic staff members to the GAA club's attitude to rugby is not possible, yet it seems inconceivable (given the profile of these individuals) that it did not have an influence on the politicisation of sport in the college.

That enmity existed between the rival clubs was evidenced again in 1917 when, with Alexander as president, the rugby club suggested that a paling should be built at the Mardyke and the pavilion partitioned, so that 'the two great factors, Rugby and Gaelic, would be permanently divided from each other'.[93] The singling out of rugby for particular disparagement in college GAA circles was further hinted in November 1919 when 'a rugby enthusiast' wrote to the *Cork Examiner* posing the question: 'to what class of games does tennis belong?'

> Is it a thoroughly Irish game or does it come under the heading of 'foreign games'? Some of the students of University College, who look upon Rugby as being everything that is bad and upon Rugby footballers as being 'outside the pale,' are doing their best to advance the game of tennis . . . I think tennis is as 'foreign' as rugby.[94]

When the Cork Colleges Committee proposed later that month 'to exclude from participating in the national pastimes those students of the schools and colleges who played foreign games', representatives of UCC GAA club, despite the large number of 'foreign' games catered for within the college precincts, voted unanimously in favour of the motion.[95] Thus a clear line of demarcation between the sporting and perceived cultural preferences of a section of the city's middle classes was instituted. The enmity was no doubt further fuelled by the rugby club's failure to cease holding practices during the 1920 hunger strikes in Cork.[96] When the rugby club received a request from its GAA counterparts not to hold rugby practices on the Mardyke for the duration of the strike, the rugby committee only discussed the submission after the IRA had called the protest off and therefore did not consider any action.[97] Mutual antipathy between the college's rugby and Gaelic clubs was summed up in the rugby club secretary's report for 1920–1: 'those enemies of the game in general and our club in particular seized on the political atmosphere of the day as an opportunity to become more aggressive. I am glad to be able to say their efforts were in vain; the game lives as every game should live on its own merits.'[98] It seems highly likely that 'anti-national' accusations emanating from the GAA club were particularly irksome for the rugby club at this point. Two months before he delivered the above-quoted report the club's secretary, G. Scanlon, had suffered the trauma of losing his brother in what the rugby club's official resolution described as a 'brutal murder . . . by armed forces of the British Crown'.[99] Michael Scanlon, a national school teacher and Commandant 1st Battalion East Limerick Brigade IRA, had been shot dead while attempting to escape military custody in Limerick. Indignity was added when the military halted his funeral motorcade in Limerick and removed the Republican flag from his coffin.[100] A week later the rugby club saw fit to officially express condolences to the brother of Christy Lucey, an IRA officer killed in Cork that week.[101] These were scarcely the words or actions of an institution that was hostile to nationalist sentiment.

Significantly, however, there seems to have been a thaw in relations by 1924. When a motion on the removal of the 'foreign games' rules was discussed at the county convention that year, the UCC club was strongly in favour, with the opinions of one college representative being summarised as follows:

> Adhesion to such a rule was an admission that Gaelic games was not up to the standards of other games and that their own rules were not in force and that they were not able to enforce them. On the main point of the Anglicising influence of foreign games, he expressed the view that that point did not any longer hold.[102]

The latter point no longer holding was no doubt partially attributable to a decisive shift in the political outlook of the college's upper echelons that had occurred in the intervening years. By 1924, the two most powerful academics in UCC, Alfred O'Rahilly and president P.J. Merriman, were nationalists. O'Rahilly has been described by John A. Murphy as being 'the best known Sinn Féin apologist in UCC' at the time, while Merriman's appointment as president was publicly wel-comed by the Cork County Board of the GAA who congratulated 'a fine type of Irishman'. Merriman (who had no apparent difficulty taking up the position of patron of the rugby club) duly ensured that one of the first group photographs taken after his appointment was 'with Gaelic friends'.[103] Moreover, this new atmosphere of Gaelic con-geniality was no doubt augmented by the departure of offensive elements such as Windle and Alexander (1919 and 1920 respectively). In addition, the process of Catholicisation that had begun during Windle's tenure probably added to a feeling of cultural ascendancy among 'Gaelic elements' in the college. In that context, it is worth pointing out that rugby players in UCC were most likely motivated by a desire to play the game that they enjoyed at school rather than any cultural imperatives. A UCC team from 1927, for instance, comprised no fewer than seven boys from either Pres or Christians, two each from Leinster schools Castleknock and Clongowes and one from Stonyhurst. As if to prove that cultural generalisations about individ-uals and institutions on the basis of sporting code were anomalous, the remaining three starting players on the team were from the apparently staunchly Gaelic Farrenferris, St Colemans and North Monastery.[104]

Cork was not the only county in the mid-1920s where dissenting voices were raised within the GAA regarding the 'ban'. At the annual convention of the Clare County Board in 1925, Rev. M. Hamilton did not see why 'Irish Gaels should be forbidden to go to Dublin to play Rugby, which was a splendid trial of strength, against France or any other country', while the chairman wondered why 'men of Clare' should 'be forbidden to compete against the All Blacks'. When a motion was put forward that the Clare representative would vote for the removal of the 'ban' at the national congress, it was passed by nineteen votes to nine.[105] The Tipperary convention had done likewise the year before when among those who voted in favour of the ban's removal was the captain of the Tipperary hurling team, Johnny Leahy. One speaker, reflecting on the fact that in Clonmel, 'some of their best Gaelic men, including their captain, were trained by rugbyites', added that he thought it 'developed their men and made good footballers of them'.[106]

On the basis of the evidence presented in this chapter so far, it seems reasonable to assert that playing or supporting rugby in Munster was far from clearly linked to any cultural or political predis-position. The separation of sport along cultural lines was more a discursive concept than a realistic reflection of the sporting and polit-ical leanings of any given individual. The ascription of meanings and identities to sports was gradual and never complete. The GAA's conflation of sport and political outlook, when applied to 'foreign' games and in this case rugby, was not grounded in reality. Antagonism appears to have only meaningfully emanated from one side of the apparent divide and rather than being a clash between 'Gael' and 'Shoneen' it can be read as a conflict between two modes of thought: those who saw as imperative the expression of nationality through sport and those who were swayed by personal conviction and social context. This becomes clearer when one looks at the actual political affiliations of rugby players and administrators in Munster.

Rugby football and political preferences

As already displayed in this chapter, the most cursory examination of the available evidence suggests that 'anti-national' representations of rugby were over-simplified and spurious. Before closely examining the political preferences of the game's followers and promoters in Munster, it is worth briefly pointing out cases where rugby was a direct channel through which nationalist sentiment and symbolism could be articulated. In this regard there were parallels with contemporary modes of political expression used by the GAA.[107] For instance, in March 1887, just one month after the GAA had institutionalised public antipathy towards the police by banning members of the RIC from the association,[108] the following report of a rugby match between Cork FC and Bandon appeared in the unionist *Cork Constitution*:

> At the termination of the game, a disgraceful scene ensued when Cork rowdies showed their unmanly disposition. There are one or two members of the Royal Irish Constabulary in the Bandon team, and right good men too, and this of course roused the ire of some of the fellows who had reason to dislike the police, and they indulged in petty general hissing towards the Bandon team. This of course, under certain circumstances, might place the Cork team in an awkward position but luckily the Bandon men know that their Cork opponents, no matter what their opinions, discountenanced anything of that kind.[109]

Clearly expressing popular antipathy towards the police through sport was not limited to the ranks of the GAA.

Sensitivity to Irish sympathy for the Boers, shown by the GAA through the naming of clubs,[110] was also displayed in a rugby context. Blackrock Road Rugby Club in Cork, for instance, was submitting team lists to the local press containing names such as 'Kruger' and 'Joubert' in 1900.[111] In the aftermath of a rugby match between Hayes' School and Storey's School in west Cork in the same year, the victorious Hayes' boys (most of whose names were decidedly Catholic) 'sang "Kruger Boys Hurra" with great gusto'.[112] Two decades later, and on the same day that the Limerick and Tipperary County GAA boards made a similar announcement, representatives of the Limerick city rugby clubs held a meeting and decided to postpone all junior and senior fixtures for the duration of the 1923 hunger strike by republican prisoners.[113] Notwithstanding the continued enforcement of tough pubic safety legislation by the Free State government and resultant difficulties in staging events comprising large gatherings of young men, this seems exceedingly likely to have been a gesture of sympathy with the hunger strikers by the rugby clubs. Pragmatic considerations were a possible explanation, yet not wholly convincing given that the Free State army more than held sway in Limerick at this point.[114] Moreover, there is no evidence of similar action being considered by Cork clubs despite the fact that the Cork hunger strikers proved the most intransigent.[115] The unilateral decision of the Limerick clubs was most likely, therefore, to have been similar in motivation to the action taken by the GAA county boards.

Politically motivated gestures were not the only means by which expressions of nationalism gainfully employed by the GAA were repeated in a rugby context. The nationalistic symbolism promoted by the GAA through the naming of clubs was, to a slight degree, evident in Munster rugby. Though Queenstown Nationals, Bandon Shamrocks and Shamrocks (Limerick) were merely a mild nod in that direction, Limerick junior clubs Faugh-a-Ballagh[116] and Emmets were a more explicit replication of the GAA experience. Indeed, GAA clubs called Faugh-a-Ballagh and Shamrocks appeared in the early twentieth century in Limerick. All these instances together are merely anecdotal and do not represent a self-consciously nationalist trend within Munster rugby. Significantly, however, it is clear that elements within the game saw rugby as a valid medium for expressing nationalistic sentiment.

By the time order was restored to Ireland in the mid-1920s, rugby football had been in formal existence in Munster for half a century. In that period the game had been played and administered by individuals from every shade of political opinion in the country. In Limerick, for instance, the downward social diffusion of rugby clearly broadened the spectrum of political beliefs accommodated within the game. The Trinity College old boys that brought the game to Limerick, aristocratic in background and educated within the imperial framework of the public school system, would most likely have been loyal to crown and empire. As pointed out in Chapter 3, a crucial bridge between classes was provided by the formation of Garryowen Football Club where the prominent Protestant businessman, W.L. Stokes, coalesced with members of the Catholic lower middle and artisan class on the club's committee. This bridge between classes also proved to be a political one. Stokes was respectfully described by the famous Limerick Fenian John Daly as 'a Unionist and he never tried to hide it',[117] while his fellow committeemen Joyce and Prendergast were nationalists and suspected Fenians. Indeed, Prendergast energetically arranged annual commemorations for the Manchester Martyrs in Limerick.[118] As earlier pointed out, both Joyce and Prendergast were elected Labour councillors in the Limerick Corporation in 1898, with Joyce eventually entering parliamentary politics as a Home Rule MP. Despite the Labour majority elected to the council in 1898, Stokes' unionist leanings did not prevent him from also securing a seat and later receiving a nomination for the position of high sheriff.[119]

This political evolution continued in the Sunday rugby tradition that Joyce, Prendergast and Stokes had been so instrumental in establishing. There is evidence that the early flagship tournament of Sunday rugby, the Transfield Cup, enjoyed, at least on one occasion, the public patronage of high-profile republicans. One exasperated correspondent to the *Limerick Leader* in 1930 reacted to 'references to "Shoneenism" on the part of rugbyites' and accusations that 'rugby has a denationalising effect on Irishmen' by recalling that in 1905, the Fenians John Daly and Tom Clarke presented medals to the Lansdowne rugby club to mark their victories in the Transfield and Junior Cup competitions.[120] The correspondent, one of the medal recipients, quoted Daly as saying:

> Some people refer to rugby as an English game, but I know it to be a game played by the people of all nations, and if you wear Irish jerseys and tights and an Irish-made ball, rugby will not do any harm to your national character. I hope when the day comes, you will be as good soldiers for Ireland as you are footballers.[121]

The broad cross-section of society attracted to rugby by the vibrancy of the junior game clearly brought diverse political affiliations with them and Daly, as one of the city's most prominent militant nationalists, probably recognised the risk of alienating elements of his support by not appearing to approve of rugby. Other overlaps occurred between rugby and republicanism in Limerick. The McInerney family, for example, were prominent in both republican and rugby circles.[122] Jim McInerney was a member of the 1st Limerick Battalion in the War of Independence and when he died in 1925, 'prominent in the procession were members of the old Lansdowne

Football Club, and Volunteers and Cumann na mBan'.[123] Dan Gallagher, later a founding member of Abbey RFC was also a prominent republican volunteer during the troubles.[124] In 1930, a correspondent to the *Limerick Leader* in expressing annoyance at the GAA's questioning of the nationality of rugby followers recalled of the revolutionary period that 'Rugbyites of all Limerick clubs, headed by the late Captain James McInerney, did their duty in the effort to secure a free Ireland.'[125] In 1950, a correspondent under the pseudonym 'Old IRA Man' wrote to the *Limerick Leader* criticising the ban on foreign games and recalling:

> I remember being at Lansdowne Road at an international rugby match either in 1919 or 1920. I had a price of £500 on my head then. Outside the grounds, armoured cars, armed military and police with their spotters were slowly patrolling up and down watching for their prey . . . I saw only a few yards away from me an old Gaelic footballer in the person of the late Austin Stack . . .[126]

More important than the veracity of the above testimony is the obvious annoyance felt by both (clearly republican) correspondents that they, by implication, were being labelled unpatriotic because of their favoured sport.

In Cork as well, rugby attracted followers from a broad range of political beliefs. W.J. Goulding, the Protestant businessman so closely involved in the early history of Munster rugby, was from a unionist family. His father, William, was elected Conservative MP for Cork city in a by-election in 1876, taking the seat of a Home Rule MP who had died.[127] Though his several other attempts to run for office were unsuccessful, he always commanded a respectable vote. Goulding junior also took an active interest in politics and in his capacity as a leading industrialist, he was a high-profile spokesman for southern unionist interests during the revolutionary period. He owed his allegiance to that section of unionist opinion that accepted the inevitability of constitutional change in Ireland after the post-1916 shift in the nature of popular nationalism. As a businessman with considerable interest in the country's future, he took a leading position in seeking the best possible deal for those of a similar background. This was exemplified by his participation in the Irish Convention of 1917–18. The Convention, an ill-fated attempt by the British government to reach a solution to the Irish question through dialogue between unionists and constitutional nationalists, was doomed to failure from the outset by Sinn Féin's decision to boycott the proceedings.[128] Besides Goulding, it had among its delegates three other high-profile rugby devotees from Cork: Sir Bertram Windle, Alfred McMullen and Thomas Butterfield.

Windle aside, the respective rugby careers of the other three delegates followed remarkably similar paths, despite representing different political outlooks. Goulding was a government nominee to the proceedings, while McMullen, another Protestant businessman, represented Cork Chamber of Commerce. Butterfield, a Catholic dentist and a nationalist, was the nominee of Cork Borough Council.[129] All three had been administrators with Cork FC and were all one-time Munster Branch presidents.

Goulding continued in his role as a spokesman for his co-religionists and in 1922 was part of a Church of Ireland delegation that met with Michael Collins to draw his attention to the mistreatment of Protestants by republican forces.[130] His fellow Irish Convention delegate, Butterfield, a member of the Irish Volunteers, had already been involved in a high-profile episode during the 1916 Rising in Cork. As lord mayor, Butterfield, along with the bishop of Cork, Daniel Cohalan, acted as an intermediary between the Volunteer leadership and the local British Army command. An agreement was reached whereby the Volunteers would hand in their weapons at Butterfield's home on condition that they would not be confiscated, thus preventing the needless bloodshed that would no doubt have accompanied a significant military operation to seize the weapons from Volunteer Hall by force.[131] Butterfield was re-elected lord mayor in 1917 and again in 1918 partially in recognition of his role in keeping the city at peace during the rebellion.[132]

Another nationalist lord mayor and MP with a direct involvement in Cork rugby was Augustine Roche, a noted businessman who simultaneously held a Westminster seat and the presidency of Cork Wanderers RFC. There was, therefore, no fundamental correlation between sporting allegiance and political ambition. Indeed, the one instance found in this research where reference to rugby involvement was intended to disparage political outlook was most notable for its farcical hypocrisy. In 1913, a correspondent to the *Southern Star* recalled that in 1909, an O'Brienite election candidate in the Mid-Cork constituency and known Fenian sympathiser, Dan Sheahan,[133] attempted to gain support from the 'Gaels of Macroom' by pointing out his opponent and fellow nationalist William Fallon's association with a rugby club in Dublin 'with the suggestion that his national record was thereby blemished'. Noting that 'human nature is frail and few of us can keep our behaviour in absolute conformity with our early ideals', the correspondent pointed out that the same Mr Sheahan had just been appointed as a vice-president of Cork County rugby club.[134] There is little evidence of militant separatism in Cork rugby, although leading republicans Tomás MacCurtain, Terence MacSwiney and P.S. O'Hegarty were all pupils at North Monastery in the period when that institution fielded a rugby team in local competitions.

The safest conclusion that can be drawn from the evidence gathered above is simply that supporting or playing rugby in Munster did not in any way presuppose rejection of Irish nationalism. The GAA's attempt to create mutually antagonistic sporting and political camps was a system of discursive invention and was far from a valid representation of the Munster rugby experience. The political outlook of rugby followers in Munster could not validly be prescribed and the local social evolution of the game is the most efficient barometer of measuring their likely political beliefs. Circumstantial evidence bolsters these suggestions. If we accept, for instance, that rugby in Munster attracted significant Catholic support – irrespective of social background – then one can safely assume that all shades of nationalist opinion were represented within the game's constituency. It seems likely, for instance, that the elite Catholic schools of Cork, so central to the vitality of rugby in the city, fell into line with similar institutions around the country and supported home rule.[135] John Horgan, who had his early schooling at Presentation Brothers College, was an eager supporter and personal friend of C.S. Parnell and an enthusiastic member of the Gaelic League.[136] In Limerick, as already pointed out, the game's broad social appeal was mirrored politically. Moreover, the clear intersection between rugby and municipal politics further illustrates the primacy of local concerns above macro-political characterisation. For the likes of Joyce, Prendergast and Stokes, involvement in rugby can only have boosted their public profile among the varying constituencies that they were attempting to court. That the mayoralty of Limerick and the presidency of Garryowen FC should have been held by the same individual on five occasions in the first decade of the twentieth century tells its own story.

The IRFU, Munster rugby and political symbolism

Apart from the external relationship between rugby football and politics in Munster, which has been dealt with above, internally, national politics has historically been an occasional source of rancour within Irish rugby. The IRFU has historically been in something of an invidious position regarding national symbolism and ceremony given that a significant section of the country's rugby-following constituency has been drawn from the Ulster Protestant community. The constitutional position of the island, therefore, impinged directly on the internal administration of Irish rugby where issues of political symbolism had to be tailored to accommodate diverse political and cultural backgrounds.

The 32-county administrative structure and cross-tradition appeal of rugby has also informed the approach of those disposed to write about the history of the game in Ireland. The officially approved histories, written in this case by Edmund Van Esbeck[137] and Seán Diffley,[138] take a benign view of any possible intersection between the sporting and political spheres, seeking to emphasise the apolitical nature of Irish rugby and stressing the ability of rugby to promote conciliation between the different traditions on the island. By contrast, the sparse academic work done on rugby and Irish politics has sought to emphasise how the island's political situation has indeed had an impact on the development of rugby in Ireland and has tended to focus on the implications of the game's cross-border administrative structure. John Sugden and Alan Bairner have rightly criticised the approach taken by Diffley and Van Esbeck.[139] The suggestion that the Irish rugby community has historically eschewed political labels and viewpoints in order to promote sporting co-operation and transcend cultural and political differences is seen as foolhardy and simplistic by Sugden and Bairner.[140] In arriving at this conclusion, however, they certainly overstress the significance of certain events in order to re-enforce their viewpoint. For instance, Sugden and Bairner imply that the existence of separate administrative bodies north and south until 1880 had some degree of political significance. There exists, however, no evidence to suggest that this 'split' was caused by sectional differences. Indeed, given that the contemporary powerbase of Dublin rugby was Trinity College and a number of surrogate clubs, it seems likely that those in positions of power in southern rugby may have had a great deal in common with their Belfast counterparts politically and socially. Moreover, northern unionists in the 1870s were extremely unlikely to have conceived of cultural identity in explicitly partitionist terms – 'Ulster' as a separate unit of political identity (notwithstanding a long-held feeling of seperateness) did not gain significant currency until the Third Home Rule Bill, an event still more than three decades in the future.[141] Hence the ascription of political significance to a disagreement between two groups of individuals from the north and the south needs to be carefully considered within the context of the political situation of the time and the background of the protagonists involved.

Sugden and Bairner are quite right, however, in arguing that rugby football could not exist in cultural isolation, independent of political events and outlooks in Ireland – an observation particularly valid in terms of the decades following independence. In 1925, the IRFU decided to replace the national flag at international matches with a flag carrying the emblems of the four provinces. This decision was designed to avoid potential controversy caused by the flying of the Union Jack at matches in Ravenhill and the Tricolour at Lansdowne Road and was seemingly endorsed by the component branches.[142] In the aftermath of a test match between Ireland and South Africa in Dublin in 1932, however, the University College Galway rugby club officially protested to the IRFU at their failure to fly the Tricolour at Lansdowne Road.[143] They called upon their sister colleges to 'lend their aid in ridding rugby of its anti-national bias'.[144] In Munster, the *Limerick Leader* rugby editorial tried to encourage the local clubs to back the colleges' campaign:

> We notice that our clubs are not exactly rushing over one another to condemn the insult to our national flag and to support the protest of the Galway University club, and on behalf of Limerick rugby supporters, we appeal to our clubs to protest against this unwarranted insult against each and every Irishman . . . in Belfast at internationals no opportunity is lost to flaunt jingoism at its worst in our faces, and surely the greater majority of clubs and supporters are not sheep to take what is an obvious insult without a protest.[145]

The Munster Branch, for its part, decided to support the IRFU's stance by agreeing not to act on an appeal by the UCC club to have the Tricolour flown at future internationals.[146] In Limerick, the clubs were beginning to react. Shannon RFC released the following statement, the terminology of which proves that the GAA was not the only sporting institution that could make appeals to national purity:

> That we the members of the above club, in registering our protest against what we can only conceive as a studied insult to every man of Irish birth, hereby call on the Irish Rugby Football Union to pledge itself against a repetition of the hurtful and un-Irish incident associated with the arrangements connected with the Irish–Springboks match at Lansdowne Road, when the governing body refused to hoist the Irish Tricolour. We as players of the game are proud of our nationality and our flag . . .[147]

Abbey RFC quickly echoed Shannon's condemnation of the IRFU, while elsewhere in the province Dolphin (Cork) and the County Tipperary clubs also registered disquiet at the Union's flag policy.[148] The *Irish Press*, which gave the issue extensive coverage and waged a campaign to have the Tricolour flown at Lansdowne Road, canvassed the opinion of ex-international rugby players in support of their position. Mick Ryan, the former Rockwell College, Munster and Ireland forward, was of the opinion that 'our status as a nation demands the recognition of our flag'.[149] When the same publication sought the position of the Limerick clubs in relation to the flag, a 'veteran rugbyite', apparently summing up the feelings of the Limerick rugby public, considered the IRFU's policy 'an insult to Irish nationalism', and added that 'the Union should have ascertained the views of the clubs in the Free State before they assumed dictatorial powers . . . [and] if the clubs were consulted there would be an overwhelming vote to fly the tricolour.'[150] As the issue was gaining more attention nationally, the press coverage intensified. On 30 January, it was reported that 'in rugby circles in Limerick that on the occasion of the international match between Ireland and England at Lansdowne Road . . . on 13th February visitors from this centre will wear the tricolour in their button holes as an act of national faith and as a protest against the insult offered by the Rugby Union to Irish nationalism.' A correspondent named 'Munsterite' wrote to the the the *Irish Press* assuring its sports editor that Munster clubs were 'doing their share' concerning the Tricolour but that 'our voice, we have long ago learned, does not reach the ears of the IRU'.[151] Eventually Limerick's high-profile senior clubs, Young Munster, Garryowen and Bohemians, backed the campaign to have the flag flown and when the IRFU decided to change its stance, the *Limerick Leader* credited the decision as 'a response to the appeals of our Limerick and other Munster clubs'.[152] The turnaround in the Union's attitude was, in fact, in deference to the wishes of the government. In a rare instance of politically motivated Irish governmental intervention in the sporting sphere, the Cumann na nGaedheal Minster for External Affairs, Paddy McGilligan, wrote to the IRFU in February asserting that he could not 'see why the international practice of flying the flag of the country in which international matches are played should not be followed at Lansdowne Rd'.[153] The IRFU immediately relented.

The flag issue is informative for a number of reasons. Firstly, it displays the sensitivity of a significant number of Irish rugby devotees to the game being perceived as being in any way anti-national. Secondly, the futility of the IRFU's attempts to keep rugby purely apolitical through symbolic compromise was underlined. In an era where public displays of Irishness were part of the broader state-building project, the symbolic value of the Tricolour being flown at Lansdowne Road cannot be underestimated. It is difficult to evaluate the role played by Munster in the controversy given that the press only drew attention to clubs that actually supported the flying of the flag, with indifference and opposition hence not quantifiable. Interestingly though, and as with the hunger strikes in 1923, the Limerick clubs acted unilaterally. Political issues in this case underscore the unique rugby identity of the city where national events and symbolism highlight the exceptionalism of the local.

Issues of national symbolism were a rare yet interesting subject of discussion at the Munster Branch committee table. In April 1933, for instance, it was proposed and agreed that the Munster Branch send a recommendation to 'the RU that the principal toast at Union dinners and functions should be Éire and not the king'.[154] When the IRFU instructed the Munster Branch to postpone a fixture between Cork Constitution and Sunday's Well as a mark of respect on the day of the funeral of King George V in 1936, the Cork Constitution delegate, P. McGrath, accused the Branch secretary of 'exceeding his duty and that he put off the match only to satisfy a certain section'.[155]

The uneasy accommodation of conflicting political outlooks that the IRFU historically strived to achieve was subjected to its sternest test in the lead-up to an international championship fixture between Ireland and Scotland in Belfast in 1953.[156] Irked at the prospect of having to stand to attention for the British national anthem (as was custom for Belfast internationals), three members of the Irish selection managed to convince the entire southern contingent of ten to refuse to take the field until after the pre-match formalities. Described by a teammate as 'rabid nationalists', Vic Rigby has plausibly suggested that the motivation of the three may have been underpinned by conspicuous contemporary concerns in the South about the imposition of the Flags and Emblems Act and revelations about sectarian bias in northern housing policy. Though not said to have been one of the ringleaders, the team captain Jim McCarthy from Cork acted as spokesman for the southern players. The situation was only resolved when the President of the Republic's High Court, Cahir Davitt, intervened and assured the players that they would never have to play international football at Ravenhill again. What could have led to an outright schism along political lines was narrowly averted.

Though already dealt with at length in a social context, one issue that exemplified the fact that Irish rugby was far from mono-cultural was the debate surrounding Sunday play. Though it had been common in Limerick since the mid-1880s, the IRFU discouraged Sunday play. Indeed in 1929, the governing body issued a letter to its respective branches banning the staging on Sundays of cup and league fixtures where gate money was taken.[157] This decision was scarcely surprising, given the likely sabbatarian sensitivities of the northern Protestants that administered the Ulster Branch and the fact that leisure time was flexibly arrangable for Leinster rugby's middle-class constituency. Tellingly, however, the attempted suppression of Sunday rugby caused considerable consternation in Munster and Connacht.

Unlike Ulster, where the staging of a Heineken Cup fixture at Ravenhill on a Sunday in 2004 led to a demonstration from the Free Presbyterian Church,[158] rugby had been played in Munster on Sundays since the late nineteenth century.[159] It was not until the staging of an interprovincial trial match on a Sunday in February 1929, however, that the Union's opposition to Sunday football became apparent. The *Limerick Leader*, stridently in favour of the retention of Sunday rugby, carried a series of editorials in 1929 on the issue that gave a colourful insight into the possible motivation for the IRFU's desire to implement a ban on the practice. It seems likely that both class and religious considerations fuelled the controversy. In terms of class, the *Leader* quoted an Irish correspondent in a cross-channel newspaper who drew attention 'to the fact that this Sunday rugby is resented inasmuch as it introduces into rugby an undesirable type of player and spectator'.[160] Similar sentiment can be gleaned in a letter from University College Dublin Rugby Club (who favoured retaining Sunday rugby) to the Union which stated that 'a rumour has now reached us that the union resolution is not a permanent ban but is a temporary expedient to deal with the problem of general discipline.'[161] That disciplinary problems should be identified as being particularly symptomatic of Sunday rugby certainly raises questions as to the Union's perception of those most likely to play and patronise rugby on the Sabbath. In Limerick, where junior rugby (mostly played on Sundays) was disproportionately violent, the Union perhaps saw the removal of Sunday rugby as a means of limiting playing and spectating opportunities for those likely to engage in disorderly behaviour on and off the field. This assertion is bolstered by the attitude of the Dublin press. As if to underline the cultural gap between the rugby establishment in Dublin and the game in Limerick, an *Irish Times* columnist referred to Sunday rugby as 'this growing evil' before asserting that 'Apart from the religious aspect of the problem, Sunday rugby is lowering the prestige, traditions and discipline of Rugby.'[162] Another column noted that 'It is considered that in recent years a rather undesirable class of player has made his appearance in the Rugby arena, due, it is averred, to Sunday football.'[163]

The *Leader*, as already noted, ran a spirited campaign through the medium of its rugby editorial to encourage the retention of Sunday rugby. Claiming that in Limerick 'we only have one ground in the city, and if matches are confined to week days our season will never end or begin,' it continued 'we in the South are inclined to attribute opposition to Sunday sports as a relic of an ancient age . . . we look on Sunday as a day of joy and if others look on it as a day of gloom, why should they not practice [sic] the tolerance the gloom is supposed to create in their souls.'[164] These implicit references to religion become clearer in later editorials where it is claimed that 'nothing will convince us but that the opposition to Sunday football is a relic of religious bias at its worst.'[165] And in a later article, 'one group believes rugby desecrates the Sabbath. Another group still believes that it only makes our Sundays a day of joy.'[166] The rugby editor 'R. Forrard' cleverly identified the latent hypocrisy in the Union's position regarding Sunday sport: 'It has been proved that the very people who object to Sunday rugby find nothing harmful in Sunday golf,'[167] having earlier made reference to a round of golf played by the Irish and English rugby union officials on the Sunday after an international match between the two countries.[168]

At official level, the Connacht Branch protested against the idea of banning Sunday rugby and were supported, albeit initially in a lukewarm manner, by their Munster counterparts. In September 1929, the Munster and Connacht Branches sent a deputation to an IRFU committee meeting seeking a reconsideration of their stance on the issue. The Munster Branch later received communication from the IRFU informing them that it was 'unanimously decided that the Union committee is unable to alter its previous rulings in regard to Sunday football'. The Munster Branch chose to ignore the ruling and resolved that 'It was unanimously agreed that all present were in favour of Sunday football.'[169] The Branch, contrary to the wishes of the IRFU, later officially decided that 'all Sunday play be carried out as heretofore and that this Branch committee give effect to the unanimous wish of the general meeting to carry out Sunday games and that the clubs be notified'.[170] Quite apart from the Munster Branch's distaste at having its autonomy infringed upon by the IRFU or the body's lack of cultural or principled objections to the idea of Sunday sport, pragmatic considerations were of particular import in this case. Given the apparent occupational patterns of certain clubs' players, Sunday was the only designated time of the week when participation in sport was a viable option. Ennis Rugby Club, for instance, insisted the banning of Sunday football 'would prevent our club from playing altogether, as the distances between clubs in Munster and Connacht are so great as to prevent the fielding of teams on half holidays in time to allow matches to be finished before dark. We strongly feel that if any such rule be passed, it would mean the finish of rugby football in most provincial towns.'[171]

In Tipperary the decision to ban Sunday rugby was met with particular hostility. Given that rugby in provincial towns most likely appealed to elements of the white-collar, and particularly the retail, sector, Sunday fixtures accommodated work schedules. Reacting to the ban, one *Nenagh Guardian* correspondent, doubting 'if it is respect for the Sabbath dictates this course of action', asserted that 'Saturday football is impossible in towns like Nenagh, Thurles, Templemore – in fact in all provincial towns where Saturday is not half-holiday. Our clubs should carefully watch any move in the direction of banning rugby on Sunday and oppose it strenuously.'[172] One possibly over-exuberant correspondent to the same publication put forward the proposal that in light of the attempted ban on Sunday rugby, a national games body could be set up to control Gaelic games and rugby with the result that the 'Dublin clubs would soon find themselves out in the cold'.[173] Forceful opposition to banning Sunday rugby also emanated from Cashel, where:

> It was pointed out that Sunday was the only day of the week when members in the country towns were free to indulge in matches and adding that such unwarranted interference in this matter of amateur sport would seriously prejudice the development of rugby, which had now gained such a large measure of public patronage, largely as a result of the holding of contests on Sundays. The suggestion that Sunday games were debased by disorderly and unruly incidents and that there was a tendency to introduce elements of unsportsmanship [sic] among players and spectators, was indignantly resented. The members pointed to the splendid spirit of healthy rivalry that had existed in County Tipperary since the formation of so many clubs during the past few years.[174]

Ultimately, the Sunday rugby controversy is a fascinating window through which one can decipher the cultural connotations of rugby football in Ireland. Objections to Sunday sport, seemingly rooted in religion and class in this case, clearly did not enjoy homogenous appeal in Munster or Connacht and by the mid-1930s, junior rugby fixtures, especially in Limerick, were mostly staged on Sundays again. Beyond the sheer practicality of Sunday football, cultural opposition to Sunday sport was evidently not widespread in Munster. Indeed, the *Limerick Leader*, on occasion, mercilessly poked fun at what the paper clearly saw as the absurdity of banning Sunday football. In one particular piece at the height of the controversy, a fictional secret agent is sent to the countryside to investigate 'Dan Inge', 'the dashing

Ballydash forward' who is suspected of playing rugby on Sundays. The agent attends a rugby match but only wins the trust of fellow spectators when he displays enough agricultural knowledge to convince them that he is a farm labourer. 'Dan Inge' is finally discovered by the agent when the former speaks while on the field of play. The agent, on hearing the voice 'knew by the very tone that Dan Inge was the speaker . . . because his courteous tone of voice immediately showed that he was a cut above the ordinary and that he had played football . . . on Saturday'.[175] This polemical and intriguing fictional article clearly indicates the extent to which issues such as class and the cultural patterns of the rural as opposed to the urban all fuelled the Sunday football debate. Clearly, what was unacceptable on religious grounds in Ulster and class grounds elsewhere was seen as no moral or cultural object in Munster or Connacht.

The IRFU's ambition to keep rugby apolitical was achieved inasmuch as rugby did not have an explicitly coherent political outlook. As the above examples display, however, a certain cultural and political fluidity permeated the game and only came to prominence when it clashed with the politics of compromise so eagerly engaged in by the IRFU. That the rugby constituencies of Munster and Connacht were at the forefront of various controversies is hardly surprising given that their inferior international selection and voting powers led to a feeling of disenfranchisement among rugby clubs in both provinces.

That separate spheres in the form of the neo-Gaelic cultural revivalists and the 'west-British' shoneens existed in Irish sport is a crude generalisation that does not adequately represent the relationship between Irish sport and politics. It has clearly been observed in this chapter that rugby was enjoyed by individuals of all political outlooks. Far from being a founding principle of the GAA, the 'ban' mentality was a contested concept, the evolutionary nature of which acknowledged both existing and potential overlaps in the respective constituencies of Gaelic games and rugby. That rugby lent itself to 'anti-national' characterisation was indicative perhaps of the perceived political bent of those who governed the game in Dublin and Belfast. The reality on the ground in Munster was much more fluid and localised than the propagandised perception promoted by the GAA allowed.

Chapter 6

Finance and Infrastructure

This chapter will examine the economic history of rugby football in Munster. Though the ideological tenets of amateurism sought to undermine any potential financial function in sport, formal clubs and governing bodies could not be run free of expense and thus had no choice but to cultivate some means of raising revenue in order to survive. In Ireland financial matters in the rugby sphere were left in the hands of the provincial branches. The cultural shift towards the concept of financial management was a slow one, however, and it was largely through the work of enterprising individuals that Munster rugby evolved from a purely participatory sporting culture to one which, out of necessity, modestly embraced the commercial imperative of modern sport. Economic and demographic scale, the geographical specificity of its popularity and the limit of its appeal to the working classes ensured that the game was never sufficiently popular in Ireland to embrace any level of professionalism until the 1990s. Therefore, though the IRFU's desire to maintain the amateur purity of the game was successful, economic reality rather than ideological adherence was at the core of this Pyrrhic victory. After a brief discussion on the commercialisation of sport in general, this chapter will initially focus on the early history of rugby as a gate-money sport in Munster. Issues that will receive particular attention will be the enclosure of grounds and the establishment of formal competitions – both fundamental developments in gate money sport. As already indicated, it will be clearly shown that the development of the game's capital infrastructure and the distribution of revenue was, for a long period, a heavily centralised process with clubs having little control over their own financial destinies. Though eagerness was always shown to balance the books, Munster rugby was not run in a businesslike manner and was ultimately heavily subsidised by the IRFU.

Modern sport as a commercial activity

One of the most observable characteristics of the Victorian and Edwardian 'revolution in sport' was the development of modern codified sport as a spectator activity. This was a gradual development and provided the rationale for the enclosure of grounds and charging for admission to sporting events. The potential for sport to generate revenue via gate money was maximised by the establishment of formal cup competitions whose popularity provided the 'market signal' for the establishment of season-long league structures.[1]

Sports in Britain that witnessed significant increases in spectator appeal from the late 1870s through to the outbreak of the First World War, such as soccer and rugby (particularly in Lancashire and Yorkshire), traded not only on the skill and entertainment on offer but also the platform they provided for expressions of civic pride and intra-regional rivalry and their ability to offer a mode of escape from the pressures of urban and industrial life.[2] Huge increases in the spectator appeal of such sports as horseracing, cricket, boxing and cycling were also witnessed in this period.[3] The revenue and, as importantly, the prestige to be gained from success in competitions created rivalry among clubs for the services of talented players and resultant abuses of the amateur ethic were inevitable. These key developments were quite regional in intensity and were intimately linked with broader social and economic conditions, with increasingly favourable levels of disposable income and spare time among the urban working classes being of particular importance.[4]

Rugby football historically had a peculiar relationship with money. The powerful RFU, which held considerable international sway over the game,[5] was deeply suspicious of commercialisation, sport spectatorship and competitions. This was symptomatic of a dogmatic desire on the part of the game's authorities to maintain amateurism in its purest form. This peculiarity was best exemplified by the secession in 1895 of twenty-two clubs in the north of England from the RFU. Though the formation of the Northern Union was occasioned by the refusal of the RFU to allow broken-time payments to players for loss of earnings through rugby participation, the causes of the split ran much deeper into the social fabric of Victorian Britain. In reality the RFU, keen to maintain middle-class hegemony over the gentlemanly game, were ill at ease with the fact that rugby in the north had become hugely popular among the industrial working classes. The resultant burgeoning popularity of cup competitions in Yorkshire and Lancashire had seen the tangible growth in the game's spectator appeal and the ability of clubs to accumulate wealth through gate money. RFU suspicions (not always unfounded) that northern clubs would be tempted to offer financial inducement to talented players led to considerable tension within the game and when compromise through payments for broken time could not be reached, a split became inevitable.[6] Though class tensions were an overriding factor in the split, it was commercialisation that fuelled the controversy.

In south-west France, where rugby became a hugely popular spectator sport with cross-class appeal before the outbreak of the First World War but particularly in the 1920s, institutionalised 'shamateurism' was historically a double-edged sword; for on the one hand it led to periodic international isolation from other rugby-playing nations while on the other it maintained domestic popularity and helped to stave off the appeal of rugby league (*le rugby à treize*).[7] Controversies of a similar nature also occurred within Welsh rugby where mass spectator and working-class appeal were precursors to suspicions of sinister practices in regards to financial remuneration of players. The Welsh rugby authorities, though also wedded to amateurism, pragmatically turned a blind eye to clandestine payments to players in order to prevent popular moves towards outright professionalism.[8]

Though the pattern clearly emerging here indicates strong class tensions within the game, a fraught relationship in rugby union between commercialisation and the raising of revenue and Victorian sporting ideals is clearly visible and fundamental. The north of England, south-west France and Wales all had shared characteristics in terms of economic and demographic structure that influenced the composition of their respective rugby constituencies. As a province, Munster differed significantly in terms of economic activity and scale – a fact tangibly reflected in the economic history of rugby in the province.[9] It is worth noting at the outset, therefore, that debates surrounding the tension between utility and profit maximisation as motivators for clubs and governing bodies, so prevalent in the economic history of British sport, are difficult to apply to Munster rugby.[10]

Early commercialisation, gate money and infrastructural development in Munster rugby

Prior to the mid-1880s, and as has already been displayed in Chapter 2, rugby was a socially exclusive pursuit of minority appeal in Munster. This lack of popularity, exacerbated by a shortage of suitable facilities and the absence of formal competitions had largely stymied any proto-commercialisation of rugby in the province. Though rugby had been played on a formal basis in Munster since at least 1872, fixtures had been sporadic, clubs ephemeral and the press largely uninterested. Throughout that decade, the game had been predominantly participatory in nature. Newspaper reports of rugby matches were rare, with press coverage being designed to notify players of upcoming fixtures. Games were played in unenclosed spaces and entry was free. From the late 1870s, however, a subtle and tentative shift occurred with efforts to promote the game as a spectator activity. Given its status as the province's most established rugby club, it was unsurprising that Cork FC was at the centre of the first meaningful attempt in the history of the province to stage a rugby event at which an admission fee would be charged.

Cork FC's efforts to secure a home fixture with a high-profile Dublin club originated in early 1878. In January, the prestigious Wanderers club from Dublin had agreed to an away fixture with Cork FC. The local club gave the match wide publicity as they had recently defeated Limerick FC in what had been the third annual fixture between the two clubs and claimed the title of 'the champion club of the South'.[11] The match was scheduled to take place at the unenclosed Cork Park, and for the local population this was apparently 'the first opportunity of witnessing the splendid game'.[12] In the event, Wanderers failed to travel, claiming that they could muster only nine players for the trip south. News of the cancellation arrived late on the eve of the match, preventing the Cork club from properly notifying the public. The 'couple of thousand' spectators who arrived at Cork Park were therefore treated to a scratch match among the players of the Cork club.[13] Later that month, Cork FC toured Dublin and played fixtures with Trinity College and Wanderers while a combined Limerick/Cork XV represented Munster in the second ever match against Lenister. At a meeting of the Irish Football Union (IFU) in November, it was decided that the same series of fixtures would take place in Cork.[14] Though the minutes of the meeting reveal little of the rationale or debate behind the decision, one can confidently speculate that the fixing of the matches for Cork was in no small part due to the lobbying of Cork's W.J. Goulding whose 'Mr Football' moniker illustrates how important an administrator he had become in Munster rugby.

Considerable planning went into the staging of the three fixtures, which were clearly seen by the Cork rugby authorities as an opportunity to showcase the game of football in the city. Crucially, the Cork club secured the use of the enclosed Mardyke cricket field for the series, thus giving the organisers an opportunity to charge admission money for the first time at a rugby match in the province. Women were to be admitted free of charge with the hope that 'in acknowledgement of this politeness, the male part of the population will not be backward in putting in an appearance, and helping those who endeavour to sustain the credit of our city, to support the necessary and heavy expenses of these visits'.[15] The first fixture, Cork v Wanderers, was scheduled for Saturday 30 November 1878, while Cork v Trinity and Munster v Leinster were fixed for the following Monday and Tuesday respectively. That Sunday was not considered a suitable day for hosting a sporting fixture was merely a reflection of common British sporting practice at the time. Significantly, details of the matches were displayed in both the sporting and the advertising columns of the local press.[16] The admission price was one shilling for men or two shillings for admission to all three fixtures.[17] As was typical of contemporary match reports in other jurisdictions, precise details on crowd numbers were not given and comments such as 'the Dyke was crowded with spectators'[18] do not even allow the most speculative of estimates to be made. It was noted, however, that students from neighbouring Queen's College Cork had not attended the Cork v Trinity match to support a number of their college colleagues who had been selected on the local XV. The *Cork Examiner,* hinting at the novelty of the entire event, commented that 'it would be in their [the students] own interest to support a movement like this which afforded them and the public in general so much gratification.'[19] The timing of the events (particularly the latter two fixtures on two winter's weekday afternoons) and the shilling entrance fee would most certainly have excluded potential working-class spectators.[20]

The financial success or otherwise of the series is unknown but it seems likely that the organisers would have been happy to cover costs, with the promotion of the game of football in general probably being the primary aim of their efforts. In addition, the Mardyke cricket field was likely to have been in far better condition than the unenclosed and notoriously wet alternative, Cork Park. The product on offer, therefore, would potentially have been of a higher standard, with an eagerness to impress the visiting Dubliners (both Wanderers and Trinity wielded considerable power in Irish rugby) likely to have been paramount in the minds of the Cork FC committee. This hypothesis is buttressed by the fact that clubs from Munster were only beginning to make their presence felt at the IFU committee table and the hosting of matches against Wanderers, Trinity College and Leinster was an ideal means of raising the profile of rugby in the province.[21]

These fixtures were rare early examples of the quasi-commerciali-sation of rugby in Munster. Indeed, some progressive administrators who clearly realised the financial imperative underlying the potential of sport were irked by the sedate pace of commercial development in

Munster. As early as December 1883, for instance, the prominent Munster Branch officer, bank official and member of Cork Football Club, John Forbes Maguire, wrote to the local press launching a bitter broadside against the state of the game of football in the city.[22] The pretext for his tirade was a recent tour to Ireland by the Wakefield Trinity club (later a professional rugby league club) and the ease with which the latter has secured victory over the local clubs. Maguire was an enterprising rugby official who three years later, along with W.L. Stokes, founded the province's first formal rugby competition in the form of the Munster Challenge Cup. In 1883, however, he was deeply concerned with what he regarded as serious structural and cultural deficiencies within the game in Munster and particularly Cork. His point of comparison for these conclusions was the touring Wakefield Trinity side and the footballing environment in which the club was nurtured. It is not known from where he derived his data but presumably as a locally notable football official he would have had occasion to converse with members of the touring Wakefield party and from there gathered significant information with which he could compare the Cork experience. On a fundamental level, he identified two key characteristics of the commercialisation and popularisation of modern sport (though he obviously did not couch it in such terms) that were of fundamental importance to the Wakefield experience but were not yet developed in Cork: the enclosure of grounds and the resultant capability to charge gate money, and the establishment of competitions.[23]

Though Cork's population was over twice that of Wakefield's, the latter had over thirty-five 'flourishing' football clubs as opposed to just three in Cork. The Wakefield Trinity club itself was reputed to have over 740 members and received subscriptions from over 1000 members at five shillings each. This was contrasted with the contemporary Cork situation where only three clubs were in existence with a combined approximate membership and annual income of 150 and £40 respectively. Maguire reserved the bulk of his envious admiration for the means by which Wakefield Trinity generated revenue through gate money. The club's policy of charging for admission to all matches yielded at least £30–£40 on each occasion. In addition, as lucrative a gate as £150 could be collected for high-profile fixtures, no doubt aided, Maguire implied, by their status as Yorkshire Cup champions. By comparison again, the Cork clubs were exclusively dependent on membership subscriptions to raise finance, with the cost of staging fixtures being left to 'the meagre funds of the clubs'.[24] Maguire, displaying a pragmatic grasp of the economic realities of modern sport, pointed to the fact that 'there is no opportunity here [in Cork] of obtaining gate money at any of the matches' and that it was 'rather strange that no other ground but the Cork Park can be obtained for the purposes of football'. In fact, the only suitable enclosed ground for football in Cork was the Mardyke cricket ground where 'the "men in authority" when applied to by the Athletic, Bicycle and Football Clubs [sic] of this city for the use of the ground, instead of using a disposition to encourage and accommodate clubs of a kindred nature to their own, either refuse altogether to accede to the application or do so in such severe and harassing conditions that it would be almost impossible to comply with them'.[25] All this was ironic given Maguire's assertion that the Cork County Cricket Club had a poor playing record and that the small crowds that they received witnessed 'an exhibition of a game bearing a much stronger resemblance to the game of skittles than cricket'.

The figures quoted by Maguire both in terms of Wakefield Trinity and the Cork clubs cannot be verified. Their accuracy or otherwise, however, is nowhere near as significant as his identification of the local rugby clubs' inability to charge gate money due to lack of enclosed grounds as a problem that stymied the contemporary prosperity of football in the city. The key role that he later played in the establishment of the Munster Cup and his admiration for Wakefield Trinity's success in the Yorkshire variant also indicates *de facto* acceptance that a lack of formal competitions was also a hindrance to the growth of football in Cork. The financial contrast between Wakefield Trinity and the Cork clubs is brought into sharper relief when one considers that the former could afford to overlook the amateur laws by paying the gifted three-quarter, Teddy Bartram, an annual stipend of £52 in the late 1870s,[26] a sum that (assuming Maguire's estimates to be roughly accurate) amounted to more than the combined annual income of the three Cork clubs. With one city situated in the midst of a nest of urban conurbations with a substantial industrial workforce with spare time and money and the other with a preponderance of service-related economic activity, considerable employment insecurity among the working classes, and situated at the southern tip of an overwhelmingly rural province, it seems obvious that the relative financial performance and popularity of football in the two cities was rooted in larger economic issues.

In the early 1880s, the period prior to the social expansion of the game in Limerick, Cork was the main rugby-playing centre of Munster. Even there, however, Maguire's complaints clearly display how the game lacked the popularity and the infrastructural sophistication to become anything equating to a gate-money sport in the

British meaning of the phenomenon. The city's lack of a critical mass of industrial workers, crucial to the urban mass appeal of spectator sport in other jurisdictions,[27] was exacerbated by a sporting culture wedded to the tenets of amateurism in which it was highly probable that the monetary aspect of sport scarcely occurred to many of those in positions of power within the game. Furthermore, and as already discernable from Maguire's letter, the availability or otherwise of grounds with suitable facilities was an issue that dominated the early history of gate-money rugby in Munster. The habitual venue for local rugby, Cork Park, was completely unusable as a commercial sports venue. The unsuitability of Cork Park for high-profile fixtures was most likely realised by the IRFU in 1886 when the national body seemingly ruled against the ground for future inter-provincial fixtures. The local reaction was hostile. In 1888, Cork footballers 'strongly disapproved of the "gate" rule in relation to inter-provincial matches', while 'all Cork players think it only their right that this year at least an inter-provincial match should be played in Cork, as it is a matter of ancient history since the last was played there.'[28]

Cork Park's problems were manifold. Not only was it a vast unenclosed expanse, but its surface was notoriously sensitive to bad weather, no doubt exacerbated by the fact that it became a popular venue for Gaelic games from the mid-1880s onwards. In addition the site had originally been covered by the tide and as a reclaimed piece of ground it would take on something of its former character when subject to heavy rain.[29] In spite of all this, it was used for the occasional high-profile fixture and had apparently improved to some extent for the staging of the inaugural Munster Cup final in 1886, with one observer moved to comment:

> Few whose acquaintance with Cork Park has been confined to the annual fugitive visit on inter-provincial days would recognise it last Tuesday when Garryowen and Bandon played the final tie for the Munster Cup. Annual experience had familiarised visitors with an exaggerated pigsty, an imitation deluge, lazy indifferent play and a handful of ill-conditioned, ill-conducted ignorant spectators. This, however, was all changed on Tuesday . . . where one rickety set of goal posts had reigned like gibbet-like grin o'er the vast expanse of gutter, at least a dozen new ones now held salutary sway at the volition of Gaelic and rugby footballers and hurlers. The wretched knot of bleary-eyed 'pub hunters' had been succeeded by thousands of healthy looking athletes, who thoroughly understood the finer points of the game, and while enthusiastic to the utmost, preserved the line of play intact in a most exemplary manner.[30]

The bulk of press comment would, however, remain critical of football facilities in Cork. Later that year, when the failure of the Tralee, Nenagh and Clanwilliam delegates to attend a Munster Branch meeting resulted in a voting majority for the Cork clubs, it was decided to stage that season's Munster v Leinster match in Cork, a decision seen as 'injudicious if it were only for the fact that a "gate" cannot be found in Cork whereas it can in Limerick'.[31] In November 1890, the result of a spell of wet weather was that 'all the clubs that make Cork Park their practising ground are not doing much work.'[32] At the beginning of the 1891–2 season the progress of the local clubs was again halted by the fact that Cork Park was 'under water', with one correspondent to *Sport* opining that 'it is a great pity that they cannot get some other place to play in . . . it is impossible to get a "gate" there [Cork Park] and I think that if an enclosed ground were rented, it would pay for itself, especially if used for cricket in the Summer.'[33] Perhaps the most withering indictment of all came in the aftermath of the Munster v Leinster fixture in 1892:

> Everybody seems to have exhausted their vocabulary in trying to find a sufficiently forcible superlative with which to characterise the state of the ground and the general conditions under which the match was contested . . . Without exaggeration the ground was covered with slush to the depth of ten inches and large pools of water were scattered around the field in plentiful abundance . . . it seems a better site could be had on one of the many elevated positions near the city. Surely a little preliminary expense would be amply repaid by the comfort of both players and spectators who naturally object to going into a muck-hole for their football.[34]

Despite such voluminous criticism, the lack of enclosed football facilities in Cork would remain a problem until the opening decade of the twentieth century. An early opportunity to solve the issue was missed when the Munster Branch rejected the option to partake in a project that would have seen the development of a proper sports ground on Cork Park. In 1891, the Cork Agricultural Society leased twenty-two acres of the Park and decided to invest £4,000 in the site to build premises along the lines of the then Ballsbridge athletic, tennis, cricket and football grounds (the modern-day Royal Dublin Showground).[35] The ambitions of the Society were apparently slow to get off the ground as it was fully seven years later before they approached the IRFU for a grant towards the building of a ground at the Park.[36] That and two further approaches from the Society in 1902 were rejected by the IRFU as 'the committee could not subscribe to any scheme for making a ground in Cork without the Munster Branch IRFU interesting themselves [sic] in the matter.'[37]

By then, in any case, the foundation of Cork Constitution FC in 1892 and that club's subsequent leasing of a ground at Turner's Cross had seen the overdue marginalisation of Cork Park as a football venue in the city. Undoubtedly bolstered by the popularity of the Munster Cup, matters improved even further in 1904 when Constitution and Cork County agreed to become joint leasees of the Western Field near Queen's College, later named the Mardyke football ground. That the development of the site was to be a truly modern project was indicated by the intention of the Constitution committee that 'a considerable sum of money would be expended in making the ground suitable, and the necessary stands, pavilions, bathrooms etc would be erected so that they hoped to make the new ground second to none in the Kingdom.'[38] The significant outlay involved would be 'more than met by increased revenue'.[39] The pace at which the grounds would be developed was dictated by the fact that Cork was chosen to host the Ireland v England international match in February 1905.

The two events of greatest importance in the history of gate-money rugby in Munster prior to the First World War were the international fixtures held in Limerick and Cork in 1898 and 1905 respectively. Both events required unprecedented planning and infrastructural investment and were designed not only to raise the profile of rugby in Munster but to showcase the respective host cities. International sporting contests of this nature were new to the province and ensuring their success was a huge challenge to respective organising committees.

When the IRFU committee decided that it was happy to resume international fixtures with Wales in the wake of the Arthur Gould controversy, Limerick was chosen as the venue for Ireland's fixture with the principality in March 1898 – a decision that had stemmed from earlier lobbying by Munster delegates at the Union's AGM that year.[40] Rugby had hitherto largely been played at the Markets Field, where Garryowen FC was the tenant club and the lease was held by a syndicate made up of club members. The local press saw the upcoming event as an important means of promoting the sport: 'it would have the effect of stimulating interest in Rugby and attracting new blood to the different clubs.'[41] The decision to play against Wales was finalised in early February, meaning that the committee established to make the arrangements for the fixture had a little over a month to convert the Limerick cricket ground into a venue capable of accommodating international football.[42] The committee itself was comprised of local notables and was presided over by bacon-curing factory owner and magistrate Joseph Matterson. Other members included the proprietor of Cruise's Royal Hotel, James Flynn; a solicitor, A. Blood Smyth;

F.G.M. Kennedy, who was manager of Guinness & Co; a prominent member of Garryowen FC and post office official F.P. Hook; and a physician, Dr O'Mara.[43] The most energetic committeeman, however, was a post office clerk, Jack O'Sullivan. A member of Garryowen FC and a former Irish international full-back, O'Sullivan was later to receive the lion's share of the credit not only for securing the fixture for Limerick but also for taking the predominant role in organising the event:

> Having once secured the event, he further determined that in the manner of its carrying out, it would mark an epoch in football history. That he succeeded in this no one who had the privilege of being present today can for a moment doubt. The arrangements for fitting up the field were altogether in Mr O'Sullivan's hands; while in the manner of receiving and entertaining the teams he was ably assisted by an influential committee of local gentlemen.[44]

Reflecting the broad popularity of rugby in Limerick, O'Sullivan had determined from the outset that 'all classes of citizens would join in making it [the international fixture] a success'.[45] To this end, local businesses were lobbied to sanction a half holiday on the afternoon of the fixture in order to allow their employees, who would otherwise be occupationally excluded, to attend the match. The response was positive and within days some of the city's principal retail outlets such as Cannock's, Todd's, McBirney's and Quinlan's agreed to close.[46] The Harbour Commissioners also agreed to grant a half holiday and the cooperation of local businesses was appreciated by the committee as 'all the assistants of the various trades in the city will have the opportunity of witnessing the match'.[47] One can reasonably assume that substantial numbers of these (mostly) Catholic white-collar workers enjoyed Sunday rugby as players and spectators.

In the space of roughly three weeks O'Sullivan's endeavours saw that the ground was enclosed and a stand with a capacity of 3,000 people was erected.[48] In addition, special trains were arranged with the Great Southern and Western Railway and the Waterford, Limerick and Western Railway to transport rugby enthusiasts from all over the country to the fixture. The estimated attendance was 15,000, 1,000 of whom were accommodated in the five-shilling covered stand; 3,000 in the three-shilling side stand with the balance paying a shilling each to watch proceedings from the terrace.[49] A post-match reflection on the weeks leading up to the event by a *Munster News* reporter conveys the extent to which the excitement surrounding the staging of the international fixture had engulfed a broad demographic within the city:

For weeks past the nascent fever has made itself felt among all classes and conditions of people, and the most unlikely victims have caught the contagion. The obscure corner of the newspapers in which in times past football reports were tolerated have all at once become the chief attraction for everyone . . . Even our lady friends show an interest in the game and a knowledge of its technicalities that is to say the least surprising . . . I have myself absorbed the prevailing microbe, in which case disastrous results may be apprehended. The boy in the street has got it; the schoolboy mixes it with his grammar; the nursery maid and the policeman have got it; it is in the warehouses and the workshops and I had almost said the workhouse as well.[50]

Indeed, the fact that the Irish team was defeated by the Welsh visitors did little to dampen the enthusiasm of local commentators, for whom the successful staging of the fixture was far more important than the on-field proceedings. Ultimately this was a sophisticated sporting fixture, clearly comparable to contemporary British developments. It was staged in a purpose-developed ground, spatially divided along class lines through varying entry fees, and linked to a large geographical catchment area by rail.

Seven seasons later, Cork would play host to international football for the first time. Munster delegates at the IRFU committee table first lobbied for an international match to be played in Cork in 1900 when a proposal at that year's AGM hoped that 'the IRFU would not overlook Cork (The Southern Capital) as a venue for an early international contest'.[51] The idea was rejected because not only was the international fixture calendar for the next two years already decided, but Cork still did not have a suitable ground to cater for a fixture of that magnitude.[52] A similar request from the Munster Branch the following season was also turned down.[53] Eventually, a special meeting of the Union was called in September 1904 when a joint request from the Cork Constitution and Cork County Football clubs to host the Ireland v England international match in February 1905 was ratified. The clubs, as leaseholders on the Mardyke football ground, agreed to pay the Union £200 to indemnify it from any loss that the staging of the fixture may have accrued.[54]

As with the earlier Limerick fixture, an energetic committee of local rugby enthusiasts was established to manage the logistical arrangements for the match. Foremost among these was the Cork County FC official, horse stud owner and bookmaker John Reese, who as chairman took a prominent role in the organisation of the international. The extensive preparation that had to be undertaken illustrates how unaccustomed Cork rugby officials were to catering for large crowds. In the

ground itself, stands had to be erected and seats installed. The committee also took it upon itself to both attract and manage the logistics of
the crowd. Rail infrastructure was critical to the commercial potential of
sport in the British Isles.[55] Not alone did the Cork committee negotiate
excursion fares with Irish railways where 'the facilities offered by the
various companies was unequalled in the history of cheap trains', they
also made arrangements with the Great Western Railway of England
for special fares from London and the south of Wales.[56] Among those
who took charge of distributing tickets was George Hutchinson, a
bicycle agent, who in his capacity as secretary of Cork Constitution had
played a central role in the initial leasing of the ground.[57]

The lowest admission price of two shillings was still comparatively
high for a rugby fixture (double the lowest admission price for the
Limerick international) and was deliberately designed to maximise the
number of spectators that the ground could cater for comfortably:
'they [the organising committee] came to this decision because they
believe that it would be much better to have 10,000 or 15,000 people
comfortable and with a good view than 20,000, many of whom would
be uncomfortable and in each other's way.'[58] Though retrospective
accusations of social exclusion are tempting here, it must be borne in
mind that the committee had also attempted (unsuccessfully) to convince the Munster Merchants Association to close retail establishments
in the city on the afternoon of the match in order to allow employees
the opportunity to attend the international.[59] Indeed, the committee
took particular exception to the action of the Merchants Association,
citing the example of Limerick establishments, all of whom had closed
for the rugby international held in that city seven years earlier.[60] It
seems likely that the admission prices did, to some extent, dictate the
social tenor of the occasion, an assertion buttressed by Gareth
Williams' observation that the 12,000 spectators that attended the
Mardyke that afternoon paid an aggregate total of £900 while the
40,000 patrons that witnessed the Wales v Ireland fixture in Swansea
that season yielded a total gate of £2,000.[61]

Reese was subject to much adulation for what was deemed a
hugely successful venture. The local press glowingly observed that

> the only reward which he desired, the only ambition that he sought
> to gratify was the reward of seeing that the first international played
> in Cork would be a credit to the name of Munster football, would
> help to place Rugby on a higher level than it had hitherto been in the
> southern province and would result in a larger measure of support
> for the game over which he had displayed such whole-hearted
> enterprise and enthusiasm and in the furtherance of which he had
> so disinterestedly performed such Herculean labours.[62]

This apparently laudable selflessness should be tempered somewhat by the suspicion that Reese was partly using the occasion as a means of self-promotion. In the column beside the weekly report of the proceedings of the international match's organising committee on 7 January 1905, for instance, there was a large advertisement for the Civility Stud, owned by none other than Reese himself.

The two international fixtures held in Munster either side of the turn of the twentieth century are historically significant for a number of reasons. Firstly, they were primarily civic rather than sporting occasions with both organising committees keen to use the international fixture as a means of bestowing a positive impression of their respective cities on the visitors. To this end, prominent local citizens were involved in the pre- and post-match ceremonial activities. The reception committee for the Limerick fixture included the mayor and the high sheriff as well as erstwhile football pioneer and prominent landowner Sir Charles Barrington.[63] In Cork, the Chamber of Commerce hosted a post match dinner for the visiting English team and officials attended by prominent local politicians and businessmen.[64] Secondly, in terms of the broader history of sport in the Victorian period and in common with Tom Hunt's observations in the case of Westmeath,[65] the role of individual agency was clearly critical in the events outlined above. Neither event may ever have taken place without the energy and enthusiasm shown by O'Sullivan and Reese respectively. Contemporary press reports indicate the ubiquity of both men in every stage of the process from the initial lobbying of the IRFU through to the development of the venues, the organisation of transport down to the minutiae of arranging ticket vendors.

The staging of these internationals, notwithstanding the time lapse between them, fuelled a gradual cultural shift in Munster rugby towards the commercial imperative of modern sport. In Limerick, for instance, it may be more than merely coincidental that within months of the international fixture, significant work was carried out by Garryowen FC on the Markets Field with the object of making the ground a more commercially viable venue. In February 1899, for example, when Limerick County would only agree to a fixture with Garryowen on condition that the gate was divided equally between the two clubs, the *Limerick Leader* considered it 'distinctly hard lines on Garryowen who have been at very heavy expense this season raising the walls around their grounds, the Markets Field and in many other ways expending money to better their enclosure all for the purpose of furthering football in Limerick and Munster'.[66]

In Cork, the arrival of the Mardyke football ground dramatically increased the gate-money capability of rugby in the city. In the case of the Queen's College club, for instance, the constant availability of a properly enclosed ground in close proximity to the city affected a clear shift in the club's revenue-generating pattern. Gate receipts had hitherto been a relatively small proportion of the club's income. This meagre contribution of gate money to the overall revenue of the club prior to the ground enclosure is evidenced by surviving club accounts from the seasons immediately preceding and postdating their tenancy at the Mardyke. In the treasurer's annual report for the season 1903–4, for instance, a fixture with Cork FC that had costs of £1 1s 4d yielded a gate of just £1 14s 9d. Fixtures the following January and February against Bective Rangers and Trinity College that had combined costs of £2 19s 11d yielded an aggregate gate of £3 12s.[67] At the end of the season, subscriptions were shown to have accounted for £28 8s out of a total income of around £43. The club was left with a debit balance of over £25, with the staging of home fixtures failing to raise near enough money to finance travelling costs.[68] In the season immediately predating the development of the grounds (1904–5), the club raised an aggregate of £16 through gate money with the remaining £45 of their total income comprising members' subscriptions.[69] The growth of the club's rugby economy in the seasons after their initial occupancy of the Mardyke is striking. In the 1907–8 season, £51 10s 10d was raised through gate receipts, including a bumper £19 gate from a fixture against Trinity College in February 1908.[70] Furthermore, subscriptions amounted to just under £36, meaning that in the short period of three seasons, gate revenue had increased dramatically in relative financial importance. Having amounted to just a third of the total collected through subscriptions in 1905, total gate money now exceeded the annual fees paid by members. Though paying annual rent of £25 on the grounds significantly decreased profit, gate receipts proved to be the difference between break even point and significant debt.

John Bale, in discussing the rationale behind the location of sports venues, pointed to the provision of outlets 'for a surrounding hinterland'.[71] Colleges were ultimately benefiting from a clear application of this rationale as the Mardyke had numerous advantages over previous venues. It was located within walking distance of the university itself and adjacent to the middle-class suburb of Sunday's Well, both locations where football enjoyed popularity. Moreover, the field was likely to have been a good deal drier than other erstwhile football venues, with a tangible improvement in the product on offer being highly likely. The inclemency of weather as a deterrent to the potential spectator was obviated by the erection of a stand. In addition, the site was well served by public transport. It was a venue already accustomed to international events of some import having (prior to its development as a football ground) hosted the Cork International Exhibition in 1902 and was connected to the city centre by the Cork and Muskerry Light Railway and the Cork Electric Tramway.[72] Though the usual series of friendly encounters and the much-unloved Munster Senior League were never likely to draw spectacular crowds, the Mardyke significantly improved matters for tenant clubs.

As will become clear below, when the building of Thomond Park and Musgrave Park is discussed, capital expenditure in Munster rugby could not be met by gate receipts alone. In a rugby economy that remained small, subsidisation was always necessary. If the 1905 international match raised the profile of Munster football and bequeathed the city of Cork with a long-sought modern football ground, it seemingly did so at considerable financial cost. In October 1906, for instance, Cork officials applied for a loan of £1,500 to pay off a debt on the Mardyke football grounds[73] – a liability no doubt accrued on the development costs for the international fixture of the previous season. The following January, the Union partially acceded by lending £500 to the Cork Football Grounds committee.[74] A joint effort by the Cork committee and the Munster Branch to secure the remaining £1,000 from the Branch failed in May,[75] while a similar request in November 1908 was partially successful in that the Union decided to lend the Munster Branch £25 per quarter for five years.[76] The ground's lessees eventually secured a mortgage of £500 in March 1909.[77] When University College Cork took responsibility for the lease in 1911, the ground was still in debt with the college agreeing to accept liability for money owed to the IRFU in connection with the project. In December 1912, the college acquired the grounds outright for a sum of £5,000.[78] Despite the optimism among those who envisaged the ground development paying for itself in the form of extra revenue, matters of scale and the competitive structure of Munster rugby militated against the fiscal capability of the project. The 12,000 spectators that witnessed the 1905 international may have comprised an unprecedented crowd by Cork standards but was, unsurprisingly, wholly unimpressive in comparison with crowds attending contemporaneous British sporting fixtures. Moreover, as Dublin would naturally remain the preferred venue for Irish home internationals, the attraction of five-figure crowds to rugby fixtures in Munster was to be a rarity.

In the three decades that spanned the foundation of the game in the province in the 1870s through to the opening decade of the twentieth century, a slow yet tangible proto-commercialisation occurred in

Munster rugby. Though commercial opportunity was most certainly not a consideration for those organising gate-paying fixtures, the necessity of progress and boosting the game's profile meant that at least some cognisance of the financial aspect of sport had to be taken by rugby administrators in Munster. The development of properly enclosed facilities in both Limerick and Cork not only made Munster a more attractive prospect for high-profile touring teams, it also ensured that domestic competitions would realise their monetary potential.

Competitions and gate money

A crucial component of the popularity of modern sport as a paying spectacle was the establishment of competitions. Within British sports historiography, for instance, rising attendances at FA Cup ties, league football, county cricket and Challenge cup games in rugby (particularly in the north) has always been identified as a crucial index of the burgeoning popularity of sport. Not only were competitions a reflection of a sport's growing appeal but they also served to stimulate interest both among potential players and spectators. Tony Collins has commented of rugby in the north of England that the 'Yorkshire Cup had brought with it an influx of new players, new spectators and new playing methods'.[79] Competitions had a crucial financial function. The mass spectator appeal of modern sport that was regulated by working-class spending power in Britain led to large-scale investment in infrastructure by clubs. The significant outlay involved in enclosing grounds, constructing stands and pavilions and ensuring the comfort of fans in the face of the vagaries of British climatic conditions was offset by the appeal of the product on offer. In order to ensure the financial viability of assets such as grounds and in the case of professional sport, players, it was necessary for clubs to provide a sufficiently regular series of competitive fixtures with spectator appeal.[80] Neil Carter has argued, using explicitly economic parlance, that the regularising of the fixture list brought about by the establishment of the Football League was designed to provide 'a regular product'.[81]

Though obviously different in scale and not affecting cultural change to the extent of professional competitions in Britain, the establishment of the Munster Senior Challenge Cup in 1886 was an event of huge significance to the financial future of the Munster Branch of the IRFU. The initial function of the cup, rather than being commercial, was the promotion and consolidation of rugby in the province, an assertion supported by the fact that the inaugural final between Garryowen and Bandon was held in the much-maligned Cork Park.

As already discussed, as an object of rugby folklore in Munster (particularly Limerick) the Senior Cup became enormously significant and would only be superseded as such in the 1990s with the combined attraction of the All-Ireland League (AIL) and the professional Munster rugby team.

In terms of finance, and bearing in mind Carter's comments on the importance of a regular product in the case of English football, the competitive culture and structure of rugby football in Munster militated against large-scale accumulation of gate-money revenue. The Munster Senior Cup, by far and away the province's most prestigious series of rugby fixtures and the Munster Branch's largest source of gate income, amounted to no more than nine, but usually approximately seven, fixtures per season. Other prestige matches such as inter-provincials were only held in Munster every second season and usually did not raise enough revenue to meet the loss incurred by sending the Munster XV to Dublin every other season. The potentially huge crowds attracted by touring teams, rather than being of significant benefit to Munster financially, were of considerable risk as the Branch had to guarantee the IRFU a minimum sum in gate revenue that the provincial committee itself would be liable for in the event of any shortfall. In 1935, for instance, the Munster Branch decided against seeking a fixture with a touring New Zealand team as the only available date fell on a Thursday, hence militating against a large crowd and increasing the possibility of a loss being made.[82] Ultimately, once the Munster Branch began to grasp some conception of the sport's potential monetary function, the proceeds of the Munster Cup were expected to both subsidise the club game and finance capital expenditure.

Unlike various spectator sports in Britain, a viable league competition did not exist in Munster rugby. The Munster Senior League never caught the rugby public's imagination and newspaper accounts frequently commented upon the sparse attendances at fixtures. When Queen's College met Cork FC in a Munster Senior League tie in 1902, for instance, 'a very meagre attendance' witnessed a match that commenced long after the advertised time.[83] Despite being entitled to keep the entire gate proceeds of league fixtures, clubs showed the lack of seriousness that they attached to the competition by frequently fielding weakened teams. Indeed, the League, for all intents and purposes, was little more than elaborate pre-cup shadowboxing. When Garryowen met Dolphin in the Munster Senior Cup in 1927, one previewer commented that 'this year has been a very lean year for the Garryowen veterans but cup tie football is as remotely [sic] different to League football as chilblains are to sunburn; and it is on record that many a frost-bitten League team has basked in the sunshine of cup victory.'[84] Cork Constitution and Garryowen showed their disdain for the League in 1930 by refusing to make room in their respective fixture lists for the series.[85] With an economically insignificant league competition, therefore, financial reliance on the Munster Cup was increased.

Reliable data on attendances at Munster Cup fixtures is unavailable with newspapers tending towards non-numerical general comments on crowd size rather than accurate estimates. When figures are given, their potential accuracy needs to be assessed in light of the fact that they were possibly no more scientific than an educated guess from the press reporter themselves. It does seem likely, however, that the Munster Cup final was limited to four-figure crowds for much of its early history. In the cup's inaugural season, Clanwilliam and Bandon did battle in an early round 'in the presence of a couple of thousand people'.[86] The *Cork Constitution* estimated that a crowd of some 3,000 spectators attended the competition's second ever final in 1887.[87] Four-figure crowds remained the norm in the pre-war period. In 1898, 3,000 spectators witnessed Garryowen and Rockwell do battle in a semi-final replay.[88] The cup's appeal apparently did not dramatically increase in the next two decades. The *Limerick Leader* estimated crowds of 4–5,000 for the finals of 1906 and 1907 respectively.[89] Significantly, both of the latter fixtures entailed a journey from Cork to Limerick for any away supporters – a factor that probably militated against crowd size. When the reverse was required of Garryowen fans for the 1903 cup final against Queen's College at Turner's Cross, Cork, for instance, the travelling support amounted to a hundred fans conveyed on a special train.[90] The vague statistics available suggest that before rugby entered an enforced hiatus in Munster brought about by the First World War, attendances fluctuated little, with an estimated 6,000 attending the Garryowen v Queen's College final in 1913.[91] The evident gradual increase seemingly reached a peak on the eve of the war. When Garryowen and Cork Constitution met in the first round in March 1914, 'there was an enormous crowd of spectators present, the gate receipts amounting to no less than £121.'[92] Clearly, cup football at club level was as attractive as the prospect of visiting touring teams. The visit of the 1905 All Blacks to Limerick, for instance, attracted what was considered a disappointing crowd of 4–5,000 people.[93]

Information on the financial history of the competition in its early decades is patchy at best, although available data suggests that the financial function of the cup evolved and increased in importance in the opening decade of the twentieth century. Indicative of the latter point is the fact that it was not until the competition's twentieth season

(1905) that the following resolution was passed by its governing committee: 'no match shall be played on a ground which is not properly enclosed and has not proper railway communication.'[94] This obvious intent to maximise admission money stemmed from what were perceived as paltry gates in the previous season's competition brought about by inconsistent and ineffective gate policies at different venues. Rockwell, for instance, returned just twenty-two shillings for two important matches, while the well-supported Cork FC club submitted £2 1s for one match. This was unfavourably compared with the £2 3s 3d returned by lowly Clonmel for their solitary cup outing.[95] The competition's auditor was unable to account for Garryowen's gate receipts as the champions had failed to furnish their accounts. Because the majority of matches were played in either Limerick's Markets Field or Cork's Mardyke grounds, the orthodox home/away fixture structure did not fluidly apply to the Munster Cup. The contemporary method of gate distribution, therefore, favoured the club that had option of ground; in other words, the club first drawn out of the hat and notionally the home team. Having paid the owner of the grounds 15 per cent of the gross gate, the Cup committee was to be given one third of the net gate and the remainder was retained by the 'home' team. In the final, the travelling team were also entitled to one third of the net gate. As with all competitions of its nature, the vagaries of the draw could ultimately mean that just one or two clubs would garner the majority of the disposable aggregate gate receipts. Coupled with the absence of a vibrant complementary league competition, the small scale of the Munster Senior Cup ensured that rugby clubs in Munster could never stake any financial future on gate money alone. The fact that clubs did not have outright ownership of grounds and that the competition was largely hosted by just one or two venues, coupled with different financial crises encountered by the Branch at various points, led to a confusing system of gate distribution that was subject to change from season to season.[96]

The financial realities of running a game with limited appeal forced the Munster Branch to control the proceeds of the Munster Cup very carefully. Therefore, though the cup was the most consistently lucrative source of gate money in Munster rugby, none of the competing clubs were ever likely to prosper from it dramatically in a financial sense due to the Branch's method of distributing the competition's proceeds. In 1929, the Branch committee fully outlined their distribution scheme: one third of the gross gates was to be pooled and divided among the competing senior clubs in the competition in the proportion of the number of matches played by each club; a club travelling outside its county was to get £15 towards travelling costs, with the Branch bearing the cost of these expenses, the renting of fields and advertising, with no expenses to be charged to the pool.[97] With the number of senior clubs standing at seven in that season, for instance, only six cup matches were guaranteed to take place (barring replays), meaning that the pool that would be divided between the competing clubs amounted to twice the average gross gate of one cup fixture. The balance, minus expenses, was retained by the Branch, who re-invested a significant proportion of its income in the form of grants to clubs. This scheme, however, floundered due to the objections of the IRFU who insisted that cup gates should be retained by the Branch committee itself.[98] Indeed, the Union withheld a promised grant of £200 to the Munster committee until they were satisfied that the desired amendments had been made to the Branch's gate-money policy.[99] What emerged was a highly centralised system of financial control whereby clubs only had indirect access to the proceeds of a competition that was made viable by the entertainment provided by their players. This change evidently had an adverse affect on the participant clubs. The *Limerick Leader*, in a characteristically sardonic response, asserted that:

> When the Rugby Union with a splendid gesture adjusted the allocation of gate money in the Cup competition, there was no revolution in Limerick Rugby, as far as we can recall. There was no appeal to the League of Nations or a funeral pyre of jerseys . . . there was just a mild little dismay, a little megrim or as the French would call it, a Papillion noir, and then like good little boys, the Limerick Rugbyites went home in a chastened mood. If our local clubs are called upon to face another band season, it is doubtful if rugby will continue in the city . . . may we look forward to a general appeal from the Munster clubs to the Union asking for a renewal of the old arrangements?[100]

Having acceded to the Union's wishes, the Branch decided to introduce a system of grants to support affiliated clubs whereby senior clubs participating in the Munster Cup would receive a grant not exceeding £50 while their junior counterparts would receive a grant not exceeding £10 which was contingent on their participation in the Munster Junior Cup.[101]

In this case, the aspiration was a good deal more generous than the actuality. Participation alone in a Branch-run competition did not yield an automatic grant. In general, grants were only awarded in lieu of expenses incurred due to travel. When one considers that travel costs for rugby clubs were theoretically not sensitive to the level of competition involved, the minority that comprised the province's senior clubs received disproportionately large grants when compared to their junior counterparts. In 1931, for instance, a total of eight senior clubs received an aggregate of £240 in travel expenses for Senior Cup matches and friendly matches outside the province. Garryowen and Cork Constitution were the principal beneficiaries, receiving £60 each with both clubs having played two away matches each in the Senior Cup and at least two friendlies each outside the province.[102] By comparison, a total of twelve junior clubs that travelled in the Munster Junior Cup received an aggregate of £60. In other words, the travel grant allowable to senior clubs (£15) was three times that allowed to junior clubs (£5). Furthermore, travel grants to junior clubs, it was resolved, were to cost the Branch a maximum of £100 for that season in spite of the fact that the committee had 'roughly £1,000 in hand'.[103]

Though the financial favouritism shown to senior clubs was illogical inasmuch as they were not subject to greater travel expense than junior clubs on a per fixture basis, it is certainly not surprising. Not only did senior clubs raise significantly more gate-receipt finance than junior clubs through the Munster Cup, but their representatives dominated the Branch committee table and therefore the financial distribution process. The former point is certainly borne out by available figures. In 1942, for instance, the profit on the Senior Cup was £624 as opposed to £132 for the Junior Cup;[104] in 1945, the Senior Cup yielded total gate receipts of £1,398 while the Junior Cup's equivalent figure was £491.[105] In 1947, the Senior Cup brought in £1,749 while the Junior Cup still languished in relative terms on £537.[106] In 1949 and in the wake of the gradual return to normality in post-Emergency Ireland, competitions took record gate receipts with the Senior and Junior Cups bringing in £2,119 and £1,155 respectively.[107] The upward trend in the Senior Cup continued in 1951 when gross receipts of £2,898 were recorded while the Junior Cup remained stable at £539.[108]

In the absence of large-scale proletarian appeal, it does not seem likely that cup attendances in Munster were as sensitive to the vicissitudes of industrial life as has been observed by Williams in the case of Welsh rugby and Collins in the case of inter-war rugby league.[109] In any case, issues of scale undermine the potential influence of any broader economic issues affecting gate receipts in Munster. Internal footballing factors were more likely to influence gate receipts than external economic trends. The vagaries of the competitions structure, for instance, could tangibly affect its revenue-generating capacity. For instance, when the 1934 Munster Cup showed a fall of £550 in total gate receipts from the previous season, it was most likely attributable to the fact that there were extra fixtures played in 1933 due to drawn ties. Bad weather also affected gates with potential spectator discomfort in largely uncovered grounds and deterioration in the quality of the product on offer due to poor playing surfaces both acting as deterrents to rugby fans. When Bohemians met Dolphin and Garryowen met Sunday's Well in a league double header in 1930, for instance, the fixtures were 'absolutely deserted' due to the weather, bar a few 'hardy souls whom one expects to find at a fixture with a local interest in, say, Greenland'.[110] In addition, rugby was simply more popular in Limerick than in Cork. Therefore, overall gate receipts in the Munster Cup were likely to be greater if Limerick teams prospered and fewer fixtures were played in Cork. When selecting the venue for the 1928 schools inter provincial match against Leinster, for instance, the rationale behind choosing Limerick lay in the fact that 'for every £ received from gates at Cork, they would get £2 and £3 at the Limerick venue.'[111] This situation remained the same more than three decades later when the *Limerick Leader* summarised the contrasting appeal of rugby in Limerick and Cork:

> A semi-final of the Munster Senior Cup in Limerick can always be counted upon to pull in well over £200 and in some cases top the £400 mark. But the 'gates' at Cork can be very disappointing. Take last Saturday's clash between Sunday's Well and Old Crescent, for example. If it was a £100 'gate' I'll be greatly surprised and I'll wager that 75 per cent of the takings were shelled out by Limerick men.

The same article ultimately concluded that if two Limerick teams reached the final 'it will be a lucky day for the Branch, for a Thomond Park decider can mean twice as much financially.'[112]

It is clear that the logistics of running a game with two centres of popularity considerably diluted the financial potential of Munster rugby. Unlike in Leinster, where all the major senior clubs were in close geographical proximity to each other, travel expenses were considerable further south.

Second wave of infrastructural development and financial crises

The three decades spanning the 1930s through to the late 1950s is the period for which the most detailed financial data on Munster rugby is available. Not only was it an era when gate receipts from cup competitions (notwithstanding some fluctuation) were increasing but it also coincided with the building of Thomond Park in Limerick and

Musgrave Park in Cork, two projects that required unprecedented infrastructural planning and financial outlay on the part of the Branch committee. The financial crises that were to ensue both at central administrative and club level offer insights into the internal functioning of Munster rugby much deeper and significant than merely the monetary. In the absence of a viable independent league competition, clubs were at the financial mercy of the Munster Branch. The committee, in turn, bore the headache of dividing its resources in such a manner as to keep clubs afloat, with the Munster Senior, Junior and Schools Cups accounting for the overwhelming majority of their revenue-raising capacity. The Branch possessed no fixed assets to speak of. UCC was the only senior club in ownership of a ground and the Branch itself was still renting the Markets Field and the Mardyke for cup fixtures. Addressing the latter point was to prove a fraught test of the administrative and financial capacity of the rugby authorities in the province.

By the early 1930s, the Munster Branch began considering the desirability of acquiring its own fixed assets in the form of grounds. The lease on the Markets Field was held by the Garryowen Athletic Company, while the Mardyke Football Grounds were now owned by University College Cork. While the Branch committee was unhappy with the rental arrangements it was subject to for the use of the Mardyke ground, there was greater urgency to develop a ground in Limerick due to the outdated facilities of the Markets Field and the Branch's failure to convince the owners to improve the venue. As Charlie Mulqueen has noted, 'the facilities there [Markets Field] grew more and more antiquated as the twentieth century progressed . . . [as the] . . . only means of washing after a match was cold water from a famous tap.'[113] Indeed, when the Leinster junior team visited Limerick in 1928, the Munster Branch gave assurances that hot baths at Cruise's Hotel would be provided for the visitors.[114] The unsuitability of the Markets Field was officially flagged as early as 1929, when the Branch wrote to the Garryowen Athletic Company claiming that they could not hold the following season's interprovincial against Leinster in Limerick unless 'the ground was re-sodded, the barbed wire removed, dressing rooms erected and the stand enlarged'.[115] In response to the unwillingness of the owners to implement such improvements, the Branch offered to buy the venue but the offer was apparently turned down.[116] The *Limerick Leader* in typically caustic mode commented of the Markets Field that 'the Archangel pitch is as damp and unsafe as ever. Limerick rugby is suffering, the gates are suffering, the poor field is suffering; in fact we never saw such suffering in all our life.'[117]

Meanwhile, the venue's committee continued to prevaricate and still had not committed to making any improvements to facilities eighteen months after the Branch's initial request.[118] Eventually, the Branch attempted to raise some money to make the necessary amendments itself. A grant of £250 was initially mooted as a potential investment in the Markets Field but it was eventually decided to withdraw the earlier threat of fixture cancellation and to divert some of what would have been rent for the Munster v Leinster interprovincial fixture in December 1930 towards improving facilities.[119] The grounds committee agreed to this suggestion and when the same body asked the Munster Branch for suggested improvements, the response gives some insight into the Spartan conditions that players were subjected to at the Markets Field: 'The suggestions were: enlarge both dressing rooms by removing the partitions, paint all inside of dressing rooms white, install basin and running water as per instruction. Install two "Elson" closets,'[120] while the following meeting decided 'that wash hand basins and lavatory accommodation be installed in the dressing rooms at the Markets Field, also that playing pitch be improved, hollows to be filled and re-sodded. Sanitary arrangements to be gone on with immediately.'[121] The mutual investment of the grounds committee and the Munster Branch in improving the Markets Field was to be of no long-term avail to the latter, however, as when an offer of £1,500 to buy the grounds in January 1931 was rejected, the rugby authorities began to look elsewhere for a venue of their own.[122] By the end of the year, a field was bought at Hassett's Cross which, after a turgidly long process of development, would become Thomond Park.

The conversion of the field at Hassett's Cross into a modern enclosed ground was a financial fiasco. Not only was the project a saga in terms of how long it took to complete but its potential cost was hopelessly underestimated. The apparently relaxed pace of progress on the new development irked the local press, who thought (wrongly) that the Branch were poised to abandon the project altogether by the autumn of 1932. Contemporary continental politics and the poetry of Yeats were invoked as metaphors to criticise the perceived blundered planning and clandestine workings of the Munster Branch:

> Limerick still lacks a proper rugby pitch and for some reason, we hear it is a question of cost of equipment, the field at Hassett's Cross will not materialise . . . It is deplorable that in a city of Limerick's size and fame we have not a suitable playing pitch for the game beloved of eighty per cent of our population. That the Inter-Pro games must go annually to Cork and, incidentally, find their best support from Limerick is equally deplorable, but what would you? Oh for a Mussolini in our rugby circles who will arise

now and go to Inisfree and instead of the mists on the bogs, tell us the stark naked truth, with all its wattles.[123]

Though the *Leader* was wrong in asserting that the project had been abandoned, the proposed venture was certainly in grave financial difficulty. It was originally estimated that the development would cost in the region of £4,000 which would be financed by £1,000 of the Branch's own funds, a grant of £1,000 from the IRFU, £20 each from fifty guarantors and a bank loan of £1,000.[124] By the beginning of 1932, however, it was discovered that the cost of levelling and enclosing the field and erecting a stand would cost a minimum of £4500 and the budget was suitably amended. A mixture of poor planning and bad luck led to a considerable budget deficit. A mistake by the appointed engineer, for instance, increased the cost of the enclosing wall by over £700.[125] By September 1934, £5,634 had already been spent on the ground, amounting to a budgetary overspend of £1,000, a situation exacerbated by the fact that the committee had yet to fund the unfinished levelling of the ground and the erection of the stand. In May 1935, the bank account set up for the development was overdrawn by £2,300. A significant increase in this indebtedness was avoided when the IRFU provided a grant of around £3,000 for the building of the stand.[126] The budgetary wishful thinking that had hitherto characterised the project was also in evidence in the forecasted costing of the new stand. The original estimate of £1,778 quickly increased to £2,300 and with the cost of dressing-room equipment and plumbing included, the final projected cost amounted to £3,135.[127]

At this stage, the slowness of the development had become a self-perpetuating problem with the half-finished ground apparently acting as a deterrent to spectators and hence depriving the committee of the much-needed funding to complete the project:

> Thomond Park is still without a stand, for players and spectators. It looks as if it will be the same bleak and desolate plateau again this year with the customary lair of mud for one to stick outside the entrance . . . It is really a shame that the work of completing the Thomond Park project is being held up for such a considerable period for it is almost impossible to get anything like a profitable attendance with the grounds in their present condition. Most of the friendly fixtures played at Thomond Park during the last two seasons attracted only a handful of spectators, while the attendance at one cup tie was well below Munster Cup gate proportions.[128]

The cost burden and planning difficulties were possibly exacerbated by contemporary economic conditions. Many of the materials needed for the project would, presumably, need to have been imported from Britain and would therefore, in some cases, have been subject to punitive tariffs from 1932.[129]

Meanwhile, the financial difficulties caused by the ground overdraft were directly affecting the management of rugby in other areas. In January 1935, trial matches for the provincial junior team were abandoned as a cost-cutting measure. Three years later, it was proposed that the practice of giving dinners to visiting interprovincial teams should be discontinued 'in view of the financial position of the Branch'.[130] It was the clubs, however, that felt the major brunt of the financial fallout occasioned by the development of Thomond Park. In 1935, travelling grants to clubs were cut by 50 per cent as a cost-cutting measure. Cork Constitution complained that 'the club was in a bad way financially and . . . the whole cause was the new ground in Limerick.'[131] With the potential cost of fulfilling away fixtures now doubled, the financial problems became widespread with the Branch committee admitting that 'the indebtedness of the Limerick ground was the reason for the clubs being in such a bad state.'[132] In November 1936, Young Munster withdrew from the Munster Senior League owing to financial difficulties with the Branch's meek acceptance of the decision indicating not only its own financial woes but also the esteem in which the league was held by its supposed promoters.[133] The following year, the committee suggested concerted action to attempt to convince the IRFU to give grants to the struggling clubs.

The situation was not helped by the Branch's decision to undertake a capital project of similar scale in Cork in 1939. The purchase of the ground that would become Musgrave Park was funded by a grant of £1,700 from the IRFU. The financial burden of properly equipping the site for rugby, however, was left to the already shaky finances of the Munster Branch. These two major capital investments continued to be drip-fed funds from the Branch and hence the pace of development remained slow. The Branch, already servicing an overdraft of £2,000 on Thomond Park, decided in 1940 to re-mortgage Musgrave Park to the tune of £500, plunging Munster rugby into yet more debt.[134] The treasurer, Jack Macaulay, warned on three separate occasions in the winter of 1941–2 of the precarious financial situation prevailing in Munster rugby, with the starkest assessment coming in March when he claimed that 'the financial position of the Branch was worse than it had been for thirty years.'[135] Financial matters seemingly stabilised over the next number of years with the Branch minute book indicating that work on developing Musgrave Park had been halted completely. Extra revenue from cup competitions was channelled into increased grants to clubs rather than ground development. From the early 1940s a scheme of special grants was introduced to help clubs and were distinct from orthodox travelling grants inasmuch as they were not in lieu of any bona fide expenses. The total of £675 spent on grants in 1945 was increased to £915 in 1946, reflecting a £350 increase in cup receipts. When a record credit balance of £2,025 was recorded in 1948, for instance, a total of £1,837 in various grades of grants was paid to clubs. A credit balance of £2,800 in 1950 saw grant expenditure of £2,300, including a generous total of £725 distributed in the form of special grants.[136]

The much-needed financial bolstering of clubs came at the expense of clearing the Thomond Park debt and the funding of much-needed developments at the Musgrave Park site. Though having been already in possession of Musgrave Park for eight years, the Branch did not begin planning the enclosure of the Cork ground until 1946, with a tender not agreed upon until 1949.[137] The lack of thorough planning that had dogged the Thomond Park project was again in evidence in 1952 when the Musgrave Park Grounds Committee sought permission to borrow £3,000 to fund the completion of the unfinished boundary wall in the now fourteen-year-old ground.[138] When the All Blacks visited Cork in 1954, the Branch was forced to continue renting the Mardyke from UCC as its own ground was still nowhere near being adequately equipped to host such a fixture. The process of building a stand at Musgrave Park, an episode that would almost bankrupt rugby football in Munster, began in 1954. In a year when all the bank accounts on Thomond Park were overdrawn, the Branch finance sub-committee, using the ground's deeds and an IRFU guarantee as security, borrowed £15,000 to build the Musgrave Park stand. The remaining £3,000 needed to fully fund the project was borrowed by the ground's two tenant clubs, Dolphin and Sunday's Well.[139] By September, the Branch's indebtedness stood at £11,095. A payment of a further £4,000 on the Musgrave Park stand a month later saw the debt increase to over £15,000.[140] This crisis occasioned a shift in grant policy with £1,000 of the £1,881 expended on grants that season being set aside for ground development rather than for clubs. By 1957, with an overdraft of over £11,000 and not in a position to finance the draining of the pitch at Musgrave Park, another finance sub-committee was set up to investigate the Branch's precarious financial position.[141] The committee's eventual report concluded that cutbacks were required and yet again it was the clubs that were deigned to shoulder this burden.

Apart from an immediate halt to capital expenditure, virtually all the recommendations directly affected the subsidisation of clubs.

Grants at all levels of rugby were cut and the long-established practice of offering grants to clubs fulfilling fixtures outside the province, and hence introducing a notionally 'national' element to the game, was to be discontinued completely.[142] In early 1958, and with the Branch's overdraft almost exceeding the permitted limit, the committee admitted that 'it was obvious that it could not continue to finance the two grounds from its present income from cup gates mainly.' It was subsequently decided that the IRFU should be approached to take over ownership of both Thomond Park and Musgrave Park and run them along similar lines as the Ravenhill ground in Belfast.[143] Their alternative solution was an immediate grant of £5,000 and a subsequent annual grant of £1,500 for ten years. It was now obvious that the rationale behind developing two grounds in relatively close chronological proximity lacked any conception of the financial sustainability of such an increase in capital expenditure. With not enough first-class fixtures per season to make either ground fund itself, Munster rugby was in a vicious financial circle whereby income from gate receipts was needed both to pay debts accrued on the two grounds and sustain the club game. Without grants to clubs, they would not be able to continue, while not servicing the debt increased the sum of interest payable.

In the spring of 1958, the IRFU intervened and established a subcommittee to investigate the financial crisis that had beset rugby in Munster.[144] Having met on three occasions, the committee reported in May. They refused either to accept the assets and liabilities of the two grounds or to offer the desired grant scheme as earlier requested by the Munster Branch. The Union committee quickly grasped the seriousness of the situation by diagnosing that the Branch's average annual surplus was 'not sufficient to meet the interest on the loans, much less to provide for payment each year of a reasonable amount off the principal'. It was further observed that the financial crisis brought about by capital expenditure was particularly exacerbated by the building of the stand at Musgrave Park. The problem was clearly not a lack of benevolence on the part of the Union. The committee calculated that since the initial purchase of Thomond Park, between grants and guarantees on loans, the Union had contributed over £22,000 to the development of the two Branch-owned grounds in Munster. The report suggested that the tenant clubs in Musgrave Park, Dolphin and Sunday's Well, should be subject to a rent increase, that grants should again be reduced and that the clubhouse built by Dolphin RFC should be used for holding dances and balls. In the event of a further deterioration, the committee vaguely yet apocalyptically concluded that the inevitable disposal of Musgrave Park would create 'a very serious situation as far as Munster rugby is concerned'.

The problems persisted and by 1960, the net overdraft had increased to almost £16,000.[145] The solutions proposed by the IRFU were ineffective in lessening the financial plight and in February 1961, the Union finally saw that additional and significant subsidisation was necessary when its financial sub-committee sanctioned an immediate grant of £5,000 to the Munster Branch. With a sudden decrease in the principal debt, interest payments became manageable and the overall financial condition of rugby football in Munster dramatically veered from critical to stable. That is not to say, however, that fundamental economic problems did not persist. The various cup competitions would always struggle to raise adequate revenue both to keep grant aid flowing to clubs and to meet the running costs of the two grounds. In the period 1961–5, for instance, average annual gate receipts of £3,880 were offset by running costs of £2,400 per annum on Musgrave Park and Thomond Park.[146] This situation was exacerbated by yearly gate receipt fluctuations. The annual interprovincial series, for instance, meandered between being a slight addition to overall gate receipts when the majority of the Munster team's games were at home to being a damaging loss-making exercise in seasons when Munster's fixtures were away from home. In 1946, the cost of Munster's trip north to play Ulster had seen the Munster Branch incur an overall loss of £200 on the series.[147] In 1948, the staging of all three interprovincial fixtures away from home had led to a loss for the Munster Branch of £300 on the series.[148] In 1953, the Branch made a loss of £80 on the interprovincial matches despite having two home fixtures.[149] Matters improved dramatically in 1955, when the committee recorded profit of over £300 on the senior interprovincials, no doubt aided by a record gate at the newly opened Musgrave Park for the visit of a star-studded Ulster side.[150] The remarkable rigidity of the competitive structure of Irish rugby that persisted into the 1990s ensured that the product provided by the Munster Senior Cup would remain the most attractive to rugby supporters in Munster.

Though dense, all this detail provides a number of key insights into the management of rugby in Munster. The first section of this chapter traced the development of the game as a commercial activity in the province from the late 1870s. But what kind of commercial activity was it? And what does the questionable financial decision-making apparent in the second half of the chapter tell us about the motivations of those charged with running rugby in Munster? Clearly, in a small-scale amateur sport run by volunteers, profit-maximisation was not a consideration.[151] There were no shareholders or other private concerns expecting a return on investment. Given that the Branch was historically committed to distributing funds in order to 'further the game', however, revenue-maximisation would have been a legitimate financial objective. Yet the construction of two purpose-built rugby grounds in Munster was never viable as a commercial venture and utterly subverted the aim of nurturing the game. Rugby in Munster was simply not adequately spectator-driven in terms of scale to justify such capital outlay for spectator facilities. The blame for the Branch's appalling financial performance lies largely with those in decision-making positions. It is worth pointing out that the combined professional capacity of those comprising the Branch committee in any given period makes the financial malaise of the middle third of the twentieth century more perplexing. Jack Macauley, who held the position of treasurer for over fifty years, was a successful mill manager; J.G. Musgrave, an official of various rank throughout the period, was one of Cork's most noted businessmen; Peter Galbraith, a committee member, was an accountant; Joshua Fitzelle, another long-serving committee man, was a butter exporter; Charlie Hanrahan was a bank manager; D.J. O'Malley was a solicitor. These were all individuals of standing who could not have been unaware of the financial burden that embarking on two capital projects would saddle the Munster Branch with. Moreover, the operational efficiency and business acumen that must have been central to some of their professional lives was clearly not transposed onto the decision-making process surrounding the ground development.[152]

The geographical structure of the game in Munster was an exacerbating factor. Neither Limerick nor Cork could ever claim to be the exclusive 'capital' or the 'cultural hearth' of rugby in Munster. As this book has shown, the cities had divergent rugby cultures that militated against an effective central ethos. Exacerbating this was traditional rivalry and resultant disharmony between the two cities in a rugby context. Generations of officials from Limerick and Cork were never willing to yield primacy to each other. Though direct evidence is lacking, it seems reasonable to speculate that the decision to develop the Cork grounds when the Limerick grounds were already heavily indebted was in some way influenced by inter-city rivalry.

In his study of the management of football clubs in England, Neil Carter has observed that human agency was a key driving force behind the modernisation of sport administration. New innovations, methods and aspirations in terms of a club's performance both on and off the field were often initially attributable to individuals.[153] This chapter has equally shown that the key events that signposted the gradual proto-commercialisation of Munster rugby in the last three decades of the nineteenth century were heavily dependent on individual agency. Men such as John Forbes Maguire, William Stokes, Jack O'Sullivan and John Reese were conspicuous by their innovativeness in comparison to those in similar positions. They made vital contributions to the gradual cultural shift that saw Munster rugby evolve from a purely participatory sporting culture to one which embraced, albeit modestly, the financial function of modern sport. The system of revenue generation that emerged from the proper enclosure of grounds and the establishment of prestige competitions was to remain strikingly rigid. In short, Munster rugby was financially dependent on the small number of prestige fixtures that comprised the Munster Senior Cup to sustain the heavily centralised system of monetary distribution. As a result, major capital expenditure was not possible without subsidisation from the IRFU. The building of not one, but two Branch-owned grounds in Cork and Limerick in the decades immediately preceding and postdating the Second World War was clearly symptomatic of a sporting culture with two centres of popularity and administrative power. Thus, civic pride and the associated tendency among individuals to promote the interests of their own city above those of the province as a whole was reflected in the commercial history of Munster rugby.

CHAPTER 7

Professionalism

The centrality of amateurism to the overall ethos of rugby union ensured that when the game 'went open' in 1995, it became the last major international sport to embrace professionalism. This development, though immediately attributable to the irresistible commercial power of satellite broadcasting, was ultimately the outcome of the game's internal contradictions. The principal contradiction, always in existence but more evident from the 1960s, was between declared support for amateurism and clandestine toleration of abuses of the amateur code. This was particularly true of the southern hemisphere unions and France. As the deference of former colonies to Britain began to erode from the 1960s, the RFU, as the foremost proponent of amateurism, began to lose its international stranglehold over rugby union. This meant that moves towards the dilution of amateurism (if not its abandonment) clearly favoured by South Africa, New Zealand, Australia and France carried much greater weight, particularly from the 1980s. Moves towards the introduction of a Rugby World Cup, for instance, were successful despite strenuous opposition from the RFU. The financial success of the tournament's inaugural and second stagings in 1987 and 1991 put considerable strain on the maintenance of amateurism.[1] This was exacerbated by agitation among players for a share of the financial windfall, exemplified by the refusal of English players to speak to the media during the 1991 Five Nations Championship without monetary compensation. It was the intervention of Rupert Murdoch and News Corporation, however, that delivered a fatal blow to amateurism in rugby union. In early 1995, Murdoch proposed the introduction of a new Super League competition that would significantly expand the financial base of rugby league in Australia. With mass defections of union players to league and its new-found riches likely, the southern hemisphere unions were left with little choice but to negotiate a separate deal with Murdoch. In April 1995, the three unions (now under the SANZAR umbrella) signed a £340 million deal with Murdoch to televise rugby union and declared

that the game was no longer amateur. Their northern hemisphere counterparts, faced with the certainty of a split in world rugby, had no
option to accept the game's new disposition.[2]

It has already been observed in Chapter 2 that the end of amateurism was met with a hostile reaction in Ireland.[3] Irish rugby officials
and press correspondents opposed the development on a mixed platform of ideological and practical considerations. For the IRFU,
amateurism was essential to the character of the game, as evidenced by
an official pronouncement in 1995:

> The IRFU will oppose the concept of payment to players to play the
> game and payment to others such as coaches, referees, touch judges
> and members of committees for taking part in the game because the
> game is a leisure activity played on a voluntary basis.[4]

Even more revealing was the opinion of then IRFU president Ken Reid:

> Let us be realistic, this could mean the end of a player pursuing a
> career outside the game and that is a sad situation. When [then
> Ireland scrum-half] Niall Hogan was conferred with his medical
> degree . . . I pointed that out.[5]

Clearly the idea that an individual qualified to practise a respectable
profession having attended a respectable school (Hogan attended
Terenure College) could conceivably consider rugby anything other
than a pastime defied Reid's assumptions of what the function of the
game was and what social cachet it should appeal to.

The sentimental musings of the IRFU were matched by legitimate
concerns as to the effect of market forces on a game built around a rigid
and conservative club system. It was obvious to commentators that the
domestic game, being built on a modest financial base and solidly
amateur in outlook, would be vulnerable to the cultural change that
professionalism would inevitably bring about. This cultural change
would come in the form of new elite-level competitions, merchandising, marketing, broadcasting deals and an international transfer
market. The IRFU had no obvious scheme in mind for coping with this
traumatic change and an overarching sense of trepidation characterised
official and press discussion on the fate of Irish rugby in the seasons
immediately following the 1995 decision. Edmund Van Esbeck, perhaps
the most vocal critic of professionalism, summed up the views of many
in late 1995:

> There is every reason now to be apprehensive about the fallout from
> the game in this country. I stated before that once professionalism
> came in the window morality and loyalty will rapidly go out the
> door. The issues were never just about paying the international

squad, or compensating them for time lost at work and for the time and effort they spent preparing for matches. An awareness of the true nature of the game in this country and the premise on which it is based made it obvious that Ireland could not sustain professionalism.[6]

The decline of club rugby

Greg Ryan has commented of the transition to professional rugby that 'Many who had invested time, emotion and sometimes their own money into the fortunes of rugby teams at the local level found that these strong community and historical reference points were being subtly altered or simply obliterated in the face of new commercial imperatives – and especially new competitions that separated the elite from the grassroots of the game.'[7] The general trend observed by Ryan was readily applicable to Munster rugby. Club rugby with its rivalries, competitions and localism came under severe pressure from the exigencies of professionalism, particularly from the turn of the twenty-first century. Before charting the rise of the Munster rugby provincial team, it is necessary to examine the development of club rugby in the professional era.

Given its long-standing significance as a focal point for the rivalries between and within cities in Munster rugby, it is necessary to set out and analyse the fate of the Munster Senior Cup in the era when the game went professional. Indeed, the evolution of the Cup's status and popularity eloquently demonstrates the cultural change that sports undergo in the context of their evolving commercial function.

In the build-up to Shannon's All-Ireland League semi-final tie against Garryowen in April 2008, the *Limerick Leader*, in a statement redolent of a different era, claimed that 'Local Limerick rugby derbies continue to capture the sporting imagination of the nation.'[8] Evidence of this enduring appeal, according to the *Leader*, was an anticipated crowd of 3,000. Rather than representing proof of the continuing appeal of the local rugby scene in Limerick, however, the predicted attendance was symptomatic of the precipitous decline in popular esteem that Irish club rugby had suffered in the previous decade. In 1992, Shannon's Munster Senior Cup ties against Garryowen and Young Munster drew an aggregate crowd of 27,000.[9] Indeed the early and mid-1990s represented something of a high watermark for club rugby in Limerick. Buoyed by the introduction of the All-Ireland League and the success of local teams in it, Limerick derbies initially retained their century-long allure. In general terms, the club game comprising the All-Ireland

League and to an increasingly lesser extent the provincial cups remained a priority for supporters and media commentators until Munster's significant breakthrough in the European Cup in 2000.

This assertion is again supported by spectator numbers. When Munster played Swansea in the province's first ever European Cup tie in November 1995, a crowd of 5,000 witnessed proceedings at Thomond Park. Just six months earlier 6,500 people had witnessed Shannon and Young Munster play out a 3-3 draw in an early round of the Munster Senior Cup.[10] This pattern persevered. In the 1996–7 season Munster and Wasps played before 6,000 spectators at Thomond Park, while that season's Munster Senior Cup final still managed to attract a crowd of 8,000 to witness a derby between Young Munster and Garryowen at the same venue. In the 1997–8 season, Munster's European ties against Harlequins and Bourgoin attracted an aggregate crowd of 13,000 while the comparable figure for two matches between Young Munster and Shannon in the All-Ireland League and Munster Senior Cup in the same season was 15,000.[11]

The first sign of change was the swift decline in popularity of the Senior Cup. For decades the prestige event on the Munster rugby calendar, the competition was, from the mid-1990s, beginning to be squeezed by the prestige of the All-Ireland League. Crucially, the Cup lost its status as the season's competitive climax to the All-Ireland League. From the mid-1990s, league success firmly supplanted the Cup in terms of clubs' ambitions – an assertion again borne out by crowd numbers. In 1991, the Cup final between Shannon and Young Munster drew 11,000 spectators to Thomond Park. When the same sides met in the final seven seasons later, a crowd of just 5,000 attended the same venue.[12] The four finals spanning the years 1991–4 inclusive drew an aggregate attendance of 43,000.[13] The equivalent figure for the finals of 1995–8 was 28,000.[14] In other words for the first four seasons of All-Ireland League competition, the Cup final was still capable of attracting an average crowd of just under 11,000. In the following four seasons, coinciding with the onset of professionalism, this average fell to just 7,000 and subsequently declined steeply. By 1999, Gerry Thornley, in advance of the Munster Senior Cup final, observed that 'Time was when the Munster Senior Cup ruled the roost during the end-of-season provincial cup fest, but now it appears to be a victim of the clubs' AIL success.'[15]

The inexorable decline continued into the twenty-first century. In 2000, what would once have been a much-anticipated weekend of rugby saw two Munster Senior Cup semi-finals between Garryowen and Shannon in Limerick and Young Munster and Constitution in Cork draw a combined crowd of less than a thousand.[16] Eventually, the competition's finale was dependent upon a rump of die-hard supporters as evidenced by the crowd of a mere 4,000 that witnessed Shannon defeat Young Munster in the 2002 final – a decline of almost two-thirds from when the teams met in the 1991 final.[17] By the mid-2000s, the once-prestigious Munster Senior Cup was largely an irrelevance to the bulk of the expanding Munster rugby constituency. From 2005, it was moved from its traditional season finale position in late spring to what was, in effect, a pre-season slot with the early rounds now played in September. The status of the competition among certain clubs in the late 2000s was clearly illustrated by withdrawals from the competition in 2009 and 2010 by Cork Constitution and Highfield respectively. Both clubs claimed that congested club and representative fixture calendars prevented them from fielding teams, with Highfield's Mick Carroll claiming that 'It's a case of priorities. Sadly, the Munster Cup is not what it used to be and for a club of our limited resources, the AIL takes precedence.'[18] The competition also fell into disrepute, with both Cork Constitution and University College Cork being thrown out amid fixture disputes in 2009 and 2010. A competition that matched and exceeded Munster's Heineken Cup attendances as late as 1997, and whose demise would have been unimaginable to the vibrant club system that had held it in such high esteem for such a long period, was now fading into insignificance.

The declining fortunes of the Munster Senior Cup were attributable to two factors. Firstly, the introduction of the All-Ireland League provided Munster clubs with a new outlet upon which they could focus their competitive energies. And secondly, the professionalisation of the provincial teams saw the club game repositioned as the 'third tier' of senior rugby in Ireland.

As already pointed out in Chapter 2, the All-Ireland League, amid some resistance from clubs, was inaugurated in the 1990–1 season. The media, assuming that the traditional dominance of the Leinster/Ulster axis would directly translate onto the new competitive club structure, considered Dublin's Wanderers favourites to take the inaugural title. Gerry Thornley of *The Irish Times*, marvelling at a training schedule that involved weights, stamina and speed work and taking into account the club's nine representatives on the Leinster squad, commented of the upcoming league that 'Only the best will survive and it is unlikely that . . . Wanderers will not be among the best.'[19] These expectations were confounded. A month after the league had started, seven encounters between clubs from Munster and Leinster has resulted in six wins for the former. This was merely a portent for the dominant pattern that was to emerge. By the end of the inaugural season, Cork Constitution were champions having defeated Garryowen in what was effectively a league decider while the much-fancied Wanderers were relegated. Limerick's First Division contingent was increased from two to three with Young Munster securing promotion from Division Two.

Limerick teams would go on to dominate the competition in the next six seasons with Garryowen and Young Munster winning a title each before Shannon won four in a row. The success of Limerick clubs was rooted in the traditional competitive culture of the game in the city. With the focal point of club rugby being hard-fought derbies played in front of passionate crowds and honed in the various cup competitions, Limerick clubs possessed a will to win unmatched by clubs from other cities. Dublin teams, accustomed to the affable atmosphere of the sub-urban ground and clubhouse, and whose senior provincial competitions were nowhere near as competitive as their schools vari-ants, struggled to cope with the hostile atmosphere at grounds such as Shannon's Thomond Park and Young Munster's Greenfields.

The All-Ireland League intensified derby matches in Limerick. A crucial First Division tie between Shannon and Garryowen in January 1992 drew an estimated crowd of 15,000 – a record for a club match in Ireland. Derby matches regularly drew crowds of over 8,000 and often above 10,000. These figures bring into sharp relief the dramatic increase in popularity enjoyed by the league in its first couple of seasons. In November 1990, for instance, one round of league fixtures attracted a cumulative crowd of 12,000 – a figure that was considered a vindica-tion of the competition at the time.[20] Crowd numbers were initially unaffected by the arrival of professionalism. In 1998, and with the provincial teams now offering professional contracts, a Limerick derby between Young Munster and Shannon was witnessed by 10,000 people while the All-Ireland League final between Shannon and Garryowen attracted an attendance of 15,000.[21]

The record set by Shannon and Garryowen in 1992 was surpassed twelve months later when Young Munster's encounter with St Mary's College, a league decider, drew a crowd of 17,000 to Lansdowne Road. The match was moved from St Mary's home ground at Templeville Road as its capacity of 5,500 could only cater for a fraction of the Limerick club's anticipated travelling support. Occasions such as these gave Limerick rugby culture, and all its associated fanfare, a national platform. Young Munster's victory, for instance, was widely perceived as being a triumph for one rugby culture over another: 'Two cultures collided. The genteel folk of St Mary's and the proletariat of Limerick.'[22] Young Munster entering Lansdowne Road, the bastion of the perceived snobbery that middle-class Dublin rugby implied, and emerging victorious was vindication of the peculiarity of Limerick rugby. This peculiarity was exemplified by the unorthodox behaviour of Young Munster fans on the occasion. Though a contingent of supporters managed to smuggle a goat into the ground, there was no such success for the club's most ostentatious supporter, an eccentric elderly woman called Dodo Reddan. Dodo was famous for parading through the rugby grounds of Limerick prior to Young Munster fixtures pushing a pram full of dogs bedecked in the black and amber of her beloved club. When she was refused permission to bring her canine companions into the Lansdowne Road grounds for the match, the press responded with opprobrium: '"A garda (pronounced gorda) let your goat in here some time ago" said an indignant steward. "It's illegal and so is the pramful of dogs. No way. No way." Who is it exactly that finds time to make laws which prevent goats from entering rugby grounds?'[23] This perceived slight served the Limerick siege mentality well and was further evidence in the popular mind that Limerick rugby was different than the rest of the country.

Though the All-Ireland League did much to amplify a long-standing Munster and, particularly, Limerick club tradition, the game underwent qualitative change in the years following the competition's initiation. With a nationwide club competition quickly garnering prestige, clubs felt pressurised to bring about cultural change, particularly in terms of training and preparation.[24] A symptom of this development was the arrival, in increasing numbers from the early 1990s, of overseas players into Irish club rugby. In 1994, the young Garryowen hooker and eventual superstar of Irish professional rugby, Keith Wood, paid the following tribute to his club mate and former All Black, Brent Anderson:

> He was a colossus to play with. He brought on everyone around him. He brought on the backs in their attitude to the game and the forwards on their skills and attitude to the game as well . . . before he came to Garryowen, there would always be a lot of shouting in the dressing room prior to kick off but this all changed when Brent arrived. The warm-ups became more careful and quiet with preparation for yourself. There is still some shouting today, but we are far more collective with our thoughts . . . this is the knock-on effect from Brent's understanding of the game.[25]

Though the role of overseas players would evolve in the years following professionalism, Anderson's encounter exemplified their initial function as a skilled caste of modernisers, bringing southern hemisphere expertise in training and preparation to the comparatively backward Irish club game. By 1992, Anderson was one of sixty-seven overseas players playing club rugby in Ireland. Amid whisperings of money exchanging hands, the IRFU threatened to ban the overseas contingent. According to Gerry Thornley, 'rumours such as "yer man is on 300 quid a week" or "so-and-so is on 18 grand a year" are proliferating . . .'[26] In 1992, the IRFU moved to curb this trend by introducing a twelve-week qualifying period and limiting to one per club the number of overseas players permitted to play competitively. In 1997, the regulations were relaxed somewhat with players resident in Ireland for two years being deemed 'native' and theretofore no longer subject to restriction. Though these regulations limited numbers, they did not stem influence. At Garryowen, New Zealand natives such as the aforementioned Anderson and John Mitchell and coach Murray Kidd contributed significantly to the club's All-Ireland League success while at Shannon, Rhys Ellison and John Langford (both of whom also played for Munster) were equally influential.

There is an extent to which clubs came to see southern hemisphere players as something of a panacea for inadequacies on the field and the training paddock. This faith was often misplaced. As former All-Ireland League player and journalist Hugh Farrelly recalled:

> I remember in the summer of 1997 the feverish excitement in Dolphin [rugby club] at the impending arrival of a 'giant Kiwi' from Southland. We had just gained promotion to Division One and were beefing up the squad for the season ahead and Steve Jackson, or the 'Messiah' as we dubbed him, was to be the fulcrum of our challenge. When he walked through the gates we were like tittering schoolgirls at a Westlife concert, even though he was a good bit smaller than the description we had been fed. It didn't work out . . . Nice guy and all that but I would rate his contribution to our season at around 2/10 . . . Two seasons later, we signed two more Kiwis, one was a 'six foot eight second row in the mould of Ian Jones', the other a 'tough tackling wing forward with a Kronfeld-like hunger for the ball'. Jones and Kronfeld? Try Mutt and Jeff.[27]

The presence of these southern hemisphere players in Irish rugby and the eagerness with which they were pursued heralded the proto-professionalisation of the All-Ireland League and was an important phase in the professionalisation of Irish rugby in general. Ireland's first professional national team coach was the New Zealander Murray Kidd, one of his successors was his fellow countryman Warren Gatland and the provincial teams all had southern hemisphere coaches appointed at some stage in the first fifteen years of their existence as professional entities.

As the delineation between the professional Munster team and the clubs that theoretically provided its players became clearer, the All-Ireland League began to suffer. The introduction of the Celtic League and the resultant congestion of the provincial teams' fixture calendars meant it was no longer tenable for elite players to serve their clubs on the field in any meaningful way. This was particularly the case with international players and players who regularly played in the European Cup. Straightforward market logic dictates that the removal of a competition's elite cohort of players reduces the quality of the product on offer. As with other trends in the professional era, the decline of the AIL was statistically evident at the gates. In the midst of Munster's Heineken Cup campaign in 2002, *The Irish Times* considered a crowd of between 2,500 and 3,000 for an AIL fixture between Cork Constitution and Shannon creditable. The same article pointed out that this attendance, far below those witnessed in the competition's heyday, was exceptionally large. Evidence of the latter was Constitution's meagre gate receipts of £68 that season for a fixture against UCD.[28]

By the mid-2000s, the position of the All-Ireland League became clearer. Though it could and, according to IRFU policy, should act as a feeder for the provincial teams, nurturing young talent and providing regular rugby for the academy players, it was permanently and unambiguously divested of the elite coterie of players that played regular Heineken Cup and Magners League rugby. When Munster, Ireland and Lions second-row Paul O'Connell turned out in the colours of his club Young Munster while recovering from injury in 2010, it was hailed as an occasion of great novelty. There was no pretence to accommodating the All-Ireland League to representative fixtures, and matches from both levels were now regularly scheduled for the same Saturday afternoon slot. This was a development that clubs gradually came to accept. In January 2011, Michael Moynihan of the *Irish Examiner*, reporting on an AIL fixture between Cork Constitution and St Mary's College, presciently observed that:

> The main rugby event on Saturday was a couple of miles west of Temple Hill in Musgrave Park, where Munster took on Glasgow a couple of hours after the AIL fixture. Although co-existing with the big show, rather than grumbling about stolen thunder, has taken Constitution a while, they've come to terms with their new status.[29]

Moynihan went on to quote Constitution's president, Der O'Riordan, who admitted that:

> 'Look, when professionalism came in first day we didn't know what to expect, what way it was going to fall . . . We didn't know if it was going to be twenty teams playing professional rugby or what.

It ended up the ideal way, with the four provincial teams, but we needed a bit of time to take that on board . . . At one stage we'd have had the attitude, 'they're taking our players'. But they're not – the players are theirs and they play with us…The mindset had to change. The days of a club player heading off once or twice a year to play for Ireland were gone and we've had to get used to the new way.'[30]

Administratively also, the club game became treated as a separate strand from professional rugby with the creation of, for instance, the Domestic Game Committee at IRFU level. In discussing the umpteenth structural change to the AIL in 2010, the chairman of the aforementioned committee, Steven Hilditch, conceded the obvious: 'I think we're putting in place something very positive but we will never again get to a point where 14,000 or 15,000 people are at an 'ordinary' shall we say AIL match.'[31] The status of club football fifteen years after the introduction of the professional game was vividly demonstrated in late 2010 when Young Munster and Shannon met in an All-Ireland League Limerick derby. Paul O'Connell, the Munster captain and talismanic international second-row, was recovering from injury and, as part of his recovery, lined out for his club, Young Munster. The presence of a player of O'Connell's stature and the scheduling of the match on a Friday under lights ensured an estimated crowd of 2,500–3,000 spectators attended the match, a very large crowd by contemporary standards.[32] That the equivalent fixture fifteen years earlier could attract a five-figure crowd and that the inclusion of senior representative players would not then have been a source of novelty neatly represents the status of the club game at the end of the first decade of the twenty-first century.

The rise of Munster Rugby

The most significant outcome of professionalisation was the meteoric rise to prominence of the provincial teams. As has been evident by the balance of emphasis in this book, the Munster representative team, much unloved for long periods, was traditionally nowhere near as central to the collective rugby mindset as the province's network of clubs. The market realities of the game's new dispensation after 1995, however, ensured that the relatively small-scale domestic club game was not a suitable foundation for professional rugby in Ireland. The limited cohort of players that were of elite standard would, therefore, need to coalesce around a small number of professional teams and the existing provincial representative structure provided a suitable model for such a development. The twenty-first-century success of the provincial teams should not blind one to the fact that in 1995, professionalising the provinces did not seem like an obvious means of preserving a meaningful domestic game.

Indeed, the Munster rugby team, despite its long amateur gestation, had a troubled birth as a professional outfit. In the period between the game going professional in 1995 and the appointment of full-time directors of rugby at the provinces in 1997, Munster occupied the ambiguous position of being an amateur representative team competing in a professional club competition.

Munster also had the challenge of convincing a somewhat doubtful public that they were worthy of the emotional investment that clubs had enjoyed a monopoly on. This was evident from Gerry Thornley's report of a match versus the Exiles upon which qualification for the inaugural European Cup hinged:

> Not that you'd have guessed it [that the stakes could hardly have been higher] from the less than deafening atmosphere around Musgrave Park generated by the 1,500 somnolent souls present. At the end of a hushed first quarter, the p.a. man startled most of us with the request that some disrespectful youngsters 'stop cheering during place kicks' after Paul Burke had landed his first kick. The surprise was that he didn't ask them to start cheering during the actual play.[33]

Once the decision was made to centralise professional rugby around the traditional provincial teams, there seemed to be a great deal of confusion as to how this team was to be administered and developed. Who would be awarded contracts? What would the value of those contracts be? Would they be part time or full time? How would the club game be accommodated among Munster's fixtures? An initial problem centred on who would coach the province. As was the contemporary fashion, the IRFU looked to foreign expertise but were spurned when first Welshman John Bevan and then New Zealander Andy Leslie refused the job having initially accepted it. Eventually Declan Kidney, a schoolteacher at PBC, was appointed as joint coach with Niall O'Donovan, Colm Tucker and Jerry Holland, stalwarts of Shannon and Cork Constitution respectively. Kidney took on the role of coaching director the following year. In its initial seasons, the province that Kidney was to coach was far from a fully professional unit. Initially the IRFU decided that one hundred contracts were to be offered to players on a tiered basis, with these in turn to be shared among the provinces. In July 1997, a total of seventy-six contracts were offered to players across the four provinces. Of these, Munster offered a modest fifteen: twelve part time and three full time. The full-time contracts were worth

£25,000 plus small win bonuses while the part-timers were to receive £7,500 per annum plus bonuses.[34] By late 1998 and with an infusion of cash from Sky Sports' coverage of the Five Nations, the IRFU had sufficient finances to contract twenty-one full-time and ten part-time players to each of the provinces.[35]

In the interim, however, the relatively parsimonious terms on offer to professional players in Ireland saw a large number of elite players on the island decamp across the Irish Sea to the parvenu English club game. In the year preceding the start of the 1997–8 season, Munster lost the services of several international and future international players including Richard Wallace, Paul Wallace, Keith Wood, Paul Burke, David Corkery and Rob Henderson.[36] Edmund Van Esbeck, somewhat dejectedly summarising contemporary developments in the autumn of 1997, railed against the lure of the English game: 'Irish rugby is a feeding ground for the English League . . . Last season what was on offer did not keep one Irish player at home. In the professional game players go where the money is and market forces obtain. Loyalty and money are not compatible bedfellows.'[37]

The fourteen months spanning the autumn of 1996 to the end of 1997 amounted to a dark period for Irish rugby. The international team, mainly comprising players based abroad, was performing appallingly. Bookended by defeats to Manu Samoa and Italy, the Irish team was also at the receiving end of a further defeat to Italy, a forty-point reversal at home to England and a heavy defeat to New Zealand. The summer of 1997 also saw the apogee of Brian Ashton's ill-fated reign as Ireland coach in the form of an infamous development tour to New Zealand, where an alarming gap in standards between the tourists and the hosts was exposed on the field.[38]

The principal problem domestically was the vague status of the provincial teams; they were neither fully professional nor amateur, they were neither clubs nor representative teams. This was further evidenced by the fact that players employed by English clubs could still, technically, play European Cup rugby for their provinces. When Shannon's Eddie Halvey joined English club Saracens in late 1995 on a contract reportedly worth £50,000 per year, the agreement included a clause allowing him to play for Munster in European competition.[39] In 1997, and in what amounted to a bleak prognosis of how professionalism would evolve, Gerry Thornley advocated making provincial players available to the fully professional London Irish club, noting that 'there was nothing to stop players from representing provinces in the European campaigns and thereafter [playing] in the English Premiership.'[40] Though players had received some payments for

European Cup matches on an ad hoc basis since 1995, professionalisation of the domestic game was proceeding in a piecemeal fashion.

At the beginning of the 1997–8 season, this state of flux was again well described by Gerry Thornley:

> All of the four provincial coaches and managers have been repeating this message mantra-like, and they know better than anyone what they're talking about. With squads of 30 or so, most have, at best, one-third of players who are full professionals, coupled with two-thirds who are semi-professionals . . . some 22 of their players are part-time and so still have the day job to take care of, during which time they are recovering from injuries, along with general wear and tear – and maybe even undergoing physiotherapy on their lunch breaks. This is not professionalism . . . Clearly the European Cup results show that Ireland only has scope for four sub-international squads to compete at this level. Given better performances, and even occasional appearances in the knock-out stages, the provinces' marketability is undersold.[41]

The idea that the club game could be completely decoupled from the provincial teams was clearly not feasible for an administrative structure made up of club representatives. This mindset was given voluminous public prominence in Edmund Van Esbeck's columns in *The Irish Times*. One of many examples was a piece in September 1995 when Van Esbeck asserted that

> . . . it is absolutely imperative that the AIL continues to be the basic element of the senior club game in this country as are the national leagues in the other home countries and France . . . There are some who believe that the AIL at least to some extent has lost its appeal as attendances fell, if not dramatically, at least to some extent last season in some areas. That, however, does not in any way diminish its crucial importance. Quite simply there is no club competition that would replace it . . .[42]

The process by which the provinces evolved into fully professional 'clubs' was, as a result of this collective mindset, an incremental process with professional players expected to remain focused on club commitments for several seasons after 1995.

Some commentators had a more realistic view of how the game should evolve. In 1998, Michael Larkin, reflecting on the contemporary state of flux of the domestic game, commented:

> . . . what is happening is far from the level of professionalism needed to succeed. The players are borrowed from clubs who still claim their first loyalty. No man can serve two masters and professional players must give full loyalty to the club/team who is paying them whether this is the province or a new club developed for the

professional game, and if it is a club wouldn't it be something to have a Limerick RFC that we could support in Europe! . . . if clubs follow the age-old tradition . . . and we fight amongst ourselves for local advantage while the rest of the world goes its own way we will be left perched at the edge of the game.[43]

Clearly the traditional prominence of the club game would have to be somewhat jettisoned if Irish rugby was going to succeed in the professional era. Moreover, the provinces would need to take on the structure of a professional administration. A significant step in this regard in Munster was taken in 1999 when a salaried chief executive was appointed for the first time. The position, when advertised, included in its remit: strategy and commercial planning, finance and administration, and marketing and sponsorship.[44]

Change, however, was slow and when success arrived it was despite the system rather than because of it. Ulster's win in the Heineken Cup final in 1999 was followed by two unsuccessful final appearances by Munster in 2000 and 2002. These achievements came in spite of the fact that players were still expected to play All-Ireland League rugby for their clubs – an expectation that became increasingly unrealistic as the provinces' stock continued to rise. In late 2000, Gerry Thornley observed that 'the clubs come a distinct third in the three-tier pyramid. And that's how it should be . . . At issue is whether they accept the inevitability of being without their international players, and even their provincial players on occasion, if AIL games clash with knock-out European games.'[45] Though pessimistic in tone, events would prove this analysis of clubs' future access to their elite players to be overly optimistic. With the introduction of the Celtic League in 2001 and its expansion to a home and away format in 2003, the provincial teams took on the appearance and feel of club-like entities. The domestic club game, in this context, found itself further marginalised. Clubs with a large cohort of contracted players, whose week-to-week availability was uncertain, began to struggle. It was scarcely a coincidence that Munster clubs' stranglehold of the All-Ireland League was broken in 2000, the year Munster reached their first European Cup final. In 2001, with seven contracted players still meaningfully on their playing roster, Young Munster struggled badly.[46] Brendan Fanning has astutely pointed out that as the European Cup continued to gather momentum, 'every surge in its power robbed the club game of more energy.'[47]

In the three seasons spanning Munster's unsuccessful final appearances, the popularity of the Munster team increased exponentially. This was clearly reflected in demand for tickets. In the early rounds of the

1999/2000 European campaign, one that would see Munster reach the competition's final, a home fixture against Pontypridd attracted 6,000 people to Thomond Park. Just over a year later, and with Munster already assured of a place in the quarter-finals, a crowd of 9,500 attended the team's final pool game against Castres in Musgrave Park.[48] From this point on, home European Cup matches were routinely sold out and overnight queuing for tickets became the norm for big matches. An estimated 35,000 Munster fans attended the 2000 European Cup final in Twickenham. When the province reached the final in 2006, an estimated 70,000 Munster fans made the trip to Cardiff and outnumbered fans of the opposition, Biarritz, by almost ten to one. By this time, plans were already in motion to increase the capacity of Thomond Park to cater for Munster's newfound popularity. The stadium, when re-opened, had almost doubled its capacity to over 25,000. Much in the contemporary style of stadium development, the new venue was designed for maximum revenue-generating capacity with ample corporate hospitality accommodation. As a multi-purpose venue, Thomond Park was now open for business as a rock concert and international soccer match venue.

A confluence of sporting and non-sporting trends led to a marked upturn in the fortunes of professional Irish rugby from 1998 onwards. Historians of sport usually, and often successfully, seek to link the success of a sport in a particular region to the prevailing social and economic conditions of that particular area in a given period. Gareth Williams, for instance, has convincingly linked a decline in the fortunes of the Welsh rugby team in the 1930s to mass working-class unemployment in depression-era Wales. In a similar vein, Phillip Dine has observed a close association between FC Lourdes' dominance of French rugby in the 1950s and a growth in the town's economy brought about by huge influxes of Christian pilgrims eager to visit the site where the Virgin Mary had allegedly appeared in 1858.[49]

In the case of Irish rugby, however, the success of the provinces and the international team from 1999 was, at best, indirectly linked to contemporary economic progress. Though the Celtic Tiger was crucial in maximising the revenue-generating capacity of the provincial team 'brands' and in sustaining crowd numbers at home and away fixtures, matters within the sport were of more immediate importance. In the first instance, a crucial ingredient in the twenty-first-century success of Irish and, by extension, Munster rugby was luck. This came in the form of a generation of players of unprecedented talent. Though this explanation may appear nebulous, it remains a fact that few generations of Munster and Ireland players were as talented as the one that matured in the first decade of the twenty-first century. Though scarcely a scientific measure of talent production, selection configurations of British and Irish Lions touring parties are one means of comparing the relative strength of elite rugby in England, Ireland, Scotland and Wales as these squads are theoretically selected on the relative merit of the four nations' elite talent pools. For the 1997 tour to South Africa, just four Irish players were selected: Peter Clohessy and Keith Wood from Munster, Eric Miller from Leinster and Jeremy Davidson from Ulster. When Clohessy withdrew, his place was taken by Paul Wallace, who had played for Munster before moving to England. For the 2001 tour to New Zealand, Irish representation increased to eight and included Munster's Keith Wood, David Wallace and Ronan O'Gara. This figure increased to twelve for the 2005 tour to New Zealand with Munster providing four players and in 2009, the touring party included sixteen Irishmen. Of the latter, eight, including the captain Paul O'Connell, were from Munster. These figures indicate that in this period Irish and, specifically, Munster players had never compared as favourably with their British counterparts.

Moreover, Munster's European Cup success was heavily dependent on the talent that the province's traditional catchment area could produce. Of the thirty-two players who started in European Cup finals for Munster between 2000 and 2008, twenty-two were from the province itself. In turn, eleven of these players were Corkmen, eight were from Limerick, two from Tipperary and one from Kerry. The remaining ten comprised two Irishmen from outside the province, five New Zealanders, two South Africans and an Australian. Though Munster did recruit from overseas, Doug Howlett was the only import that could credibly be classed as having been an international player of repute. Crucially, practically all of the native players began playing rugby before the onset of the Celtic Tiger and emerged from the Munster team's traditional sources of recruitment. The half-back pairing of Ronan O'Gara and Peter Stringer, for instance, had forged their successful partnership as mini-rugby players at Cork Constitution and subsequently as schools players at PBC. Forwards such as Jerry Flannery, Keith Wood and Anthony Foley had been successful schools players at St Munchin's in Limerick, while players such as John Hayes, Eddie Halvey and Alan Quinlan started their careers at junior clubs before graduating to senior rugby at All-Ireland League level. These are players who would most likely have played rugby irrespective of economic conditions or whether the game was amateur or professional.

If the Celtic Tiger was not a crucial ingredient in player recruitment, it most certainly provided the revenue needed for player retention, bolstered the marketability and popularity of the Munster team and, by extension, the Munster brand. Increased levels of disposable income, improved transport and road networks and cheap air travel all facilitated Munster's off-field success. In terms of the latter, for instance, Munster came to prominence in a time when the province's busiest airport in Cork saw passenger numbers more than double from around 1,500,000 in 1999 to over 3,000,000 in 2008.[50] In this context travelling away to support rugby teams was a realistic prospect for a larger cross-section of society, something that companies such as Ryanair gainfully took advantage of. In 2005, Ryanair launched a Dublin–Biarritz route early in order to coincide with Munster's Heineken Cup quarter-final against the French team that season.[51] The airline routinely scheduled extra flights for big matches and skillfully cloaked their commercial interest in rugby in the language of interprovincial banter. In 2009, when Leinster defeated Munster in the Heineken Cup semi-final, Ryanair offered Munster fans refunds of €100 for flights booked to Edinburgh in anticipation of reaching the final. A Ryanair spokesman claimed that 'Since many of these couldn't bear to watch the Leinster "Ladyboys" in Edinburgh we offer them the chance to cancel their flights and get a refund.'[52]

It is also likely that the evolution of Irish identity and the country's political economy in the Celtic Tiger era also contributed to the appeal of Munster. John Fitzgerald commented in 2000 that contemporary Irish success owed 'much to the enthusiasm with which Ireland . . . approached the globalisation of its economy and the opening up of its society to outside influences.'[53] In some ways, Munster can be seen as a sporting prototype of this development. The team's success was heavily dependent upon foreign capital in the form of Sky television's coverage of the Heineken Cup. In addition, Munster's success was not measured in domestic success but by performance in pan-European competition. Though an essentially local identity was very successfully constructed around the team, the manner in which this identity was sold was symptomatic of the slick, corporate machine-like efficiency that characterised much of the contemporary *zeitgeist*.

From the middle of the 2000s, more serious attention was given to Munster's merchandising capability. Club shops were opened to cater for ever-increasing demand for Munster merchandise and subsidiary brands such as the Thomond Park fashion brand and the Thomond Reserve selection of wines appeared. In acknowledgement of the fact that a large proportion of the province's new support base came from outside the traditional club system, and a Munster Supporters Club was established in 1999, offering a season ticket scheme. Though membership numbered a modest 500 in 2001, subsequent success increased that number to 11,000 by the end of the 2000s.[54] In 2007 Munster appointed a full-time marketing manager, Glyn Billinghurst, whose aim it was 'to build the club and put it in position to be the biggest club in the world'.[55] The scale of the Munster team's evolution as a professional club was evident in a *Limerick Leader* interview with former coach Niall O'Donovan in 2009 when he recalled: 'Our first game was in Dooradoyle against Leinster in 1998. Declan and myself, Jerry Holland as manager, Colm Tucker was an advisor and Dave Mahedy was fitness coach, that was the entire backroom team and there was less than 300 people at the game that day.'[56] That Munster versus Leinster would subsequently become a much-vaunted sporting rivalry would, in all likelihood, have been unimaginable to the crowd present that afternoon.

Conclusion

History and the modern 'Munster Rugby' phenomenon

'Munster is a state of mind or, if you like, a state of heart. And rugby is the great unifying force. This was true a century ago and hasn't changed'[1] Such were the sentiments of the celebrated Irish sports journalist Con Houlihan in the aftermath of the Munster rugby team's Heineken Cup final defeat at the hands of Leicester Tigers in 2002. Houlihan's comments typified much of the public discourse that began to surround the Munster rugby team as it became increasingly successful in European competition from the beginning of the twenty-first century. A consistent media image emerged which saw Munster rugby as being successful because it was unique. Relative to the rest of Ireland but particularly Leinster, Munster and the team's home ground in Limerick, Thomond Park, came to be seen as the spiritual nuclei of Irish rugby. This spirit was built upon notions of regional identity, community solidarity and humble social roots. Episodes such as the Munster team's victory over the New Zealand All Blacks in 1978 and the manner in which such events have been popularly positioned within a linear progression of a Munster rugby tradition have sustained the implicit assumption that the modern-day success of the Munster team is in some way a congruent outcome of the game's historical development in the province. This has been principally mediated through journalists in both newspapers and the plethora of populist monographs that have been published in recent years.[2]

The widely held twenty-first-century view of the Munster rugby 'tradition' is at odds with the findings of this book. In terms of popular identification, the preceding chapters have illustrated how local ties always superseded any provincial solidarity. Indeed localisation was the essence of Munster rugby. With loyalty to one's own city and club paramount, the administration of rugby in Munster was a fraught exercise at provincial level – an aspect of the game's history most vividly demonstrated, perhaps, by the management of the game's infrastructure in the province. Moreover, within the cities themselves, rugby in Limerick and Cork developed along distinct historical tangents with different social and cultural characteristics.

These divergent experiences were expressed most obviously, perhaps, in the varying socio-geographical appeal of rugby in the two cities. Put simply, rugby in Limerick was a game of the inner city, while in Cork, it had a clear suburban bias. Limerick rugby built upon and nurtured parochial sentiment. In turn, the pre-eminence of Garryowen and that club's ability to inculcate cross-class civic pride imbued Limerick rugby with a populist flavour facilitating a multi-layered identification with place. More importantly, the junior game had a strong *de facto* administrative structure, allowing rugby to stave off competition from other codes. Among Garryowen's founders were individuals who took an active interest in movements closely associated with working-class self-improvement, and the club's nurturing of junior Sunday rugby can legitimately be interpreted as an extension of this mindset. Charles Korr has commented of the early history of West Ham United that 'A shared interest surrounded the club, its players and supporters and also what might also be called its "role."'[3] This is a useful framework for considering the early significance of Garryowen. The club's pursuit of the best junior talent gave the social profile of its ranks a cross-class quality, while a shared sense of community pride among the middle-class men who dominated the club's committee meant that Garryowen resembled more a civic institution than a private club. The emergence of other senior clubs in the twentieth century, especially (the hitherto junior) Young Munster and Shannon only strengthened the popular cultural significance and the primacy of locality in Limerick rugby. Anthony Foley recalled, of his childhood in the 1970s, trips to Angela Cowhey's pub in St Mary's parish after his father had played in matches for Shannon RFC. The pub, club and parish remained synonymous with each other.[4]

The leading Cork clubs, by contrast, possessed much less in the way of association with place. This rootlessness gave Cork clubs something of the character of private recreational and social institutions for young gentlemen.[5] The junior game in Limerick, played on Sundays and giving rise to inter-parish rivalry, was not replicated in Cork. Junior rugby was limited to the second XVs of a small cohort of senior clubs whose members were spatially dispersed yet socially analogous in background. The game's adoption by elite educational institutions influenced its social character and rugby in Cork became a means of professional networking. Geographical configuration of clubs was, therefore, critical. For even though Limerick rugby attracted middle-class men of various levels in significant numbers, its penetration of inner-city communities brought individuals from the lower ranks of the social ladder into the game.

Any potential social homogeneity in Munster rugby is further diluted by the history of the game in provincial towns. Here the game was dependent on the enthusiasm of men with exposure to urban life satisfying the local demand for professional skills and devoting significant portions of their spare time to organising and sustaining rugby clubs. As the support for Sunday rugby among provincial town clubs suggests,[6] a critical mass of players and other administrators was most likely provided by retailers of different levels and skilled workers.

The respective histories of rugby in Limerick, Cork and the province's smaller towns represent three distinct strands within the province's social history. The intra-province social variations were as conspicuous, therefore, as any similarities. Yet the progress of Munster rugby in the professional era has led to a remarkable re-imagination of the game's history in the province – one that strives to underline social homogeneity. On the reverse of the commemorative DVD celebrating Munster's 2006 Heineken Cup victory, the following synopsis of the team's supposed uniqueness is given:

> Munster Rugby's proud tradition and competitive spirit have seen them emerge as one of the world's best supported rugby teams. For many of its fans, Munster is more than just a team, it's a way of life, and the 'red thread' of history that fuses its proud legacy with an honest style of playing has captured the hearts and minds of sports enthusiasts the world over.[7]

These sentiments, a slightly elaborated version of Houlihan's, can be read as the 'officially' marketed perception of Munster rugby midway through the opening decade of the twenty-first century and symptomatic of the dominant media discourse surrounding the team's success. This discourse, I would suggest, had a number of mythologised facets. Firstly, Munster's accomplishments, rather than being unprecedentedly novel, were seen as another chapter in a glorious tradition of success in which the 1978 victory over the touring All Blacks was the seminal moment. Secondly, Munster rugby was unique relative to the rest of the country. In Munster, and as already indicated, rugby was seen to inculcate a sense of community and place, symbolically enshrined in Thomond Park. Munster was seen as special because of its humble parochialism, awareness of its roots and the classless nature of the game in the south. Much of this was mediated through their apparent traditional domestic rivalry with Leinster – the highpoints of which were the 2006 and 2009 Heineken Cup semi-finals between the teams – and, in a rugby sense, the attendant cultural clash between the two provinces. When strung together, these mediated discursive threads have given the Munster team and fans a powerful sense of their own traditional uniqueness.

A brief analysis of the mythical components of the modern 'tradition' will serve to underline how the local variations and complex set of loyalties illustrated in the preceding chapters can easily become subsumed into an altogether more simplified historical conception to accommodate the needs of the present.

In a general sense, the shift in emphasis from club to province is worthy of note. This book has shown that in terms of Munster rugby, issues of interest to the social historian are predominantly accessible through analysis of the club game. The popular imagination was almost exclusively concerned with club rugby prior to the transition to professionalism in the mid-1990s, as exemplified by Charles Mulqueen's *Story of Munster Rugby* which was published in 1993. The book comprises seventeen chapters, thirteen of which are concerned with the workings of the club game and primarily the Munster Senior Cup. The Munster provincial XV and their record against touring teams form the subject matter of the remaining four. Significantly, the interprovincial championship, which accounted for the vast majority of the Munster XV's fixtures in the amateur era, scarcely merits a mention in the entire publication.[8] Apart from occasional jousts with touring teams then, the Munster rugby team ranked far below the province's constituent clubs in terms of popular identification. Indeed, as late as 1995 and in the aftermath of the province's maiden fixture in the Heineken European Cup against Swansea, one observer commented of the match: 'Munster supporters who normally support All Ireland League teams probably felt relieved that the two points on offer had no bearing on the fortunes of their favourite team and consequently had a thoroughly enjoyable afternoon.'[9]

As illustrated in Chapter 2, the representative XV was frequently most notable for becoming embroiled in the murky internal politics of Munster rugby. As late as February 1976, just two years before the famous victory over the All Blacks, the Munster Branch committee conceded that 'the present division of 3/2 North and South Munster in alternate years did not always lend to the best selection committee.'[10] Though the Munster team's historical competitiveness in matches against touring teams is beyond doubt, the position of some of these fixtures within the 'glorious' Munster rugby tradition takes on a different light if analysed within their contemporary historical contexts.

When Munster defeated Australia in 1967, the *Limerick Leader* commented that the game was played 'on a gluepot of a surface in front of a crowd that rarely got worked up . . . these Wallabies, fielding more or less their "second team", were a tired looking bunch.'[11] Indeed, one of the principal talking points surrounding the match was the non-inclusion of Garryowen prop Tom Carroll in the Munster team. Unimpressed with the official reasoning that Carroll was too light, the *Limerick Leader* observed that it 'would indeed be interesting to know the difference in weight between himself and [the player selected in favour] Phil O'Callaghan'.[12] No such weigh-ins were necessary for one *Leader* reader who diagnosed Carroll's non-selection in local vernacular: 'the reason for his omission, I would say, he had not got the pull behind him. Sure how could he have the chance with three Cork selectors? 'Nuff said.'[13] When a similar victory over Australia was achieved in 1981, the same publication commented that 'the quality of the opposition was to say the least suspect', with the Australians fielding 'very much a second string outfit'.[14]

The outstanding example of a past fixture being taken out of context for the sake of modern purposes is the 1978 victory over the All Blacks. In 2005, the mythical qualities of 1978 were underlined when the match was the subject of a 200-plus-page volume by journalist Alan English. The book strings together a chronologically disparate collection of anecdotes, mainly about Limerick rugby, and arbitrarily links them to a detailed account of the circumstances surrounding the 1978 victory, thus implicitly creating an historical continuum of a glorious Munster rugby tradition.[15] Significantly, the book's title, *Stand Up and Fight*, refers to a song that was only adopted by the Munster team in the 1999/2000 season.[16] Hence the anecdotes, the 1978 victory and the twenty-first-century context in which the book was written are all subsumed into one linear progression. Some of English's anecdotal material takes on a different light when analysed in specific contexts. The author's random mention of Ter Casey, for instance, presumably serves the function of underlining the egalitarian nature or 'ordinariness' of Munster rugby. Casey, a dock labourer, was part of a very successful Young Munster club side in the late 1920s and early 1930s and was selected to play for Ireland on two occasions – a notable achievement given the middle-class hegemony of Irish international teams. Yet at almost the precise moment that Casey was gaining provincial and international honours, and as described in Chapter 2, the Limerick press was campaigning for a breakaway body to administer Limerick rugby due to the perceived Cork bias in the selection of the Munster rugby team.[17] Moreover, the extent to which Casey and his teammates at Young Munster would mentally have conceived of 'Munster rugby' as a coherent sporting entity is highly questionable. This obvious disunity, therefore, renders spurious the implicit inclusion of Casey in the Munster rugby 'tradition'.

The 1978 victory has served as a useful chronological staging post for the dubious re-imagination of Munster rugby in more ways than one. The twenty-first-century mystique of Thomond Park, for instance, owes much to the All Blacks victory. It has already been noted in Chapter 6 that Thomond Park was in many ways a monument to inefficient planning, symptomatic of the historical administrative disunity of Munster rugby. Moreover, until at least the closing years of the twentieth century, the ground was most clearly positioned in the popular imagination as the site of important club fixtures and as the shared home venue for popular local clubs Shannon and Bohemians. When writing in the *Limerick Leader* the day after the 1978 Munster victory, Charlie Mulqueen's most instinctive point of reference was the local club game when fishing for comparison: 'Scenes reminiscent of those which marked Shannon's [rugby club] first ever win in the Munster Senior Cup in 1960 were witnessed by the record crowd at Thomond Park yesterday . . .'[18] Mulqueen stressed the typically boisterous atmosphere of Thomond Park in a style that prefigured much of the twenty-first-century eulogising of the ground. Yet Thomond Park owed its reputation in 1978 to intense club encounters in the Munster Senior Cup and was more famous as a graveyard of ambition for visiting Cork clubs than as a crucible of provincial identity. Indeed, the Munster team split their home games evenly between Thomond Park and Cork's Musgrave Park until well into the professional era. The 'sacred' ground in Limerick, beyond one fixture in 1978, had no cultural or emotional link whatsoever with the Munster rugby team prior to the onset of success in Europe. This lack of tradition is constantly inadvertently emphasised by journalistic hyperbole. In an article in the *Irish Examiner* in 2007 for instance, a rugby reporter having observed that 'there is solid substance to the argument that Munster rugby is consecrated, and is in the service of God', waxed lyrical on the subject of Thomond Park:

> Thomond Park has mystique, it has an aura all its own. It touches the Munster players in ways they cannot describe, it touches the fans likewise. It makes those players bigger, stronger, faster, it gives them power they never thought they had, but, conversely, it reduces the opposition, stifles them, handcuffs them, weakens them. How else to describe the concussive hit by little Seamus Dennison on Stu Wilson, in 1978? How else to describe the fact that, for the only time in that all-conquering tour, the All-Blacks

> were held scoreless? How else to describe all the massive Heineken
> Cup wins, the Miracle Match win over Gloucester, the demolition
> of Bath, the last-death win over Saracens, all games in which the
> Munster players were giants, the opposition reduced to ghostly
> imitations of themselves?[19]

John Bale has appositely observed of the sports stadium that 'It possesses . . . an authentic sense of place which is, above all, that of being inside and belonging to your place both as an individual and as a member of a community, and to know this without reflecting on it.'[20] The 1978 victory has clearly, in this sense, functioned as the foundation myth for Munster's 'traditional' prowess at Thomond Park.

Apart from being able to reflect on a proud playing record and celebrate its spiritual home in Limerick, the imagined Munster rugby community takes pride in its classlessness. The ubiquity of press comments such as 'the players are ordinary Joe Soaps, brought up in the local community and therefore conscious of the bigger picture'[21] and 'It's . . . been well documented that Munster players are playing for their parish, neighbours and families, and can scarcely walk down their local streets without being recognised'[22] are designed to inculcate a humble image of the team complete with a marked sense of place. In addition, Munster are seen to subvert the quintessential middle-class image associated with Irish rugby in general. Con Houlihan, who earlier stressed the century-long provincial harmony of Munster rugby, observed again in 2002 that despite its strong middle-class roots, 'rugby in Cork is now classless.'[23] Eoin Murphy, a journalist with *Star Sunday*, later made the exalted claim that 'the Munster squad comprises of players from all over the province that recognise no class system', before going on to give a list of clubs from Cork and Limerick in his 2006 account of the 'Munster rugby phenomenon'.[24]

This perception is brought into sharper relief when Munster are subject to comparison with their apparently more affluent rivals in Leinster. Kevin Myers recently summed up, in slightly exaggerated terms, the journalistic perception of the social divergence between Munster and Leinster: 'In the hacks' cliche view, Munster is more authentic, more vital, more plain people of Ireland, whereas Leinster is effete, lisping, insecure.'[25] Myers' irreverent outlook has been augmented by the views of specialist sport commentators. Gerry Thornley has characterised the Munster/Leinster rivalry as 'a clash of cultures',[26] while Tony Ward has described Munster's antipathy for their rivals thus: 'Leinster represent, to those outside the Pale [Dublin and its environs] what England do to the rest of the rugby world . . . The "fancy Dan" stereotype fits . . .' Ward goes on to implicitly apply historical connotations by describing the rivalry as a clash between 'two tribes'.[27] This journalistic commentary along with the lampooning of Dublin rugby by Paul Howard in his Ross O'Carroll Kelly series of books has facilitated the creation of a binary system of identification in which the two provinces represent divergent social constituencies.

The Munster/Leinster rivalry, ultimately, is a myth loosely based on reality.[28] It has already been observed in this book that one of the few issues upon which the Cork and Limerick rugby constituencies historically found consistent common ground was a mutual sense of grievance at what was seen as an anti-Munster bias in the selection of the Irish international XV. Both implicit and outright criticism of the international selection policy was frequent in the Limerick and Cork press throughout the amateur era and nurtured, in Munster, a sense of slight against Leinster rugby.[29]

Despite the bitterness emanating from Munster, however, a tangible popular rivalry between Munster and Leinster, involving players and fans alike, simply did not exist in the amateur era. The competition in which Munster and Leinster annually met, the interprovincial championship, palpably failed to capture the public imagination throughout its history. Crowds never consistently flocked to see the apparent rivalry between Munster and Leinster consummated on the field of play. Taking the decade that framed that 1978 victory, for instance, in 1973 a crowd of fewer than five hundred paid to watch Munster play Leinster in Cork. The following season, the *Limerick Leader*, without any recourse to phrases such as 'tribal warfare' or 'cultural clash', reported soberly that the meeting of Munster and Leinster had been 'one of the dreariest and boring that even the Interprovincial Championship, not exactly renowned for the high standard of entertainment that it throws up, has produced for some time'.[30] In the same year as the victory over the All Blacks, rivalry between the provinces was meagre, to the extent that the *Limerick Leader* was moved to comment after the Munster/Leinster fixture: 'there are those who believe that the Interprovincial Championship has outlived its usefulness. I'm not one of them and I don't believe that there are many in Munster who would like to see them pass by altogether, although a new system may be evolved which could give the series added appeal.'[31] In 1986, a Munster selector meekly admitted in the aftermath of a turgid interprovincial campaign for the team that 'we have never been the outstanding province. Munster has always suffered in comparison to Leinster and Ulster in terms of standards.'[32]

Given the lacklustre appeal of the Munster/Leinster rivalry and interprovincial rugby in general evident in these instances, it seems somewhat peculiar that modern commentators attach such retrospective significance to the apparent rivalry. Tony Ward, a television and press commentator whose playing career with both Munster and Leinster spanned the period covered by the above examples, suggested in 2008 that 'When red runs out against blue it is personal . . . the same as it ever was . . . Over the years, whether the game was in Cork, Limerick or Dublin, Munster against Leinster was always the main event.'[33] Given the recent admission of Liam Toland, another former player turned journalist, that the 2009 Magners League clash in Limerick would attract far more Leinster fans alone than the entire attendance at his Munster/Leinster debut in 1995,[34] it seems that any substantial rivalry between the two provinces is a very recent development. In that sense, the twenty-first-century creation of a binary identity system involving the two provincial rugby teams further fulfils the function of underlining the supposed uniqueness of Munster rugby and adds another compelling chapter to the mythical narrative.

As Chapter 3 of this book displayed, any assertions of widespread classlessness in Munster rugby are highly illusory. Seven of the eight Cork-born players on the Heineken Cup-winning squad in 2006, for instance, were the products of fee-paying education and were drawn from clubs with no traditional sense of locality. Clearly no latter-day parochial metamorphosis had occurred in Cork rugby and the same patterns of the game's social appeal that had taken root in the city more than a century earlier still held firm. If Munster was no monolith in terms of class, neither was Limerick. In fact, this book has clearly argued that what set Limerick and Cork rugby apart was the differing manner in which middle-class men in both cities felt that the game ought to function. The true heritage of Munster rugby's parochialism, therefore, is *one* aspect of the social history of *Limerick* rugby.

A more astute judgement of modern Munster rugby has frequently been posited by Tom Humphries. In 1993, Young Munster, a club, as has been observed, with a profound traditional attachment to locality in Limerick and a socially diverse player and fan base, defeated St Mary's College from Dublin to win the All-Ireland League. In 2006, Humphries' analysis of Munster rugby was somewhat at odds with that of the bulk of his colleagues inasmuch as he was able to draw a clear distinction between past and present:

> . . . we appreciate that for the men and women working in the coalmines and ironworks and assembly lines of Limerick the [Heineken] cup is a fantastic escape from the drudgery of everyday life. That alone makes Munster 'different' . . . It was only yesterday Young Munster were touchy about anyone calling their home

> patch the Killing Fields and Garryowen, their well-to-do neigh-
> bours, were slugging it out with them for the new-fangled All
> Ireland league and people used to injunct against any slagging of
> Limerick rugby because Young Munster were 'sound like.' Now all
> of Munster has appropriated Young Munster's soundness . . .[35]

The facetious and exaggerated tone of Humphries' language and his
famed distaste for rugby does not detract from the genesis of his
argument. What marginal classlessness or in this case 'soundness'
that existed historically in Munster rugby had, by 2006, been adopted
as a legitimate channel of description for the rugby tradition of the
entire province.

Reaction to Humphries' article was predictably hostile. One correspondent to *The Irish Times* caustically stated that 'his [Humphries']
facile understanding of Munster rugby would be amusing were it not
for the column inches it enjoys.'[36] This assertion is far greater testament
to the power of a popularly mediated historical discourse than it is to
the correspondent's 'understanding' of Munster rugby. Conboy has
asserted that the historical representation of nationality in the contemporary press is 'not just "a story which people tell about themselves in
order to lend meaning to their social world" . . . but one which can be
powerfully amplified by the mediation of these stories through the
pages of the popular press, entering into an extended dialogue as they
do with millions of readers every day with the symbols and the narra-
tives of community imagined historically'.[37] Issues of scale aside, this
paradigm is clearly applicable to Munster rugby. The amplification of
historical aberrations such as the 1978 victory over the All Blacks and
the creation of a self-perception engendering selective aspects of a more
complex past, in this case the apparent traditional egalitarianism of
Munster compared to Leinster, creates the sense of belonging cherished
by all 'imagined communities'. The requirement of nations to 'have
"oublié bien des choses"'[38] implies a selectivity of historical perspective
gainfully indulged in by media commentaries of Munster rugby. The
'phenomenon' that became Munster rugby from 2000 onwards was
rooted in the present. In the context of a society and a sport that changed
a great deal in the decades either side of the turn of the twenty-first
century, Munster rugby provided an easily accessible psychic sense of
place where a physical one was more difficult to realise.[39]

Munster rugby in context

Its traditional resonance with public school values, its association with
the British imperial mission and the dogged pervasiveness of

amateurism has given global rugby a homogenous historical identity that recent scholarship has begun to unravel and dispel. In reality the rugby world has historically been diverse.[40] While countries such as England and Scotland strived to maintain middle-class hegemony, others such as Wales, France and New Zealand facilitated mass working-class participation. Though the game played second fiddle to 'native' sporting codes in Ireland, Australia and North America, it was elevated to a position of national cultural importance in Wales and New Zealand. While the language of public school gentlemanly conduct influenced the game to some extent in all countries, violent confrontation and partisanship frequently defined the game for periods in Wales and France.

This regional study of Irish rugby has shown that most of the contradictions inherent in the game's global history were perceptible in differing levels within one province. In both Limerick and Cork, products of the British public school and ancient university system were directly involved in the early organisation of rugby and no doubt attempted to impose their own values upon the evolution of the game. Yet rugby in Munster was far from an imperial game. Indeed many of rugby's players and followers were most likely hostile to empire and in numerical terms, nationalists of different hues probably came to dominate club ranks by the end of the nineteenth century. There was no neat delineation between political outlook and sporting choice in Ireland. In addition, though aspects of the Muscular Christian ideology were apparent in discourses surrounding the game, inter-community partisanship directed the nature of Munster rugby to a much more obvious extent. Rugby was fluid. What provided one individual with recreational opportunities among those of similar profession and background provided another with a means of expressing community pride.

Another major finding of this book is that the character of rugby in Munster was a product of the social and economic context in which it evolved. As an urban game in a disproportionately rural society, rugby happily existed as a minority sport. The structure of the Irish economy and resultant demographic trends ensured that Munster rugby was spared the poisonous confrontations caused by professionalism in England and France. In Limerick and Cork the game followed divergent social tangents that mirrored different urban sporting patterns observed in Britain.[41] While the game successfully harnessed community pride in Limerick, it was part and parcel of middle-class ambition in Cork. The game's popularity in provincial towns was again intimately linked to economic structure. As trading centres for agricultural hinterlands, there was a clear demand for professional expertise of different varieties in provincial towns. The individuals who satisfied this need, most of whom presumably had exposure to urban life and middle-class education, merely brought their favoured sporting pursuits with them. From the mid-1990s, the coincidence of the Celtic Tiger, professionalism in rugby union, and increased globalisation of sport through mass media brought about colossal change in Munster rugby. Increasingly affordable air travel and the growing prestige of pan-European rugby competition gave Munster rugby a mass following it had never previously enjoyed. There was no historical precedent for the modern cultural resonance of Munster rugby. The 'red thread of history' so eagerly promoted in the era of satellite television and mass digital media was in reality a richly multi-coloured tapestry.

APPENDIX

A note on sources

It is only in recent years that Irish historians have slowly come to recognise the value of sport as a subject of enquiry. This has been visible in the inclusion of sport-related material in general works of synthesis. R.V. Comerford included an entire chapter on sport in his *Inventing the Nation*,[1] while Richard English's treatment of the GAA in his history of Irish nationalism (2006) is a good deal more satisfactory and nuanced than the efforts of Robert Kee in a work of similar scope published thirty-four years earlier.[2] Most impressive of all, perhaps, was the coverage given to a relatively wide range of sport in Diarmaid Ferriter's *The Transformation of Ireland*, where sporting themes are skilfully woven into the author's extensive exploration of Irish society in the twentieth century.[3]

Two developments have influenced the shift in emphasis in more recent works. Firstly, a tendency among historians in Ireland to recognise the significance of sport has no doubt emerged. From a position, perhaps, of being viewed as an object of frivolity, the Irish historical mind is beginning to grasp the social, political and cultural importance of sport. Critical to this progress has been the growth, from the 1990s, of a small body of professional historical work on the subject. The most pervasive theme within this literature has been the intersection between sport and identity politics in Ireland. In addition, a dramatic reconsideration of the history of Gaelic games has taken place. Works by Cronin,[4] Rouse[5] and Garnham[6] have strived (if not to decouple Gaelic games and nationalism) to present a critical view of the GAA's relationship with politics and also to encourage more analyses of the Association as a social and sporting body. The culmination of these efforts was the publication in 2009 of a landmark collection of essays that opened up several new avenues of enquiry into the history of Gaelic games.[7] Quality works on the social history of Irish sport, however, remain few and far between. Exceptions to this include Neal Garnham's *Association Football and Society*[8] and Tom Hunt's remarkable local study of Westmeath.[9] Heavily influenced by the work of British

241

historians, these books successfully analyse significant themes in Irish social history through the prism of sport.

Within this expansion of Irish sporting historiography, rugby remains largely ignored. The general surveys written by the journalists Edmund Van Esbeck,[10] Seán Diffley[11] and Charlie Mulqueen,[12] though containing useful detail, are limited in analytical ambition. Though some works have explored the relationship between rugby and national identity, particularly in the context of the game's thirty-two county structure,[13] little has been written on the social history of the game. Moreover, existing research has done little to challenge the pervasive perception that rugby has historically been a middle-class anglophile game. Indeed, the work of Michael Mullan, for instance, takes the assumption of a neat social and cultural binary division between Gaelic games and sports of British origin as the starting point for his work on the 'bifurcation of Irish sport'.[14] This paradigm also informs Patrick McDevitt's work on 'muscular Catholicism' in which the author states, for example, that:

> By creating the GAA, Irishmen were performing a deliberate act of heresy in the face of the cultural imperialism and political dominance of Great Britain . . . By repudiating the central rituals of the British imperial religion, they rejected the tenet that team games were symbolic of the superiority of British manhood.[15]

Rugby, by implication, is lumped together with a variety of sports of British origin standing at variance with the broad social appeal (Mullan) and cultural message (McDevitt) of Gaelic games. The validity of this assumption has not been corroborated by detailed academic research. Given the extent to which recent work has demolished historical pre-conceptions about Irish cricket,[16] this over-simplified view of Irish rugby is in need of detailed re-consideration.

Approaches in this book have also been heavily influenced by readings on the history of rugby football in other countries. My focus on the fluidity and localisation of the game has been informed by the work of Tony Collins on English rugby,[17] Gareth Williams on Wales and the home nations,[18] and Phillip Dine on France.[19] These works, along with volumes on the game in other parts of the world,[20] have proven that despite the ubiquity of its public school image, rugby is a game that has been experienced in a remarkably varied range of social and cultural settings in those parts of the world where the game took root. This book attempts to display how this varied nature could be experienced within one province and, ultimately, clearly aims to address a significant gap in the historiography of modern Irish sport and society. Minimal research has facilitated the blossoming of crass simplification and spurious myth-making in the historical discourse of Irish sport. This work has not only attempted to challenge static, one-dimensional assumptions but also to use rugby as a means of analysing the communities within which it was played and supported.

Sources and methods

A wide range of source material of varying usefulness was consulted in the research of this book. Newspapers, minute books, contemporary published work, trade directories and census returns provided the bulk of the primary evidence. Given that several dozen newspapers were operating at any given time in the province in the period covered by the book, an exhaustive survey of all press material would not have been possible. As this work is primarily focused on Limerick and Cork, newspapers from the two cities are cited extensively. In Cork, the unionist *Cork Constitution*, hostile to the GAA, gave rugby significant if not extensive coverage. The nationalist *Cork Examiner* was slightly more detailed but both papers certainly under-reported. As rugby evolved from a quasi-private pastime to a public spectacle, coverage in both papers increased. Rugby reporting moved from small notices in the news digest to detailed reports in the specialist sports pages. In Limerick, the *Limerick Chronicle* provided patchy coverage, while the more populist *Limerick Leader* covered rugby extensively. In addition, the *Leader* was the only newspaper that carried frequent editorial pieces on rugby. These, though treated with circumspection, were particularly valuable in assessing the social and cultural role of rugby in the city. Provincial newspapers were consulted on specific themes. The *Southern Star*, the *Nenagh Guardian* and the *Kerry Sentinel*, for example, provided useful detail for areas outside the two main cities where rugby enjoyed popularity.

The surviving minutes of the Munster Branch committee (1927–78) were a source of considerable importance. The minute books were remarkably detailed due to two factors. First, the slow turnover of officials and resultant administrative continuity of Munster rugby aided detailed record-keeping of meetings. In addition, the Branch committee oversaw practically every facet of rugby in Munster and sub-committees were rarely convened. A large volume of vital data, therefore, was available in the minute books and some 80,000 words in transcribed notes were taken from them. The minute books of the Irish Rugby Football Union from 1874 were also useful, although Van Esbeck consulted them extensively for his history of Irish rugby. Much of the information within the Union's minutes, therefore, was already in the public domain before research for this book was carried out. The minute books of Queen's/University College Cork RFC were the only club records to which the author gained access. Covering the period 1905–25, the minutes contained much useful detail and offered an insight into the internal workings of a rugby club in the opening decades of the twentieth century.

Methodological obstacles hampered the usefulness of census returns. Due to the preponderance of generic Catholic names on lists of rugby teams and officials and the inevitable replication of common names in cities, sample sizes were generally small. Moreover, the successful cross-referencing of names sufficiently esoteric to avoid replication cannot be deemed conducive to representative samples. Sample sizes as empirically convincing as those gathered by Hunt in his study of Wesmeath were never, therefore, going to be possible when researching population units as large as Limerick and Cork cities. Census returns have been employed, therefore, as a means of bolstering anecdotal evidence rather than as a significant statistical base for the socio-economic material in this book. In addition, the patchiness of press reporting and the size of the subject area precluded extensive quantitative research of the type pioneered by Tranter and successfully adapted by Hunt.[21]

Notes and References

INTRODUCTION

1 The following works, while wholly inadequate as explanations of why Munster rugby has changed, give a flavour of the characteristics of the modern Munster rugby 'phenomenon': A. English, *Stand up and fight: The Day Munster Beat the All Blacks* (London: Yellow Jersey, 2005); H. Farrelly, *Munster Rugby Giants* (Dublin: The O'Brien Press, 2001); E. Murphy, *Munster Rugby: The Phenomenon* (Meath: Maverick House, 2006); A. English, *Munster: Our Road to Glory* (Dublin: Penguin, 2006).

2 Much of what follows in this section is based on R. Holt, *Sport and the British: A Modern History* (Oxford: Oxford University Press, 1989); N.L. Tranter, *Sport, Economy and Society in Britain, 1750–1914* (Cambridge: Cambridge University Press, 1998); W. Vamplew, *Pay Up and Play the Game* (Cambridge: Cambridge University Press, 1989). One notable dissenter to this viewpoint is Allen Guttmann who argues that the creation of modern sport is linked to the embracing of the scientific *weltanschauung* in the West in the eighteenth century; see A. Guttmann, *From Ritual to Record: The Nature of Modern Sports* (New York: Columbia University Press, 1978).

3 For the classic account of this process, see J.A. Mangan, *Athleticism in the Victorian and Edwardian Public School* (Cambridge: Cambridge University Press, 1981).

4 See Tranter, *Sport, Economy and Society*, pp. 13–31.

5 See Vamplew, *Pay Up and Play the Game*, pp. 51–76.

6 For a comprehensive treatment of rugby and public school values, see T. Collins, *Rugby's Great Split: Class, Culture and the Origins of Rugby League Football* (London: Frank Cass, 1998) and T. Collins, *A Social History of English Rugby Union* (London: Routledge, 2009).

7 See T. Mason, *Association Football and English Society, 1863–1914* (Brighton: Harvester Press, 1981).

8 For an account, see N. Garnham, *Association Football and Society in Pre-Partition Ireland* (Belfast: Ulster Historical Foundation, 2004).

9 F. D'Arcy, *Horses, Lords and Racing Men: The Turf Club, 1890–1990* (The Curragh: Co. Kildare Turf Club, 1991), p. 139; T. Hunt, *Sport and Society in Victorian Ireland: The Case of Westmeath* (Cork: Cork University Press, 2007), pp. 39–74.

10 B. Griffin, *Cycling in Victorian Ireland* (Dublin: Nonsuch, 2006)

11 Richard Holt has recently reminded us that the GAA was founded at a critical moment in the global history of sport. See R. Holt 'Ireland and Victorian

Sporting Revolution', in M. Cronin, P. Rouse and W. Murphy (eds), *The Gaelic Athletic Association, 1884–2009* (Dublin: Irish Academic Press, 2009), pp. 33–46.

12 C. Ó Gráda, *Ireland: A New Economic History, 1780–1939* (Oxford: Clarendon Press, 1990), pp. 213–14.

13 Figures derived from W.E. Vaughan and A.J. Fitzpatrick, *Irish Historical Statistics: Population, 1821–1971* (Dublin: Royal Irish Academy, 1978), pp. 8–10.

14 *Census of Ireland 1901.*

15 Derived from Vaughan and Fitzpatrick, *Population*, pp. 32–5.

16 T.W. Guinnane, *The Vanishing Irish: Households, Migration and the Rural Economy in Ireland, 1850–1914* (Princeton, NJ: Princeton University Press, 1997), p. 122.

17 Bandon's population fell from 10,179 in 1821 to 3,122 in 1911 partly due to the decline of the local textile industry. See A. Bielenberg, *Cork's Industrial Revolution, 1780–1880: Development or Decline?* (Cork: Cork University Press, 1991), p. 119.

18 Guinnane, *Vanishing Irish*, p. 122.

19 Ibid., p. 123.

20 D. Fitzpatrick, *Irish Emigration, 1801–1921* (Dublin: Economic and Social History of Ireland Society, 1984), p. 4. The impressive scale of emigration is underlined on pages 5 and 6.

21 The percentage, in this case, of the cohort aged 5–24 that decreased from census to census.

22 Derived from Guinnane, *Vanishing Irish*, p. 102.

23 From 17.9 to 36.1 million. See N. Tranter, *Population since the Industrial Revolution: The Case of England and Wales* (London: Croom Helm, 1973), p. 42.

24 *Census of Ireland 1901.*

25 A. Fahy, 'Place and Class in Cork', in P. O'Flanagan and C. Buttimer (eds), *Cork History and Society: Interdisciplinary Essays on the History of an Irish County* (Dublin: Geography Publications, 1993), pp. 793–812.

26 Bielenberg, *Cork's Industrial Revolution*, p. 119.

27 Ibid., p. 124.

28 G. Ó Tuathaigh, *Ireland before the Famine, 1798–1848* (Dublin: Gill & Macmillan, 1984), p. 120.

29 J.J. Lee, *The Modernisation of Irish Society, 1848–1918* (Dublin: Gill & Macmillan, 1973), pp. 5–36.

30 M. Murphy, 'The Working Classes in 19th Century Cork', *Journal of the Cork Historical and Archaeological Society*, vol. 85, no. 241 (1980), p. 31.

31 Ibid., pp. 28–30.

32 S. Lewis, *A History and Topography of Limerick City and County* (Dublin: Mercier Press, 1980), p. 128. Originally published in 1837 as part of the same author's *A Topographical Dictionary of Ireland*.

33 Ibid., p. 124.

34 J. Hill, *The Building of Limerick* (Cork: Mercier Press, 1991), p. 150.

35 Ibid., p. 150.

36 See M. Cronin, *Country, Class or Craft? The Politicisation of the Skilled Artisan in Nineteenth-Century Cork* (Cork: Cork University Press, 1994), p. 6.

37 R.W. Breach and R.M. Hartwell, *British Economy and Society, 1870–1970* (Oxford: Oxford University Press, 1972), p. 382.

38 D. Fitzpatrick, 'The Disappearance of the Farm Labourer in Ireland, 1841–1912', *Irish Economic and Social History*, 7 (1980), p. 87.

39   See *Farming since the Famine: Irish Farm Statistics, 1847–1996* (Central Statistics Office, Dublin, 1997), p. 89.

40   Ibid., pp. 78–9.

41   S. O'Donnell, *Clonmel, 1840–1900: Anatomy of an Irish Town* (Dublin: Geography Publications, 1998), pp. 18–21.

42   In the case of Cork and the surrounding region, see D. Dickson, *Old World Colony: Cork and South Munster, 1630–1830* (Cork: Cork University Press, 2005), pp. 420–2.

43   In the broader Irish context, Rouse has made a convincing case for this viewpoint. See P. Rouse, '*Sport* and Ireland in 1881', in A. Bairner (ed.), *Sport and the Irish: Histories Identities, Issues* (Dublin: University College Dublin Press, 2005), pp. 7–11.

44   Mangan, *Athleticism*.

45   I. D'Alton, 'Keeping Faith: An Evocation of the Cork Protestant Character, 1820–1920', in O'Flanagan and Buttimer, *Cork History and Society*, p. 781.

46   T. West, *Midleton College: A Tercentenary History* (Cork: T. West, 1996), pp. 26–7.

47   G. Williams, 'Rugby Union', in T. Mason (ed.), *Sport in Britain: A Social History* (Cambridge: Cambridge University Press, 1988), p. 321.

48   See, for example, *Cork Constitution*, 5 January 1870.

49   West, *Midleton College*, pp. 26–7.

50   Lee, *Modernisation*, p. 13.

51   J.W.P. Rowledge, *A Regional History of Railways. Vol. 16: Ireland* (Cornwall: Atlantic Transport Publications, 1995), pp. 244–5.

52   S.C. Jenkins, *The Cork, Blackrock and Passage Railway* (Oxford: Oakwood Press, 1993), p. 37.

53   Ibid.

54   Rowledge, *Railways*, pp. 244–5.

55   For the social and political aspects of Irish rail development, see K. O'Connor, *Ironing the Land: The Coming of the Railways to Ireland* (Dublin: Gill & Macmillan, 1999).

56   T. Ferris, *Irish Railways: A New History* (Dublin: Gill & Macmillan, 2008), p. 46; Rowledge, *Railways*, pp. 103–24.

57   Lee, *Modernisation*, p. 13.

58   Ibid., p. 74.

1. Origins

1   R. Holt, 'Working-Class Football and the City: The Problem of Continuity', *British Journal of Sports History*, vol. 3, no. 1 (1986), p. 5.

2   For a broad-ranging analysis of pre-modern leisure, see H. Cunningham, *Leisure in the Industrial Revolution* (London: Croom Helm, 1980). The adaptation of pre-modern sport to modern society has been clearly elucidated in Holt, *Sport and the British*, pp. 57–73.

3   This could vary within one region, as was the case with Cornish hurling. See N. Elias and E. Dunning, *The Quest for Excitement: Sport and Leisure in the Civilising Process* (Oxford: Blackwell, 1986), pp. 184–8.

4   Collins, *Rugby's Great Split*, pp. 1–5; Mason, *Association Football*, pp. 9–20; D. Russell, *Football and the English: A Social History of Association Football in England, 1863–1995* (Preston: Carnegie Publishing, 1997), pp. 5–21.

5   For a full account of this process, see Mangan, *Athleticism*.

6   Russell, *Football*, p. 9.

7   N.L. Tranter, 'The Chronology of Organised Sport in Nineteenth-Century Scotland. Part I: Patterns', *International Journal of the History of Sport*, vol. 7, no. 2 (1990), p. 192.

8   Collins, *Rugby's Great Split*, p. 7. For an historiographical discussion of the Webb Ellis myth, see D. Booth, *The Field: Truth and Fiction in Sport History* (London: Routledge, 2005), pp. 116–18.

9   See *The Irish Times*, 23 January 1968.

10 E. Van Esbeck, *One Hundred Years of Irish Rugby* (Dublin: Gill & Macmillan, 1974), p. 7.

11 *The Irish Times*, 26 November 1962.

12 N. Garnham, *The Origins and Development of Football in Ireland, Being a Reprint of R.M. Peter's Irish Football Annual, 1880* (Belfast: Ulster Historical Foundation, 1999), p. 4.

13 Ibid., p. 2; J. Mahon, *A History of Gaelic Football* (Dublin: Gill & Macmillan, 2000), p. 1.

14 *Freeman's Journal*, 28 January 1764.

15 *Freeman's Journal*, 20 April 1793.

16 *Freeman's Journal*, 25 July 1839.

17 *The Irish Times*, 2 September 1865.

18 *The Irish Times*, 20 October 1866.

19 For a critique, see D.L Andrews, 'Welsh Indigenous! And British Imperial? Rugby, Culture and Society, 1890–1914', *Journal of Sport History*, vol. 18, no. 3 (Winter 1991), pp. 335–49.

20 The mythical historical lineage claimed by historians of Gaelic games has been critiqued by Mike Cronin. See, for example, M. Cronin, 'Fighting for Ireland, Playing for England? The Nationalist History of the Gaelic Athletic Association and the British Influence on Irish Sport', *International Journal of the History of Sport*, vol. 15, no. 3 (December 1998), pp. 35–56.

21 *Limerick Leader* (hereunder 'LL'), 7 November 1936.

22 Ibid.

23 *Sunday Independent*, 4 August 2002.

24 Elias and Dunning, *The Quest for Excitement*, pp. 186–7.

25 *The Irish Times*, 23 January 1968.

26 P.D. Mehigan, *History of Gaelic Football*, quoted in E. Corry, *Catch and Kick* (Dublin: Poolbeg, 1989), pp. 5–6.

27 *The Irish Times*, 17 September 1946.

28 T. Hayes, 'Hurling', in T. Collins, J. Martin and W. Vamplew, *Encyclopedia of Traditional British Rural Sports* (London: Routledge, 2005), p. 167.

29 *Cork Examiner* (hereunder 'CE'), 21 April 1874.

30 *CE*, 28 April 1874.

31 *Tralee Chronicle*, 15 April 1879.

32 *Kerry Sentinel*, 19 January 1878.

33 *Tralee Chronicle*, 1 October 1878.

34 *Kerry Sentinel*, 24 January 1878.

35 *Tralee Chronicle*, 4 November 1879.

36 *Kerry Sentinel*, 18 October 1878.

37 Corry, *Catch and Kick*, p. 7.

38 National Library of Ireland (hereafter NLI), MS 9515, Account Book and Records of Kilruane Football Club, 1876–1880.

39 Partrick Bracken has noted as much. See P. Bracken, *Foreign and Fantastic Field*

Sports: Cricket in County Tipperary (Thurles: Liskaveen Books, 2004), p. 71.

40 *Guy's Postal Directory of Munster, 1886* (Cork: Francis Guy and Co., 1886), p. 48.

41 NLI, MS 9515.

42 *Guy's Postal Directory, 1886*, p. 746.

43 Ibid., p. 197.

44 IRFU Minutes, 6 December 1876.

45 NLI, MS 9515.

46 *CE*, 26 February 1878.

47 *CE*, 12 March 1878.

48 Van Esbeck, *Irish Rugby*, p. 10.

49 Adrian Harvey, on the balance of evidence, favours the claim of Trinity above that of Guy's Hospital. See A. Harvey, 'The Oldest Rugby Club in the World?' *Sport in History*, vol. 26, no. 1 (April 2006), pp. 150–2.

50 Van Esbeck, *Irish Rugby*, p. 15.

51 *The Irish Times*, 6 December 1860.

52 *The Irish Times*, 20 November 1867.

53 Ibid.

54 Van Esbeck, *Irish Rugby*, p. 16.

55 T. West, *The Bold Collegians: The Development of Sport in Trinity College Dublin* (Dublin: Lilliput Press, 1991), p. 26.

56 *The Irish Times*, 12 December 1863, 10 June 1865.

57 Garnham, *Origins and Development of Football in Ireland*, p. 5.

58 Van Esbeck, *Irish Rugby*, p. 19.

59 *Sport*, 11 February 1882.

60 Van Esbeck, *Irish Rugby*, p. 24.

61 *Munster Branch Irish Rugby Football Union: Official Fixtures and Information Booklet, Season 2003–2004*, p. 61.

62 IRFU Minutes, List of affiliated clubs, 1884–5.

63 West, *Midleton College*, p. 23.

64 Ibid.

65 *CE*, 21 February 1873.

66 *CE*, 7 December 1874, 5 January 1876.

67 The theme of rugby and suburbanisation is fully explored in Chapter 3.

68 IRFU Minutes, 3 March 1875.

69 IRFU Minutes, 19 March 1875, 4 October 1876.

70 *The Irish Times*, 10 October 1876.

71 IRFU Minutes, 15 October 1877.

72 *The Irish Times*, 3 March 1876.

73 *The Irish Times*, 3 April 1876.

74 University College Cork Archives, College Register.

75 Corry, *Catch and Kick*, p. 7.

76 Marcus de Burca, *The GAA: A History* (Dublin: Gill & Macmillan, 1999), pp. 5–14.

77 Hunt, *Westmeath*, pp. 124–5.

78 Bracken, *Foreign and Fantastic Field Sports*, pp. 56–70.

79 P. Dine, *French Rugby Football: A Cultural History* (Oxford: Berg 2001).

80 J. Phillips, 'The Hard Man: Rugby and the Formation of Male Identity in New Zealand', in John Nauright and T.J.L. Chandler (eds), *Making Men: Rugby and Masculine Identity* (London: Frank Cass, 1996), p. 71. It is important, however, not to overstress the importance of the rural 'pioneer' dynamic in New

Zealand rugby as Phillips has been accused of doing. See G. Ryan, 'Rural Myth and Urban Actuality: The Anatomy of All Black and New Zealand Rugby, 1884–1938', in G. Ryan (ed.), *Tackling Rugby Myths: Rugby and New Zealand Society, 1854–2004* (Dunedin: University of Otago Press, 2005), pp. 33–54.

81 Similar to the pattern observed by Tranter in the case of Stirling. See N.L. Tranter, 'The Chronology of Organised Sport in Nineteenth-Century Scotland: A Regional Study. Part III: Causes', *International Journal of the History of Sport*, vol. 7, no. 3 (1990), p. 365.

2. Overview since 1880

1 Garnham, *Origins and Development of Football in Ireland*, p. 65.
2 Ibid.
3 Ibid., p. 84.
4 See *Guy's Postal Directory of Munster 1886*, p. 456.
5 Garnham, *Origins and Development of Football in Ireland*, p. 76.
6 Ibid., pp. 68–70.
7 Ibid., pp. 104–20.
8 Ibid., p. 104.
9 M. Quane, 'Ennis Grammar School', *North Munster Antiquarian Journal*, 10 (1966), p. 43.
10 *Cork Constitution*, 4 October 1881.
11 *Cork Constitution*, 4 February 1882.
12 *Cork Constitution*, 22 February 1882.
13 *Cork Constitution*, 19 October 1882.
14 See below, pp. 113–14.
15 A. Metcalfe, 'Football in the Mining Communities of East Northumberland, 1882–1914', *International Journal of the History of Sport*, vol. 5, no. 3 (1988), pp. 269–91.
16 Hunt, *Westmeath*.
17 Ibid., p. 227.
18 A. O'Riordan, 'The Diffusion of Selected Team Sports in Cork, 1858–1995', unpublished MA thesis, National University of Ireland Cork, 1997, p. 50.
19 See below Chapter 3.
20 For a full expansion of this theme, see ibid.
21 *Cork Constitution*, 11 January 1886.
22 *Sport*, 30 September 1897.
23 *Sport*, 6 November 1886.
24 *Sport*, 3 December 1887.
25 *Sport*, 19 December 1891, 26 December 1891.
26 *Southern Star*, 22 January 1898.
27 *LL*, 15 November 1899.
28 *Sport*, 4 February 1893.
29 *CE*, 9 November 1910.
30 *Sport*, 21 October 1882.
31 *Kerry Sentinel*, 6 March 1895.
32 *LL*, 18 March 1899.
33 *Sport*, 11 October 1890.
34 *Sport*, 29 November 1890.
35 *Southern Star*, 24 November 1894.
36 *Southern Star*, 4 December 1897.

37 *Kerry Sentinel*, 11 November 1884.
38 *Southern Star*, 18 July 1896.
39 *Southern Star*, 7 November 1896.
40 *Nenagh Guardian*, 29 September 1906.
41 *CE*, 7 March 1894.
42 *Cork Constitution*, 27 January 1903.
43 *Cork Sportsman*, 29 January 1910.
44 *Sport*, 20 October 1888.
45 *Sport*, 11 April 1891.
46 *Sport*, 7 October 1893.
47 C. Mulqueen, *The Murphy's Story of Munster Rugby* (Cork, 1993), pp. 121–3.
48 UCC RFC Minutes, 10 October 1911. UC/MB/CS/RF/1.
49 *CE*, 8 February 1895.
50 *The Irish Times*, 24 January 1896.
51 *Weekly Irish Times*, 28 September 1901.
52 *CE*, 27 December 1909; *LL*, 12 April 1911.
53 See Chapter 6.
54 Ibid.
55 IRFU Minutes, 2 November 1877, 20 November 1878, 12 February 1879, 11 June 1879. IRFU M/01.
56 *The Irish Times*, 24 October 1879.
57 *LL*, 14 April 1924.
58 Van Esbeck, *Irish Rugby*, p. 60.
59 *Sport*, 25 January 1890.
60 *Sport*, 26 January 1895; *CE*, 24 January 1895.
61 *CE*, 4 February 1895.
62 *LL*, 24 January 1898.
63 IRFU Minutes, Clubs 1884–5. IRFU M/03.
64 IRFU Minutes, Clubs 1884–5. IRFU M/03.
65 *Sport*, 23 October 1886, 30 October 1886.
66 *Sport*, 11 December 1886.
67 *Sport*, 19 January 1889.
68 *The Irish Times*, 19 January 1891.
69 *Sport*, 19 January 1889.
70 *The Irish Times*, 25 January 1892.
71 *Sport*, 27 January 1894.
72 *LL*, 13 January 1909
73 *LL*, 9 January 1911.
74 *LL*, 9 December 1912.
75 IRFU Minutes, 1 January 1907. IRFU M/03.
76 *Cork Sportsman*, 26 December 1908.
77 *Cork Sportsman*, 30 January 1909.
78 *CE*, 21 September 1910.
79 *LL*, 10 October 1910.
80 Tranter, *Sport, Economy and Society*, p. 13.
81 See Chapter 6.
82 *LL*, 27 November 1905.
83 *CE*, 2 February 1914.
84 UCC RFC Minutes, 3 February 1915. UC/MB/CS/RF/2.
85 *The Quarryman*, vol. 3, no. 1 (December 1915).

86　*LL*, 4 November 1916.

87　*LL*, 9 November 1914.

88　*CE*, 13 November 1914.

89　UCC RFC Minutes, 22 November 1915. UC/MB/CS/RF/2.

90　Van Esbeck, *Irish Rugby*, p. 91.

91　*The Irish Times*, 31 May 1915.

92　Van Esbeck, *Irish Rugby*, pp. 77–80.

93　Collins, *English Rugby Union*, p. 49.

94　H. Hanna, *The Pals at Suvla Bay* (Dublin: E. Ponsonby Limited, 1916), p. 14.

95　Quoted in ibid., p. 29.

96　This is a remark frequently made in general terms about Irish recruitment. See, for example, P. Orr, *Field of Bones: An Irish Division in Gallipoli* (Dublin: Lilliput Press, 2006), pp. 14–22.

97　Ibid., p. 16.

98　Occupations taken from 1911 census enumerator forms.

99　UCC RFC Minutes, Annual Report 1914–15. UC/MB/CS/RF/2.

100　See P. Orr, '200,000 Volunteers', in J. Horne (ed.), *Our War: Ireland and the Great War* (Dublin: Royal Irish Academy, 2008), pp. 63–94.

101　For a discussion in the Irish context, see M. Staunton, 'The Royal Munster Fusiliers in the Great War, 1914–1919', unpublished MA thesis, University College Dublin, 1986, pp. 75–86.

102　*University College Cork Record of Students Past and Present Engaged in the War 1914–1919* (Cork: University College Cork, 1919). University College Cork Archives.

103　*The Quarryman*, vol. 3, no. 1 (December 1915).

104　See Staunton, 'Royal Munster Fusiliers'.

105　*LL*, 29 December 1916. Census enumerator form 1911.

106　*LL*, 17 September 1915. Census enumerator form 1911.

107　See below, p. 101.

108　*LL*, 13 December 1918, 5 May 1919.

109　R. Graves, *Goodbye to All That* (London: Penguin, 1960), p. 229.

110　See Chapter 5.

111　*The Irish Times*, 24 January 1921.

112　IRFU Minutes, 15 March 1920. IRFU M/03.

113　UCC RFC Minutes, Secretary's Report, 1920–1. UC/MB/CS/RF/2

114　UCC RFC Minutes, Secretary's Report, 1921–2. UC/MB/CS/RF/3.

115　UCC RFC Minutes, 29 January 1923. UC/MB/CS/RF/3.

116　P. Hart, *The IRA and its Enemies: Violence and Community in County Cork, 1916–1923* (Oxford: Oxford University Press, 1998), p. 103.

117　Ibid.

118　*The Irish Times*, 4 January 1924.

119　Munster Branch Committee Minutes (hereunder 'MBCM'), 6 October 1927.

120　MBCM, 6 January 1928.

121　MBCM, 15 November 1928.

122　*The Irish Times*, 7 March 1925.

123　MBCM, 15 November 1928.

124　*LL*, 9 October 1926.

125　*LL*, 28 September 1935.

126　*LL*, 20 February 1937.

127　IRFU Papers, List of Munster clubs, gate receipts and numbers of members. Undated (c.1932). F/060

128 MBCM, 1927–32, List of affiliated clubs.

129 Various, *Christians: The First Hundred Years* (Cork, 1989), p. 57.

130 This victory is analysed in further detail in Chapter 3.

131 IRFU Minutes, 15 June 1921. IRFU M/03.

132 *The Irish Times*, 16 April 1928.

133 *The Irish Times*, 8 December 1930.

134 IRFU Papers, List of Munster clubs, gate receipts and numbers of members. Undated (c.1932). F/060.

135 *LL*, 10 December 1924.

136 *LL*, 2 December 1932.

137 *LL*, 14 January 1933.

138 Ibid.

139 This is discussed fully in Chapter 6.

140 *LL*, 11 January 1941. The interprovincial match between Munster and Leinster in 1944 was cancelled because of interrupted train services. See *CE*, 18 April 1944.

141 MBCM, AGM 1942.

142 *LL*, 22 February 1941.

143 *LL*, 6 January 1943.

144 *LL*, 21 September 1940.

145 MBCM, 27 November 1940.

146 MBCM, 23 April 1942.

147 MBCM, 10 June 1943.

148 MBCM, 3 December 1942.

149 *The Irish Times*, 6 October 1945.

150 MBCM, 8 February 1944.

151 MBCM, 10 April 1944.

152 MBCM, 10 June 1943, AGM 1943.

153 P.J. Lynch to Rupert Jeffares, 29 June 1943. IRFU Papers, F/100.

154 MBCM, 11 June 1953.

155 Though the 1960s is often singled out as a decade of unprecedented change in Ireland, apportioning static timeframes to gradual processes is flawed. See B. Fallon, *An Age of Innocence: Irish Culture, 1930–1960* (Dublin: Gill & Macmillan, 1999), p. 257.

156 For the effect of broadcasting on sport in a British context, see J. Hill, *Sport, Leisure and Culture in Twentieth-Century Britain* (Basingstoke: Palgrave, 2002), pp. 47–53.

157 For an overview, see D. Ferriter, *The Transformation of Ireland, 1900–2000* (Dublin: Profile Books, 2005), pp. 540–50; see also R.F. Foster, *Luck and the Irish: A Brief History of Change* (London: Allen Lane, 2007), pp. 7–36.

158 For the English context, see Collins, *Rugby Union*, pp. 183–93. For an example of the effect of evolving mass media on sport, see Russell, *Football and the English*, pp. 195–200.

159 MBCM, 12 October, 1967, 19 January 1968.

160 MBCM, AGM, 6 December 1969.

161 MBCM, 13 November 1969, 9 April 1970.

162 *Munster Rugby News*, vol. 3, no. 1 (October 1993), p. 12.

163 MBCM, 14 September 1972.

164 See N. Carter, *The Football Manager: A History* (London: Routledge, 2006), pp. 83–4.

165 D. McAnallen, '"The Greatest Amateur Association in the World?" The GAA and Amateurism', in Cronin, Murphy and Rouse, *The Gaelic Athletic Association*, pp. 157–83.

166 Collins, *Rugby Union*, p. 186; Dine, *French Rugby*, p. 119.

167 MBCM, 1 October 1965.

168 MBCM, 26 November 1965.

169 MBCM, 28 September 1966.

170 MBCM, 16 June 1967.

171 MBCM, 3 May 1973.

172 MBCM, 14 September 1972, 16 May 1974.

173 McAnallen, '"The Greatest Amateur Association in the World?"' p. 176.

174 MBCM, 11 November 1976.

175 *Munster Rugby News*, vol. 4, no. 1 (September 1994), p. 22.

176 C. Ó Gráda, *A Rocky Road: The Irish Economy since the 1920s* (Manchester: Manchester University Press, 1997), p. 115.

177 MBCM, 10 October 1974.

178 This point is expanded in the concluding chapter.

179 *The Irish Times*, 26 November 1984.

180 *The Irish Times*, 9 March 1985.

181 *The Irish Times*, 16 April 1985.

182 *Irish Independent*, 19 October 1985.

183 For a useful account, see B. Fanning, *From There to Here: Irish Rugby in the Professional Era* (Dublin: Gill & Macmillan, 2007); see also L. O'Callaghan and M. Cronin, '"Without its Clubs, Rugby Union is Nothing": Resisting and Embracing Professional Rugby in Ireland', in G. Ryan (ed.), *The Changing Face of Rugby: The Union Game and Professionalism since 1995* (Newcastle: Cambridge Scholars Press, 2008), pp. 130–46. This subject and its effects on Munster rugby will provide much of the subject matter for the Conclusion.

184 See T. Collins, 'The First Principle of our Game: The Rise and Fall of Amateurism, 1886–1995', in Ryan, *The Changing Face of Rugby*, pp. 1–19.

185 *The Irish Times*, 3 June 1995.

186 O'Callaghan and Cronin, '"Without its Clubs, Rugby Union is Nothing"', pp. 143–4.

187 See Conclusion.

3. Class and Community

1 *Cork Constitution*, 13 February 1903.

2 *Cork Constitution*, 11 February 1903, 13 February 1903.

3 Quoted in *Cork Constitution*, 11 February 1903.

4 See, for example, Williams, 'Rugby Union', p. 322; M. Cronin, *Sport and Nationalism in Ireland: Gaelic Games, Soccer and Irish Identity since 1884* (Dublin: Four Courts Press, 1999), Introduction.

5 Healy was one of the most revered Limerick sportsmen of all time. As with all figures of this nature, separating myth from reality in accounts of his life and sporting career can frequently be difficult. Anecdotes about his life, therefore, are treated with a reasonable level of circumspection. For an interesting example of one such account, see D. O'Shaughnessy, *A Spot So Fair: Tales from St Mary's* (Limerick: Margo Press, 2001), pp. 94–7.

6 Such was the assessment posited in *The Irish Times*, 30 September 2008.

7   Author's calculations. Based on appendicised list of Irish rugby internationals in Van Esbeck, *Irish Rugby*, pp. 185–201.

8   Following details of religion and occupation taken from 1911 census enumerator forms for Dublin.

9   Here I am only interested in the social significance of these institutions; the ideological implications are dealt with in Chapter 4.

10 See *Cork Constitution*, 6 December 1879, 30 December 1879.

11 *Cork Constitution*, 6 December 1879.

12 Williams, 'Rugby Union', p. 321.

13 See, for example, *Cork Constitution*, 5 January 1870.

14 For a treatment of the spread of British games across the empire, see J.A. Mangan, *The Games Ethic and Imperialism* (London: Viking, 1986).

15 *The Quarryman*, vol. 1, no. 4 (April 1914).

16 See, for example, *Francis Guy's Postal Official and General Directory of the County and City of Cork, 1875–6* (Cork: Francis Guy and Co., 1876).

17 UCC RFC Minutes, Secretary's report, 1912–13. UC/MB/CS/RF/2.

18 *The Skull and Crossbones: A Centenary History of University College Cork RFC* (Cork: University College Cork RFC, 1974).

19 *The Quarryman*, vol. 1, no. 4 (April 1914).

20 Ibid.

21 *The Quarryman*, vol. 1, no. 5 (May 1914).

22 T. Champion, 'Urbanisation, Suburbanisation, Counterurbanisation and Reurbanisation', in R. Paddison (ed.), *Handbook of Urban Studies* (London: Sage, 2001), p. 148.

23 Fahy, 'Place and Class in Cork', p. 793.

24 Ibid., p. 802.

25 M. Cronin, 'From the "Flat o' the City" to the Top of the Hill: Cork since 1700', in H.B. Clarke (ed.), *Irish Cities* (Cork: Mercier Press, 1995), p. 61.

26 Ibid., p. 62.

27 See, for example, *CE*, 22 November 1874, 6 January 1875, 5 January 1876.

28 *The Quarryman*, vol. 1, no. 4 (April 1914)

29 Ibid.

30 *Francis Guy's Postal Directory of Cork 1876*.

31 *The Quarryman*, vol. 1, no. 4 (April 1914).

32 See, for instance, *Cork Constitution*, 2 February 1888.

33 *The Quarryman*, vol. 1, no. 5 (May 1914).

34 *Cork Constitution*, 16 March 1896.

35 *CE*, 22 November 1874, 7 December 1874.

36 *Sport*, 18 December 1886.

37 The following statistics are taken from *Guy's Cork Directory 1876*, p. 509.

38 Ibid., p. 511.

39 *The Quarryman*, vol. 1, no. 5 (May 1914).

40 Ibid.

41 Garnham, *Origins and Development of Football in Ireland*, p. 77.

42 J.A. Murphy, *The College: A History of Queen's/University College Cork, 1845–1995* (Cork: Cork University Press, 1996), p. 46.

43 J.J. Horgan, *From Parnell to Pearse: Some Recollections and Reflections* (Dublin: Browne & Nolan, 1948), p. 147.

44 Garnham, *Origins and Development of Football in Ireland*, p. 76.

45 *Cork Constitution*, 4 October 1881.

46   Garnham, *Origins and Development of Football in Ireland*, pp. 77, 155; *Purcell's Cork Almanac 1882*, p. 58.
47   *The Quarryman*, vol. 2, no. 1 (December 1914).
48   Garnham, *Origins and Development of Football in Ireland*, p. 63.
49   See Chapter 1.
50   *The Quarryman*, vol. 2, no. 2 (January 1915).
51   *Guy's Cork Almanac 1911* (Cork, 1911), p. 561.
52   M. Huggins, 'Second-Class Citizens? English Middle-Class Culture and Sport, 1850–1910: A Reconsideration', in J.A. Mangan (ed.), *A Sport-Loving Society: Victorian and Edwardian Middle-Class England at Play* (London: Routledge, 2006), p. 24.
53   Detailed in Chapter 1.
54   *Limerick Chronicle*, 5 November 1881.
55   Ibid; *Sport*, 5 November 1881.
56   Rugby men such as Fred Hook and W.L. Stokes were listed as members of the LPYMA (see *Limerick Chronicle*, 6 November 1880); Stokes, along with Barrington and another rugby patron, A.W. Shaw, were leading members of the Limerick Athletic and Bicycle Club in 1884 (see *Limerick Chronicle*, 27 March 1884). Several members of Limerick FC including the ubiquitous Stokes attended the AGM of Leamy's School FC in 1886 (see *Sport*, 9 October 1886).
57   See, for example, *Irish Times*, 25 April 1878.
58   *Irish Times*, 22 February 1926.
59   S. Pašeta, *Before the Revolution: Nationalism, Social Change and Ireland's Catholic Elite, 1879–1922* (Cork: Cork University Press, 1999), p. 82.
60   Ibid., pp. 36–40.
61   For working-class solidarity and division, see Cronin, *Country, Class or Craft?*, pp. 170–96. See also M. Cronin, 'Parnellism and Workers: The Experience of Cork and Limerick', in F. Lane and D. Ó Drisceoil (eds), *Politics and the Irish Working Class* (Basingstoke: Palgrave, 2005), pp. 140–53.
62   *Sport*, 1 November 1884.
63   *Sport*, 19 January 1884.
64   *LL*, 21 February 1902, 24 February 1902.
65   *Sport*, 4 October 1884.
66   B. Donnelly, 'Michael Joyce: Square Rigger, Shannon Pilot and MP', *Old Limerick Journal*, 27 (Autumn 1990), pp. 42–44.
67   E. McKay, 'The Limerick Municipal Elections, January 1899', *Old Limerick Journal* (Winter 1999), pp. 3–10.
68   See Chapter 4.
69   *LL*, 18 April 1910.
70   Collins, *Rugby's Great Split*, p. 19.
71   For the social and political overtones of Limerick marching bands, see J. McGrath, 'Music and Politics: Marching Bands in Late Nineteenth-Century Limerick', *North Munster Antiquarian Journal*, 6 (2006), pp. 97–106.
72   S. Ó Ceallaigh, 'Great Limerick Athletes, No. 198: Tom Prendergast of St Michael's', *LL*, 9 March 1957.
73   Ibid.
74   For a summary of rational recreation in a British context, see Holt, *Sport and the British*, pp. 136–48.
75   For a discussion on this in a British context, see ibid., pp. 42–3.

76 *Sport*, 4 November 1893; *Limerick Chronicle*, 18 March 1886.
77 *Sport*, 29 September 1888.
78 *Sport*, 22 December 1894.
79 Garnham, 'Accounting for the Early Success of the Gaelic Athletic Association', *Irish Historical Studies*, vol. 34, no. 133 (May 2004), pp. 65–78.
80 McGrath, 'Music and Politics'; F. Lane, 'Music and Violence in Working-Class Cork: "The Band Nuisance", 1879–82', *Saothar*, 24 (1999), pp. 17–32.
81 See J. Lowerson, 'Sport and the Victorian Sunday: The Beginnings of Middle-Class Apostasy', in Mangan, *A Sport-Loving Society*, pp. 179–99.
82 D. McAnallen, 'Sabbatarianism Versus the Gaelic Athletic Association in Ulster, 1884–1920', unpublished paper, 2008. My thanks to the author for providing me with a draft copy of this work.
83 *Sport*, 22 February 1887.
84 *Sport*, 15 February 1887.
85 *Sport*, 22 February 1887.
86 *Sport*, 15 February 1887.
87 *Sport*, 26 March 1887.
88 *Sport*, 24 September 1887.
89 *Sport*, 10 December 1887.
90 *Sport*, 4 February 1888.
91 See *CE*, 4 January 1886, 5 April 1886.
92 *Sport*, 13 November 1886. The teams were: Midleton, Ballintemple, Kinsale Green Rovers, Shamrocks, Trinity, Shandon and Queenstown.
93 *CE*, 8 March 1886.
94 Based on study of the *CE*, January, February and March 1886.
95 For a match report, see *CE*, 5 February 1886.
96 As evidenced by a report of a match between them and Cork Nationals. See *Sport*, 3 March 1888.
97 *Sport*, 8 October 1887.
98 *CE*, 24 January 1894; *Purcell's Cork Directory 1894*, p. 64.
99 E. Van Esbeck, *100 Years of Cork Constitution Football Club* (Cork, 1992), p. 16. It is unclear where precisely Van Esbeck took this quote from.
100 *Sport*, 25 February 1888.
101 *Sport*, 13 March 1886.
102 *CE*, 8 March 1886.
103 L. Ó Tuama, *Where He Sported and Played. Jack Lynch: A Sporting Celebration* (Dublin: Blackwater Press, 2000), p. 3.
104 I have been unable to find corroborating evidence of this either in contemporary Cork newspapers or in IRFU records.
105 *United Irishman*, 18 March 1899.
106 *LL*, 17 February 1899.
107 *LL*, 2 April 1900.
108 *LL*, 24 January 1908.
109 *LL*, 4 January 1901.
110 See Chapter 5.
111 *LL*, 27 October 1911.
112 *Sport*, 12 February 1887.
113 *CE*, 3 January 1913.
114 *CE*, 1 November 1910. Occupations and residence taken from *Guy's Cork Directory 1910* (Cork, 1910).

115 R. Henchion, *Bishopstown, Wilton and Glasheen: A Picture of Life in Three Western Suburbs of Cork from Early Days to Modern Times* (Cork: Dahadore Publications, 2001), pp. 33–4; Various, *75 Years of Rugby: Highfield RFC, 1930–2005* (Cork: Highfield RFC, 2005). The founding members were from faultlessly middle-class backgrounds. The Pope brothers were the sons of a banker; Archibald Hughes was the son of a legal clerk; Henry Seymour was the son of a sea-faring chief steward; Victor Walsh was the son of a naval officer; Jim Mack was the son of a tramway engineer; George Ellard was the son of a corporation ganger; Richard and Thomas Gibson were the sons of a national school teacher; Tony McTighe was the son of an army pensioner; Henry Newman was the son of a Jewish merchant taylor; Tom Carman was the son of a Methodist accountant. Details taken from 1911 census enumerator forms.

116 The Garrison club were mentioned as being 'well to the front this year' in 1890. See *Sport*, 1 November 1890.

117 *CE*, 1 November 1912.

118 For the origins of elite Catholic education in Ireland see Pašeta, *Before the Revolution*, pp. 28–36.

119 *Cork Constitution*, 1 March 1890. The schools were: CBC, Presentation, Dixon's Academy, Latchford's Academy, Carmichael School, Cork Grammar, Midleton College, St Nicholas'.

120 *Sport*, 14 December 1895; *Cork Weekly News*, 10 February 1900.

121 *Cork Constitution*, 20 March 1900.

122 *Cork Sportsman*, 12 February 1910.

123 *CE*, 21 August 1888.

124 Various, *Christians: The First Hundred Years*, p. 13; Pašeta, *Before the Revolution*, p. 38.

125 1911 Census enumerator forms.

126 For anti-intellectualism in British public schools, see Mangan, *Athleticism*, pp. 106–10.

127 *Cork Sportsman*, 5 February 1910.

128 *Cork Sportsman*, 12 February 1910.

129 *The Collegian, 1931* (Cork, 1931), p. 19.

130 A point eloquently made in relation to Cork by Maura Cronin. See M. Cronin, 'Place, Class and Politics', in J.S. Crowley, R.J.N. Devoy, D. Linehan and P. O'Flanagan (eds), *Atlas of Cork City* (Cork: Cork University Press, 2005), p. 202.

131 UCC RFC Minutes, 15 February 1927. UC/MB/CS/RF/3.

132 Various, *Christians: The First Hundred Years*, pp. 376 and 383.

133 For a pictorial representation of this contrast, see Devoy et al., *Atlas of Cork City*, pp. 317–18.

134 1911 census enumerator forms.

135 Ibid.

136 D'Alton, 'Keeping Faith', p. 781.

137 C. O'Flynn, *There is an Isle: A Limerick Boyhood* (Cork: Mercier Press, 1998), p. 19.

138 See R.F. Foster, *The Irish Story: Telling Tales and Making it Up in Ireland* (London: Allen Lane, 2001), pp. 164–86.

139 F. McCourt, *Angela's Ashes* (London: Harper, 1996). See C. O'Flynn, *A Writer's Life* (Dublin: Obelisk Books, 2001), pp. 294–303.

140 See Chapter 4.

141 *LL*, 10 November 1919. See Chapter 5.
142 *LL*, 7 May 1920.
143 *LL*, 22 April 1925.
144 *LL*, 22 February 1924.
145 *LL*, 26 September 1924.
146 For the historical geography of Limerick city, see E. O'Flaherty, 'Three Towns: Limerick since 1691', in Clarke, *Irish Cities*, pp. 177–90.
147 Ibid., p. 186.
148 *LL*, 27 January 1908, 18 January 1909.
149 MBCM, List of affiliated clubs c.1927–30.
150 Ibid.
151 The quality of literature on the history of the parish is varied. The nostalgic work of Criostóir O'Flynn and Denis O'Shaughnessy, though useful, veers towards hyperbole and clearly overly romanticises a parish where life must have been difficult for a significant number of inhabitants. See O'Shaughnessy, *A Spot so Fair* and O'Flynn, *There is an Isle*. By far the best piece of research on the history of St Mary's parish is John McGrath's excellent thesis. See J. McGrath, 'Sociability and Socio-Economic Conditions in St Mary's Parish Limerick, 1890–1950', unpublished MA thesis, Mary Immaculate College, University of Limerick, 2006.
152 McGrath, 'St Mary's Parish', p. 82.
153 See *Sport*, 1 December 1888. Garryowen had in excess of forty-five players attending training sessions at this point.
154 See McGrath, 'St Mary's Parish', p. 83.
155 Munster Branch Committee Minutes, 11 June 1953.
156 *LL*, 11 May 1908.
157 See O'Shaughnessy, *A Spot so Fair*, p. 94.
158 McGrath, 'St Mary's Parish', p. 106.
159 Ibid., p. 86.
160 O'Shaughnessy, *A Spot so Fair*, p. 11.
161 Based on a study of the 1901 census enumerator form for Athlunkard Street.
162 *LL*, 7 May 1920.
163 McGrath, 'St Mary's Parish', p. 112.
164 Ibid., p. 78; *LL*, 15 January 1930, 2 June 1928.
165 Daly to Jeffers, 25 March 1929, IRFU Papers, F/062.
166 MBCM, 3 April 1929.
167 Daly to Jeffers, 25 March 1929, IRFU Papers, F/062.
168 MBCM, 15 April 1930.
169 The last mention of Abbey as an active club in the Munster Branch records was, inevitably, for a disciplinary infraction in February 1934. MBCM, 23 February 1934.
170 MBCM, 10 April 1944.
171 Recollection of Paddy Reid, quoted in McGrath, 'St Mary's Parish', p. 117.
172 MBCM, 4 March 1945.
173 See Chapter 4.
174 Following details taken from O'Shaughnessy, *A Spot so Fair*, pp. 35–8.
175 See below, p. 137.
176 *LL*, 19 December 1932.
177 Ibid.
178 *LL*, 11 April 1925.

179   *LL*, 3 October 1931.
180   *Cork Weekly News*, 21 March 1903.
181   *LL*, 14 April 1905.
182   *Sport*, 29 September 1888.
183   *LL*, 15 February 1911.
184   *LL*, 24 October 1923.
185   *LL*, 7 March 1953, 21 March 1953, 23 March 1953.
186   Van Esbeck, *Irish Rugby*, pp. 187 and 217.
187   See Collins, *Rugby's Great Split*, pp. 32–3.
188   M. O'Flaherty, *The Story of Young Munster Rugby Football Club* (Limerick, 1995). p. 13
189   *Sunday World*, 16 March 2008.
190   Van Esbeck, *Irish Rugby*, p. 95.
191   *LL*, 16 April 1928.
192   See McGrath, 'St Mary's Parish', pp. 18–76.
193   *LL*, 16 April 1928.
194   Census enumerator forms 1911.
195   F. Kinirons, 'The Spiritual Home of Rugby: The Growth, Spread and Development of Rugby in Limerick', unpublished MA thesis, University of Limerick, 2006; McGrath, 'St Mary's Parish', p. 126.
196   See C. Mulqueen, *Limerick's Rugby History* (Limerick, 1978), p. 149; *LL*, 28 March 1938.
197   MBCM, List of affiliated clubs c.1927; *LL*, 25 June 1928.
198   *LL*, 16 June 1928.
199   W.F. Mandle, 'W.G. Grace as a Victorian Hero', *Historical Studies*, 19 (1980), pp. 353–68.
200   For a summary, see M. Taylor, 'Football, History and Memory: The Heroes of Manchester United', *Football Studies*, vol. 3, no. 2 (October 2000), pp. 25–7.
201   T. Mason, '"Our Stephen, Our Harold": Edwardian Footballers as Local Heroes', in R. Holt, J.A. Mangan and P. Lanfranchi (eds), *European Heroes: Myth, Identity, Sport* (London: Routledge, 1998).
202   S. Ó Ceallaigh, 'Great Limerick Athletes (no. 52): James O'Connor of Limerick City', *LL*, 7 November 1953.
203   Ibid.
204   *LL*, 7 March 1911.
205   O'Shaughnessy, *A Spot so Fair*, p. 128.
206   Matt the Thresher was representative of all that Kickham saw as being virtuous in Irish manhood. See C.J. Kickham, *Knocknagow* (New York: Garland, 1979).
207   *LL*, 15 January 1930.
208   *LL*, 9 November 1910.
209   Mulqueen, *Limerick's Rugby History*, p. 114.
210   S. Ó Ceallaigh, 'Great Limerick Athletes (No. 55): Charlie McGill of Limerick City', *LL*, 28 November 1953.
211   *LL*, 24 February 1930.
212   *LL*, 15 January 1930.
213   *LL*, 24 February 1930.
214   *LL*, 6 February 1932.
215   *LL*, 30 February 1932.
216   O'Flynn, *There is an Isle*, p. 93.

217 *LL*, 3 April 1912.
218 *LL*, 10 March 1911.
219 *LL*, 2 March 1929.
220 *LL*, 16 March 1929.
221 *LL*, 8 March 1930.
222 Tony Mason, for instance, was grimly dependent on a list of casualties from a Scottish stadium disaster to compile a sample of British football supporters. See Mason, *Association Football*, pp. 154–6. This is a point also made by Tom Hunt regarding his similar difficulties in researching spectator sport in Westmeath; see, Hunt, *Westmeath*, p. 218.
223 *Sport*, 24 January 1891.
224 *LL*, 5 December 1931.
225 *LL*, 22 October 1932.
226 *LL*, 22 February 1930.
227 *LL*, 17 February 1934.
228 Ibid.
229 *LL*, 2 May 1960.
230 C. Kenneally, *Maura's Boy: A Cork Childhood* (Cork: Mercier Press, 1996); C. Kenneally, *Small Wonders* (Cork: Mercier Press, 2005).
231 Kenneally, *Small Wonders*, p. 134.
232 Kenneally, *Maura's Boy*, p. 11.
233 Ibid., p. 90.
234 Kenneally, *Small Wonders*, p. 134.
235 Collins, '"The First Principle of our Game"'.
236 See Dine, *French Rugby*, pp. 41–60.

4. VIOLENCE AND MASCULINITY

1 *Heineken Cup Final: Official Match Day Programme* (Cardiff, 2002), pp. 7–8.
2 See Conclusion.
3 In this case Rev. J.G. Guinane, long-time Old Crescent delegate to the Munster Branch and elected president of the Branch in 1959. Guinane has a certain resonance with the tyrannical priest and rugby coach character in the Ross O'Carroll Kelly series of novels. See, for example, P. Howard, *The Mis-education of Ross O'Carroll Kelly* (Dublin: The O'Brien Press, 2001).
4 Jeffrey Hill, some years ago, expressed concern at the preoccupation of sport historians with larger questions of social history as a means of legitimising their work at the expense of considering the potential autonomy of cultural practices. See J. Hill, 'British Sports History: A Post-Modern Future?', *Journal of Sport History*, vol. 23, no. 1 (1996).
5 Mangan, *Athleticism*, p. 27.
6 M. Phillips, 'Golf and Victorian Sporting Values', *Sporting Traditions*, vol. 6, no. 2 (May 1990), pp. 121–2.
7 T.J.L. Chandler, 'The Structuring of Manliness and the Development of Rugby Football at the Public Schools and Oxbridge', in Nauright and Chandler, *Making Men*, p. 25.
8 Holt, *Sport and the British*, p. 174.
9 For a comprehensive treatment, see ibid., pp. 86–116.
10 Garnham, *Origins and Development of Football in Ireland*, p. 55.
11 Collins, *Rugby Union*, pp. 30–6; M. Huggins, *The Victorians and Sport* (London: Hambledon Continuum, 2004), pp. 54–7.

12   Collins, *Rugby's Great Split*; Collins, *Rugby Union*, pp. 22–46.

13   See T. Collins, 'The Ambiguities of Amateurism: English Rugby Union in the Edwardian Era', *Sport in History*, vol. 26, no. 3 (December 2006), pp. 386–405.

14   Collins, *Rugby's Great Split*, p. 125.

15   J.W. Martens, 'Rugby, Class, Amateurism and Manliness: The Case of Rugby in Northern England, 1871–1895', in Nauright and Chandler, *Making Men*, p. 36.

16   Collins, *Rugby Union*, pp. 78–9.

17   Garnham, *Origins and Development of Football in Ireland*, p. 47.

18   'Conclusion', in Nauright and Chandler, *Making Men*, p. 246.

19   See above, p. 68.

20   Garnham, *Origins and Development of Football in Ireland*, p. 62.

21   IRFU Minutes, 4 October 1876.

22   Collins, *Rugby Union*, pp. 42–3.

23   I. Wallace, 'Aspects of Education in Nineteenth-Century Fermoy', unpublished MEd thesis, University College Cork, 1986, p. 205

24   Ibid., p. 206.

25   Ibid., p. 250.

26   *Endowed Schools, Ireland, Commission. Report of Her Majesty's Commissioners Appointed to Inquire into the Endowments, Funds, and Actual Condition of all Schools Endowed for the Purpose of Education in Ireland; Accompanied by Minutes of Evidence, Documents, and Tables of Schools and Endowments*, 1857–8 [2336-I] [2336-II] [2336-III] [2336-IV]

27   West, *Midleton College*, p. 23.

28   J. Fleming and S. O'Grady, *St Munchin's College Limerick, 1796–1996* (Limerick, 1996), pp. 198–9.

29   Ibid.

30   Mulqueen, *Munster Rugby*, pp. 148–60.

31   MBCM, 6 January 1946.

32   MBCM, 11 June 1953.

33   Pašeta, *Before the Revolution*, p. 148.

34   Mangan, *Athleticism*, pp. 106–10.

35   *Sport*, 18 January 1886.

36   *The Quarryman*, vol. 2, no. 2 (January 1915).

37   UCC RFC Minutes, 13 March 1906. UC/MB/CS/RF/1.

38   *CE*, 26 November 1909.

39   *QCC*, vol. 5, no. 5 (May 1909), p. 123.

40   *Cork Sportsman*, 28 November 1909.

41   *Cork Sportsman*, 4 December 1909.

42   These were the occupations listed for Ernest Capper, James Morrish and Humphrey Moynihan. See 1911 Census enumerator forms, Cork city.

43   *Cork Sportsman*, 11 December 1909.

44   *Cork Sportsman*, 18 December 1909.

45   *Cork Sportsman*, 26 December 1909.

46   *Cork Sportsman*, 26 March 1910.

47   *Cork Sportsman*, 23 January 1909.

48   *LL*, 5 April 1909.

49   *LL*, 4 January 1924.

50   *LL*, 17 December 1923.

51   *LL*, 17 February 1934.

52 *Cork Constitution*, 3 January 1889.
53 *Cork Weekly News*, 2 April 1898.
54 Irish Rugby Football Union Minutes, 6 April 1898, 5 May 1898. IRFU M/03.
55 EHD Sewell, 'The Past Rugby Football Season', *Fortnightly Review*, vol. 83, no. 497 (May 1908), p. 882.
56 *Cork Sportsman*, 2 January 1909.
57 *LL*, 5 April 1909.
58 *CE*, 17 November 1923.
59 *CE*, 15 November 1923.
60 *LL*, 21 March 1900.
61 *LL*, 27 April 1908.
62 *LL*, 26 April 1909.
63 *Irish Independent*, 31 May 1910.
64 *LL*, 8 March 1922.
65 These sample statistics were derived from a study of the Munster Branch IRFU minute books across the fifteen-season period 1927–42.
66 *The Irish Times*, 28 May 1928.
67 MBCM, 19 March 1927.
68 MBCM, 28 January 1932.
69 *LL*, 2 March 1942.
70 MBCM, 15 October 1942.
71 MBCM, 12 March 1942.
72 MBCM, 5 April 1930.
73 MBCM, 26 March 1927.
74 MBCM, 6 October 1927.
75 *LL*, 29 November 1929.
76 *LL*, 19 September 1927.
77 *LL*, 1 November 1930.
78 *LL*, 13 November 1930, 30 December 1930.
79 *LL*, 17 March 1911.
80 *LL*, 28 November 1931.
81 *LL*, 19 January 1933, 28 February 1935, 3 December 1936.
82 E. Dunning and K. Sheard, *Barbarians, Gentlemen and Players: A Sociological Study of the Development of Rugby Football* (Oxford: Robertson, 1979), p. 14.
83 Ibid., p. 112.
84 Ibid., p. 272.
85 MBCM, 19 October 1927.
86 MBCM, 12 March 1942.
87 *LL*, 7 February 1927.
88 Travelling grants were distributed at the end of each season. See MBCM.
89 MBCM, 31 March 1928.
90 Purcell to Mercier (Leinster Branch), 15 April 1928, IRFU Papers F/062.
91 Jeffares to O'Brien, 8 October 1928, IRFU Papers F/062.
92 MBCM, 1 September 1932.
93 MBCM, 10 May 1934.
94 MBCM, 3 December 1936.
95 *LL*, 22 November 1924.
96 *LL*, 23 February 1929.
97 See, for example, MBCM, 26 January 1948.
98 Data gathered from MBCM.

99   O'Shaughnessy, *A Spot So Fair*, pp. 35–6.
100   These details are taken from the 1911 census enumerator forms.
101   Holt, *Sport and the British*, pp. 173–4.
102   MBCM, 4 February 1928.
103   MBCM, 15 February 1928.
104   *The Irish Times*, 28 May 1928.
105   *LL*, 19 April 1930.
106   See Dine, *French Rugby*, p. 68.

5. Politics and Culture

1   MBCM, 18 March 1966.
2   J. Sugden and A. Bairner, *Sport, Sectarianism and Society in a Divided Ireland* (Leicester: Leicester University Press, 1993), p. 57.
3   Paul Rouse, 'Why Irish Historians Have Ignored Sport: A Note', *History Review*, xiv (2003) p. 74.
4   *Dáil Debates*, vol. 1, col. 2143, 16 November 1922.
5   *Dáil Debates*, vol. 35, col. 667, 5 June 1930.
6   P. Puirséal, *The GAA in its Time* (Dublin: Ward River Press, 1984), p. 32.
7   Academic histories of Irish sport have been keen to underline this irony. See, for example, Cronin, 'Fighting for Ireland, Playing for England?'; Garnham, 'Accounting for the Early Success of the Gaelic Athletic Association'.
8   P. Rouse, 'The Politics and Culture of Sport in Ireland: A History of the GAA Ban on Foreign Games: Part One: 1884–1921', *International Journal of the History of Sport*, vol. 10, no. 3 (December 1993), p. 334.
9   Ibid.
10   Mullan, 'Bifurcation'.
11   Ibid., p. 57.
12   *Cork Constitution*, 7 January 1888.
13   *Cork Constitution*, 5 January 1888.
14   *Cork Constitution*, 5 February 1900.
15   Rouse, 'Ban', p. 341.
16   Ibid., p. 348.
17   Ibid., p. 349.
18   Ibid., p. 352.
19   V. Comerford, *Inventing the Nation: Ireland* (London: Arnold, 2003), p. 220.
20   M. Cronin, 'Enshrined in Blood: The Naming of Gaelic Athletic Association Grounds and Clubs', *The Sports Historian*, vol. 18, no. 1 (May 1998) p. 90.
21   Garnham, 'Accounting', p. 71.
22   *CE*, 20 April 1885.
23   *Sport*, 12 February 1887.
24   J. Cronin, *Munster GAA Story* (Ennis: Clare Champion, 1986), p. 27.
25   *Sport*, 22 November 1890.
26   J. Ó Muircheartaigh and T.J. Flynn, *Princes of Pigskin: A Century of Kerry Footballers* (Cork: The Collins Press, 2007), p. viii; Comerford, *Inventing the Nation*, p. 222. In the introduction to the former, Con Houlihan records the seemingly dubious speculation that Gaelic football became popular in Kerry because it was safer than rugby and easier for spectators to understand.
27   *CE*, 28 February 1887.
28   Garnham, *Association Football*, p. 23.
29   Hunt, *Westmeath*, pp. 156, 178.

30 Collins, *Rugby's Great Split*, pp. 185–7.

31 *LL*, 8 March 1899, 27 March 1899.

32 *LL*, 1 March 1905.

33 *LL*, 31 May 1907.

34 *LL*, 25 January 1901.

35 *LL*, 10 November 1919.

36 Ibid.

37 *LL*, 7 February 1925.

38 *LL*, 19 April 1926.

39 *LL*, 10 December 1923.

40 *LL*, 5 March 1924.

41 *LL*, 2 February 1929.

42 *LL*, 10 March 1924.

43 *LL*, 2 February 1929.

44 See, for instance, *Southern Star*, 24 December 1892; see also IRFU Minutes, Affiliated clubs 1884–5. Clonakilty and Bandon were the only two clubs outside of Cork and Limerick cities to affiliate to the IRFU that season.

45 According to IRFU records, the original Clonakilty Rugby Club was founded in 1882. IRFU Minutes, Affiliated clubs 1884–5.

46 *Southern Star*, 12 November 1892.

47 *Southern Star*, 24 December 1892.

48 *Southern Star*, 14 January 1893.

49 *Sothern Star*, 4 November 1893.

50 *Southern Star*, 25 January 1896.

51 *Southern Star*, 1 February 1896.

52 *CE*, 3 August 1896.

53 Ibid.

54 Ibid.

55 *Nenagh Guardian*, 4 October 1913.

56 *Nenagh Guardian*, 20 June 1925.

57 Cronin, *Munster GAA Story*, pp. 384–5.

58 Ibid.

59 *Southern Star*, 23 June 1906.

60 *Southern Star*, 7 July 1906.

61 *Cork Sportsman*, 10 October 1908.

62 *Cork Sportsman*, 31 October 1908.

63 *Cork Sportsman*, 7 November 1908.

64 B.M. Coldrey, *Faith and Fatherland: The Christian Brothers and the Development of Irish Nationalism, 1838–1921* (Dublin: Gill & Macmillan, 1988), pp. 193–4.

65 See ibid., pp. 66–70. See also Pašeta, *Before the Revolution*, pp. 40–4.

66 S. O'Faoláin, *Vive Moi!* (London: Sinclair Stevenson, 1993), p. 104.

67 See D. Fitzgerald, *How to Play Gaelic Football* (Cork: Guy and Co., 1914).

68 Rev. Bro. Austin, *Presentation Brothers College Cork 1887–1954: The Story of Pres* (Cork: Presentation Brothers, 1954), p. 65.

69 *The Collegian, 1917*.

70 Various, *Christians: The First Hundred Years*, p. 179.

71 Ibid., p. 21.

72 *Southern Star*, 6 April 1918.

73 Ibid.

74 *CE*, 28 November 1919.

75   Ibid.
76   *CE*, 1 December 1919.
77   *CE*, 19 November 1919.
78   *CE*, 1 December 1919.
79   *The Collegian, 1919*, p. 72.
80   Senia Pašeta makes this point well in terms of elite Catholic schools and their choice of sport, although she does not acknowledge the chronological advantage that rugby enjoyed over Gaelic games. See Pašeta, *Before the Revolution*, pp. 40–5.
81   *CE*, 25 November 1919.
82   *The Collegian, 1919*, p. 41.
83   Ibid.
84   *The Quarryman*, vol. 1, no. 1 (December 1913).
85   Pearson was elected president of the rugby club in 1909. UCC RFC Minutes, 5 November 1909. UC/MB/CS/RF/1.
86   Murphy, *The College*, p. 200.
87   See, for example, UCC RFC Minutes 5 November 1905, 8 November 1905. UC/MB/CS/RF/1.
88   Murphy, *The College*, p. 200.
89   Ibid., pp. 204–5.
90   *CE*, 26 November 1909.
91   See, for example, UCC RFC Minutes, 3 February 1915. UC/MB/CS/RF/2.
92   Murphy, *The College*, p. 200.
93   UCC RFC Minutes, 20 November 1917. UC/MB/CS/RF/2.
94   *CE*, 24 November 1919.
95   *CE*, 28 November 1919.
96   For an account of the strikes, see Hart, *The IRA and its Enemies*, pp. 74–86.
97   UCC RFC Minutes, 4 November 1920, 13 November 1920. UC/MB/CS/RF/2.
98   UCC RFC Minutes, 12 January 1921. UC/MB/CS/RF/2.
99   UCC RFC Minutes, 4 November 1920. UC/MB/CS/RF/2.
100 *LL*, 29 October 1920. See also P. O'Farrell, *Who's Who in the Irish War of Independence* (Dublin: Mercier Press, 1980), p. 143.
101 UCC RFC Minutes, 13 November 1920. UC/MB/CS/RF/2.
102 *CE*, 11 February 1924.
103 Murphy, *The College*, pp. 215, 217. O'Rahilly was from Listowel, Co. Kerry. He joined Sinn Féin in 1916 and was imprisoned on Spike Island from January to June 1921. See O'Farrell, *Who's Who*, p. 130.
104 UCC RFC Minutes, 15 February 1927. UC/MB/CS/RF/3.
105 *Nenagh Guardian*, 31 January 1925.
106 *Nenagh Guardian*, 23 February 1924.
107 For the GAA and nationalistic symbolism and iconography, see Cronin, 'Enshrined in Blood'.
108 Rouse, 'Ban', p. 343.
109 *Cork Constitution*, 2 March 1887.
110 Cronin, 'Enshrined in Blood', p. 96.
111 See, for example, *Cork Constitution*, 11 January 1900.
112 *Southern Star*, 8 December 1900.
113 *LL*, 7 November 1923.
114 See M. Hopkinson, *Green Against Green: The Irish Civil War* (Dublin: Gill & Macmillan, 1988), p. 345; Hart, *The IRA and its Enemies*, p. 117.

115 Hart, *The IRA and its Enemies*, pp. 125–6.

116 First mentioned as a club taking part in the Limerick junior rugby tournament in 1887. See *Sport*, 15 February 1887.

117 *LL*, 25 January 1904.

118 See, for example, *LL*, 20 November 1899.

119 McKay, 'Limerick Municipal Elections', p. 8.

120 The veracity of this story is questionable given that Clarke was living in America at this time.

121 *LL*, 7 December 1930.

122 Peter Hart has asserted that the two Limerick battalions of the IRA were divided along class lines and that the more 'white collar' 1st Battalion was made up of men from rugby clubs. This has been challenged by John McGrath, who has speculated that the working-class-orientated 2nd Battalion most likely comprised men from rugby clubs as well. See P. Hart, 'The Social Structure of the Irish Republican Army, 1916–1923', *The Historical Journal*, vol. 42, no. 1 (1999), p. 216; McGrath, 'St Mary's Parish', p. 120.

123 *LL*, 16 February 1925.

124 McGrath, 'St Mary's Parish', p. 110.

125 *LL*, 16 February 1910.

126 *LL*, 4 March 1950.

127 B. Walker, *Parliamentary Election Results in Ireland, 1801–1922* (Dublin: Royal Irish Academy, 1978), p. 121.

128 R.B. McDowell, *The Irish Convention, 1917–18* (London: Routledge, 1970); J.J. Lee, *Ireland, 1912–1985: Politics and Society* (Cambridge: Cambridge University Press, 1989), p. 36.

129 McDowell, *The Irish Convention*, pp. 219–24.

130 R.B. McDowell, *Crisis and Decline: The Fate of Southern Unionists* (Dublin: Lilliput Press, 1997), p. 135.

131 G. White and B. O'Shea, *'Baptised in Blood': The Formation of the Cork Brigade of the Irish Volunteers, 1913–1916* (Cork: Mercier Press, 2005), pp. 106–9.

132 A. O'Callaghan, *The Lord Mayors of Cork, 1900 to 2000* (Cork: Inversnaid Publications, 2000), pp. 38–40.

133 Sheehan defeated Fallon by 2,824 votes to 1,999. See Walker, *Parliamentary Election Results*, p. 337. Nationalist politics was factional in this constituency. Sheehan, a journalist, represented the interests of labourers, was a member of the Land and Labour Association, and had become a supporter of the William O'Brien faction which emerged from 1903, while Fallon was representative of the mainstream Irish Party led by John Redmond. See P.G. Lane, 'The Land and Labour Association, 1894–1914', *Journal of the Cork Historical and Archaeological Society*, 98 (1993), pp. 90–106.

134 *Southern Star*, 11 October 1913.

135 See Pašeta, *Before the Revolution*, pp. 46–9.

136 Horgan, *Parnell to Pearse*, p. 92.

137 Van Esbeck, *Irish Rugby*.

138 S. Diffley, *The Men in Green: The Story of Irish Rugby* (Dublin: Gill & Macmillan, 1973)

139 See Sugden and Bairner, *Sport, Sectarianism and Society*, pp. 52–63.

140 Ibid., p. 54.

141 B. Walker, *Dancing to History's Tune: History, Politics and Myth in Ireland* (Belfast: Queen's University Belfast, 1997), p. 115.

142   Daly to Jeffares, 2 February 1932. IRFU Papers.
143   F.J. Mangan, Sec UCD RFC, to Jeffares, 31 January 1932. IRFU Papers.
144   *Irish Press*, 4 January 1932.
145   *LL*, 9 January 1932.
146   MBCM, 28 January 1932.
147   *LL*, 16 January 1932.
148   *LL*, 6 February 1932.
149   *Irish Press*, 25 January 1932.
150   *Irish Press*, 26 January 1932.
151   *Irish Press*, 4 February 1932.
152   *Irish Press*, 13 February 1932.
153   McGilligan to Clarke, 5 February 1932. IRFU Papers.
154   MBCM, 27 April 1933.
155   MBCM, 5 February 1936.
156   The following paragraph is based on V. Rigby, 'The Riddle of Ravenhill', paper presented at Sport History Ireland Third Annual Conference, NUI Galway, February 2007. My thanks to the author for providing me with a copy of this work.
157   MBCM, 3 April 1929.
158   http://news.bbc.co.uk/2/hi/uk_news/northern_ireland/3387255.stm [accessed 23 July 2007].
159   See above, pp. 76–81.
160   *LL*, 9 February 1929.
161   IRFU Papers, F101/1, UCD to IRFU, 25 November 1929.
162   *The Irish Times*, 14 October 1929.
163   *The Irish Times*, 28 September 1929.
164   *LL*, 5 October 1929.
165   *LL*, 23 November 1929.
166   *LL*, 30 November 1929.
167   *LL*, 7 December 1929.
168   *LL*, 9 February 1929.
169   MBCM, 10 October 1929.
170   MBCM, 15 December 1929.
171   *LL*, 2 October 1929.
172   *Nenagh Guardian*, 5 October 1929.
173   *Nenagh Guardian*, 16 November 1929.
174   *Nenagh Guardian*, 26 October 1929.
175   *LL*, 12 October 1929.

6. Finance and Infrastructure

1   Vamplew, *Pay Up and Play the Game*, p. 64
2   See ibid., pp.56–72; Collins, *Rugby's Great Split*, pp. 29–60; Holt, *Sport and the British*, pp. 159–78; Tranter, *Sport, Economy and Society*, pp. 54–7.
3   Tranter, *Sport, Economy and Society*, p. 17.
4   The social and economic context in which sport was modernised in Britain has been outlined in Chapter 1.
5   Gareth Williams has characterised the International Rugby Board in the mid-1880s as being 'virtually a puppet of the RFU'. Williams, 'Rugby Union', p. 317. Indeed, the RFU held a veto over the IRB until 1948.
6   See Collins, *Rugby's Great Split*.

7   P. Dine, 'Money, Identity and Conflict: Rugby League in France', *The Sports Historian*, vol. 16 (1996), pp. 90–108.

8   Williams, 'Rugby Union', p. 317.

9   For the economy of the province, see the Introduction.

10   These debates are best explored in the work of Wray Vamplew. See Vamplew, *Pay Up and Play the Game*; see also, W. Vamplew, 'The Economics of a Sports Industry: Scottish Gate-Money Football, 1890–1914', *Economic History Review*, vol. 15, no. 4 (November 1982), pp. 549–67.

11   *CE*, 4 January 1878.

12   *CE*, 7 January 1878.

13   Ibid.

14   IRFU Minutes, 5 November 1878.

15   *CE*, 30 November 1878.

16   Ibid.

17   Ibid.

18   *CE*, 4 December 1878.

19   *CE*, 3 December 1878.

20   Given the insecurity of employment suffered by artisans and laborers in Cork, the entrance fee was arguably prohibitively expensive; see Cronin, *Country, Class Or Craft?*, pp. 28–9.

21   Though Rathkeale had briefly affiliated to the IFU in 1875, it was not until meetings in 1877 that Munster were properly represented in the form of Limerick FC and later Cork FC. See IRFU Minutes, 15 October 1877, 24 October 1878, 5 November 1878.

22   Much of what follows is based on Maguire's letter published in the *Cork Weekly News*, 1 December 1883.

23   See Hunt, *Westmeath*.

24   *Cork Weekly News*, 1 December 1883.

25   *Cork Weekly News*, 1 December 1883.

26   Collins, *Rugby's Great Split*, p. 50.

27   Ibid., pp. 32–48; Vamplew, *Pay Up and Play the Game*, pp. 63–8. For a good example of how an entire nation's fortunes in a game can be sensitive to the economic vicissitudes of industrial life, see Gareth Williams, 'From Grand Slam to Great Slump: Economy, Society and Rugby Football in Wales during the Depression', *The Welsh History Review*, 11 (June 1983), pp. 338–57.

28   *Sport*, 1 December 1888.

29   *Sport*, 17 December 1892.

30   *Sport*, 24 April 1886.

31   *Sport*, 23 October 1886.

32   *Sport*, 15 November 1890.

33   *Sport*, 24 October 1891.

34   *Sport*, 17 December 1886.

35   *Sport*, 19 December 1891.

36   IRFU Minutes, 27 March 1899.

37   IRFU Minutes, 14 February 1902, 15 December 1902.

38   *Cork Weekly News*, 20 February 1904.

39   Ibid.

40   IRFU Minutes, AGM 20 January 1898.

41   *LL*, 24 January 1898.

42   *LL*, 6 February 1898.

43 *LL*, 9 March 1898. Occupations taken from *Guy's Postal Directory of Munster 1886* (Cork, 1886), pp. 621–74.
44 *Munster News*, 19 March 1898.
45 *LL*, 9 March 1898.
46 *LL*, 12 March 1898.
47 *LL*, 16 March 1898.
48 *LL*, 23 February 1898.
49 *LL*, 16 March 1898.
50 *Munster News*, 19 March 1898.
51 IRFU Minutes, AGM 19 January 1900.
52 Ibid.
53 IRFU Minutes, 15 November 1901.
54 IRFU Minutes, 10 September 1904, 5 November 1904.
55 See Vamplew, *Pay Up and Play the Game*, pp. 47–8; Hunt, *Westmeath*, pp. 224–6.
56 *CE*, 2 February 1905.
57 Occupation taken from *Purcell's Cork Almanac 1904* (Cork: Purcell's, 1904).
58 *CE*, 9 February 1905.
59 *CE*, 7 February 1905.
60 *CE*, 8 February 1905.
61 Williams, 'Rugby Union', p. 316. Williams' figures seem accurate. The press claimed that 10,000 spectators were present when the teams entered the field. Allowing for the unprecedented scale of the fixture and concomitant logistical issues, it seems perfectly plausible that 2,000 additional spectators entered the ground after kick-off.
62 *CE*, 13 February 1905.
63 *LL*, 9 March 1898.
64 *CE*, 1 February 1905.
65 Hunt, *Westmeath*, p. 117.
66 *LL*, 15 February 1899.
67 Treasurer's Report of Queen's College Rugby Football Club 1904, UCC Archives, 10 Nov/05 UC/OUNCIL/21/345 (1)
68 Ibid.
69 University College Cork RFC, Income and Expenditure 1904–5. UCC Archives, UC/COUNCIL/21/61(2).
70 Accounts for Queen's College Rugby Football Club for season 1907–8, UCC Archives UC/OFFICERS/7/11.
71 J. Bale, *Sports Geography* (London: E&F Spon, 1989), p. 78.
72 The suitability of the site for football is obvious from an inspection of a map of the 1902 exhibition venue. See *Cork International Exhibition 1902: Official Guide* (Cork, 1902), p. 7.
73 IRFU Minutes, 10 October 1906.
74 IRFU Minutes, 1 January 1907.
75 IRFU Minutes, 2 May 1907.
76 IRFU Minutes, 7 November 1908.
77 Hurley to IRFU Secretary, 4 December 1945, IRFU Papers.
78 Hurley to IRFU Secretary, 4 December 1945, IRFU Papers.
79 Collins, *Rugby's Great Split*, p. 24.
80 Vamplew, *Pay Up and Play the Game*, p. 54.
81 Carter, *The Football Manager*, p. 19.
82 *LL*, 21 September 1935.

83 *Cork Weekly News*, 8 March 1902.
84 *LL*, 5 February 1927.
85 MBCM, 4 September 1930.
86 *Cork Weekly News*, 13 March 1886.
87 *Cork Constitution*, 4 April 1887.
88 *Cork Weekly News*, 2 April 1898.
89 *LL*, 16 April 1906, 22 April 1907.
90 *Cork Weekly News*, 18 April 1903.
91 *LL*, 31 March 1913.
92 *LL*, 18 March 1914.
93 *LL*, 29 November 1905; *Cork Weekly News*, 2 December 1905.
94 *CE*, 18 February 1905.
95 Ibid.
96 MBCM. These issues comprised a large proportion of the Munster Branch Committee's business.
97 MBCM, 10 January 1929.
98 MBCM, 15 October 1936.
99 MBCM, 10 September 1930.
100 *LL*, 24 September 1932.
101 MBCM, 5 April 1930.
102 MBCM, 24 April 1931.
103 MBCM, 4 June 1931.
104 MBCM, AGM 1943.
105 MBCM, 6 January 1946.
106 MBCM, 20 May 1948.
107 MBCM, AGM 1950.
108 MBCM 13 June 1952.
109 See Williams, 'From Grand Slam to Grand Slump'; T. Collins, *Rugby League in Twentieth-Century Britain* (London: Routledge, 2006).
110 *LL*, 11 October 1930.
111 MBCM, 4 February 1928.
112 *LL*, 7 April 1962.
113 Mulqueen, *Limerick's Rugby History*, p. 73.
114 MBCM, 15 February 1928.
115 MBCM, 10 January 1929.
116 MBCM, 14 February 1929.
117 *LL*, 4 January 1930.
118 MBCM, 22 October 1930.
119 Ibid.
120 MBCM, 6 November 1930.
121 MBCM, 13 November 1930.
122 MBCM, 28 January 1931.
123 *LL*, 15 October 1932.
124 MBCM, 4 June 1931.
125 MBCM, 12 April, 1934.
126 MBCM, 29 April 1937.
127 MBCM, 29 April 1937, 29 July 1937.
128 *LL*, 26 September 1936.
129 See M. Daly, *Industrial Development and Irish National Identity, 1922–1939* (New York: Syracuse University Press, 1992), p. 62.

130 MBCM, 3 January 1935, 18 October 1934.

131 MBCM, 15 October 1936.

132 Ibid.

133 MBCM, 27 November 1936.

134 MBCM, 17 October 1940.

135 MBCM, 12 March 1942.

136 MBCM, 1 June 1950.

137 MBCM, 27 June 1946, 30 May 1949.

138 MBCM, 6 February 1952.

139 MBCM, 4 February 1954.

140 MBCM, 23 September 1954, 22 October 1954.

141 MBCM, 13 June 1957.

142 Report of Munster Branch Finance Sub-Committee, June 1957, MBCM, 25 June 1957.

143 MBCM, 20 February 1958.

144 What follows in this paragraph is taken from 'Report and Recommendations of the Special Sub-Committee Appointed to Examine the Financial Structure of the Munster Branch', MBCM.

145 MBCM, 4 February 1960.

146 Derived from figures quoted in MBCM, 20 May 1965.

147 MBCM, AGM 1946.

148 MBCM, AGM 1948.

149 MBCM, 21 March 1953.

150 MBCM, 6 March 1955.

151 The profit-maximisation versus utility maximisation debate, as examined in the context of professional British sport by Wray Vamplew, is not applicable here. See Vamplew, *Pay Up and Play the Game*, pp. 77–111.

152 Occupations taken from 1911 census enumerator forms.

153 Carter, *The Football Manager*, p. 50.

7. PROFESSIONALISM

1 Collins, 'The First Principle of Our Game'.

2 Ibid., p. 15.

3 See O'Callaghan and Cronin, 'Without its Clubs Rugby Union is Nothing'.

4 Ibid., p. 136.

5 *The Irish Times*, 24 June 1995.

6 *The Irish Times*, 19 December 1995.

7 Ryan, 'Introduction', p. xi.

8 *Limerick Leader*, 30 April 2008.

9 *The Irish Times*, 27 January 1992, 27 April 1992.

10 *The Irish Times*, 13 April 1995.

11 *The Irish Times*, 13 October 1997, 16 March 1998, 18 May 1998; *Sunday Independent*, 21 September 1997.

12 *Sunday Independent*, 28 April 1991; *The Irish Times*, 18 May 1998.

13 *Sunday Independent*, 28 April 1991, 25 April 1993: *The Irish Times*, 27 April 1992.

14 *The Irish Times*, 20 May 1996, 12 May 1997, 18 May 1998.

15 *The Irish Times*, 15 May 1999.

16 *The Irish Times*, 20 November 2000.

17 *The Irish Times*, 24 May 2002.

18 *Irish Examiner*, 20 November 2010.

19   *The Irish Times*, 17 September 1990.
20   *The Irish Times*, 20 November 1990.
21   *The Irish Times*, 16 March 1998; *Sunday Independent*, 26 April 1998.
22   *The Irish Times*, 15 February 1993.
23   Ibid.
24   See O'Callaghan and Cronin, 'Without its Clubs Rugby Union is Nothing', pp. 139–41.
25   *Munster Rugby News*, September 1994, p. 5.
26   *The Irish Times*, 3 February 1992.
27   *Irish Examiner*, 7 February 2003.
28   *The Irish Times*, 22 January 2002.
29   *Irish Examiner*, 22 October 2010.
30   *Irish Examiner*, 20 January 2011.
31   *Irish Examiner*, 22 October 2010.
32   *Irish Examiner*, 29 November 2010.
33   *The Irish Times*, 11 December 1995.
34   *The Irish Times*, 17 July 1997.
35   *The Irish Times*, 18 December 1998.
36   *The Irish Times*, 15 August 1997.
37   *The Irish Times*, 6 September 1997.
38   See Fanning, *From There to Here*, pp. 58–83.
39   *The Irish Times*, 12 December 1995.
40   *The Irish Times*, 28 October 1997.
41   *The Irish Times*, 7 October 1997.
42   *The Irish Times*, 7 December 1996.
43   *Old Crescent RFC Official Programme Season 1998–99*.
44   *The Irish Times*, 5 February 1999.
45   *The Irish Times*, 28 November 2000.
46   *The Irish Times*, 5 December 2001.
47   Fanning, *From There to Here*, p. 209.
48   *The Irish Times*, 22 November 1999; *Sunday Independent*, 21 January 2001.
49   Dine, *French Rugby*, pp. 120–1.
50   Dublin Airport Authority plc Annual Report and Financial Statements 2009. www.daa.ie
51   *The Irish Times*, 9 February 2005.
52   *The Irish Times*, 7 May 2009.
53   Quoted in P. Kirby, 'Contested Pedigrees of the Celtic Tiger', in P. Kirby, L. Gibbons and M. Cronin (eds), *Reinventing Ireland: Culture, Society and Global Economy* (London: Pluto, 2002), p. 29.
54   http://www.mrsc.ie/membership.aspx [accessed 16 June 2011].
55   *Limerick Leader*, 7 February 2007.
56   *Limerick Leader*, 7 May 2009.

6. Conclusion

1   C. Houlihan, 'State of the Heart', *Rugby Ireland*, vol. 3, no. 7 (June 2002).
2   English, *Stand Up and Fight*; Farrelly, *Munster Rugby Giants*; Murphy, *Munster Rugby*; English, *Munster: Our Road to Glory*.
3   C. Korr, 'West Ham United Football Club and the Beginnings of Professional Football in East London', *Journal of Contemporary History*, vol. 13, no. 2 (April 1978), p. 230.

4   See A. Foley, *Axel: A Memoir* (Dublin: Hachette, 2008), p. 19.

5   For the contrast between clubs centred on civic pride and those based on private 'clubability', see Collins, *Rugby's Great Split*, p. 17.

6   See above, pp. 175–177.

7   See *Munster: The Brave and the Faithful: The Official Commemorative DVD* (Iris Productions, 2006).

8   Mulqueen, *Munster Rugby*, p. 5.

9   *Munster Rugby News*, vol. 5, no. 3 (December 1995), p. 12.

10   MBCM, 2 February 1976.

11   *LL*, 28 January 1967.

12   *LL*, 21 January 1967.

13   Ibid.

14   *LL*, 18 November 1981.

15   English, *Stand up and Fight*.

16   Fanning, *From There to Here*, p. 127.

17   See above, p. 54.

18   *LL*, 1 November 1978.

19   *Irish Examiner*, 21 June 2007.

20   J. Bale, *Landscapes of Sport* (Leicester: Leicester University Press, 1994), p. 132.

21   *Irish Examiner*, 18 October 2006.

22   *Irish Times*, 11 April 2006.

23   Houlihan, 'State of the Heart'.

24   Murphy, *Munster Rugby*, pp. 64–5.

25   *Irish Independent*, 22 January 2009.

26   *The Irish Times*, 11 April 2006.

27   *Irish Independent*, 31 March 2009.

28   In the myth theory of David Henige, myth does not necessarily presuppose fabrication. See D. Henige, *Historical Evidence and Argument* (Madison, WI: University of Wisconsin Press, 2005), p. 118.

29   See, for instance, above, pp. 39–40.

30   *LL*, 28 October 1974.

31   *LL*, 16 December 1978.

32   *Irish Times*, 2 December 1986.

33   Tony Ward, *Irish Independent*, 27 September 2008.

34   *The Irish Times*, 3 April 2009.

35   *The Irish Times*, 29 May 2006.

36   *The Irish Times*, 1 June 2006.

37   M. Conboy, 'A Tale of Two Battles: History in the Popular Press', *Media History*, vol. 13, no. 2 (2007), pp. 257–71.

38   B. Anderson, *Imagined Communities: Reflections on the Origins and Spread of Nationalism* (London: Verso, 1991).

39   For more on place in modern Ireland, see J.J. Lee, 'A Sense of Place in the Celtic Tiger', in H. Bohan and G. Kennedy (eds), *Are We Forgetting Something?* (Dublin: Veritas, 1999), pp. 71–93.

40   Collins, '"The First Principle of our Game"'.

41   For a classical outline of these social patterns, see Holt, *Sport and the British*, Chapters 2 and 3.

6. Appendix: A note on sources

1   Comerford, *Inventing the Nation: Ireland*, pp. 212–35.

2 R. English, *Irish Freedom: The History of Irish Nationalism* (London: Macmillan, 2006); R. Kee, *The Green Flag: A History of Irish Nationalism* (London: Penguin, 1972).
3 Ferriter, *The Transformation of Ireland*.
4 Cronin, *Sport and Nationalism in Ireland: Gaelic Games, Soccer and Irish Identity since 1884*; Cronin, 'Fighting for Ireland, Playing for England?'
5 Rouse, 'Ban'.
6 Garnham, 'Accounting for the Early Success of the Gaelic Athletic Association'.
7 Cronin, Rouse and Murphy, *The Gaelic Athletic Association*.
8 Garnham, *Association Football*.
9 Hunt, *Westmeath*.
10 Van Esbeck, *Irish Rugby*.
11 Diffley, *The Men in Green*.
12 Mulqueen, *Munster Rugby*.
13 D. Hassan, 'Rugby Union, Irish Nationalism and National Identity in Northern Ireland', *Football Studies*, vol. 6, no. 1 (2003), pp. 5–18; J. Tuck and J. Maguire, 'Making Sense of Global Patriot Games: Rugby Players' Perceptions of National Identity Politics', *Football Studies*, vol. 2, no. 1 (1999), pp. 26–54; Sugden and Bairner, *Sport, Sectarianism and Society*.
14 M. Mullan, 'The Devolution of the Irish Economy in the Nineteenth Century and the Bifurcation of Irish Sport', *International Journal of the History of Sport*, vol. 13, no. 2 (1996), pp. 42–60.
15 P. McDevitt, 'Muscular Catholicism: Nationalism, Masculinity and Gaelic Team Sports, 1884–1916', *Gender & History*, vol. 9, no. 2 (August 1997), pp. 262–84.
16 See, in particular, Hunt, *Westmeath*, pp.113–40. See also Bracken, *Foreign and Fantastic Field Sports*; M. O'Dwyer, *The History of Cricket in County Kilkenny: The Forgotten Game* (Kilkenny: O'Dwyer Books, 2006).
17 Collins, *Rugby's Great Split*; Collins, *English Rugby Union*.
18 D. Smith and G. Williams, *Fields of Praise* (Cardiff: University of Wales Press, 1980); G. Williams, 'Rugby Union', in T. Mason (ed.), *Sport in Britain: A Social History* (Cambridge: Cambridge University Press, 1988), p. 321.
19 Dine, *French Rugby*.
20 Ryan, *The Changing Face of Rugby*; J. Nauright and T.J.L. Chandler (eds), *Making Men: Rugby and Masculine Identity* (London: Frank Cass, 1996).
21 Tranter, 'The Chronology of Sport in Nineteenth-Century Scotland: A Regional Study. Part I: Patterns'.

Bibliography

Primary sources

(i) *Archival*

IRISH RUGBY FOOTBALL UNION, LANSDOWNE ROAD, DUBLIN 4
IRFU Papers
IRFU Minute Books 1874–1920

IRISH RUGBY FOOTBALL UNION MUNSTER BRANCH, PEARSE ROAD,
    BALLYPHEHANE, CORK
Munster Branch Committee Minute Books 1927–77

UNIVERSITY COLLEGE CORK ARCHIVES
Queen's/University College Cork Rugby Football Club Minute Books 1905–30
Queen's/University College Cork Rugby Football Club Income and
    Expenditure Statement 1904–5
Queen's/University College Cork Rugby Football Club Treasurer's Report
    1905
Queen's/University College Cork Rugby Football Club Accounts Statements
    1907–8
Queen's/University College Cork Rugby Football Club Proposed Rules c.1907
College Register 1870–1900
*University College Cork Record of Students Past and Present Engaged in the War
    1914–1919*
Miscellaneous Letters

NATIONAL ARCHIVES OF IRELAND
Census of Ireland 1911 Enumerator Forms (online)

CORK ARCHIVES INSTITUTE
Cork Young Men's Society Membership/Subscription List 1891
Cork Young Men's Society Membership List 1904
Monkstown Golf Club Statement of Accounts 1917–18

NATIONAL LIBRARY OF IRELAND
Account Book of Kilruane Football Club 1976, MS 9515

(ii) *Official Publications*

Census of Ireland 1891

Census of Ireland 1901

Cork International Exhibition 1902: Official Guide (Cork, 1902)

Endowed Schools, Ireland, Commission, Report of Her Majesty's Commissioners Appointed to Inquire into the Endowments, Funds, and Actual Condition of all Schools Endowed for the Purpose of Education in Ireland; Accompanied by Minutes of Evidence, Documents, and Tables of Schools and Endowments, 1857–8 [2336-I] [2336-II] [2336-III] [2336-IV]

Farming since the Famine: Irish Farm Statistics 1847–1996 (Dublin: Central Statistics Office, 1997)

Heineken Cup Final: Official Match Day Programme (Cardiff, 2002)

Munster Branch Irish Rugby Football Union: Official Fixtures and Information Booklet, Season 2003–2004

Parliamentary Debates Dáil Éireann 1922–

Parliamentary Debates Seanad Éireann 1922–

(iii) *Directories and Works of Reference*

Francis Guy's Postal Official and General Directory of the County and City of Cork 1875–6

Guy's Cork Directory 1910

Guy's Cork Almanac 1911

Guy's Postal Directory of Munster 1886

Purcell's Cork Almanac 1882

Purcell's Cork Directory 1894

Purcell's Cork Almanac 1904

Vaughan, W.E. and Fitzpatrick, A.J., *Irish Historical Statistics: Population, 1821–1971,* (Dublin: Royal Irish Academy, 1978)

(iv) *Newspapers and Periodicals*

Clare Sentinel

Cork Constitution

Cork Examiner

Cork Sportsman

Cork Weekly News

Freeman's Journal

Irish Examiner

Irish Independent

Irish Press

Kerry Sentinel

Limerick Chronicle

Limerick Leader

Munster News

Munster Rugby News

Nenagh Guardian

QCC
Quarryman
Rugby Ireland
Southern Star
Sport
Sunday Independent
Sunday World
The Collegian
The Irish Times
Tralee Chronicle
United Irishman

Secondary sources

(i) *Items Published Before 1920*

Fitzgerald, D. *How to Play Gaelic Football* (Cork: Guy and Co., 1914)

Hanna, H, *The Pals at Suvla Bay* (Dublin: E. Ponsonby Limited, 1916)

Lewis, S. *A Topographical Dictionary of Ireland* (London: S. Lewis and Co., 1837)

Marshall, Rev. F. (ed.), *Football: The Rugby Union Game* (London: Cassell and Co., 1892)

Sewell, E.H.D. 'The Past Rugby Football Season', *Fortnightly Review*, vol. 83, no. 497 (May 1908)

(ii) Journal Articles and Book Chapters

Andrews, D.L. 'Welsh Indigenous! And British Imperial? Rugby, Culture and Society 1890–1914', *Journal of Sport History*, vol. 18, no. 3 (Winter 1991), pp. 335–49

Champion, T. 'Urbanisation, Suburbanisation, Counterurbanisation and Reurbanisation', in R. Paddison (ed.), *Handbook of Urban Studies* (London: Sage, 2001)

Chandler, T.J.L. 'The Structuring of Manliness and the Development of Rugby Football at the Public Schools and Oxbridge', in J. Nauright and T.J.L. Chandler (eds), *Making Men: Rugby and Masculine Identity* (London: Frank Cass, 1996)

Collins, T. 'The First Principle of our Game: The Rise and Fall of Amateurism, 1886–1995', in G. Ryan (ed.), *The Changing Face of Rugby: The Union Game and Professionalism since 1995* (Newcastle: Cambridge Scholars Publishing, 2008), pp. 1–19

Collins, T. 'The Ambiguities of Amateurism: English Rugby Union in the Edwardian Era', *Sport in History*, vol. 26, no. 3 (December 2006), pp. 386–405

Collins, T. 'History, Theory and the "Civilising Process"', *Sport in History* (2005), pp. 289–306

Conboy, M. 'A Tale of Two Battles: History in the Popular Press', *Media History*, vol. 13, no. 2 (2007), pp. 257–71

Cronin, M. 'From the "Flat o' the City" to the Top of the Hill: Cork since 1700',
  in H.B. Clarke (ed.), *Irish Cities* (Cork: Mercier Press, 1995), pp. 55–68

Cronin, M. 'Place, Class and Politics', in J.S. Crowley, R.J.N. Devoy, D. Linehan
  and P. O'Flanagan (eds), *Atlas of Cork City* (Cork: Cork University Press,
  2005), pp. 202–8

Cronin, M. 'Parnellism and Workers: The Experience of Cork and Limerick',
  in F. Lane and D. Ó Drisceoil (eds), *Politics and the Irish Working Class*
  (Basingstoke: Palgrave Macmillan, 2005), pp. 140–153

Cronin, M. 'Enshrined in Blood: The Naming of Gaelic Athletic Association
  Grounds and Clubs', *The Sports Historian*, vol. 18, no. 1 (May 1998), pp.
  90–104

Cronin, M. 'Fighting for Ireland, Playing for England?' The Nationalist History
  of the Gaelic Athletic Association and the British Influence on Irish Sport',
  International Journal of the History of Sport, vol. 15, no. 3 (December 1998),
  pp. 35–56

Curry, G., Dunning, E. and Sheard, K. 'Sociological Versus Empiricist History:
  Some Comments on Tony Collins's "History, Theory and the 'civilising
  process'"', *Sport in History*, vol. 26, no. 1 (2006), pp. 110–23

D'Alton, I. 'Keeping Faith: An Evocation of the Cork Protestant Character,
  1820–1920', in P. O'Flanagan and C. Buttimer (eds), *Cork History and
  Society: Interdisciplinary Essays on the History of an Irish County* (Dublin:
  Geography Publications, 1993), p. 755–92

Dine, P. 'Money, Identity and Conflict: Rugby League in France', *The Sports
  Historian*, vol. 16 (1996), pp. 90–108

Donnelly, B. 'Michael Joyce: Square Rigger, Shannon Pilot and MP', *Old
  Limerick Journal*, 27 (Autumn 1990), pp. 42–4

Fahy, A. 'Place and Class in Cork', in O'Flanagan and Buttimer (eds), *Cork
  History and Society: Interdisciplinary Essays on the History of an Irish County*
  (Dublin: Geography Publications, 1993), pp. 793–812

Fitzpatrick, D. 'The Disappearance of the Farm Labourer in Ireland, 1841–
  1912', *Irish Economic and Social History*, 7 (1980), pp. 66–92.

Garnham, N. 'Accounting for the Early Success of the Gaelic Athletic
  Association', *Irish Historical Studies*, vol. 34, no. 133 (May 2004), pp. 65–78

Harvey, A. 'The Oldest Rugby Club in the World?' *Sport in History*, vol. 26, no.
  1 (April 2006), pp. 150–2

Hart, P. 'The Social Structure of the Irish Republican Army, 1916–1923', *The
  Historical Journal*, vol. 42, no. 1 (1999), pp. 207–31

Hassan, D. 'Rugby Union, Irish Nationalism and National Identity in
  Northern Ireland', *Football Studies*, vol. 6, no. 1 (2003), pp. 5–18

Hayes, T. 'Hurling', in T. Collins, J. Martin and W. Vamplew, *Encyclopedia of
  Traditional British Rural Sports* (London: Routledge, 2005), p. 167

Hill, J. 'British Sports History: A Post-Modern Future?', *Journal of Sport History*,
  vol. 23, no. 1 (1996), pp. 1–19

Holt, R. 'Working-Class Football and the City: The Problem of Continuity',
  British Journal of Sports History, vol. 3, no. 1 (1986), pp. 5–17

Holt, R. 'Ireland and the Victorian Sporting Revolution', in M. Cronin, P. Rouse and W. Murphy (eds), *The Gaelic Athletic Association, 1884–2009* (Dublin: Irish Academic Press, 2009)

Huggins, M. 'Second-Class Citizens? English Middle-Class Culture and Sport, 1850–1910: A Reconsideration', in J.A. Mangan (ed.), *A Sport-Loving Society: Victorian and Edwardian Middle-Class England at Play* (London: Routledge, 2006)

Kirby, P. 'Contested Pedigrees of the Celtic Tiger', in P. Kirby, L. Gibbons and M. Cronin (eds), *Reinventing Ireland: Culture, Society and Global Economy* (London: Pluto, 2002)

Korr, C. 'West Ham United Football Club and the Beginnings of Professional Football in East London', *Journal of Contemporary History*, vol. 13, no. 2 (April 1978), pp. 211–32

Lane, F. 'Music and Violence in Working-Class Cork: "The Band Nuisance". 1879–82', *Saothar*, 24 (1999), pp. 17–32

Lane, P.G. 'The Land and Labour Association 1894–1914', *Journal of the Cork Historical and Archaeological Society*, 98 (1993), pp. 90–106

Lee, J.J. 'A Sense of Place in the Celtic Tiger', in H. Bohan and G. Kennedy (eds), *Are We Forgetting Something?* (Dublin: Veritas, 1999), pp. 71–93

Lowerson, J. 'Sport and the Victorian Sunday: The Beginnings of Middle-Class Apostasy', in J.A. Mangan (ed.), *A Sport-Loving Society: Victorian and Edwardian Middle-Class England at Play* (London: Routledge, 2006), pp. 179–99

McAnallen, D. '"The Greatest Amateur Association in the World?' The GAA and Amateurism', in M. Cronin, W. Murphy and P. Rouse, *The Gaelic Athletic Association, 1884–2009* (Dublin: Irish Academic Press, 2009), pp. 157–83

McDevitt, Patrick, 'Muscular Catholicism: Nationalism, Masculinity and Gaelic Team Sports, 1884–1916', *Gender & History*, vol. 9, no. 2 (August 1997), pp. 262–84

McGrath, J. 'Music and Politics: Marching Bands in Late Nineteenth-Century Limerick', *North Munster Antiquarian Journal*, 6 (2006), pp. 97–106

McKay, E. 'The Limerick Municipal Elections, January 1899', *Old Limerick Journal* (Winter 1999), pp. 3–10

Mandle, W.F. 'W.G. Grace as a Victorian Hero', *Historical Studies*, 19 (1980), pp. 353–68

Martens, J.W. 'Rugby, Class, Amateurism and Manliness: The Case of Rugby in Northern England, 1871–1895', in J. Nauright and T.J.L. Chandler, *Making Men: Rugby and Masculine Identity* (London: Frank Cass, 1999), pp. 32–49

Mason, T. '"Our Stephen, Our Harold": Edwardian Footballers as Local Heroes', in R. Holt, J.A. Mangan and P. Lanfranchi (eds), *European Heroes: Myth, Identity, Sport* (London: Routledge, 1998)

Metcalfe, A. 'Football in the Mining Communities of East Northumberland, 1882–1914', *International Journal of the History of Sport*, vol. 5, no. 3 (1988), pp. 269–91

Mullan, M. 'The Devolution of the Irish Economy in the Nineteenth Century and the Bifurcation of Irish Sport', *International Journal of the History of Sport*, vol. 13, no. 2 (1996), pp. 42–60

Murphy, M. 'The Working Classes in 19th Century Cork', *Journal of the Cork Historical and Archaeological Society*, vol. 85, no. 241 (1980)

O'Callaghan, L. and Cronin, M. '"Without its Clubs, Rugby Union is Nothing": Resisting and Embracing Professional Rugby in Ireland', in G. Ryan, *The Changing Face of Rugby* (Newcastle: Cambridge Scholars Publishing, 2008), pp. 130–46

O'Flaherty, E. 'Three Towns: Limerick since 1691', in H. Clarke (ed.), *Irish Cities* (Cork: Mecier Press, 1995), pp. 177–90

Orr, P. '200,000 Volunteers', in J. Horne (ed.), *Our War: Ireland and the Great War* (Dublin: Royal Irish Academy, 2008)

Phillips, J. 'The Hard Man: Rugby and the Formation of Male Identity in New Zealand', in J. Nauright and T.J.L. Chandler, *Making Men: Rugby and Masculine Identity* (London: Frank Cass, 1999), pp. 70–90

Phillips, M, 'Golf and Victorian Sporting Values', *Sporting Traditions*, vol. 6, no. 2 (May 1990)

Quane, M. 'Ennis Grammar School', *North Munster Antiquarian Journal*, 10 (1966), pp. 27–46

Rouse, P. 'The Politics and Culture of Sport in Ireland: A History of the GAA Ban on Foreign Games, 1884–1971. Part One: 1884–1921', *International Journal of the History of Sport*, vol. 10, no. 3 (December 1993), pp. 333–60

Rouse, P. 'Why Irish Historians Have Ignored Sport: A Note', *History Review*, xiv (2003), pp. 67–73

Rouse, P. '*Sport* and Ireland in 1881', in A. Bairner (ed.), *Sport and the Irish: Histories Identities, Issues* (Dublin: University College Dublin Press, 2005), pp. 7–11

Ryan, G. 'Rural Myth and Urban Actuality: The Anatomy of All Black and New Zealand Rugby, 1884–1938', in G. Ryan (ed.), *Tackling Rugby Myths: Rugby and New Zealand Society, 1854–2004* (Dunedin: Otago University Press, 2005), pp. 33–54

Stokvis, R, 'Sport and Civilisation: Is Violence the Central Problem?' in E. Dunning and C. Rojek (eds), Sport and Leisure in the Civilising Process: Critique and Counter-Critique (London: Macmillan, 1992), pp. 121–36

Taylor, M. 'Football, History and Memory: The Heroes of Manchester United', *Football Studies*, vol. 3, no. 2 (October 2000), pp. 24–41

Tranter, N.L. 'The Chronology of Sport in Nineteenth-Century Scotland: A Regional Study. Part I: Patterns', *International Journal of the History of Sport*, vol. 7, no. 2 (1990), pp. 188–203

Tranter, N.L. 'The Chronology of Organised Sport in Nineteenth-Century Scotland: A Regional Study. Part III: Causes', *International Journal of the History of Sport*, vol. 7, no. 3 (1990), pp. 365–87

Tuck, J. and Maguire, J. 'Making Sense of Global Patriot Games: Rugby Players' Perceptions of National Identity Politics', *Football Studies*, vol. 2, no. 1 (1999), pp. 26–54

Vamplew, W. 'The Economics of a Sports Industry: Scottish Gate-Money Football, 1890–1914', *Economic History Review*, vol. 15, no. 4 (November 1982), pp. 549–67

Williams, G. 'From Grand Slam to Great Slump: Economy, Society and Rugby Football in Wales during the Depression', *The Welsh History Review*, 11 (June 1983), pp. 338–57

Williams, G. 'Rugby Union', in T. Mason (ed.), *Sport in Britain: A Social History* (Cambridge: Cambridge University Press, 1988), pp. 308–43

(iii) *Books*

Anderson, B. *Imagined Communities: Reflections on the Origins and Spread of Nationalism* (London: Verso, 1991)

Austin, Rev. Bro., *Presentation Brothers College Cork, 1887–1954: The Story of Pres* (Cork: Presentation Brothers, 1954)

Bairner, A. (ed.), *Sport and the Irish: Histories, Identities, Issues* (Dublin: University College Dublin Press, 2005)

Bale, J. *Sports Geography* (London: E. and F.N. Spon, 1989)

Bale, J. *Landscapes of Sport* (Leicester: Leicester University Press, 1994)

Bielenberg, A. *Cork's Industrial Revolution, 1780–1880: Development or Decline?* (Cork: Cork University Press, 1991)

Bohan, H. and Kennedy, G. (eds), *Are We Forgetting Something?* (Dublin: Veritas, 1999)

Booth, D. *The Field: Truth and Fiction in Sport History* (London: Routledge, 2005)

Bracken, P. *Foreign and Fantastic Field Sports: Cricket in County Tipperary* (Thurles: Liskaveen Books, 2004)

Breach, R.W. and Hartwell, R.M. *British Economy and Society, 1870–1970* (Oxford: Oxford University Press, 1972)

Carter, N. *The Football Manager: A History* (London: Routledge, 2006)

Clarke, H.B. (ed.), *Irish Cities* (Cork: Mercier Press, 1995)

Coldrey, B.M. *Faith and Fatherland: The Christian Brothers and the Development of Irish Nationalism, 1838–1921* (Dublin: Gill & Macmillan, 1988)

Collins, T. *Rugby's Great Split: Class, Culture and the Origins of Rugby League Football* (London: Frank Cass, 1998)

Collins, T. *Rugby League in Twentieth-Century Britain* (London: Routledge, 2006)

Collins, T. *A Social History of English Rugby Union* (London: Routledge, 2009)

Collins, T., Martin, J. and Vamplew, W. (eds), *Encyclopedia of Traditional British Rural Sports* (London: Routledge, 2005)

Comerford, R.V. *Inventing the Nation: Ireland* (London: Arnold, 2003)

Corry, E. *Catch and Kick* (Dublin: Poolbeg, 1989)

Cronin, J. *Munster GAA Story* (Ennis: Clare Champion, 1986)

Cronin, M. *Country, Class or Craft? The Politicisation of the Skilled Artisan in Nineteenth-Century Cork* (Cork: Cork University Press, 1994)

Cronin, M. *Sport and Nationalism in Ireland: Gaelic Games, Soccer and Irish Identitysince 1884* (Dublin: Four Courts Press, 1999)

Cronin, M., Rouse, P. and Murphy, W. (eds), *The Gaelic Athletic Association, 1884–2009* (Dublin: Irish Academic Press, 2009)

Cunningham, H. *Leisure in the Industrial Revolution* (London: Croom Helm, 1980)

Daly, M. *Industrial Development and Irish National Identity, 1922–1939* (New York: Syracuse University Press, 1992)

D'Arcy, F. *Horses, Lords and Racing Men: The Turf Club, 1890–1990* (The Curragh: Co. Kildare Turf Club, 1991)

De Burca, M. *The GAA: A History* (Dublin: Gill & Macmillan, 1999)

Devoy, R.J.N., Linehan, D. and O'Flanagan, P. (eds), *Atlas of Cork City* (Cork: Cork University Press, 2005)

Dickson, D. *Old World Colony: Cork and South Munster, 1630–1830* (Cork: Cork University Press, 2005)

Diffley, S. *The Men in Green: The Story of Irish Rugby* (London: Pelham Books, 1973)

Dine, P. *French Rugby Football: A Cultural History* (Oxford: Berg 2001)

Dunning, E. and Sheard, K. *Barbarians, Gentlemen and Players: A Sociological Study of the Development of Rugby Football* (Oxford: Robertson, 1979)

Dunning, E. and Rojek, C. (eds), *Sport and Leisure in the Civilising Process: Critique and Counter-Critique* (London: Macmillan, 1992)

Elias, N. and Dunning, E. *The Quest for Excitement: Sport and Leisure in the Civilising Process* (Oxford: Blackwell, 1986)

English, A. *Stand up and Fight: The Day Munster Beat the All Blacks* (London: Yellow Jersey, 2005)

English, A. *Munster: Our Road to Glory* (Dublin: Penguin, 2006)

English, R. *Irish Freedom: The History of Irish Nationalism* (London: Macmillan, 2006)

Fallon, B. *An Age of Innocence: Irish Culture, 1930–1960* (Dublin: Gill & Macmillan, 1999)

Fanning, B. *From There to Here: Irish Rugby in the Professional Era* (Dublin: Gill & Macmillan, 2007)

Farrelly, H. *Munster Rugby Giants* (Dublin: The O'Brien Press, 2001)

Ferris, T. *Irish Railways: A New History* (Dublin: Gill & Macmillan, 2008)

Fitzpatrick, D. *Irish Emigration, 1801–1921* (Dublin: Economic and Social History of Ireland Society, 1984)

Fleming, J. and O'Grady, S. *St Munchin's College Limerick, 1796–1996* (Limerick: St. Munchin's College, 1996)

Foley, A. *Axel: A Memoir* (Dublin: Hachette, 2008)

Foster, R.F. *The Irish Story: Telling Tales and Making it Up in Ireland* (London: Allen Lane, 2001)

Foster, R.F. *Luck and the Irish: A Brief History of Change* (London: Allen Lane, 2007)

Garnham, N. *The Origins and Development of Football in Ireland, Being a Reprint of R.M. Peter's Irish Football Annual, 1880* (Belfast: Ulster Historical Foundation, 1999)

Garnham, N. *Association Football and Society in Pre-Partition Ireland* (Belfast: Ulster Historical Foundation, 2004)

Graves, R. *Goodbye to All That* (London: Penguin, 1960)

Griffin, B. *Cycling in Victorian Ireland* (Dublin: Nonsuch, 2006)

Guinnane, T.W. *The Vanishing Irish: Households, Migration and the Rural Economy in Ireland, 1850–1914* (Princeton, NJ: Princeton University Press, 1997)

Guttmann, A. *From Ritual to Record: The Nature of Modern Sports* (New York: Columbia University Press, 1978)

Hart, P. *The IRA and its Enemies: Violence and Community in County Cork, 1916–1923* (Oxford: Oxford University Press, 1998)

Henchion, R. *Bishopstown, Wilton and Glasheen: A Picture of Life in Three Western Suburbs of Cork from Early Days to Modern Times* (Cork: Dahadore Publications, 2001)

Henige, D. *Historical Evidence and Argument* (Madison, WI: University of Wisconsin Press, 2005)

Hill, J. *Sport, Leisure and Culture in Twentieth-Century Britain* (Basingstoke: Palgrave Macmillan, 2002)

Hill, J. *The Building of Limerick* (Cork: Mercier Press, 1991)

Holt, R. *Sport and the British: A Modern History* (Oxford: Oxford University Press, 1989)

Holt, R., with J.A. Mangan and P. Lanfranchi (eds), *European Heroes: Myth, Identity, Sport* (London: Routledge, 1998)

Hopkinson, M. *Green Against Green: The Irish Civil War* (Dublin: Gill & Macmillan, 1988)

Horgan, J.J. *From Parnell to Pearse: Some Recollections and Reflections* (Dublin: Browne & Nolan, 1948)

Horne, J. (ed.), *Our War: Ireland and the Great War* (Dublin: Royal Irish Academy, 2008)

Howard, P. *The Mis-education of Ross O'Carroll Kelly* (Dublin: The O'Brien Press, 2001)

Huggins, M. *The Victorians and Sport* (London: Hambledon Continuum, 2004)

Hunt, T. *Sport and Society in Victorian Ireland: The Case of Westmeath* (Cork: Cork University Press, 2007)

Jenkins, S.C. *The Cork, Blackrock and Passage Railway* (Oxford: Oakwood Press, 1993)

Kickham, C.J. *Knocknagow* (New York: Garland, 1979)

Kee, R. *The Green Flag: A History of Irish Nationalism* (London: Penguin, 1972)

Keogh, D. *Twentieth-Century Ireland: Nation and State* (Dublin: Gill & Macmillan, 1994)

Kenneally, C. *Maura's Boy: A Cork Childhood* (Cork: Mercier Press, 1996)

Kenneally, C. *Small Wonders* (Cork: Mercier Press, 2005)

Kirby, P., Gibbons, L. and Cronin, M. (eds), *Reinventing Ireland: Culture, Society and Global Economy* (London: Pluto, 2002)

Lane, F. and Ó Drisceoil, D. (eds), *Politics and the Irish Working Class* (Basingstoke: Palgrave Macmillan, 2005)

Lee, J.J. *The Modernisation of Irish Society, 1848–1918* (Dublin: Gill & Macmillan, 1973)

Lee, J.J. *Ireland, 1912–1985: Politics and Society* (Cambridge: Cambridge University Press, 1989)

McCourt, F. *Angela's Ashes* (London: Harper, 1996)

McDowell, R.B. *The Irish Convention, 1917–18* (London: Routledge, 1970)

McDowell, R.B. *Crisis and Decline: The Fate of Southern Unionists* (Dublin: Lilliput Press, 1997)

Mahon, J. *A History of Gaelic Football* (Dublin: Gill & Macmillan, 2000)

Mangan, J.A. *Athleticism in the Victorian and Edwardian Public School* (Cambridge: Cambridge University Press, 1981)

Mangan, J.A. *The Games Ethic and Imperialism* (London: Viking, 1986)

Mangan, J.A. (ed.), *A Sport-Loving Society: Victorian and Edwardian Middle-Class England at Play* (London: Routledge, 2006)

Mason, T. *Association Football and English Society, 1863–1914* (Brighton: Harvester Press, 1981)

Mason, T. (ed.), *Sport in Britain: A Social History* (Cambridge: Cambridge University Press, 1988)

Mulqueen, C. *Limerick's Rugby History* (Limerick: Limerick Leader, 1978)

Mulqueen, C. *The Murphy's Story of Munster Rugby* (Cork, 1993)

Murphy, E. *Munster Rugby: The Phenomenon* (Meath: Maverick House, 2006)

Murphy, J.A. *The College: A History of Queen's/University College Cork, 1845–1995* (Cork: Cork University Press, 1996)

Nauright, J. and Chandler, T.J.L. (eds), *Making Men: Rugby and Masculine Identity* (London: Frank Cass, 1996)

O'Callaghan, A. *The Lord Mayors of Cork, 1900 to 2000* (Cork: Inversnaid Publications, 2000)

O'Connor, K. *Ironing the Land: The Coming of the Railways to Ireland* (Dublin: Gill & Macmillan, 1999)

O'Donnell, S. *Clonmel, 1840–1900: Anatomy of an Irish Town* (Dublin: Geography Publications, 1998)

O'Donnell, S. *Clonmel, 1900–1932: A History* (Clonmel: Marlfield Publications, 2009)

O'Dwyer, M. *The History of Cricket in County Kilkenny: The Forgotten Game* (Kilkenny: O'Dwyer Books, 2006)

O'Faoláin, S. *Vive Moi!* (London: Sinclair Stevenson, 1993)

O'Farrell, P. *Who's Who in the Irish War of Independence* (Dublin: Mercier Press, 1980)

O'Flaherty, M. *The Story of Young Munster Rugby Football Club* (Limerick: Leader Print, 1995)

O'Flanagan, P. and Buttimer, C. (eds), *Cork History and Society: Interdisciplinary Essays on the History of an Irish County* (Dublin: Geography Publications, 1993)

O'Flynn, C. *There is an Isle: A Limerick Boyhood* (Cork: Mercier Press, 1998)

O'Flynn, C. *A Writer's Life* (Dublin: Obelisk Books, 2001)

Ó Gráda, C. *Ireland: A New Economic History, 1780–1939* (Oxford: Clarendon, 1990)

Ó Gráda, C. *A Rocky Road: The Irish Economy since the 1920s* (Manchester: Manchester University Press, 1997)

Ó Muircheartaigh, J. and Flynn, T.J. *Princes of Pigskin: A Century of Kerry Footballers* (Cork: The Collins Press, 2007)

Orr, P. *Field of Bones: An Irish Division in Gallipoli* (Dublin: Lilliput Press, 2006)

O'Shaughnessy, D. *A Spot so Fair: Tales from St Mary's* (Limerick: Margo Press, 2001)

Ó Tuama, L. *Where He Sported and Played. Jack Lynch: A Sporting Celebration* (Dublin: Blackwater Press, 2000)

Ó Tuathaigh, G. *Ireland before the Famine, 1798–1848* (Dublin: Gill & Macmillan, 1984)

Paddison, R. (ed.), *Handbook of Urban Studies* (London: Sage, 2001)

Pašeta, S. *Before the Revolution: Nationalism, Social Change and Ireland's Catholic Elite, 1879–1922* (Cork: Cork University Press, 1999)

Puirséal, P. *The GAA in its Time* (Dublin: Ward River Press, 1984)

Rowledge, J.W.P. *A Regional History of Railways. Vol. 16: Ireland* (Cornwall: Atlantic Transport Publications, 1995)

Russell, D. *Football and the English: A Social History of Association Football in England, 1863–1995* (Preston: Carnegie, 1997)

Ryan, G. (ed.), *Tackling Rugby Myths: Rugby and New Zealand Society, 1854–2004* (Dunedin: Otago University Press, 2005)

Ryan, G. (ed.), *The Changing Face of Rugby: The Union Game and Professionalism since 1995* (Newcastle: Cambridge Scholars Publishing, 2008)

Smith, D. and Williams, G. *Fields of Praise* (Cardiff: University of Wales Press, 1980)

Sugden, J. and Bairner, A. *Sport, Sectarianism and Society in a Divided Ireland* (Leicester: Leicester University Press, 1993)

Tranter, N.L. *Sport, Economy and Society in Britain, 1750–1914* (Cambridge: Cambridge University Press, 1998)

Tranter, N.L. *Population since the Industrial Revolution: The Case of England and Wales* (London: Croom Helm, 1973)

Vamplew, W. *Pay Up and Play the Game* (Cambridge: Cambridge University Press, 1989)

Van Esbeck, E. *One Hundred Years of Irish Rugby* (Dublin: Gill & Macmillan, 1974)

Van Esbeck, E. *100 Years of Cork Constitution Football Club* (Cork: Cork Constitution Football Club, 1992)

Various, *75 Years of Rugby: Highfield RFC, 1930–2005* (Cork: Highfield RFC, 2005)

Various, *Christians: The First Hundred Years* (Cork: Christian Brothers, 1989)

Various, *The Skull and Crossbones: A Centenary History of University College Cork RFC* (Cork: University College Cork RFC, 1974)

Walker, B. *Parliamentary Election Results in Ireland, 1801–1922* (Dublin: Royal Irish Academy, 1978)

Walker, B. *Dancing to History's Tune: History, Politics and Myth in Ireland* (Belfast: Queen's University Belfast, 1997)

West, T. *The Bold Collegians: The Development of Sport in Trinity College Dublin* (Dublin: Lilliput Press, 1991)

West, T. *Midleton College: A Tercentenary History* (Cork: T. West, 1996)

White, G. and O'Shea, B. *'Baptised in Blood': The Formation of the Cork Brigade of the Irish Volunteers, 1913–1916* (Cork: Mercier Press, 2005)

(iv) *Unpublished material*

Kinirons, F. 'The Spiritual Home of Rugby: The Growth, Spread and Development of Rugby in Limerick', unpublished MA thesis, University of Limerick, 2006

McAnallen, D. 'Sabbatarianism Versus the Gaelic Athletic Association in Ulster, 1884–1920', unpublished paper, 2008

McGrath, J, 'Sociability and Socio-Economic Conditions in St Mary's Parish Limerick 1890–1950', unpublished MA thesis, Mary Immaculate College, University of Limerick, 2006

O'Riordan, A. 'The Diffusion of Selected Team Sports in Cork, 1858–1995', unpublished MA thesis, National University of Ireland Cork, 1997

Rigby, V. 'The Riddle of Ravenhill', paper presented at Sport History Ireland Third Annual Conference, National University of Ireland Galway, February 2007

Staunton, M. 'The Royal Munster Fusiliers in the Great War, 1914–1919', unpublished MA thesis, University College Dublin, 1986

Wallace, I. 'Aspects of Education in Nineteenth-Century Fermoy', unpublished MEd thesis, University College Cork, 1986

(v) *Audio-Visual/Internet*

Munster: The Brave and the Faithful: The Official Commemorative DVD (Iris Productions, 2006), http://news.bbc.co.uk/2/hi/uk_news/northern_ireland/3387255stm [accessed 23 July 2007]

Dublin Airport Authority, Plc Annual Report and Financial Statements 2009, www.daa.ie [accessed 16 June 2011]

http://www.mrsc.ie/Membership. aspx [accessed 16 June 2011]

Index